Essays on the Works of Erasmus

edited by

Richard L. DeMolen

New Haven and London Yale University Press 1978

Designed by John O. C. McCrillis and set in IBM
Journal Roman type. Printed in the United States
of America by The Murray Printing Co., Westford,
Massachusetts.

Published in Great Britain, Europe, Africa, and
Asia (except Japan) by Yale University Press, Ltd.,
London. Distributed in Australia and New Zealand
by Book & Film Services, Artarmon, N.S.W.,
Australia; and in Japan by Harper & Row,
Publishers, Tokyo Office.

Library of Congress Cataloging in Publication Data

Main entry under title:

Essays, on the works of Erasmus.
    Includes index.
    1. Erasmus, Desiderius, d. 1536—Criticism and
interpretation—Addresses, essays, lectures.
2. Theology—Addresses, essays, lectures.
3. Thompson, Craig Reingwalt, 1911–
I. DeMolen, Richard L. II. Title.
PA8518.A1E8   199.492   78-3481
ISBN 0-300-02177-1

Contents

Preface

This collection of essays owes its genesis to a group of scholars who were conducting research at the Folger Shakespeare Library in the spring of 1974. They wanted to commemorate the sixty-fifth birthday of Craig R. Thompson, Felix E. Schelling Professor of English Literature at the University of Pennsylvania, on June 25, 1976, by preparing a *Festschrift* in his honor. Since Professor Thompson has devoted so much of his scholarship to Erasmus, we thought it fitting to assemble a collection of essays on the individual works of Erasmus that would attempt to provide an interpretation of each work in terms of a central theme. With this in mind, I invited fourteen Erasmians to write on one each of the major works of the Prince of Humanists. The results can be found on the following pages. The volume is a tribute to Professor Thompson and a confirmation of the importance of Erasmus's *Opera omnia* by an international body of scholars: specialists in such diverse areas as English literature, the classics, philosophy, European history, theology, French literature, and church history. Moreover, in an effort to identify a common theme running through nineteen major works of Erasmus, I have contributed an introductory essay of my own and have prepared an index to the collection itself.

I wish to thank the contributors for their generous assistance in assembling and editing this volume; and I am grateful to Louise M. Kamenjar, Dr. Willard T. Daetsch, and Simone Ferguson for translating four of the essays. I likewise wish to express my gratitude to Dean Vartan Gregorian and Professor Joel Conarroe of the University of Pennsylvania for their sustained support.

Writing to William Blount, Lord Mountjoy, in September of 1508, Erasmus provided a eulogistic thought which is appropriate for this occasion as well:

> Admittedly it is the way of authors to fill a great part of their prefaces with compliments to those to whom they dedicate their writings, and it seems but the proper tribute to true goodness that the recollection thereof should be handed down to posterity, which is better done by books than by any other memorials.*

---

*The Correspondence of Erasmus, trans. R. A. B. Mynors and D. F. S. Thomson (Toronto, 1975), 2:144.

Introduction

Opera Omnia Desiderii Erasmi: Rungs on the Ladder to the *Philosophia Christi*

RICHARD L. DeMOLEN

> Please explain to her [Lady Anna van Borssele] how much greater is the glory she can acquire from me, by my literary works, than from the other theologians in her patronage. They merely deliver humdrum sermons; I am writing books that may last for ever. Their uneducated nonsense finds an audience in perhaps a couple of churches; my books will be read all over the world, in the Latin west and in the Greek east and by every nation.[1]
>
> [Erasmus to Jacob Batt, December, 1500]

The title Prince of Humanists had not yet been earned by the young Austin canon who penned this letter, and yet the very same priest was abundantly aware of his own intellectual gifts and the power of the printed word.[2] During his lifetime (ca. 1469 to 1536) Erasmus published about one hundred works (if one groups together his various *apologiae* and declamations). His attitude toward these publications was very different from that of Martin Luther, who wished to see his treatises buried after his death. In a letter to a theologian at Louvain, Martin Dorp, dated May 1515, Erasmus explained that he wrote his books and treatises in order to serve "some useful purpose": "What I have aimed at in publishing all of my books was to serve some useful purpose through my efforts, and, if I fell short of this, at least to avoid doing any harm to anyone. . . ." He was anxious, above all, that his works contribute to the development of religious perfection. To insure this, he deliberately disavowed anything he had written up to May 1515 that might inhibit piety: "I would not want anything I wrote in jest to be in any way detrimental to Christian piety. Just give me a reader who understands what I wrote, who is fair and honest, who is eager for knowledge, and not bent on criticism."[3]

Erasmus also believed that learning supports piety, arguing that true piety must be based on genuine learning and must lead to moral action. Toward the end of his life, when he was living in Freiburg, Erasmus penned a letter (February 1530) to some Franciscan friars in which he continued to emphasize his double-edged goal: "Let them read the list of his works and they will see how much this decrepit old man has contributed to learning and to true

1

piety."[4] It will be the purpose of this introduction to substantiate Erasmus's declaration that he offered the reading public only works that served to enhance learning and Christian piety.[5] Early in his career he wrote to Richard Foxe, the bishop of Winchester (January 1, 1506), and defined piety in terms of his conception of Christianity as "that true and perfect kind of friendship which consists in dying with Christ, living in Christ, and forming one body and one soul with Christ."[6]

Erasmus perceived the direction that his writing program would take before he left the monastery of the Canons Regular of Saint Augustine at Steyn. In 1489 or about that date, he identified a thoroughly religious program of studies to Cornelis Gerard, a fellow canon at a nearby Augustinian monastery, and attributed his change of direction to this friend: "since you kindly remind me of this, I have decided for the future to write nothing which does not breathe of the atmosphere either of praise of holy men or of holiness itself."[7] Erasmus's decision, however, did not mean that he was going to abandon the study of the classics which he had enjoyed from his boyhood, for these works served his purpose by "showing up men's vices" and, at the same time, by emphasizing the pursuit of virtues by other members of society. Erasmus reasoned as follows: those men who object to the study of the classics "fail to perceive how much moral goodness exists in Terence's plays, how much implicit exhortation to shape one's life" is to be found in the literature of the ancients.[8] He believed that the study of the classics was a useful adjunct for those who wished to attain moral perfection. He grew tired of those monks and theologians who railed against the classics under the pretext that they undermined Christian doctrine by promoting paganism. In a letter to a Hebrew scholar at Basel, Wolfgang Faber Capito, dated February 26, 1517, Erasmus urged the continuing study of the three major classical languages as an aid to uncovering the meaning of Christ's teachings:

> I could wish that those dreary quibblings could be either done away with or at least cease to be the sole activity of theologians, and that the simplicity and purity of Christ could penetrate deeply into the minds of men; and this I think can best be brought to pass if with the help provided by the three languages we exercise our minds in the actual sources.[9]

The example of Christ was held up both to aged scholar and young child. Writing to Adolph of Burgundy in 1499, Erasmus reminded the ten-year-old boy that he must follow Christ: "Finally, I shall add something I would wish you to lay very closely to heart: let it be one of your firmest convictions that nothing so well becomes the noble and well born as religious devotion. This is no idle advice, for I know by experience that royal courts contain those who neither hesitate to believe, nor blush to say, that Christ's teaching is no matter that

need concern noblemen but should be left to priests and monks. Stop your ears
to their deadly siren-song, and follow where your mother and Batt are beckon-
ing."[10] Erasmus called his program of reform to the attention of the whole
world.

In response to repeated requests for a bibliography of his writings, Erasmus
drew up a catalogue and sent it to John Botzheim, a canon at Constance, in
letter form under date of January 30, 1523. He also sent the very same catalogue
of his lucubrations to Hector Boece on March 15, 1530.[11] These catalogues
divide Erasmus's writings into the following nine major "orders" or divisions:
The first category consisted of works which dealt with instruction on classical
letters (*ad institutionem literarum*). Under this classification he listed twenty-
one titles (with eighteen subtitles under Lucian and the "Dialogues"), including
On Copia of Words and Things, the *Colloquies, On Civility of Manners for
Boys,* the *Dialogue on the Ciceronian,* and *On the Instruction of Boys.* The
second division consisted exclusively of the *Adages,* which Erasmus described
in a letter to Servatius Roger, prior of the monastery at Steyn (July 8, 1514),
as "a profane work, of course, but most helpful for the whole business of
education";[12] the third division contained only his *Epistles.* Though Erasmus
identified the first three divisions separately, they are related, since all of the
individual works in these divisions contribute in some way to improving the
writing of classical letters. Erasmus regarded these works as preliminary to his
writings on morality and piety. (We see an expression of this idea in the letter
to Servatius, referred to above, where Erasmus characterized *On Copia of
Words and Things* as "a useful handbook for future preachers".) Erasmus's
fourth division consisted of works on morality. It included thirteen titles (with
eight subdivisions under the name of Plutarch), among them the *Praise of Folly,*
the *Instruction of a Christian Prince,* and the *Complaint of Peace.* The fifth and
largest division represented works on piety and included the *Handbook of the
Christian Soldier,* the *Method of True Theology,* and *On Preaching.* Concerning
the *Handbook,* Erasmus observed in his letter to Servatius (July 8, 1514) that
"many people testify that it has fired them with religious enthusiasm." The
sixth, seventh, eighth, and ninth categories were related to works on piety but
enjoyed a separate classification in Erasmus's scheme. The sixth division consisted of only two titles, the New Testament and the *Paraphrases of the New
Testament.* The seventh and ninth divisions represented the Church Fathers: the
seventh included works by the Greek Fathers, Saint John Chrysostom, Saint
Athanasius, Origen, and Saint Basil (with eight subdivisions under the names
of Chrysostom and Athanasius); the ninth consisted of nine separate titles and
represented the works of the following Latin Fathers: Saint Jerome, Saint Cyprian, Saint Hilary, Saint Irenaeus, Saint Ambrose, Lactantius, Saint Augustine,
and Alger of Liège. The eighth division contained twenty-two separate titles,

among them various *Apologiae,* including *The Antibarbarians* and *A Discourse on the Freedom of the Will.*

By the middle of the second decade of the sixteenth century, Erasmus had been lauded for his wisdom and received many letters of praise for his dedication to learning. Dean John Colet of St. Paul's Cathedral observed in one of these letters, dated June 20, 1516:

> Indeed, Erasmus, I am surprised at the fertility of your mind, which conceives so many projects, and brings such important works to birth, day after day, in such perfection, especially when you have no fixed abode, and are not assisted by any great or certain emoluments.[13]

Erasmus's devotion to his studies greatly exceeded his desire for material comforts and represents a further indication of his personal devotion to Christ and of his trust in Divine Providence. Many of his correspondents were also impressed by Erasmus's virtue, which is the best indication of all that the prince of humanists was adhering to his belief in the importance of imitating Christ. Writing to Erasmus in August of 1516, John Watson, a fellow of Peterhouse, Cambridge, marveled at the combination of brilliance and virtuousness that he saw in Erasmus:

> I am constantly more and more impressed, when I see Erasmus growing greater as he advances in years, and showing himself every day in a new and more exalted character. You are celebrated everywhere in Italy, especially among the learned of the highest note. It is incredible how favourably your *Copia* is everywhere received; and your *Moria* regarded as the highest wisdom. . . . Your fame is spread throughout all the Christian world; but as others enlarge on the riches of your varied learning or extraordinary eloquence, nothing strikes me so much as the modesty with which you are ready to take the lowest place, while the general suffrage sets you in the highest. The kind of literary skill which you enjoy is apt to inflate the possessor of it, and as it puts him in a peculiar class, to separate him from familiarity with his kind; but you are all generosity in communicating yourself to others; and having for your object the welfare of all, you do not despise the friendship of any. Therefore wherever you are, you so live as to seem present everywhere in Christendom, and will continue to live by the immortality of your fame and the noble monuments you will leave behind you.[14]

And there were others who praised him as well. Capito underscored Watson's observation in a letter to Erasmus, dated September 2, 1516: "You have left behind you here a sort of odour of your kindness and consummate literature, with which you attach to yourself Princes and Nobles, Prelates and People."[15]

Erasmus succeeded in attracting such a diverse following because he consciously strove to do so. In pursuing his goal of teaching piety to all, he appealed to members of every class and distinction.

But it would be misleading to suggest that every reader of Erasmus's works found only good things to report about them. Such was not the case. Guillaume Budé, the eminent French humanist, was only one of his unfavorable critics. Budé found fault with Erasmus's efforts to reach the minds of the uneducated masses and suggested that he was damaging his reputation by composing works for boys. In response, Erasmus defended his actions and reiterated his major goal in a letter to Budé, dated October 28, 1516:

> As for the risk you point out, of my name being obscured by so many trifling books, this in very truth does not give me the slightest uneasiness. Whatever celebrity, rather than glory, my lucubrations have earned for me, I would willingly and most cheerfully set it aside, if I am allowed to do so. Different people find pleasure in different studies. Some are capable of one thing, some of another. All have not the same genius. It is my fancy to devote my thoughts to such commonplace matters, in which, however, I find less frivolity and more profit than in some subjects which their authors think so magnificent. Finally, he whose single aim it is, not to exhibit himself, but to do some good to others, is not concerned so much with the splendour of the matters in which he is engaged, as with their utility; and I shall not refuse any task even more despised than that despised little *Cato,* if I see that it will conduce to the promotion of honest study. Such things are written, not for a Persius or a Laelius, but for boys and blockheads.[16]

Utility was the driving purpose behind the writing program on holiness that Erasmus first conceived while yet a student preparing for ordination at Steyn. It remained so throughout his long career as a scholar and theologian. One should not be surprised, therefore, to find Erasmus laying aside his works on theology and the Church Fathers in the late 1520s in order to instruct boys in good manners and the elements of writing Latin prose. Boys and blockheads were just as important to his *philosophia Christi* as nobles and princes. To quote Craig R. Thompson: "His witty, vivid presentation of men and manners, his literary and educational writings, urbane and tolerant spirit, and conception of Christian piety made him memorable."[17] In his own work on the *Instruction of a Christian Prince,* Erasmus summarized his definition of a Christian by posing a question and offering a reply:

> Who is truly Christian? Not he who is baptized or anointed, or who attends church. It is rather the man who has embraced Christ in his innermost feelings of his heart, and who emulates Him by his pious deeds.[18]

In taking up nineteen of Erasmus's works one by one, I shall discuss where and why Erasmus pursued his goal to teach all men how to be truly Christian.

EPISTLES (ca. 1484-)

The letters of Erasmus are a remarkable inheritance because they reveal rather clearly the mind and personality of their author. Between 1514 and his death in 1536 about twenty editions of Erasmus's letters appeared in print.[19] Erasmus was conscious of his epistolary talents as an adolescent and, more importantly, was aware of the significance of his letters when he reached full manhood. Writing to Beatus Rhenanus in 1520, Erasmus recalled his earliest efforts: "although when I was a young man . . . I wrote very many letters, yet I hardly wrote any for publication . . . indeed, I did nothing more than amuse myself, as it were, expecting nothing less than that my friends should copy out and preserve such trifles."[20] As early as 1505, Erasmus conceived the idea of publishing his letters. In that year he addressed a letter to Francis Theodoricus, prior of the monastery at Hemsdonck, instructing him to "help in collecting, as far as possible, the letters which I have written to various persons with more than usual care—as I have an idea of publishing one book of Epistles."[21]

Having achieved greatness in the second decade of the sixteenth century, Erasmus decided to edit his correspondence in order to stop, or at least impede, the publication of his letters by unauthorized editors. He even went so far as to destroy some of his correspondence: "I myself, having come into possession of many of my letters by chance, burned them, for I realized that they were being preserved by very many people."[22] Nevertheless, unauthorized collections of Erasmus's letters appeared regularly after 1516. Johann Froben introduced the scheme at Basel as early as August of 1515 by printing a modest collection of four letters (*Damiana elegeia*). He was followed by Peter Gilles, secretary of the city of Antwerp, who edited two larger editions of the correspondence that were printed by Thierry Martens at Louvain in October of 1516 (*Epistolae aliquot . . .*) and in April of 1517 (*Aliquot epistolae sane quam elegantes . . .*). Froben reprinted the latter edition in January of 1518.

It seems almost certain that Erasmus had a hand in many of these early editions. Concerning the October 1516 edition, Erasmus admitted that "I was myself rather a conniving than a consenting party."[23] Finally, in August of 1518, Beatus Rhenanus, scholar and afterward biographer of Erasmus at Basel, edited "without authorization" a collection of the correspondence (*Auctarium . . .*, Basel: Froben). Others were to follow. Like all its predecessors, the August 1518 edition only served to irritate and agitate the republic of belles lettres. Many of his correspondents objected to having their views aired publicly and others felt slighted because their letters were not included. Writing to Rhenanus in 1520, Erasmus observed, "For you know how unhappy was the issue of those epistles, of which you first undertook the editing."[24]

Rhenanus's edition was followed by a second effort in October of 1519 (*Farrago nova epistolarum . . .*, Basel: Froben). Erasmus's reaction can be found in his prefatory letter to Rhenanus in the January 1522 edition (*Epistolae . . . ad diversos et aliquot*).[25] It is hardly complimentary: in order to prevent the publication of unauthorized letters, "I sent you a medley (*farraginem*), giving you authority to select, and even to make corrections, in case there should be anything that seemed likely to injure my own reputation, or seriously to embitter anybody's feelings. . . . And yet even in that collection enough was found to excite in some breasts animosities of quite a tragic sort."[26] Shortly after the appearance of the *Farrago,* Adrian Barland (or Baerland) edited still another edition, entitled *Epistolae aliquot selectae ex Erasmicis,* which was printed by Thierry Martens in December of 1520.[27] Throughout the remaining years of Erasmus's life publishers printed a new edition of his letters nearly every year.

Beginning with the 1522 collection of letters (*Epistolae . . . ad diversos et aliquot*), Erasmus henceforth supervised the editing of his own correspondence. He set forth his reasons for doing so in his prefatory letter to Rhenanus:

> I, therefore, permitted some to be published, first, in order that people, having their appetite satisfied, might cease from demanding more, or at any rate abstain from any intention of publication, when they saw that I had myself set my hand to the business; next, that the letters might be issued with some selection and in a more correct form than as they existed in several copies; and, finally, that they might contain less of the bitter ingredient. With this design I have revised the Farrago, cleared up some points which had been unfairly construed, expunged some passages by which the too tender and irritable minds of some people had been offended, and softened others.[28]

Furthermore, Erasmus supervised other succeeding editions of his correspondence. I shall refer only to those of August 1529 (*Opus epistolarum . . .*, Basel: Froben), September 1531 (*Epistolae Floridae . . .* Basel: Herwagen), and February 1536 (*Opus epistolarum . . .*, Basel: Herwagen). In the prefatory epistles to these editions, Erasmus expressed his views on the nature of the epistolary genre and his methodology as editor.

To begin with, Erasmus insisted that letters should represent reality and feeling: "letters of that genuine kind, which represent, as in a picture, the character, fortune, and feelings of the writer, and, at the same time, the public and private condition of the time."[29] Genuine letters were not merely literary exercises.[30]

Speaking from experience, however, he discouraged others from publishing nonliterary letters during their own lifetimes: "Therefore if anything of this sort is to be published, I would not advise anyone to bring it out in his lifetime, but rather commit it to some secretary to edit after your death."[31] His reasons for restricting the publication of personal correspondence were well founded: (1) both friends and foes will take offense and (2) one's reputation will suffer on account of the unevenness and inconsistency in the letters: "Whence it happens that with inexperienced persons we fall under the suspicion of inconstancy, when the variation they observe is to be ascribed to a difference of age and of feeling, a change of persons and circumstances."[32]

Having suffered from the fact that many of his letters were misinterpreted and read out of context, Erasmus advised the reader, in his 1529 prefatory epistle, "that there are none of my lucubrations for which I care less than my Epistles." And yet we might ask why, then, did he spend so much effort collecting, discarding, and editing his letters? How could he justify his labors on the 1529 edition, in which he "divided the whole work into Books, so that the reader may find more readily what he seeks," in which he "added the day and year at the foot of each letter," and printed an "Index with the names of the persons and the numbers of the Books and Epistles" in order to "show who writes to whom, and how many letters"? If his correspondence was really of no consequence, why did he bother to take "the greatest pains that passages likely to produce much irritation should be either omitted or at any rate softened"?[33] I think that the answer to these questions is obvious: Erasmus took seriously the editing of his correspondence because he wanted his letters to serve his cause. Some four months before his death in July of 1536, Erasmus penned an epistolary preface to the 1536 edition of his correspondence in which he emphasized the importance of his reputation and the part his correspondence played in achieving his goal:

> Within the last few days, I determined to look over some confused heaps of papers, partly for the sake of one or two letters which I wished to be published, and partly in order to destroy some documents which others might, perhaps, publish after my death, or even during my life . . . I have not for some years taken any pains to preserve any copies of my own [letters], partly because I had not clerks enough to write them all out, and partly because in answering so many correspondents I am forced to write some and to dictate others, without preparation. I was also a little ashamed of the former publications . . . I have brought these matters to your notice, candid readers, that you may not too lightly believe everything to be mine above which my name is written; and also that you may not think Erasmus has no one to take his part but a few gossips . . .[34]

Since Erasmus saw some of his letters as divisive, he wanted to destroy them and to publish only those letters that would serve his underlying purpose.

THE BOOK OF THE ANTIBARBARIANS (1494/95; 1520)

One of the earliest treatises of Erasmus was written in part while he was living in the monastery of the Austin Canons at Steyn: The *Antibarbarorum liber* was begun about 1489 ("before he attained his twentieth year").[35] Erasmus completed it about 1494/95, when he was in the employment of Henry of Bergen, the bishop of Cambrai. It finally appeared in print in May of 1520 and was reprinted in September, November, and December of the same year. Moreover, it was published about a dozen times during the author's lifetime.[36] Begun as an oration, the *Book of the Antibarbarians* was written in its final form as a dialogue. When it was conceived, it was to have consisted of four books, of which only two were completed and only part one survives. Book One offered a vigorous defense of classical letters. Book Two, no longer extant, sketched the practice of rhetoric and presented the major arguments of its critics. Books Three and Four defended rhetoric and poetry, respectively.[37]

The two completed books were revised by Erasmus at Bologna (about 1506) and, together with the materials for the remaining chapters, were given to Richard Pace at Ferrara in 1521, but were lost sometime thereafter. Erasmus refers to this incident in his correspondence. He seems to have believed that his work still existed somewhere, in the hands of a conspirator who would eventually publish it posthumously. In 1551, Roger Ascham wrote from Augsburg to Jerome Froben, claiming that he had received a manuscript copy of the work in 1549; but he was not sure whether he had the complete text or some abridgment, or whether it was the same as the section that had been published but was now out of print.[38] Book One, in its older form, existed in several copies; and since it was too well known to be suppressed, Erasmus revised it again and printed it at Basel in 1520. In the dialogue so published, the scene of the colloquy was laid at a country house in the neighborhood of Bergen, a market town and port in Brabant. As the book appears to have been shown to Robert Gaguin, the leading French humanist, in this form (about August 1495), it may be conjectured that the plan of so arranging it was adopted at Bergen during Erasmus's first residence there with the bishop of Cambrai.[39]

The purpose of the *Book of the Antibarbarians* was to launch an attack against the enemies of classical literature—those sixteenth-century schoolmen, whether lay or cleric, who preferred the crude conventions of medieval Latin to classical letters. The theme of the various conversations centered, therefore, on the reasons for the decline in the *optimae artes* of the sixteenth century and the utility of classical learning. The function of scholarship, according to Erasmus, was to elucidate revelation. Direct revelation, by which the apostles were guided, had long ago ceased to be operative. In defending the classics against ignorant schoolmasters, magistrates, monks, and theologians, Erasmus cautioned the reader against an uncritical reading of them. Pure poetry was not necessarily a vehicle for impure and godless thought; nor, on the other hand, was bad Latin a guarantee of true piety. Indeed, one could praise God and, at the same time, aspire to a classical purity of form.

For Erasmus and his contemporaries, the purity and elegance of Latin and the forms of prose and poetry were burning issues of the day, the essence of the new culture, and the subject of conflict between the old and the new. Writing to John Sapidus, a teacher of Latin, in the prefatory letter to the *Antibarbari,* Erasmus recalled: "In my childhood, polite letters were wholly banished from our schools of learning. Not only was assistance from books and teachers lacking, but there was no reward to stimulate my ability. Moreover, the whole world tried to frighten me away from the study of polite letters and to push me in the other direction. . . . I began to hate all those who I knew were insensible to the humanities; I fell in love with those who delighted in them."[40] For Erasmus, as well as the ancients, revelation was not so much a deposit as a quest, never ending, never amenable to definitive formulation. The *studia humanitatis* (including Latin and Greek literature, rhetoric, history, and moral philosophy) furnished standards of taste and permanent models of excellence. Erasmus's defense of the classics rested on his belief that there was no such thing as "Christian" erudition; there was only a secular erudition. By means of "true" erudition man was ennobled. Speaking through the character of Batt, Erasmus reflected:

> The man whose life is pure has done nobly. But in doing nobly he serves merely his own interests, or at the most his influence is exerted on only the few individuals with whom he lives. But if to his upright character erudition is allied, how much more beautifully and widely will his virtue flourish, as if a torch had been lighted? If one is a member of that group who are able to commit to letters the finest reflections of the mind, that is, if he is not only learned but eloquent, necessarily the influence of such a man is most widely spread, not merely to his intimate friends, not only to his contemporaries and to his neighbors, but also to foreigners, to posterity, to the most distant inhabitants of the earth. Untaught virtue dies with its author unless it is handed down to posterity in writings. Not the lands, nor the seas, nor the long succession of ages prevent trained erudition from reaching all humanity in its flight. I do not wish to raise here the invidious comparison whether the blood of the martyrs or the pen of scholars did more to advance the cause of our religion. I do not disparage the glory of the martyrs which no

one can reach even by the greatest eloquence. But so far as our advantage is concerned, we owe almost more to some heretics than to our martyrs themselves. And while there have been a great number of martyrs, scholars have been few. The martyrs in dying diminished the number of Christians; the learned writers by their persuasiveness have increased it.[41]

Thus the *Book of the Antibarbarians* addressed itself directly to Erasmus's major goal. Through learning and eloquence the virtuous man can advance the cause of his religion. Christianity will be enriched by "the pen of scholars."

ADAGES (1500–)

As a collection of popular sayings, epigrams, proverbs, and anecdotes, the *Adagia* is a silent tribute to the immense reading of its author. It was reprinted some forty times during his lifetime and was constantly enlarged as edition succeeded edition.[42] The work brought both fame and fortune. Beginning as a collection of 818 adages in 1500 (*Adagiorum collectanea . . .*, Paris: J. Philippi) gathered from Latin and Greek literature, it ended as a collection of 4,151 adages in 1536 (*Adagiorum chiliades . . .*, Basel: J. Froben and N. Episcopius).[43] In the later editions, the adages were arranged in groups of 1,000 (per book) and subdivided into hundreds: each adage was followed by a commentary that sought to clarify its meaning or its origin. Ostensibly Erasmus published these adages in an effort to aid the reader in improving his style of writing Latin. The fact that his *Adagiorum collectanea* and *Adagiorum chiliades* enjoyed so many editions during the author's lifetime attests to their popular appeal. In his 1500 dedicatory letter to Lord Mountjoy, Erasmus emphasized their utility:

> So I put aside my nightly labours over a more serious work and strolled through diverse gardens of the classics, occupied in this lighter kind of study, and so plucked, and as it were arranged in garlands, like flowerets of every hue, all the most ancient and famous of the adages. . . . I foresaw that while this labour of mine might bring no credit to its author, nevertheless it was likely to bring some profit and pleasure to its prospective readers: those, I mean, who dislike the current jargon and are searching for greater elegance and a more refined style. . . . I felt sure that though they might not admire it as a work of great artistry, at least they would be glad to welcome it on the ground of extreme usefulness. . . . You may draw upon it for all purposes; to find something that will charm by means of a clever and apposite metaphor, or bite with incisive wit; give pleasure by pointed brevity, or delight by brief pointedness . . . they do not merely decorate your style; they are equally helpful in giving strength as well.

But there was a deeper motivation too, Erasmus underscored the point that an eloquent style of writing could serve the church:

> . . . When these are found, I repeat (and I need not list them all), does it
> never occur to you that this manner of expression contains not merely vain
> display but rather a genuine element of sanctity, appropriate to religious
> topics? So for many reasons it seemed to me I had undertaken no vain or
> unprofitable task in attempting to instruct, or at least interest, studious
> youth, as well as I could, in a method of composition which a great many
> learned and pious authors have found good reason to pursue.[44]

Moral instruction was at the heart of the *Adages*. Whoever observed the wise
sayings of the ancients and the Church Fathers would be led to a virtuous life
in imitation of Christ. Writing in the *Dulce bellum inexpertis,* which first appeared in his 1515 edition of the *Adagia,* Erasmus noted that

> The end and aim of the faith of the Gospel is conduct worthy of Christ.
> Why do we insist on those things which have nothing to do with morality,
> and neglect the things which are like pillars of the structure—once you take
> them away, the whole edifice will crumble at once? Finally, who will believe
> us, when we take as our device the Cross of Christ in the name of the Gospel,
> if our whole life obviously speaks of nothing but the world?[45]

The youthful Christian was here enjoined to follow the message of the Gospel
by renouncing the temptations of the world, the devil, and the flesh. Morality
alone supports the weight of the Cross.

In a letter to Guillaume Budé, dated June 19, 1516, Erasmus spoke of the
philosophical and theological content of the adages. He admitted that "in the
Adages, a fragmentary work, how often do I roam into the fields of Philosophy
and Theology, forgetting, as it may seem, the immediate subject, and take a
higher flight than the occasion demands."[46] For a discussion of the other
purposes for which the adages were written, see Mrs. Phillips's essay on the
history of the *Adagia.*

THE HANDBOOK OF THE CHRISTIAN SOLDIER (1503)

With conviction and grace, Erasmus drafted the first complete expression of
his *philosophia Christi* in the *Enchiridion militis christiani* (i.e. Christian Soldier's Dagger or Handbook) in 1501 and published it two years later. His
formula was undogmatic, and yet it was nothing less than "a method of morals,"
as he himself put it.[47] In preparation for life's inevitable encounters with the
world and the devil, Erasmus urged the Christian knight to fortify himself with
virtue and knowledge of the classics and the works of the Church Fathers. He
was speaking to all men, whatever their age and station in life, when he wrote:

> If you are inflamed by lust, acknowledge your weakness and deny yourself
> somewhat more, even of lawful pleasures; assign yourself an additional

number of chaste and moral duties. If you are enticed by greed or avarice, increase your charitable donations. If you are attracted by empty fame, humble yourself that much more in every respect.[48]

One of Erasmus's most popular works, the *Enchiridion,* according to the *Bibliotheca Belgica* (1964), enjoyed some fifty-one Latin editions (in addition to translations into German, English—there were ten editions between 1533 and 1576—, French, Dutch, and Spanish) during the lifetime of the author.[49] It was conceived as a handbook that could be carried about and was composed specifically at the request of a woman who had asked Erasmus to instruct her wayward husband, Johann Poppenruyter, in virtue. Writing to John Botzheim in January of 1523, Erasmus described these circumstances:

> The *Enchiridion militis christiani* was begun by me nearly thirty years ago when staying in the castle of Tournehem, to which we were driven by the plague which depopulated Paris. The work arose out of the following incident. A common friend of mine and of Batt was in the castle—a man whose wife was a lady of singular piety. The husband was no one's enemy so much as his own, a man of dissolute life, but in other respects an agreeable companion. He had no regard for any clergyman except me; and his wife, who was much concerned about her husband's salvation, applied to me through Batt to set down some . . . sense of religion, without his perceiving that it was done at the insistence of his wife. For even with her it was a word and a blow, in soldier's fashion. I consented to the request and put down some observations suitable to the occasion. These having met the approval even of learned persons, and especially of Jean Vitrier [the warden of a Franciscan community at Saint-Omer], a Franciscan friar of great authority in those parts, I finished the work at leisure, after the plague (then raging everywhere) had routed me out of Paris and driven me to Louvain.[50]

Throughout the treatise Erasmus calls the reader to the *divinae scripturae fontes.* He wished to create a world that was inhabited by men, who preferred the example of Christ to that of Judas Iscariot. Erasmus's formula was both Christocentric and universal in its application. Writing to Budé in June of 1516, Erasmus underscored the originality of his theme: "In the *Enchiridion,* I ventured to differ widely from our own age, without being deterred by the authority of anyone."[51]

The *Handbook of a Christian Soldier* is divided into two parts. The first part analyzes the nature of man and his purpose on earth, while part two provides a discussion of twenty-two "rules" for "living a Christian life." It concludes with a section that proposes remedies for such vices as lust, avarice, ambition, pride and haughtiness, and anger and revenge. Erasmus reminded the reader at the

very end of the treatise that one should study the classics in order to obtain
moral guidance in this life on earth, which he described as "a type of continual
warfare." In the dedicatory letter to his friend Johann Poppenruyter (dated
1501), Erasmus justified his interest in good letters and sacred scriptures:

> I shall try to cause certain malicious critics, who think it the height of
> piety to be ignorant of sound learning, to realize that, when in my youth
> I embraced the finer literature of the ancients and acquired, not without
> much midnight labour, a reasonable knowledge of the Greek as well as the
> Latin language, I did not aim at vain glory or childish self-gratification, but
> had long ago determined to adorn the Lord's temple, badly desecrated as it
> has been by the ignorance and barbarism of some, with treasures from other
> realms, as far as in me lay; treasures that could, moreover, inspire even men
> of superior intellect to love the Scriptures. But, putting aside this vast
> enterprise for just a few days, I have taken upon myself the task of pointing
> out to you, as with my finger, a short way to Christ.[52]

And this handbook on piety bore fruit. Writing to Master John, a former tutor
to Archduke Philip, on November 2, 1517, Erasmus exclaimed: "The *Enchiridion* is read everywhere; and it is making many people either good, or at
any rate—we do hope—better than they were."[53] What more could Erasmus
expect? Ernst-W. Kohls shifts his focus and draws attention to the theological
content of the handbook.

THE PRAISE OF FOLLY (1511)

This literary triumph was written in the course of a week in late summer
of 1509 and revised and published in 1511. Erasmus described it as "a playful
booklet too light to become a theologian, too caustic to befit Christian meek-
ness."[54] The *Moriae encomium* enjoyed some forty editions, including French
and German translations, during the lifetime of its author, and was certainly
one of his best-known works.[55] Erasmus set forth the reasons that motivated
him to write it in his dedicatory letter to Sir Thomas More:

> So I beg you to accept this short essay as a souvenir of your comrade, but
> also to acknowledge and cherish it, inasmuch as it has been dedicated to you
> and is no longer mine, but yours. For there will perhaps be some wrangling
> critics who will falsely assert either that these trifles are too airy to be quite
> suitable to a theologian's pen, or that they are more sarcastic than suits the
> modesty of a Christian. They will loudly accuse me of imitating the Old
> Comedy or some kind of Lucianic satire, and of attacking the whole world
> with my teeth. Now as for those who find the triviality and humour of the

theme offensive, I should like them to reflect that this is no vein of my own invention, but reflects the habitual practice of great writers of the past. . . . So let them make up stories about me if they wish, alleging that I have sometimes played draughts for recreation, or ridden a hobbyhorse if they would rather; for, considering that every way of living is permitted its appropriate recreation, it would be monstrously unfair to allow no diversion whatever of those who pursue literary studies, especially if nonsense leads to serious matters and absurd themes are treated in such a way that the reader whose senses are not wholly dulled gains somewhat more profit from these than from some men's severe and showy demonstrations. . . . For, as there is nothing more frivolous than to handle serious topics in a trifling manner, so also there is nothing more agreeable than to handle trifling matters in such a way that what you have done seems anything but trifling. Others will judge me; but unless my vanity altogether deceives me, I have written a Praise of Folly without being altogether foolish.[56]

Through this medium, Erasmus launched an attack on those sycophantic theologians who practiced the letter of the law and ignored its spirit: "Such is the erudition and complexity they all display that I fancy the apostles themselves would need the help of another holy spirit if they were obliged to join issue on these topics with our new breed of theologian."[57] Erasmus was impatient with such scholastic thinkers and insisted on a return to Scripture as a basis for theological discussion:

> Yet all the while they are so happy in their self-satisfaction and self-congratulation, and so busy night and day with these enjoyable tomfooleries, that they haven't even a spare moment in which to take a single look at the gospel or the letters of Paul.[58]

In addition to singling out the theologians, Erasmus chose as targets the professional activities of many others, arguing that "We won't go into every kind of life, it would take too long, but will pick out some outstanding examples from which it will be easy to judge the rest."[59] Those who were singled out included the scientist, the schoolmaster, the poet, the grammarian, the orator, the writer, the monk, the monarch, the courtier, the pontiff, the cardinal, the bishop, and the priest. Erasmus poked fun at the foibles and failings of these and others in order to underscore his observation that "all mortals are fools, even the pious." It is indeed because of their foolishness that Christ "by the folly of the cross and through his simple, ignorant apostles, to whom he unfailingly preached folly . . . taught them to shun wisdom, and made his appeal through the example of children, lilies, mustard-seed and humble sparrows, all foolish, senseless things, which live their lives by natural instinct alone, free from care or purpose."[60] This is the reason, according to Folly, why Christ insisted that his disciples learn to depend on him for their sustenance and grace. She was convinced that Christian piety was akin to folly and that there was a closer affinity between Christianity and folly than between Christianity and wisdom.

She also observed that the "biggest fools" appeared to be those who have been "wholly possessed by zeal for Christian piety." These people represented "the very young and the very old, women and simpletons." It is they who "squander their possessions, ignore insults, submit to being cheated, make no distinction between friends and enemies, shun pleasure, sustain themselves on fastings, vigils, tears, toil, and humiliations, scorn life and desire only death."[61] In short, it is these people who pursue the *philosophia Christi* and it is these people whom Erasmus wants all men to emulate. Erasmus also reminded his readers that "Christ seems to have taken special delight in little children, women and fishermen." It is therefore not surprising that Erasmus spent so much of his productive life writing textbooks for the education of children and handbooks on piety for adult laymen. He emphasized the unique qualities of children in this passage from the *Praise of Folly*:

> It's a fact that as soon as the young grow up and develop the sort of mature sense which comes through experience and education, the bloom of youthful beauty begins to fade at once, enthusiasm wanes, gaiety cools down and energy slackens.[62]

Writing to John of Louvain, a Franciscan in Amsterdam, on January 2, 1518, Erasmus noted that his *Moria* had gone through twelve editions and had aroused the ire of monks and theologians. Moreover, he observed with surprise that this work was being read in the classroom by schoolchildren: "though indeed I did take pains to admit nothing in it, that would be corrupting to that age; for as to your fear, that the reading of it might alienate them from all religion, I do not understand what that means. Is there any danger of all religion being disliked, because something is said against those who are superstitiously religious. . . ? Indeed I will say more freely still, I would that priests and people were such true followers of the religion of Christ, that those who are now the only persons called Religious would not appear religious at all."[63] Erasmus insisted here and in the following letter to Martin Dorp (May 1515) that his purpose in writing the *Moriae encomium* was "to admonish, not to cause pain; to be of benefit, not to vex; to reform the morals of men, not to oppose them."[64] Clarence Miller enriches our knowledge of Erasmus as a stylist by drawing attention to his use of proverbs in the *Praise of Folly*.

ON COPIA OF WORDS AND THINGS (1512)

Erasmus's *De duplici copia verborum ac rerum commentarii duo* was begun in Paris in the mid-1490s as a textbook for boys enrolled in the next to the highest form or class, who were learning how to write elegant Latin. In time it served other purposes as well. Erasmus, in his letter to Servatius Roger, saw it as a "useful handbook for future preachers."[65] The text was not finished, however, until 1511 at the suggestion of Dean Colet, who had only recently established a school at St. Paul's. Erasmus dedicated the work to the dean when it appeared in print in 1512. From then until 1536, some eighty-five editions, periodically revised and enlarged, appeared regularly under various titles.[66]

The work itself was subdivided into two books—hence the "commentarii duo" in the title: Book 1 provided ways of enriching the student's vocabulary by the use of schemes and tropes and through discussions of methods of varying one's writings, in chapters on synonymy, enallage, antonomasia, periphrasis, metaphor, allegory, catachresis, onomatopoeia, metalepsis, metonymy, synecdoche, aequipollentia, comparatives, change of relatives, amplification, hyperbole, etc. Book 2, on the other hand, provided discussions on how to use partition, enumeration of antecedents, enumeration of causes, enumeration of effects and consequences, description, digression, epitheton, amplification, extenuation, multiplication of propositions, proof, example, similitude, judicial examination, embellishment, and so forth. Erasmus assumed that the mastery of these skills would enable the fifteen-year-old boy to analyze classical literature on his own: it was merely the means to an end.

In his dedicatory epistle to Dean Colet, dated April 29, 1512, Erasmus emphasized the importance of providing children "with an excellent literary education from their earliest years. For you are profoundly aware both that the hope of the country lies in its youth—the crop in the blade, as it were—and also how important it is for one's whole life that one should be initiated into excellence from the cradle onwards."[67] Since Erasmus saw education as the means to winning young souls to Christ, his *De copia* was an instrument designed to further Colet's lifetime commitment to the conversion of boys into Christian soldiers: "So I have chosen to dedicate to the new school these two new commentaries *De copia,* inasmuch as the work in question is suitable for boys to read and also, unless I am mistaken, not unlikely to prove helpful to them."[68] Erasmus also defended the work against the charges of Guillaume Budé that it was unworthy of its author in a letter dated October 28, 1516: "The *Copia* which we despise (for on this point we are certainly in the same lobby) has been extolled by a great many persons of no ordinary sort, who maintain that no work I have ever written is more clever or equally useful."[69]

Through the use of this treatise, Erasmus hoped to reach child and adult alike and to turn their attention to the powers of persuasive eloquence. The future success of Christianity itself depended upon the ability of mortal men to communicate its gospel message to others. Virginia W. Callahan turns her attention to a bibliographical survey of the *De copia* in order to reveal how previous scholarship has interpreted it.

THE INSTRUCTION OF A CHRISTIAN PRINCE (1516)

Begun in 1515, this treatise was first published in 1516, under the title *Institutio principis christiani,* and reinforced a theme that had appeared in the adage "Dulce bellum inexpertis" in the previous year. It enjoyed some twenty editions during the lifetime of the author. [70]

Erasmus dedicated the work to the sixteen-year-old Prince Charles (afterward Emperor Charles V) in an attempt to persuade him to pursue a policy of peace in his future role as king and emperor. Returning to an earlier injunction, Erasmus insisted that this young prince must be carefully taught, for "the seeds of morality must be sown in the virgin soil of his spirit so that little by little they may grow and mature through age and experience, to remain firmly implanted throughout the course of life. Nothing remains so deeply and tenaciously rooted as those things learned in the first years." [71] The ethics of Christianity would serve as the foundation for Erasmus's advice to Charles, who was asked to read the *Proverbs* of Solomon, *Ecclesiasticus,* the *Book of Wisdom,* and the Gospels—in that order—together with the *Apophthegmata,* the *Morals* and *Lives* of Plutarch, the works of Seneca, Plato, the *Politics* of Aristotle, the *Offices* of Cicero, and excerpts from Herodotus and Xenophon, Sallust and Livy, providing that the impressionable young mind was protected from any objectional passages that might appear in these latter works.

Erasmus also insisted that a good prince must encourage the education of his subjects: "A prince who is about to assume control of the state must be advised at once that the main hope of a state lies in the proper education of its youth. . . . As a result of this scheme of things, there will be no need for many laws or punishments, for the people will of their own free will follow the course of right." [72] Erasmus advised the prince to know his people and to make judgments only after careful study of the situation. The function of power, he noted, is not to extend the "boundaries of one's realm, but to enrich it." War, above all, is to be avoided, except as a last resort. He bade the prince to remember that Aristotle answered the following question in his *Politics:*

> What does the average man demand in his prince? Is it the figure of Nereus, or the strength of Milo, or the stature of Maximinus, or the wealth of Tantalus? No; it is none of these things. What is the answer then? He must have

virtue in its highest and purest form and he must be content with a golden mean in his private affairs.[73]

Virtue should be the mark of a good prince, just as justice should be his goal. For Erasmus there was only one master of Christian men, He "who alone is in all ways to be imitated."[74] The *Instruction of a Christian Prince* called the attention of the prince to the *philosophia Christi*. With the help of a good prince, honest magistrates and public officials, holy priests, wise schoolmasters, just laws, and good habits, he was certain that his philosophy of Christ would gain public support: all it required was the example of good men. Writing to Capito on February 26, 1517, Erasmus spoke of the future in optimistic terms:

> When I see that the highest sovereigns of Europe, Francis of France, Charles the King Catholic, Henry of England and the Emperor Maximilian, have set all their warlike preparations aside, and established peace upon solid, and, as I trust adamantine foundations, I am led to a confident hope, that not only morality and Christian piety, but also a genuine and purer literature may come to renewed life or greater splendour.[75]

THE APOLOGIES (1515-)

Beginning in 1515, Erasmus answered the charges of his critics by addressing *apologiae* or defenses of his positions to them in the form of epistles or tracts. During the remainder of his life he published some thirty apologies, including those to Martin Dorp, a theologian at Louvain, who criticized parts of his *Praise of Folly* and the *Novum Instrumentum* (1515-); Jacques Lefèvre d'Etaples, the Parisian theologian, who accused Erasmus of impiety when he observed that Christ was described in his *Novum Instrumentum* as "a little lower than the angels" in Hebrews 2:7 (1517, 1518, 1520–21); Jacobus Latomus, a theologian at Louvain, who objected to Erasmus's defense of the Hebrew language (1517–19, 1521); those scholars who criticized his work on the Apostolic Epistles (1518); Jan Briard, the vice-chancellor at Louvain, who pointed out errors in his *Praise of Marriage* (1519, 1521, 1522); those "barbarians" who opposed the study of the classics in the form of the *Book of the Antibarbarians* (1520); Edward Lee, the archbishop of York after 1531, who accused Erasmus of denying Christ's equality with the Father (Arianism) in 1520; those theologians at Louvain who accused him of heresy in 1520; those theologians who found fault with his interpretation of "In principio erat sermo" in St. John's Gospel, in which Erasmus substituted *speech* ("sermo") for *word* ("verbum") in 1520–21; Diego López de Zuñega (Stunica), a theologian at Alcala, who also accused Erasmus of Arianism and criticized his notes on the New Testament (1521–25); Nicholas Egmondanus, a Dutch Carmelite theologian (Erasmus referred to him as the "camelite"), who objected to Erasmus's interpretation of Paul's Epistle to the Corinthians (1521–22, 1525); Christoph von Utenheim, the bishop of Basel, to whom Erasmus addressed the treatise *On the Prohibition of Eating Meat*, who attacked Erasmus's criticisms of fasting, abstinence, the number of holy days of obligation, and his advocacy of marriage for priests (1522–23, 1532); Sanctius Carranza of Miranda, a theologian at Salamanca, who objected to Erasmus's notes on the New Testament (1522–23); Ulrich von Hutten, a German humanist and nationalist, to whom Erasmus addressed his *Sponge to Wipe Away the Aspersions of Hutten*, who accused Erasmus of cowardliness by not joining forces with Luther (1523); Martin Luther in the form of his *De libero arbitrio diatribe* (1524) and the *Hyperaspistes* (1526–27); Peter Sutor, a theologian at the Sorbonne, who suggested that Erasmus's New Testament undermined the church by calling the Vulgate into question (1525); Josse van Clichthove, who criticized his theological positions (1526); Noel Beda, the syndic of the Faculty at the Sorbonne, who accused Erasmus of heresy and sought to condemn his *Paraphrases*, his edition of the New Testament, and his *Enchiridion* (1526–29); in defense of his seal: *Terminus: concedo nulli* (1528); those Spanish monks who accused him of heresy (1528–29); those Franciscans who opposed his annotations on Saint Paul's Epistle to the Romans (1529); Gerardus Noviomagus (or Geldenhouwer), who accused Erasmus of opposing the Lutheran cause (1529); Albert Pio, the prince of Carpi, who also accused Erasmus of heresy (1529, 1531–32); Louis de Carvajal, a Spanish Franciscan who criticized Erasmus's New Testament (1529–30); those theologians at Strasbourg who called for a return to the primitive church, under the title of *Against the Pseudoevangelicals of Strasbourg* (1530); in defense of his position on piety against Eustace of Sichem (1531); and Peter Cursius (or Corsi) against the charges that he misinterpreted the proverb "Myconius calvus" (1535).

Though Erasmus personally abhorred quarreling and rancor, his patience broke under the strain of being accused of harming religion and of heresy itself. In a letter to Louis Baer, rector of the university at Basel (dated March 30, 1529), Erasmus reasoned, "it is a kind of denial of faith not to speak up against a charge of heresy."[76] It should not be surprising that most of his defenses are aimed at those scholastic theologians, labeled as "fools" in his *Praise of Folly* of 1511, who accused him of impiety. Throughout the *apologiae*, Erasmus is concerned with returning to the essential beliefs of Christianity, with stripping away the accumulated pious practices of the institutional church in order to get at the essentials. In drawing a distinction between Christocentric doctrines and manmade customs, he wished to stimulate the growth of the church by promoting Christian living. Nevertheless, as Lewis W. Spitz points out: "Erasmus was perfectly orthodox and 'correct' on all matters of dogma. His long *apologies* are replete with assertions that he had wished only to spread the true faith and that he had always been true to the ecclesiastical teaching office in all submissiveness and obedience. . . . His test was whether a doctrine had been approved by the church, not merely whether it was to be found in the Scriptures or was validated by early tradition."[77]

Erasmus quietly accepted the invectives of those who labeled him as "rude, coarse, stupid, ignorant, a block, a dolt, a fool,"[78] but when it came to charging him with heresy, he shrugged off his reserve and prepared moderate and reasoned defenses of his particular position. For it was no longer merely a matter of inherent flaws in his personality that was of concern but an attack on his belief in Christ. Erasmus set forth the reasons for these attacks in his letter to Baer (or Ber) of March 30, 1529:

> It is not obscure for what frivolous reasons these people first attacked me. To the great advantage of theology I cultivated languages and polite literature, which they now pretend to admire, although more than forty years ago they left no stone unturned to destroy and uproot them when they were just beginning to spring up. And that was the seed of this present tragedy. I exhorted the theologians that, leaving aside their little questions which have more of ostentation than of piety, they should betake themselves to the very sources of the Scriptures and to the ancient Fathers of the Church. Moreover, I did not wish that scholastic theology should be abolished, but that it should be purer and more serious. That, unless I am mistaken, is to favour, not to hurt it. I exhorted the monks to be what they said they were, namely, dead to the world, to trust less to external ceremonial, and to embrace rather true piety of soul. Is this wishing well or ill to the monks? . . . Never have I contemned the constitutions and rites of the Church, nor taught that they were to be contemned; but I have given preference to the precepts of God; I have shown the progression from ceremonies to better things; and if by the negligence of man anything foreign to them has crept in, I have indicated how such might be corrected, a thing which the Church has often done.[79]

Earlier, Erasmus had expressed indignation when he learned of the charges made against him by Lefèvre in his commentaries on Saint Paul's Epistles. Writing to Wolfgang Capito on December 6, 1517, he observed: "Within fourteen days after reading Lefèvre's criticism I had finished my Apology: the sole object of which is to repel the charge of impiety and blasphemy, which I know not by whose instigation, he had brought against me."[80] Some two months later he addressed another letter to Guillaume Budé (dated February 22, 1518) in which he emphasized his belief in Christ's divinity and expressed a hope for reconciliation: "To spend your life in the cause of friendship is considered laudable; but for the sake of a friend to admit yourself to be a blasphemer against Christ is not only madness, but impiety. . . . Let him [Lefèvre] change, if he can, the passage in which he lacerates me, and I shall do my best to suppress the Apologias in which I defend myself."[81] Erasmus desired an end to this dispute because it was damaging the cause of Good Letters and was draining away his energies from the pursuit of sacred studies. Cuthbert Tunstall, afterward bishop of London, in a letter dated September 14, 1517, reminded him of this fact:

> There is one thing I regret—that, while composing an Apology against this writer [Lefèvre], you have lost the time in which you might have written what would have been more useful to posterity. Do therefore bestow your first attention upon the revision of your Notes on the New Testament, which, in consequence of your promise, is greedily expected by everybody. Having deserved well of profane literature and won immortal fame in its service, you will do well, if you spend the remainder of your life in the illustration of Sacred Letters. Posterity will infer that the studies which concern the salvation of the soul have been dearer to you than those which afford mere amusement, when the latter have most attracted you in youth, but the former, embraced in mature years, have been deemed a worthy occupation for your age.[82]

Erasmus published the first collection of his apologies in October 1521 (part 1) and February 1522 (part 2) at the press of Froben in Basel. He described these works in his subtitle as "vindications" of his position and not as "excuses" ("non satis circunspecte sunt calumniati"). The volume included his *apologiae* against Diego López Zuñega, James Latomus, Jan Briard, those who had objected to his interpretation of "in principio erat sermo," Edward Lee, and Jacques Lefèvre d'Etaples. The border of the title page of this volume betrayed the mood of the author: it consists of humanlike representations of the Seven Deadly Sins.

It is John Olin's opinion that "the letter to Dorp [composed in May 1515 but not published until August in a collection of letters (the *Auctarium*) printed by Froben] is perhaps Erasmus's most important *apologia* and is extremely valuable in understanding *The Praise of Folly* within the context of Erasmus's aims and lifework."[83] In this letter to Dorp, Erasmus refers once again to his major purpose in writing books:

> For reasons such as this I have persuaded myself to guard my writings from any harmdoing or vengeance and to avoid contaminating them with

so much as a mention of evil. Nor did I have any intentions in the *Folly* different from those in my other works, although the method may have differed. In the *Enchiridion* I simply set down a design for Christian living. In the pamphlet *The Education of a Prince* I publicly advised in what subjects a prince ought to be instructed. . . . So for the *Folly;* the same thing was done there under the semblance of a jest as was done in the *Enchiridion.* I wanted to admonish, not to cause pain; to be of benefit, not to vex; to reform the morals of men, not to oppose them.[84]

Here, in 1515, Erasmus identified the common theme that pervaded all of his treatises. Myron P. Gilmore, in his essay, discusses in greater detail the meaning and significance of Erasmus's apology to Martin Dorp.

THE NEW TESTAMENT (1516)

As early as 1505, Erasmus began work on a text of the New Testament that was to be based in part on the surviving Greek manuscripts. He wrote to Dean Colet of his intentions late in 1504:

I am now eager, dear Colet, to approach sacred literature full sail, full gallop; I have an extreme distaste for anything that distracts me from it, or even delays me. But the ill will of fortune, which has ever regarded me with steadfast hostility, is the reason why I have not been able to free myself from these vexations. . . . Three years ago, indeed, I ventured to do something on Paul's Epistles to the Romans, and at one rush, as it were, finished four volumes; and would have gone on, but for certain distractions, of which the most important was that I needed the Greek at every point. Therefore for nearly the past three years I have been wholly absorbed by Greek. . . . I have gone through a good part of Origen's work; under his guidance I think I have achieved worthwhile results, for he reveals some of the wellsprings, as it were, and demonstrates some of the basic principles of the science of theology.[85]

Erasmus's earlier efforts at preparing annotations on Saint Paul's Epistle to the Romans failed because he lacked expertise in Greek. He realized as early as 1501 that he would need to perfect his knowledge of that language if he wanted to understand the writings of the Church Fathers on the New Testament and to get closer to the actual words of Christ. However, progress was slow. In his July 8, 1514, letter to Servatius Roger, Erasmus assured the prior at Steyn that he was "resolved to live and die in the study of the Scriptures. I made these my work and my leisure."[86]

Erasmus's New Testament was finally published in Basel by Froben in March of 1516 under the title *Novum Instrumentum.* He dedicated this *New Instru-*

ment to Pope Leo X. Erasmus was justified in renaming his New Testament, for it included an impressive number of innovations: a preface to the annotations, an exhortation ("Paraclesis") to the readers, an *apologia* for the Greek text, a Latin translation that differed somewhat from Saint Jerome's Vulgate text, and an explanation of his methodology. Erasmus also added a preface before each one of the Gospels and Epistles and provided over 1,000 notes both to help explain given passages and to call the reader's attention to the way of Christ. Throughout the annotations, Erasmus condemned superstition, ignorance, and false piety. In a letter to Dorp (May 1515) he explained his methodology: "I have translated the entire New Testament according to the Greek original, with the Greek appended directly to allow for quicker comparison. I added notes separately in which, partly by proofs and partly by the authority of early theologians, I show that what I emended was not changed rashly, lest my corrections should lack credence or my emendations be easily altered."[87]

Erasmus's *Paraclesis* was an exhortation to the reader to follow the *philosophia Christi* as well as an eloquent plea for the vernacular translation of Scripture. It was obvious to him that he could achieve a following among Christians only if they understood the words of Christ; and the best way to achieve such understanding was by urging the translation of the New Testament into vernacular languages:

> Indeed, I disagree very much with those who are unwilling that Holy Scripture, translated into the vulgar tongue, be read by the uneducated, as if Christ taught such intricate doctrines that they would scarcely be understood by very few theologians, or as if the strength of the Christian religion consisted in men's ignorance of it. The mysteries of kings, perhaps, are better concealed, but Christ wishes his mysteries published as openly as possible. I would that even the lowliest women read the Gospels and the Pauline Epistles. And I would that they were translated into all languages so that they could be read and understood not only by Scots and Irish but also by Turks and Saracens. Surely the first step is to understand in one way or another.[88]

Further on in the *Paraclesis,* Erasmus defined his *philosophia Christi:* "what else is the philosophy of Christ, which He himself calls a rebirth, than the restoration of human nature originally well formed? . . . If we seek a model for life, why does another example take precedence for us over that of Christ himself?"[89] Catherine Jarrott focuses her essay on Erasmus's commentary on the Pauline epistles and the development of his philosophy of Christ.

In preparing the first edition of his New Testament, Erasmus, according to his prefatory letter, collated ten Greek manuscripts, one dating back to the tenth century. However, we now know that most of these manuscripts were incomplete and of fairly recent origin; hence they were of little value. As a result of these limited sources and a careless job of proofreading, there were a small number of serious errors and a larger number of typographical errors in the 1516 edition. Even so, the demand for the *Novum Instrumentum* was so great that it was quickly sold out. Erasmus was applauded for his labors by many of the leading scholars of his day, including Johann Oecolampadius, Bishop Richard Foxe, Sir Thomas More, Henry Bullock, and John Watson. In replying to Watson on January 13, 1517, Erasmus declined to talk about the merits of his edition but did emphasize his purpose in publishing it, "that we have striven our utmost by our humble industry to commend the philosophy of Christ to virtuous minds."[90]

Erasmus sought to allay criticism of his work by dedicating his New Testament to the pope. His dedicatory letter of August 8, 1516, tried to emphasize the conservative nature of the text and his reliance on the Church Fathers:

> For by this labour, we do not intend to tear up the old and commonly accepted edition, but to emend it in some places where it is corrupt, and to make it clear where it is obscure; and this not by the dreams of my own mind, nor, as they say, with unwashed hands, but partly by the evidence of the earliest manuscripts, and partly by the opinion of those, whose learning and sanctity have been confirmed of the authority of the Church— I mean Jerome, Hilary, Ambrose, Augustine, Chrysostom, and Cyril. Meantime we are always prepared either to give our reasons, without presumption, for anything which we have rightly taught, or to correct, without grudging, any passage where as men we have unwittingly fallen into error.[91]

This letter to Leo X shows clearly that Erasmus was ready to retract any statement or translation of his that was based on erroneous evidence. All he asked for was a fair reading. Before actually publishing his text, he submitted it to the bishop of Basel, in whose jurisdiction he was living. The bishop accepted it without question. After it had appeared in print, Erasmus also submitted it to William Warham, archbishop of Canterbury; two doctors of theology, Louis Baer of Paris and Wolfgang Capito of Basel; Gregory Reisch, the prior of the Carthusians at Freiburg; Bishop John Fisher; Domenico Cardinal Grimani; Raffaele Cardinal Riario—all of whom praised it; and finally to Pope Leo X, who, according to Erasmus, sent him two letters of approbation.

With so much praise, Erasmus felt confident that he had satisfied all of the requirements that had been laid down by the Lateran Council (1512-17) on this matter. But his critics thought otherwise. Before the end of 1517, Erasmus was angrily criticized for issuing a new translation of Scripture without the express authority of a general church council. Erasmus answered the charge by asking his adversaries if they knew whether or not Saint Jerome had been required to submit his Vulgate to a church council before it had been completed. In a letter to Bullock dated August 1516, Erasmus observed, "I believe it was written first, and approved afterwards; and the same may take place with respect to my edition, though that is a thing I neither solicit nor expect."[92]

No sooner was the first edition out when Erasmus decided to correct it and to publish a second edition. He hoped in this way to satisfy his wrangling critics. Writing to Marcus Laurinus, the dean of St. Donatian at Bruges, on April 5, 1518, Erasmus spoke openly of his intentions: "But these wrangling critics, naturally stupid and rendered doubly blind by the malady of evil-speaking, believe, I fancy, that it has been my intention to supersede entirely the translation [of Saint Jerome] which we have in use, and which in several places, I myself prefer to the reading of the Greek copies; whereas all that I have done is to translate the text which I found in the Greek manuscripts, pointing out in the notes which reading I approve or disapprove. . . . I show by manifest proofs, that in a multitude of passages our version is depraved, but not so far as to endanger the Faith; and I point out how Cyprian, Jerome, and Ambrose agree with the Greek manuscripts."[93]

Erasmus fought an almost uphill battle when he attempted to improve the accuracy of the Vulgate. So entrenched had that Latin version of the Scriptures become by the sixteenth century that Erasmus decided to retain the text of Saint Jerome when he issued his third edition in 1522. Erasmus was, nevertheless, disappointed that a number of his readers had missed the whole purpose of his labors. His letter to Cardinal Wolsey of May 18, 1517, reiterates his lifelong commitment to piety and the instruction of children that lay at the base of his scriptural studies:

> At any rate I have taken every precaution, that nothing should proceed from me, which would either corrupt the young by obscenity, or in any way hinder piety, give rise to sedition, or draw a black line across any one's character. Whatever exertions I have hitherto made, have been made for the assistance of honourable studies and the advancement of the Christian religion; and all persons on every side are thankful for what has been done, except a few theologians and monks, who have no wish to be wiser or better than they are. May I lose the favour of Christ, if I do not desire that whatever I have of talent or of eloquence should be wholly dedicated to His glory, to the Catholic Church, and to sacred studies.[94]

This was an eloquent statement by Erasmus of his orthodox religious position some six months before Martin Luther drew the attention of Christendom to his Ninety-five Theses. Who could have been more catholic in his concern for the church than Erasmus, who preferred peace and harmony to revolt or sedition?

The second edition of the New Testament required a change in title, and Erasmus decided to name it the *Novum Testamentum*. His new edition appeared in 1519 (a third edition in 1522, a fourth in 1527, and a fifth in 1535) and included a justification for each book and an expanded discussion of his methodology (known as the *Ratio verae theologiae,* which was first published in 1518) and enlarged annotations. Ignoring the criticisms of his foes, Erasmus also published an entirely new translation of the Greek text which differed considerably from that of the Vulgate. Erasmus explained to Antonio Pucci, an ecclesiastical official, on August 26, 1518, the plan of his second edition of the New Testament:

> Having first collated several copies made by Greek scribes, we followed that which appeared to be the most genuine; and having translated this into Latin, we placed our translation by the side of the Greek text, so that the reader might readily compare the two, the translation being so made, that it was our first study to preserve, as far as was permissible, the integrity of the Latin tongue without injury to the simplicity of the Apostolic language.
>
> Our next care was to provide that any sentences, which had before given trouble to the reader, either by ambiguity or obscurity of language, or by faulty or unsuitable expressions, should be explained and made clear with as little deviation as possible from the words of the original, and none from the sense; as to which we do not depend upon any dreams of our own, but seek out the writings of Origen, Basil, Chrysostom, Cyril, Jerome, Cyprian, Ambrose, or Augustine. Some annotations were added (which have now been extended), where we inform the Reader, upon whose authority this or that matter rests, relying always upon the judgment of the old authors.[95]

It was Erasmus's intention to clarify the meaning of Scripture by determining its actual words. This could only be done by returning to the original Greek language in which it was first written and then by comparing it with later Latin translations. The study of theology itself depended on this kind of clarity. Erasmus underscored his interest in reforming theology in the same letter to Pucci referred to above: to "theology, which is almost too prevalent in the Schools, is to be added a knowledge of the original sources; it is to this result that our work especially leads."[96] Clarity of meaning would lead theologians to the actual teachings of Christ and put more emphasis on what he defined as necessary doctrine than on what later scholastic theologians have tended to emphasize. But in promoting such a program Erasmus only succeeded in antagonizing these very same theologians. They were outraged that he was suggesting to all of Christendom that theology might be harboring false ideas by giving undue emphasis to certain matters of faith and morals.

THE CHURCH FATHERS (1516-)

To support his textual studies of Scripture, Erasmus turned to the writings of the Church Fathers. He relied heavily on their learning and judgments. He discovered in their writings a keen appreciation for the study of Scripture and for its application to the lives of individuals. Erasmus succeeded in publishing the *opera* of the following Church Fathers: the letters of Saint Jerome (in four volumes) appeared in July of 1516, the works of Saint Cyprian in 1520, Arnobius and Saint Athanasius in 1522, Saint Hilary in 1523, Saint Irenaeus in 1526, Saint Ambrose in 1527, Saint Augustine in 1528-29, Lactantius (a single work) in 1529, Saint John Chrysostom and Alger in 1530, Saint Gregory Nazianzen in 1531, Saint Basil in 1532, and Origen posthumously in 1536.

Jerome and Origen were the two most important influences on Erasmus, and he valued their writings above all the others. He expressed his great admiration for both men by composing biographies of them, which he attached to his critical editions and in which he acknowledged their rational syntheses of classical and Christian learning. Throughout Erasmus's writings it is evident that he preferred the ancient Church Fathers to such medieval scholastic theologians as Saints Thomas Aquinas and Bonaventure, and the reason should not be surprising: the ancient Church Fathers, with their knowledge of ancient languages and history, were closer to the sources of Christianity and emphasized in their own writings the importance of imitating Christ. In a letter to Pope Leo X, dated April 29, 1515, Erasmus detailed his admiration for Saint Jerome:

> I saw that St. Jerome was so completely the first among Latin theologians, that we might almost call him the one person worthy of that name. What a fund in him of Roman eloquence, what skill in languages, what a knowledge of antiquity and of all history, what a retentive memory, what a perfect familiarity with mystic literature, above all, what zeal, what a wonderful inspiration of the divine breath! He is the one person who at the same time delights by his eloquence, teaches by his erudition, and ravishes by his holiness.[97]

Erasmus wanted to edit the works of Saint Jerome in order to promote Christian piety. Later on in the above letter he concludes: "I do not myself expect any other outcome of my exertions, but that Christian piety may obtain some aid from the memorials of Jerome. He, for whose sake I undergo this labour, will abundantly recompense me for it."[98] Christ was never far from his thoughts. Erasmus had begun work on the letters of Saint Jerome even before he started his study of the New Testament. He delayed it only because he saw the letters as an adjunct to Scripture. Erasmus's edition of Saint Jerome was judicious. It retained both Greek and Hebrew spellings and made a concerted effort to designate those letters that he regarded as spurious or doubtful. His notes display both erudition and restraint: a delicate balance.

Erasmus used the format of the preface to his critical editions to emphasize his Christocentric perceptions. Two examples will suffice. The first is taken from Erasmus's edition of Saint Hilary (1523). The prefatory letter (dated January 5, 1523) was addressed to John Carondelet, the archbishop of Palermo:

> When life leaves us, when faith is in the mouth rather than the heart, when we lack knowledge of the Sacred Scriptures, we drive men to believe what they do not believe, to love what they do not love, to understand what they do not understand. What is coerced cannot be sincere, and what is not voluntary cannot please Christ.[99]

The second example is taken from Erasmus's dedicatory letter to King John III of Portugal, dated March 24, 1527, in the *Chrysostomi lucubrationes* (Basel, 1527), which had also been scheduled to be inserted in his 1530 edition of Saint John Chrysostom; but when the king declined to acknowledge it, Erasmus withdrew the letter. The dedicatory letter urges the preacher to inspire Christian piety by promoting the study of Scripture:

> A preacher will readily find a means of winning over his audience if he succeeds in getting people to know and love what they are learning. One can find in the Scriptures an abundance of material for charming and captivating pious hearts, without searching for bait in witty phrases from poets and mimes. If the teacher is on fire, he will easily set others aflame. If he deeply enjoys the things he preaches, he will easily inspire his listeners with that same feeling. This heart, this golden tongue [of Chrysostom] which was aimed at the secular forum was diverted by Christ to the preaching of the gospel.[100]

Erasmus's efforts won the plaudits of many men of learning. Francois Deloynes, a French humanist, described his reaction to the edition of Saint Jerome's letters in an epistle to Erasmus dated November, 1516: "and the works of Jerome are in hand, a laborious task, which was reserved for the strength of a Hercules, that is, of an Erasmus; in which I seem to see Jerome himself by your care and diligence come back to light, and anticipate the promised day of Resurrection."[101] But Erasmus was also aware of the fact that his work sometimes aroused the ire of readers. In an effort to pacify his critics, he promised restraint. Erasmus referred to this subject in a letter to Louis Baer, dated January 1, 1517, where he also emphasized his didactic purpose:

> I only endeavour by my small exertions to promote the general instruction. It has been thought that I express myself in some places with too much heat; but those who think so do not take into account the want of due respect with which sacred literature and the writings of the Fathers are received. While I was pushing on through my work, although my indignation was repeatedly curbed by reason, I could not in every case hide my feelings. But I was afterwards forced to be more restrained by the extreme scrupulosity of some of my friends. For indeed, if it can be done, I should wish to assist study in such a way as not to offend any mortal being. If I do not always succeed in this; I am comforted by the consciousness of rectitude, and by the consideration that up to this time I have the approval of the most approved persons; and we may well hope that what now satisfies the candid will in time satisfy all. At any rate I trust that I shall never be pleased with anything that is false in learning or religion, even in my own books.[102]

Erasmus pledged to Baer and to his other friends that henceforth he would pursue his scholarship with regard for the eyes of the beholder as well as for truth itself. Since truth required impartiality, he weighed the merits and shortcomings of the writings of the Church Fathers. In a letter to John Botzheim (August 19, 1529) Erasmus justified his dissensions from the Church Fathers by observing that these mortal men "sometimes fall into heretical error." For example, he noted that "Jerome translated and interpreted the Prophets and yet he often admitted that he could not understand their meaning."[103] Erasmus's powers of discrimination mark him as a man of great strength and originality. He bent his full faculties to the task of uncovering the meaning of Scripture, but without offending "any mortal being." It was, to quote Deloynes, a "laborious task, which was reserved for the strength of Hercules."

THE COMPLAINT OF PEACE (1517)

Querela pacis was written in 1516 at the request of John le Sauvage, chancellor of Brabant, and dedicated to the bishop of Utrecht, Philip of Burgundy. It appeared in print in December of 1517. Some thirty-four editions, including German and Dutch translations, were published before 1536.[104] In raising objections to war, Erasmus naturally turned to the Old and New Testaments, where he freely quoted from the Psalms, Isaiah, Saints Paul, Matthew, John, and Luke. Erasmus not only condemned wars between nations but hostilities that took place between members of a family or among scholars, particularly theologians and monks. He especially abhorred warfare among Christians, and, in turn, was repelled by the fact that the very instruments of war, namely guns, were frequently blessed by the clergy before the start of a battle, and not infrequently named after an apostle or decorated with the images of saints.

The Complaint of Peace called true Christians back to Christ. It held up the image of the Prince of Peace in order to promote concord: after all, "truly Christ doth no other thing, commanding them to learn one certain thing of Him: to be meek of mind and not fierce."[105] But Erasmus was not content with merely condemning wars and those who participated in them, he sought to find a way to permanent peace. He thought he saw a solution to this crisis in the second decade of the sixteenth century when three young rulers sat on three of the leading thrones of Europe: Francis I of France, Charles I of Spain, and Henry VIII of England. Through his friendship with each of them and through the persuasive power of the written and printed word, he hoped to convince these rulers to seek only peaceful solutions to any of their future difficulties:

> I pray thee, O thou Christian prince, if thou be truly a Christian, behold the image of thy Prince. Observe and mark how He entered into His Kingdom, how He proceeded, how He departed hence; and thou shalt easily understand how He would have thee to rule . . . that peace and concord might be the sum and conclusion of all thy care and rule.[106]

Erasmus went so far as to ask these princes to sue for peace at any price: "Sometimes peace must be bought. And if thou calculate what war shall consume and waste, and that thou shalt keep thy citizens from destruction, it shall seem, although thou didst buy it full dearly, to be bought for little. And when a great deal more besides the blood of thy citizens should have been spent in war, thou shalt reckon how great and manifold evils thou eschewdest and how much goodness thou defendedst; so shalt thou not repent thee of thy expenses and charges."[107] Human life was obviously of greater value than money or material goods.

Erasmus also directed other petitions to the papacy and to Christian men in general. On May 21, 1515, he wrote to Pope Leo X, pleading with him not to resort to war even for the purpose of repelling the Turks and recovering the Holy Land:

> . . . those savage beasts, will not withstand the roar of our Leo, and truculent though they be, they shall feel, yes, they shall feel the unconquerable strength of our gentle Leo, and they will be impotent before a Pontiff armed

more with piety than with might of numbers, and who bears into battle the immortal assistance of the Heavenly Power.[108]

It was far better to subdue the Turks by setting a good example before them than by force of arms. Prior to this letter, he addressed one to Anthony of Bergen under date of March 14, 1514, in which he promoted peace among all men, but especially among Christians:

> I often wonder what it is that drives the whole human race, not merely Christians, to such a pitch of frenzy that they will undergo such effort, expense, and danger for the sake of mutual destruction. . . . For us, who boast of naming ourselves 'Christians' after Christ who preached and prac- tised naught save gentleness, who are members of one body, one flesh, quickened by the same spirit, nurtured upon the same sacraments, joined in union to a single head, called to the same eternal life, hoping for that supreme communion whereby, even as Christ is one with the Father, so we too may be one with him—how can anything in this world be so im- portant as to impel us to war, a thing so deadly and so grim that even when it is waged with perfect justification no man who is truly good approves it?[109]

Moreover, Erasmus lamented the consequences of man's aggressive nature on the future of Christendom, but saw signs of hope in Divine Providence: "I can see vast disturbances in the making, and what their outcome will be is not clear; may God in his mercy vouchsafe to quiet the storm that now afflicts Christen- dom."[110] Erasmus placed his faith in man's future in the mercy of God.

PARAPHRASES OF THE NEW TESTAMENT (1517–)

According to Wallace K. Ferguson, Erasmus emphasized the *philosophia Christi* in his studies on Scripture, but he also revolutionized that study: "Eras- mus introduced a new note into biblical interpretation by demonstrating the part played by human authorship and error. He insisted on treating the Bible as a human document, to be studied in the light of modern historical and philological knowledge. He said little, it is true, about dogma; but he had much to say about the philosophy of Christ."[111] After the New Testament appeared in 1516, John Colet and other scholars urged Erasmus to prepare paraphrases of the books of the New Testament that would expand upon the meaning of the texts.

The *Paraphrase of St. Paul's Epistle to the Romans* was published at the end of 1517 and was dedicated to Domenico Cardinal Grimani, a patron of letters. It was followed in turn by the paraphrases of Corinthians and Galatians (in

1519); by Ephesians, Timothy, Titus, and Philemon, together with the Epistles of Peter and Jude (in 1520); by Philippians, Colossians, Thessalonians, and the Epistles of John, James, and Saint Paul to the Hebrews (in 1521); by the Gospel of Saint Matthew (in 1522); by the Gospels of Mark, Luke, and John (in 1523); and by the Acts of the Apostles (in 1524).[112] Moreover, collected editions of these paraphrases appeared in 1524, 1532, and 1534, and certain paraphrases (for example, the Gospel of Saint Matthew and Saint Paul's Epistle to the Corinthians) were translated into German as early as 1521. So popular did this work become that during the reign of King Edward VI (1547–53), the Paraphrases in English were ordered to be placed alongside the Bible in every parish church in England: John Byddell had earlier printed Leonard Cox's translation, titled *The Paraphrase of Erasmus . . . upon ye Epistle of . . . Paule unto . . . Titus* (about 1535), and Nicholas Udall, Thomas Caius, and John Old et al. translated a two-volume edition of the Paraphrases in 1548–49 that was used by the Church of England. These paraphrases, unlike Erasmus's edition of the New Testament and his annotations, provided a single interpretation of the text that reflected the considerable erudition and good judgment of its author.

Erasmus set forth the circumstances surrounding his writing of the *Paraphrases* in a letter to an unknown recipient, dated November 1517:

> I send, meantime, our Paraphrase upon the Epistle of Paul to the Romans, which is our latest offspring; for, being now employed in the most troublesome of all literary labours, I mean, in the revision of the text of the New Testament I am wont to refresh my mind with such relaxation, when tempted by satiety to steal away from work. They thus serve as my ball or my die, sending me back with fresh vigour to my task. . . . Perhaps I may deal with the other Epistles in the same way, if I find this first taste is not displeasing to the palates of my readers. For it is wonderful how much hazard there is, even in these matters; so that it often happens that where you expect the most appropriation, you carry away a poor return; and on the other hand, where you expect no favour at all, you come in for a great amount of praise.[113]

In an earlier letter of October 31, 1517, Erasmus wrote to Peter Barbier, an official at the court of King Charles I of Spain, expressing pleasure at the wonderful reception that was given to his *Paraphrase on St. Paul's Epistle to the Romans* by men of learning. He regarded this epistle as "the principal and most excellent part of the New Testament." Taking advantage of the opportunity, Erasmus employed the prologue to this edition to urge the reader to "commit himself wholly unto Christ."[114] Moreover, in a dedicatory letter to Archduke

Ferdinand of Austria which accompanied his edition of the Gospel of Saint
John, he advised even princes to imitate the message of the Gospel: "A prince
does not preach and teach the Gospel, but he does observe, practice, and fulfill it."[115] Albert Rabil, Jr., discusses the paraphrases as instruments of Christian
reform and as an expression of Erasmus's *philosophia Christi.*

THE COLLOQUIES (1518--)

The *Colloquia* originated as exercises for the teaching of Latin to boys during
the time when Erasmus was supporting himself and pursuing theological studies
at the University of Paris (1495 to 1499). They were never meant to be published, and when they did appear in an unauthorized edition, edited by Beatus
Rhenanus and printed by Johann Froben in November of 1518, Erasmus was
distinctly annoyed. Under pressure, he finally approved their publication in
1519. The text of the *Colloquies* is of an intensely personal nature. Erasmus
chose the names of his own pupils to identify the various speakers. He did so
deliberately in an effort to make the study of Latin more attractive to his
youthful readers. It is clear from the design of this book that Erasmus had
mastered the arts of teaching before he had published his first book! So popular
did this work become that within a year of its appearance it was reprinted
in Paris, Antwerp, Louvain, London, and again in Basel by Froben himself. It
has been estimated that eighty-seven reprints appeared before Erasmus's
death.[116]

The *Colloquies* enjoyed such great success because it was an immensely useful
book: both grammar-school boys and style-conscious adults benefited from
its novel approach to writing. But it was also much more than a book on rhetoric. According to Craig R. Thompson: "The result was a book of unusual
variety: debates on moral and religious questions: lively arguments on war,
government, and other social problems; advice on how to train husbands, wives,
and children; discourses on innkeepers, beggars, pets, horse thieves; on methods
of study or of sleep or of burial; on diet and on sermons—all this and much
more."[117] As usual, uppermost in Erasmus's mind was his *philosophia Christi.*
He was anxious to persuade everyone, from the tender-aged child to the aging
adult, that the best means to heaven was through the imitation of Christ in
the Gospels. In his *De utilitate colloquiorum* (1526), Erasmus reminded his
readers that even though "Socrates brought philosophy down from heaven
to earth; I have brought it even into games, informal conversations, and drinking
parties. For the very amusements of Christians ought to have a philosophical
flavor."[118]

Even earlier though, in his 1522 colloquy entitled *The Godly Feast,* which was
"in some ways the most typical and has always been one of the most popular"

of the colloquies,[119] Erasmus stressed the importance of "obeying the commandments of the Gospel." Speaking through the characters Eusebius and Timothy, he observed:

> *Eusebius:* Does he [i.e. the doorkeeper in the form of a statue of Saint Peter] seem to you an uncivil porter who at one and the same time warns us to avoid sin and turn to the pursuit of godliness; next, warns us that we do not attain to the true Christian life by works of the Mosaic law but through gospel faith; finally, that the way to life eternal is by obeying the commandments of the Gospel?
>
> *Timothy:* And look: the path on the right shows us presently an exquisite little chapel. On the altar Jesus Christ gazes heavenward, whence his Father and the Holy Spirit look out, and he points to heaven with his right hand while with his left he seems to beckon and invite the passerby.
>
> *Eusebius:* Nor does he receive us in silence: you see in Latin, "I am the way, and the truth, and the life"; in Greek, "I am Alpha and Omega"; in Hebrew, "Come, ye children, hearken unto me; I will teach you the fear of the Lord."[120]

Christ commanded the faithful to imitate his example.

Erasmus revised and added to his *Colloquies* regularly. In 1519, for example, he added an appendix to them in which he addressed himself to the Protestant cause:

"I clearly bore witness to my thorough opposition to the Lutheran teaching. At that time I warned Luther privately—he had written to me first—to act with sincerity and with that moderation which befits one who professes the Gospel."[121] Erasmus found fault specifically with Luther's cause because Luther and his followers failed to imitate the example of Christ in the Gospel. Yet, in spite of his opposition to Lutheranism, portions of the *Colloquies* were held to be heretical by the Sorbonne as early as May of 1526. In an attempt to satisfy these critics and others, Erasmus wrote a defense of them (*De utilitate colloquiorum,* dated May 21, 1526) which he appended to his edition of June 1526. Erasmus emphasized the pedagogical purpose of his work: "Now if someone protests that it is undignified for an old man to play in this childish fashion, my answer is: 'I don't care how childish, if only it's useful.' And if graybeard grammar masters are commended for coaxing youngsters with bits of cake into wanting to learn the rudiments, I don't think I should be reproached for attracting youth with like zeal to refinement of Latin speech and to godliness. . . . But to implant from the start a taste for excellence in young minds *is* urgent. Moreover, I'm not sure anything is learned better than what is learned as a game."[122]

Thoroughly practical in his approach to learning and pedagogy, Erasmus never forgot that the real object of education was Christian piety. He willingly played the part of "a fool" in order to entice young minds to learn of Christ and to imitate his way of life: "And this little book, if taught to ingenuous youth, will lead them to many more useful studies: to poetry, rhetoric, physics, ethics, and finally to matters of Christian piety. I have played the part of a fool in making myself eulogist of my own writings, but I was forced to it, partly because of the villainy of slanderers, partly because of service to Christian youth, for whom we must do all we can."[123]

Erasmus took the trouble to answer his critics because he wanted to promote goodwill and to uproot blind judgment. He implored his adversaries to end their bitterness and dissension, and to advance "the fellowship of the heavenly Jerusalem."[124] Erasmus also perceived that the way of Christ was something other than "a dismal mode of life." Christ was not a pessimist: he loved life and urged his followers to enjoy it. Erasmus, speaking through the character Hedonius, describes his own conception of Christ: "Completely mistaken, therefore, are those who talk in their foolish fashion about Christ's having been sad and gloomy in character and calling upon us to follow a dismal mode of life. On the contrary, he alone shows the most enjoyable life of all and the one most full of true pleasure."[125] Erasmus added a new perspective to Christian life, one that combined piety and joy and was rooted firmly in the image of Christ himself. Sister Geraldine Thompson examines the meaning of the *Colloquies* in terms of Erasmus's use of invention.

THE METHOD OF TRUE THEOLOGY (1518)

The *Ratio verae theologiae* was first written as prefatory material for the 1516 edition of the New Testament. It was later expanded and printed separately at Louvain in November of 1518 under the title: *Ratio seu methodus compendio perveniendi ad veram theologiam.* Eighteen editions appeared during the lifetime of the author.[126] In fashioning this theological treatise, Erasmus drew upon Scripture and such Church Fathers as Origen, and Saints Basil, Gregory Nazianzen, Athanasius, Cyril, John Chrysostom, Jerome, Ambrose, Hilary, and Augustine.

In this handbook for students of theology, Erasmus impressed upon his readers the importance of attaining a virtuous life before embarking on the study of theology. He also insisted on the learning of Hebrew, Greek, and Latin and the mastery of the *studia humanitatis* (including dialectic, rhetoric, arithmetic, music, poetry, and history) as preliminary skills to the study of theology. The theological curriculum itself consisted of the following subjects: exegesis, especially the study of the Church Fathers, church history, civil and ecclesiastical law, and ethics. Finally, Erasmus devoted attention to the methodology for interpreting figurative language. He encouraged allegorical interpretation of both classical and Christian texts in order to teach morality. Writing to John Botzheim on August 19, 1529, he justified his own interpretations of certain figures of speech or tropes in the New Testament by arguing that Saint Jerome had removed "all the Hebrew tropes [from the Old Testament] despite Augustine's vain protests." For Erasmus, Scripture was more than "a merely human product" since "the essence of Scripture lies in its meaning not in its words."[127] In one of the following essays, Father Georges Chantraine examines the idea of mystery in Erasmus's view of exegesis.

The Method of True Theology was soon attacked by theological adversaries; among them was Jacob Latomus of Louvain, who criticized Erasmus for his emphasis on piety in the formation of the theologian. Indirectly, Erasmus responded to this charge by underscoring the importance of virtue in the life of a theologian, in his letter to Bishop Fisher, dated April 2, 1519:

> I had said in my *Method* that piety and edification are theology's good side. Latomus attacks this view and demonstrates at length that to be a theologian is not equivalent to being pious. But I fear, in the future, if they carry on, some may say that to be a theologian is not equivalent to being a wise man. . . . The folly of it all: while we are wasting our labours and the peace of others in such wrangling, we count ourselves as saints, as theologians and as Christians: But, meanwhile, where is Christian peacefulness, where is simplicity, and where are our happy blithesome games in the fields of Scriptures?[128]

Erasmus insisted that theologians as spokesmen for the Church should assume responsibility, paying particular attention to the encouragement of concord and order. In his dedicatory letter of June 1, 1523 (Allen, *EE*, V, Ep. 1365) to Archbishop Albert of Brandenburg (which appeared in a new edition of the *Ratio*), Erasmus discussed the religious strife that was then consuming the world and his own efforts toward securing peace:

> It is part of my unhappy fate that my old age has fallen on these evil times. We must implore the Lord Jesus that He, who alone has the power to do so by his spirit, will turn the hearts of the Christian people to the love of peace and concord. . . . And yet what is our religion if peace be gone? The world would be no darker if you were to extinguish the sun. For my part I would rather be a grocer in the possession of Christian tranquillity, and rejoicing in evangelical simple-mindedness, than the greatest and most renowned theologian in the world, and be involved in these dissensions. I, at any rate,

for my own part, am devoting all my strength to eliminating this poison from the inmost fibres of my heart, recovering the simplicity and peace of the Gospel spirit, and composing myself to that habit of mind in which I may appear with all confidence before the judgment seat of Christ, to which perhaps tomorrow or any day I may be summoned.[129]

Erasmus was staunchly committed to securing Christian tranquillity, and he devoted his energies to achieving it in the spirit of the Gospel. Lewis W. Spitz has identified and summarized Erasmus's pursuit of the Gospel message in terms of his *philosophia Christi:* "Erasmus constantly stressed the imitation of Christ, the exemplar of virtue and wisdom, an imitation which involved the mystic and spiritual indwelling of Christ in the human heart, not merely the outward mimicking of his actions—as one would copy the charity of a saint, for example."[130]

A DISCOURSE ON THE FREEDOM OF THE WILL (1524)

De libero arbitrio diatribe seu collatio (*A Diatribe or Discourse on the Freedom of the Will*) was published in September 1524, at presses in Basel, Antwerp, and Strasbourg, and appeared in some seven editions during the author's lifetime.[131] Erasmus described the work as follows in a letter to John, the elector of Saxony (March 2, 1526): "I gave the book a very modest title, calling it a discussion or conference. I do not assume the role of a judge, but of one who is questioning and discussing, meanwhile laying aside all authority except that of Holy Scripture."[132] Throughout the treatise Erasmus insisted that salvation without freedom of choice was a non sequitur. He argued that the belief in man's free will rests on Scripture, the Church Fathers, ancient philosophers, and human reason itself. He concluded that "the will is not powerless though it cannot attain its end without grace."[133] Erasmus based this conclusion on the following reasoning:

I ask what merit can a man arrogate to himself if whatever, as a man, he is able to achieve by his natural intelligence and free choice, all this he owes to the one from whom he receives these powers? And yet God himself imputes this to our merit, thus we do not turn our soul away from his grace, and that we apply our natural powers to simple obedience. And this surely goes to show that it is not wrong to say that man does something and yet attributes the sum of all that he does to God as its author, from whom it has come about that he was able to ally his own effort with the grace of God. . . . Here there is nothing that a man can arrogate to his own strength and yet, with sure confidence, he may hope for the reward of eternal life from God, not because he has merited it with his good deeds, but because it seemed in accordance with God's goodness to promise it to those who trust in Him.

According to Erasmus, God required man to cooperate freely with His saving grace:

> It is man's part to pray without ceasing that God will impart and increase in us his Spirit, giving thanks if anything is done well by us, that we may marvel at his power in all things, everywhere wondering at his wisdom, everywhere loving such goodness. This way of viewing the matter seems to me also completely plausible, for it agrees with Holy Scripture, and answers to the confession of those who, once for all dead to the world, are buried together with Christ in baptism, that the flesh having been mortified, they afterward may live and act in the Spirit of Jesus, in whose body they have been implanted by faith.[134]

Uppermost in Erasmus's mind was the need to "live and act in the Spirit of Jesus," and this could only be accomplished if the individual participated willingly and actively in the imitation of Christ's life.

Luther responded to Erasmus's tract in December of 1525 with his *De servo arbitrio* (*The Bondage of the Will*), in which he flatly rejected Erasmus's argument and accused him of impiety, insisting that man could not effect his salvation without Christ's prior saving grace. Erasmus answered Luther in the *Hyperaspistes* (*The Heavenly Armed Soldier*) which was published in two parts (March 1526 and September 1527). In this work Erasmus accused Luther of being a dogmatist and extremist, who in his enthusiasm for Scripture rejected reason as a second source of truth.

Though Erasmus sympathized with the original purpose of the Protestant Reformation, he refused to join that movement. He recoiled at the thought of a revolutionary band that lacked sincerity and fomented discord. He tried to explain his reasons in the following letter to Martin Bucer, the reformer of Strasbourg, on November 11, 1527:

> However it was the duty of the leaders of the movement, if Christ was their goal, to refrain not only from vice, but even from the appearance of evil; and to offer not the slightest stumbling block to the Gospel, studiously avoiding even practices which, although allowed, are not yet expedient. Above all they should have guarded against all sedition. If they had handled the matter with sincerity and moderation, they would have won the support of the princes and bishops: for they have not all been given up for lost. And they should not have heedlessly wrecked any thing without having something better, ready to put in its place. . . . So I could wish that with your

good sense you would strive to the end that this movement, however it began, may through firmness and moderation in doctrine and integrity of conduct be brought to a conclusion worthy of the Gospel. To this end I shall help you to the best of my ability. As it is, although the host of monks and certain theologians assail me with all their artifices, nothing will induce me wittingly to cast away my soul.[135]

It was obvious that Erasmus wanted the Church to undergo the reforms these men were advocating, but he was quite unwilling to divorce himself from the institutional Church. He described his undogmatic position and his allegiance to the Church and Holy Scripture in his *Discourse on the Freedom of the Will:* "so far am I from delighting in 'assertions' that I would readily take refuge in the opinion of the Skeptics, wherever this is allowed by the inviolable authority of the Holy Scriptures and by the decrees of the Church, to which I everywhere willingly submit my personal feelings, whether I grasp what it prescribes or not."[136]

Throughout the controversy with Luther, Erasmus preached moderation to Protestants and Catholics alike. He sought to build a church that promoted greater faith but fewer dogmas, one that was based exclusively on Christ's teachings and precepts. He abhorred the thought of a divided Christendom, of two hostile camps that would promote dogmatism and eschew tolerance. Erasmus encouraged the Lutheran cause at the outset because he saw in it the possibility of restoring the "philosophy of Christ." He expressed this idea in a letter, dated December 6, 1520, to Lorenzo Cardinal Campeggio:

So I have favored Luther; I have favored the good points I noticed in him, or which I believed to be there. Actually, I favored not him but the glory of Christ. At the same time, I also noticed things in him which made me feel somewhat uneasy and suspicious. Consequently when he, of his own accord, provoked me with a letter I seized the opportunity at once to give him some careful advice as to what I thought he should avoid. My purpose was that, once his natural qualities were corrected and purified, he might with rich results and also with great glory and profit for Christ restore for us the philosophy of the gospel which had almost become cold from neglect.[137]

But when the leaders of Protestantism discarded "the philosophy of the gospel" and adopted revolutionary positions, Erasmus refused to support them. How could he reconcile the actions of Luther with those of his exemplar, the Prince of Peace? In his accompanying essay, Brian A. Gerrish examines the positions of Erasmus and Luther on the question of free will.

DIALOGUE ON THE CICERONIAN (1528)

The *Dialogus Ciceronianus* appeared in print for the first time in 1528. There were eight editions during the author's lifetime.[138] Erasmus dedicated the work to Johann Vlatten, a humanist-statesman in the service of the duke of Cleves, on February 14, 1528. The *Ciceronian* was presented in the form of a dialogue between the two anti-Ciceronians (Bulephorus and Hypologus) and one Ciceronian (Nosoponus). Most of the discussion takes place in the latter's study. Bulephorus begins the assault by pointing out some of Cicero's imperfections as a stylist: (1) he lacked a sense of humor; (2) he was too verbose; (3) he was not always reliable; (4) he lacked skills in certain literary genres; and (5), most serious of all, Cicero's writing was irrelevant to the moral issues of the day. Since Ciceronian writers used only words that had been found in Cicero's writings, it was virtually impossible for them to express Christian concepts in a language that had never dealt with such ideas.

Erasmus also argued that he perceived "neopagan" ideas in contemporary Ciceronian writings, masked behind certain stylistic conventions. In turn, Ciceronian writers accused Erasmus of being a fraud and dubbed him "Er-rasmus" in an effort to discredit his works. As the coup de grace, Erasmus concluded his treatise by observing that some of the major Latin writers in the period after Cicero, who were admired by all Ciceronians, were totally un-Ciceronian in style. In the end, Bulephorus and Hypologus (with Erasmus incognito) persuade Nosoponus that he is suffering from a malady and that the only remedy lies in abandoning his allegiance to Ciceronianism. In one of the following essays, Emile V. Telle discusses the *Ciceronian* as a comedy, emphasizing its popularity in terms of its humorous content.

Despite the satirical quality of this work, Erasmus stressed the point in his dedicatory letter to Vlatten that he wrote this dialogue not to ridicule Ciceronians per se but to warn his readers against the neopagan ideas that were imbedded in Ciceronian texts and to lead them to a greater appreciation of Christian piety. Speaking through the character Bulephorus, Erasmus noted in the last few pages of the *Ciceronian* that "The liberal arts, philosophy, and oratory are learned to the end that we may know Christ, that we may celebrate the glory of Christ."[139]

ON THE INSTRUCTION OF BOYS (1529)

The *Declamatio de pueris statim ac liberaliter instituendis* (*Declamation on the Immediate and Kindly Instruction of Boys*) drew the readers' attention to two key words in its title, *immediate* and *kindly*. Erasmus advocated instruction in the *studia humanitatis* that was to begin early in the life of a child and was to be accompanied by kindness. According to W. H. Woodward, Erasmus's *On the Instruction of Boys* is the "ripest of his educational tracts."[140] In it, one finds the often quoted phrase of Erasmus that "Men are not born, they are made." This maxim serves as the theme of his treatise.

In his preface, Erasmus indicated that he composed this work during his stay in Italy between 1506 and 1509. Moreover, he viewed it as a complement to his *De copia*. It was not published, however, until September of 1529 in Basel by Froben. At least four other editions appeared in the same year in Cologne, Antwerp, Strasbourg, and Paris. Some ten editions appeared in Erasmus's lifetime.[141] The work was dedicated to the young duke William of Cleves (1516–92), who sent Erasmus a silver cup in appreciation of the honor.

The treatise is a synthesis of classical and contemporary ideas and methods. Erasmus drew from Greek and Latin sources, especially from the Old and New Testaments, Plutarch, and Quintilian, but he also borrowed from Marsilio Ficino, Pico della Mirandola, Robert Gaguin, John Colet, and others. In turn, Erasmus influenced such educational theorists as Thomas Elyot, Juan Luis Vives, and Johann Amos Comenius. It is the last-named educator to whom Jean-Claude Margolin devotes his attention in the following collection of essays. Erasmus summarized his methodology as follows:

> My principles of method then are briefly these. First, do not hurry, for learning comes easily when the proper stage is reached. Second, avoid a difficulty which can be safely ignored or at least postponed. Third, when the difficulty *must* be handled, make the boy's approach to it as gradual and as interesting as you can.[142]

Boys were to be lured to learning by making it as interesting as possible. Erasmus also insisted that the progress of the individual child depended on these three conditions: (1) innate capacity, (2) the skilled application of instruction and guidance, and (3) proficiency through practice. In addition to making learning interesting and keeping the individuality of the child in mind, Erasmus stressed the importance of employing a qualified and sympathetic schoolmaster. Indeed, the success of education depended largely on the skill of the teacher:

> Seeing, then, that children in the earliest stage must be beguiled and not driven to learning, the first requisite in the Master is a gently sympathetic manner, the second a knowledge of wise and attractive methods. Possessing these two important qualifications he will be able to win the pupil to find pleasure in his task.[143]

Erasmus valued education because it taught children how to be virtuous and how to be of service to the state and to their God:

For I hesitate not to affirm that those things which men covet for their sons—health, riches, and repute—are more surely secured by virtue and learning—the gifts of education—than by any other means. True, the highest gifts of all no man can give to another, even to his child, but we can store his mind with that sound wisdom and learning whereby he may attain to the best. . . . Your children are begotten not to yourself, but to your country; not to your country alone, but to God.[144]

ON CIVILITY OF MANNERS FOR BOYS (1530)

De civilitate morum puerilium was first printed in Basel by Froben in 1530. Erasmus dedicated it to an eleven-year-old boy, Henry of Burgundy, Lord of Veere. Two other editions appeared in the same year (one in Cologne, the other in Paris). It has been estimated that some thirty editions appeared during the lifetime of the author, including translations in German (1531) and English (1532).[145] Moreover, throughout the seventeenth, eighteenth, nineteenth, and twentieth centuries, translations of the work appeared in German, Dutch, French, and Spanish.

Erasmus wrote this work on etiquette for children. He did so by maintaining a simple and clear Latin style which could be easily understood by school-age readers. He offered them advice on how to behave in church, at play, in the school dormitory, how to dress and walk correctly. In addition to imitating good manners, Erasmus also insisted in his introduction to the work that children should pursue the liberal arts and be trained as responsible members of society. Moreover, they should be instructed in piety as early as possible. Writing to John and Stanislaus Boner, sons of Severin Boner, a Polish nobleman, on December 12, 1532, Erasmus emphasized the importance of cultivating piety in young children:

> There is nothing better for man than devotion to God, and its seeds must be implanted in small children bit by bit right along with their mother's milk. . . . And yet, there is nothing more natural for us than virtue and learning, and if you took these away from man he would cease to be a man.[146]

In addition, Erasmus made the point that education placed an obligation on the recipient that called him to a life of public service: "he is not educating you for himself but for Christ and the good of your country."[147] In an earlier letter to Severin Boner, Erasmus stressed the importance of early education in the sound formation of young minds: "For you appreciated the fact that we understand most thoroughly and remember most accurately the things we imbibe in those early years when we are still impressionable and . . . adaptable to any habit."[148] More important still was the character of the nurse or tutor who first instructed the child in the elements of piety and learning. In his letter to John and Stanislaus Boner, Erasmus described the young child as "free from any defects and, like soft wax, is plastic and readily copies any and every habit found in his model."[149] Genuine piety in the nurse and first teacher begets piety in the young. Franz Bierlaire discusses the influence of *On Civility of Manners for Boys* in the sixteenth century.

ON PREACHING (1535)

Ecclesiastes, sive de ratione concionandi (*Ecclesiastes: On the Art of Preaching*), divided into four books, was begun by Erasmus about 1523 but was not completed and printed until 1535. There were four editions before Erasmus's death in 1536.[150] Throughout the work, Erasmus urges the preacher to base his sermons on Scripture in an effort to reform society along Christian lines. He provided the preacher with a battery of illustrations and examples to support his efforts. Erasmus dedicated the treatise to Christopher von Stadion, the bishop of Augsburg, only after he had learned of the senseless execution of his friend Bishop Fisher, at whose request he had undertaken the composition of the work.

Part 1 deals with those qualities, whether natural or acquired, that ought to be cultivated in a good preacher. Erasmus specifically condemned those preachers who preferred to pursue wealth and fame rather than to serve Jesus Christ. In relating a story about a Franciscan preacher named Robert de la Lice, who epitomized greed, Erasmus, speaking through the mouth of a conventional Franciscan, commented on his qualities:

> It was not your eloquence that drew those tears, but the compassion which I then felt for you, and a concern that one of such happy talents should choose rather to serve the world than Jesus Christ.[151]

Just as Erasmus saw man in terms of flesh and spirit, so he interpreted the Bible in terms of its literal and spiritual meanings. The spiritual meaning of Scripture referred to its allegorical or tropological (i.e. moral) sense. It was the allegorical sense that Erasmus found the hardest to explain because it was not self-evident. Though he was willing to set aside the literal or historical meaning of a scriptural passage when it conflicted with Christ's teachings or with morality itself, Erasmus maintained the importance of using historical and allegorical interpretations in combination with one another, since the allegorical and tropological senses of Scripture ultimately depend on their historical foundation. Above all, however, Erasmus was concerned with identifying the meaning of Scripture so that it could be made applicable to human conduct. Moral action lay at the heart of his exegesis.

Nevertheless, Erasmus was aware of man's limited knowledge and his inability to comprehend every passage in Scripture. In his *Discourse on the Freedom of the Will,* for example, Erasmus had acknowledged that man's mind is unable to freely understand all the mysteries of Scripture:

> For there are some secret places in the Holy Scriptures into which God has not wished us to penetrate more deeply and, if we try to do so, then the deeper we go, the darker and darker it becomes, by which means we are led to acknowledge the unsearchable majesty of the divine wisdom, and the weakness of the human mind.[152]

Robert G. Kleinhans sees *On Preaching* as a means to uncovering the mind and intentions of its author. He develops this theme in the last of the following essays.

Shortly after the appearance of *Ecclesiastes,* Erasmus expressed chagrin at the tumultuous conditions in which Christendom found itself, but he also took time to reiterate the lifelong goal of his writing program. The following excerpt is from a letter composed at Basel and was addressed to Damian a Goes, a humanist-statesman in the service of King John III of Portugal, on August 18, 1535:

> If the Lord would only take me to his rest and away from the mad world: so far am I from desiring the long life you are invoking for me. If my writings have helped anyone to attain pure piety I am glad. I am not concerned about fame and wish that I were not burdened with it.[153]

These touching words from the Prince of Humanists, within a year of his death, should serve as a reminder to us all that Erasmus of Rotterdam died convinced that he had not only preached the philosophy of Christ but had lived it as well. In an earlier letter to Jean Morin (November 30, 1531), Erasmus confessed that "I would have had a mitre too, except that I have preferred to serve Christ rather than men."[154] The glory of his life was in the living of it. In serving Christ he exposed the vanities of mortals and the follies of organized society with the grace and charm of his engaging personality. And yet, no doubt, greater glory awaited this man of peace and compassion when he reached his Maker and laid bare his immortal soul that had been purified by a lifetime's commitment to "the glory of Christ" and to Christian piety. Throughout his life and his works, Erasmus sought to bridge learning and piety: "from the body to the spirit, from the visible world to the invisible, from letter to mystery . . . as if by the rungs of Jacob's ladder."[155]

NOTES

1. *The Correspondence of Erasmus,* trans. R. A. B. Mynors and D. F. S. Thomson (Toronto, 1974), 1 : 301–02. Hereafter cited as *CWE.*

2. There are a number of good biographies of Erasmus. For three of the best, see Roland H. Bainton, *Erasmus of Christendom* (New York, 1969); Johan Huizinga, *Erasmus and the Age of Reformation,* trans. F. Hopman (New York, 1924, etc.); and Margaret Mann Phillips, *Erasmus and the Northern Renaissance* (London, 1949, and New York, 1950, etc.). The reader should also consult two recent collections of interpretive essays: *Erasmus,* ed. T. A. Dorey (London, 1970), and *Erasmus of Rotterdam: A Quincentennial Symposium,* ed. R. L. DeMolen (New York, 1971). For an edited collection of Erasmus's writings and letters, see my volume in the Documents of Modern History series, entitled *Erasmus* (London and New York, 1973).

3. Erasmus to Martin Dorp, May 1515, trans. John C. Olin, *Desiderius Erasmus: Christian Humanism and the Reformation* (New York, 1965), pp. 57, 78.

4. Erasmus, *Opus Epistolarum,* ed. P. S. Allen et al. (Oxford, 1906–58), vol. 8, Ep. 2275, p. 365, ll. 68–69. Henceforth cited as *EE.*

5. I am obviously not the first person to arrive at such a conclusion. E.-W. Kohls and R. R. Post et al. have sought to determine the origins of the *philosophy of Christ* in Erasmus's earliest writings, notably the *De contemptu mundi.* See Kohls, *Die Theologie des Erasmus,* 2 vols. (Basel, 1966) and Post, *The Modern Devotion* (Leiden, 1968), pp. 658–80. For a useful discussion of the twin themes of *pia doctrina* and *docta pietas* in Erasmus's letter to Paul Volz (August 14, 1518) and his *Ratio verae theologiae* (1518), see chapter 2 of Georges Chantraine's *'Mystère' et 'Philosophie du Christ' selon Erasme* (Namur-Gembloux, 1971). Moreover, Sister Geraldine Thompson has demonstrated in her study of Erasmus's satirical writings that he wrote in order "to alert a great new reading public to a richer understanding of truth and goodness." See her *Under Pretext of Praise: Satiric Mode in Erasmus' Fiction* (Toronto, 1973).

6. *CWE,* 2 : 103.

7. Ibid., 1 : 51.

8. Ibid., p. 59.

9. Translated by Barbara Flower in Johan Huizinga's *Erasmus and the Age of Reformation* (New York, 1957), p. 221.

10. *CWE,* 1 : 185.

11. Erasmus to John Botzheim, Jan. 30, 1523, in *EE,* vol. 1, Ep. 1, pp. 38–42, and Erasmus to Hector Boece, March 15, 1530, in ibid., vol. 8, Ep. 2283, pp. 373–77.

12. *CWE,* 2 : 299–300.

13. Francis M. Nichols, trans., *The Epistles of Erasmus,* 3 vols. (London, 1901–17), 2 : 287.

14. Ibid., 2 : 334–35.

15. Ibid., p. 379.

16. Ibid., p. 415.

17. Craig R. Thompson, ed., *The Colloquies of Erasmus* (Chicago and London, 1965), p. xiii.

18. Erasmus, *The Education of a Christian Prince,* trans. Lester K. Born (New York, 1936), p. 153.

19. Nichols, *Epistles,* 1 : xxi–xxxvii, provides us with an informative survey of the various editions of Erasmus's letters. The reader should compare Nichols's findings with those of P. S. Allen in his *EE,* vol. 1, appendix 7, pp. 593–602. Neither author accounts for all of the editions of the correspondence that have survived until now.

20. This letter served as the preface to Erasmus's *Epistolae ad diversos* (Basel, 1521).

For a partial translation, see J. W. Binns's interesting essay, "The Letters of Erasmus," in *Erasmus,* ed. T. A. Dorey (London, 1970), pp. 57–58.

21. Nichols, 1 : 390.

22. Erasmus, *Catalogus Lucubrationum* (1523, 1524), trans. J. W. Binns, in *Erasmus,* ed. T. A. Dorey, p. 56.

23. Erasmus to Guillaume Budé, Oct. 20, 1516, in Nichols, *Epistles,* 1 : xxix.

24. Erasmus to Beatus Rhenanus, May 27, 1520, in Nichols, 1 : lxxvii. This letter was later published as a prefatory epistle to Erasmus's *Epistolae ad diversos* (Basel, 1521).

25. Allen, *EE,* 1 : 600, gives the date of this edition as August 31, 1521, taking it from the title page, but this date is incorrect, seeing that one of the letters in the volume has the date November 21, 1521.

26. Erasmus to Beatus Rhenanus, May 27, 1520, Nichols, 1 : lxxvii.

27. This edition was missed by Nichols and not recorded by Allen until volume 3 of his *EE* (appendix 12, pp. 627–29). See Alöis Gerlo, ed., *Erasme et la Belgique* (Brussels, 1969), p. 9.

28. Nichols, 1 : lxxviii–lxxix.

29. Erasmus to Beatus Rhenanus, May 27, 1520, Nichols, 1 : lxxxi.

30. D. F. S. Thomson maintains that the earliest letters of Erasmus to Servatius Roger were literary exercises. See Thomson, "Erasmus as a Poet in the Context of Northern Humanism," *The Guilden Passer* 47 (1969): 187–210. Erasmus, however, would not have regarded such exercises as letters. See his definition of a letter in epistle to Beatus Rhenanus, May 27, 1520, Nichols, 1 : lxxxi.

31. Erasmus to Beatus Rhenanus, May 27, 1520, Nichols, 1 : lxxxi.

32. Ibid., 1 : lxxxii.

33. Erasmus to the Reader, *Opus epistolarum* (Basel, 1529), Nichols, 1 : lxxxiii.

34. Erasmus to Friendly Readers, February 20, 1536, in *Opus epistolarum* (Basel, 1536), trans. Nichols, *Epistles,* 1 : lxxxvii, xc, xci.

35. See Allen, *EE,* vol. 4, Ep. 1110, p. 279. The letter to John Sapidus, ca. June 1520, served as the preface to Book 1 of the *Antibarbari.*

36. For a discussion of this and other matters, see Kazimierz Kumaniecki's introduction to his critical edition of the *Antibarbarorum liber,* in *Opera Omnia Desiderii Erasmi Roterodami* (Amsterdam, 1969), vol. 1, pt. 1, pp. 7–32.

37. See Nichols's edition of *The Epistles of Erasmus,* 1 : 100–02, and Albert Hyma's *The Youth of Erasmus* (New York, 1968), pp. 182–204.

38. Roger Ascham to Jerome Froben, June 10, 1551, in *The Whole Works of Roger Ascham,* ed. J. A. Giles, 3 vols. (London, 1864–65), vol. 1, pt. 2, pp. 288–90.

39. *EE,* vol. 1, appendix 5, pp. 587–90.

40. Hyma, *Youth of Erasmus,* p. 185.

41. Ibid., pp. 200–01.

42. Ferdinand van der Haeghen and Marie-Thérèse Lenger, *Bibliotheca Belgica* (Brussels, 1964), 2 : 382–86.

43. Margaret M. Phillips gives the number of adages in the 1536 edition as 4,251. See her edition, *The 'Adages' of Erasmus* (Cambridge, 1964), p. 3.

44. *CWE,* 1 : 257–58.

45. See Mrs. Phillips's translation in *The 'Adages' of Erasmus,* p. 346.

46. Nichols, 2 : 282.

47. *CWE,* 2 : 87.

48. *The Enchiridion of Erasmus,* trans. Raymond Himelick (Bloomington, Ind., 1963), p. 166.

49. Van der Haeghen and Lenger, *Bibliotheca Belgica* (1964), 2 : 838–42.

50. Nichols, 1 : 337-38. The translation has been modified in places.

51. Ibid., 2 : 282.

52. *CWE*, 2:53.

53. Nichols, 3:116.

54. *EE*, vol. 1, Ep. 222, p. 460, II. 26-27.

55. See Betty Radice's introduction to her translation of *Moriae encomium*, titled *Praise of Folly* (London, 1974), p. 7.

56. *CWE*, 2:163-64.

57. Erasmus, *Praise of Folly*, trans. Radice, p. 81.

58. Ibid., p. 84.

59. Ibid., p. 73.

60. Ibid., pp. 108-09.

61. Ibid., p. 110.

62. Ibid., p. 35.

63. Nichols, 3:209.

64. Olin, trans., *Christian Humanism and the Reformation*, p. 60.

65. *CWE*, 2:300.

66. See Herbert D. Rix, "The Editions of Erasmus' *De Copia*," *Studies in Philology* 43 (1946): 595-618.

67. *CWE*, 2:226.

68. Ibid., p. 227.

69. Nichols, 2:416.

70. Van der Haeghen and Lenger, *Bibliotheca Belgica* (1964), 2:865-66.

71. Erasmus, *The Education of a Christian Prince*, trans. Lester K. Born (New York, 1936), p. 140.

72. Ibid., pp. 212-13.

73. Ibid., p. 189.

74. Ibid., p. 177.

75. Nichols, 2:506.

76. John J. Mangan, trans., *Life . . . of Desiderius Erasmus of Rotterdam*, 2 vols. (New York, 1927), 2:312, and *EE*, vol. 8, Ep. 2136, p. 120.

77. Lewis W. Spitz, *The Religious Renaissance of the German Humanists* (Cambridge, Mass., 1963), pp. 226-27.

78. See Erasmus, *Opera omnia*, ed. Jean Le Clerc (Leiden, 1703-06), 9:317C-D.

79. Mangan, *Life . . . of Desiderius Erasmus*, 2:312-13.

80. Nichols, 3:179.

81. Ibid., p. 265.

82. Ibid., p. 62.

83. Olin, *Christian Humanism and the Reformation*, p. 56.

84. Ibid., pp. 59-60.

85. *CWE*, 2:86-87. For a useful discussion of Erasmus's exegesis, see John B. Payne, "Toward the Hermeneutics of Erasmus," in *Scrinium Erasmianum*, ed. J. Coppens (Leiden, 1969), 2:13-49.

86. Translated by Flower in Huizinga, *Erasmus and the Age of Reformation*, p. 216.

87. Olin, *Christian Humanism and the Reformation*, p. 90.

88. Ibid., pp. 96-97.

89. Ibid., pp. 100, 102.

90. Nichols, 2:454.

91. Ibid., p. 316.

92. Ibid., p. 325.

93. Ibid., 3:325-26.

94. Ibid., pp. 385-86.

95. Ibid., pp. 430-32.

96. Ibid., p. 431.

97. Ibid., 2:201.

98. Ibid., p. 203.

99. Hans J. Hillerbrand, trans., *Erasmus and His Age* (New York, 1970), p. 169.

100. Ibid., p. 197.

101. Nichols, 2:440–41.

102. Ibid., pp. 451–52.

103. *EE*, vol. 8, Ep. 2206, p. 260.

104. Van der Haeghen and Lenger, *Bibliotheca Belgica* (1964), 2:1017.

105. Erasmus, *The Complaint of Peace,* trans. William H. Hirten (New York, 1946), p. 24.

106. Ibid., p. 20.

107. Ibid., p. 44.

108. Mangan, *Life . . . of Desiderius Erasmus,* 1:395.

109. *CWE,* 2:280.

110. Ibid., pp. 279–80.

111. Wallace K. Ferguson, ed., *Erasmi Opuscula: A Supplement to the Opera Omnia* (The Hague, 1933), pp. 225–26.

112. Ferdinand van der Haeghen, *Bibliotheca Erasmiana* (Ghent, 1893), cites 1520 editions of the Paraphrase of the Gospel of Saint Matthew and the Paraphrase of the Epistles of Saint James. See pp. 149 and 143 of his *Bibliotheca Erasmiana.*

113. Nichols, 3:163–64.

114. Erasmus, *Opera Omnia,* ed. Jean Le Clerc (Leiden, 1703–06), 7:771–72.

115. Ibid., pp. 493–94.

116. Thompson, *The Colloquies of Erasmus,* p. xxv.

117. Ibid., p. xxvi.

118. Ibid., p. 630.

119. Ibid., p. 47.

120. Ibid., p. 50.

121. Erasmus to Duke George of Saxony, Dec. 12, 1524, trans. Hillerbrand, *Erasmus and His Age,* p. 179.

122. Thompson, *Colloquies,* p. 625.

123. Ibid., p. 633.

124. Ibid., p. 637.

125. Ibid., p. 549.

126. Van der Haeghen and Lenger, *Bibliotheca Belgica* (1964), 2:1040.

127. Erasmus to John Botzheim, Aug. 19, 1529, in *EE*, vol. 8, Ep. 2206, p. 260.

128. Jean Rouschausse, trans., *Erasmus and Fisher: Their Correspondence* (Paris, 1968), pp. 67–69.

129. Robert B. Drummond, trans., *Erasmus: His Life and Character* (London, 1873), 2:187–88.

130. L. W. Spitz, *The Religious Renaissance of the German Humanists,* p. 225.

131. Van der Haeghen, *Bibliotheca Erasmiana* (1893), p. 20.

132. Hillerbrand, *Erasmus and His Age,* p. 191.

133. Erasmus, *De Libero Arbitrio,* trans. E. Gordon Rupp et al. under the title *Luther and Erasmus: Free Will and Salvation* (Philadelphia, 1969), p. 79.

134. Rupp et al., *Luther and Erasmus,* pp. 84–85, 86.

135. Translated by Flower in Huizinga, *Erasmus and the Age of Reformation,* pp. 245–46.

136. Rupp et al., *Luther and Erasmus,* p. 37.

137. Hillerbrand, *Erasmus and His Age,* p. 159.

138. Van der Haeghen, *Bibliotheca Erasmiana* (1893), p. 75.

139. Erasmus, *Dialogue Ciceronianus,* trans. Izora Scott under the title *Controversies over the Imitation of Cicero* (New York, 1910), p. 129.

140. William H. Woodward, *Desiderius Erasmus: Concerning the Aim and Method of Education* (Cambridge, 1904, and New York, 1964), p. 27.

141. Jean-Claude Margolin, ed., *Declamatio de pueris statim ac liberaliter instituendis: Etude critique, traduction et commentaire* (Geneva, 1966), p. 127.

142. Woodward, trans., *Concerning the Aim and Method of Education*, p. 217.

143. Ibid., p. 203.

144. Ibid., pp. 185, 187.

145. Van der Haeghen, *Bibliotheca Erasmiana* (1893), pp. 29–30.

146. Hillerbrand, *Erasmus and His Age*, pp. 256–57.

147. Ibid., p. 257.

148. Ibid., p. 253.

149. Ibid., p. 257.

150. Van der Haeghen, *Bibliotheca Erasmiana* (1893), p. 78.

151. John Jortin, trans., *The Life of Erasmus,* 3 vols. (London, 1808), 2:215.

152. Rupp et al., *Luther and Erasmus*, p. 38.

153. *EE*, vol. 11, Ep. 3043, p. 207.

154. Hillerbrand, *Erasmus and His Age*, p. 256.

155. Erasmus, *The Handbook of a Christian Soldier,* trans. Margaret E. Aston in "The Northern Renaissance," *The Meaning of the Renaissance and Reformation,* ed. R. L. DeMolen (Boston and London, 1974), p. 90.

1 Ways with Adages

MARGARET MANN PHILLIPS

The history of the *Adagia,* covering most of Erasmus's long working life, can be approached from two positions: the beginning and the end. We can ask ourselves the double question: what do we know of the inception of the book and is it possible to arrive at a definition of its final true character?

When and why did Erasmus develop the idea of a collection of proverbs? To date the answer is probably, very early. There is a proverb, later to be cited in the *Adagia,* in his first recorded letter, written apparently at the age of fourteen.[1] And one of the few approachable people who inspired his boyhood, Rudolph Agricola, was associated for him with a proverb: *Quid canis et balneo?* as he wrote in the first *Collectanea,* and this memory was maintained in the *Adagiorum Opus* to the end.[2] From the beginning he had a liking, which amounted to reverence, for the sayings consecrated by time. Not only were proverbs cherished by the authors he most admired—and the strongest influence here may have been Jerome—but they represented in tabloid form his deep urge to rediscover the wisdom of the past. Here we feel the great gulf between ourselves and the men of the Renaissance, for whom Erasmus was speaking when he wrote about the "allurements of Antiquity" as conferring "an exceptional amount of elegance and grace when they have come to form part of the accepted idiom and the daily coin of language. Proverbs improve with age exactly as wines do."[3] The revolution in taste of the early nineteenth century has given a prestige to originality which obscures the delight found by the early humanists in well-worn coin of phrase, the more hackneyed the better. For Erasmus, indeed, the old *was* the new, much newer than the products of more recent centuries.

Perhaps Erasmus was attracted to proverbs because he was Dutch. The Dutch have always had a special facility for pithy sayings, and it was not hard to find in his own language what seemed like echoes of the ancient voices. But the *Adages* seem to have been associated more particularly with England. The collection had been begun in Paris, but it was for an Englishman, Lord Mountjoy; and it was discussed in Oxford, where it had particular encouragement from the prior of the house of Austin Canons where Erasmus lodged, Richard Charnock. Charnock was a friend of Colet's and they spoke together about the brilliant stranger. But we may be sure that it was not Colet who wished Erasmus

to go on with the *Adages*. Erasmus's letter of October 1499 shows clearly
enough that Colet thought his friend had spent enough time on "the rocks
of the Sirens." To him, as to mistaken critics of a later age, the *Adages* may
have been merely pagan trifles. The developed Aldine *Adagia* must have made
him change his mind.[4]

It was the success of the slight and jejune performance of 1500 which
launched Erasmus on the lifelong amusement and effort of construction which
became the *Adagiorum Opus*.

If one attempts to define the ultimate result, one thing at least is clear: it is
not to be judged, like most books, by the author's purpose. In other cases it
is often enough to ask, what was the author's objective and did he achieve it?
With the *Adages,* no; it is an organic growth. Erasmus certainly had a clear
aim at the outset, which he describes in the preface-letter to Mountjoy,[5] and it
amounts to aids for the writer or speaker who wishes to embellish his prose;
a pedagogical aim, parallel with the *De copia* and the *De conscribendis epistolis,*
fruits of his teaching period, of which the first drafts date from about this
time. There was the additional need to explain obscure allusions in the classical
texts, as Erasmus points out,[6] where ignorance of the meaning of a proverb may
stand in the way of a correct reading. It was to be an exercise in comprehension
and in the achievement of *copia.*

But as the book grew through nearly forty years, these humble aims became
enclosed in the immense accretion like the grain of sand in an oyster. The book
came to represent the author's mind in the same way as a long-built-up library
can be a reflection of the owner's tastes and development. He said at first that
it was a task without glamor or prestige, not allowing for flowers of rhetoric,
dealing with things "so tiny, so humble, that not only do they not attract
ornaments of speech and fluent writing but they repel everything of the sort."[7]
But that was near the beginning, when some of the uses of the *Adagia* were yet
in the future, and it is amusing to see him at this time (1508) rejecting the
reproach that he has not spent on his work the nine years recommended by
Horace, with the typically Erasmian argument that you might spend nine years
on a hundred items, but when it came to Thousands you would have to proceed
more quickly.[8] He was not then envisaging a process that would continue till
he died; nor did he expect to live until nearly seventy. In 1524, however, he
wrote: "A year ago the *Adages* came out augmented and corrected in many
places. And a new edition is ready. I promise that I am going to do this as
long as I live."[9]

To arrive at any assessment of what is surely one of the most original books
ever written, though compiled so largely from borrowed material, we must
look at the result rather than the aim, and begin by deciding what it is not. A

collection of proverbs, certainly, but obviously not merely that (Erasmus insisted from the beginning that he was not compiling a dictionary of proverbs).[10] It is not systematic, nor is it haphazard; nor is it a book to be read straight through. It is not a sheaf of stories and anecdotes, though they form a large part of it; it is not, as the compilers of the *Index Librorum Prohibitorum* seem to have thought, a subversive repertory of hidden topical allusions, though these are there. It is not the mouthpiece of any circle of humanists, nor a boosting platform for any individual or cause, though there are frequent, usually complimentary, mentions of contemporaries. It is decidedly one man's work, yet its structure is more severe than that of the usual commonplace book. It expresses one person's view of the world of his time, but linked continuously with a historical background and literary and ethical standards of a high order. His reader met not only Erasmus but the classics. We may attempt to follow the widening process that was the result of a lifelong *commerce des livres,* as one and another facet of Erasmus's reading struck him, and thus arrive at a definition of the book.

By 1508 the pedagogical aim had already been extended to teach the right attitude toward textual study and criticism. It was an age for waging war in the cause of clarification. Corrupt texts abounded, and the *Adagia* abounds in examples of Erasmus's campaign. He suggests emendations or variant readings, sometimes to be accepted by future generations of scholars, sometimes not. He discusses the views of others, usually with tact and respect (an exception is Apostolius). In a long comment on the mysterious phrase *Non nostrum onus, bos clitellas (LB,* 2.9.84), he begs the reader not to decide against him too quickly if his reading differs from that of other scholars; *labentur hi quoque, qui libros emendant,* and he adds that Aldus is not to be held responsible for all the misreadings in the Aldine edition of Cicero's letters. He will defend Aldus, *tum quia doctus est, tum quia amicus.* Errors are often the fault of typesetters rather than editors; a passage of Varro is "vilely corrupt, not only because of the times but by the fault of those common printers who seem to have only this one object in view, the destruction of all good books." In another place (*fricantem refricere*) he discusses two readings of Plato, and remarks that at one time he followed an incorrect one because the Greek text was not at hand: "it seemed right to inform the reader of this, in case anyone should work up a grievance against me on the grounds that I had rashly changed a passage of Plato."[11]

Some authors, like Andrea Alciati or Paolo Bombace, are mentioned with the highest praise. When a criticism is implied, great care is taken not to offend: giving a translation of a Greek epigram, he first transcribes the version of John Argyropoulos and then adds one of his own, giving his reasons, and adding: "I am not saying this to cast aspersions on a man whose scholarship deserves the thanks of liberal studies, but so that young readers may profit by the criticism; for this is mainly written for them." Similarly, he queries Domizio Calderini, but calls him *vir alioqui probe doctus.*[12]

Two of the most revealing passages about his task as a textual critic are in *Quis aberret a janua?* and *Amazonum cantilena.* In the first it is a question of a misreading in Greek, θύ꒤ας for θή꒤ας. "It often happens that an error in an archetype is carried on from one book to another. I am not saying this because I want to start a dispute, if anyone feels differently: that is beside our purpose, and also I know what a ticklish thing it is to alter anything in such important authors. However, I will bring out the conjectures I have made. If they seem likely to anyone, he can follow my opinion; if not, the old view will have all the more authority for having been called in question. On this point the learned will pronounce. I have done my duty as a commentator by exposing what I have found in the authors and what seems likely to me." On *Amazonum cantilena* he admits himself puzzled, and proposes the reading *mazonomon* (a dish in which food was brought into a banquet, denoting luxury). "But this is just a dream of mine, until something more certain is put forward by the learned. And no one need despair of that, since every day new authors are brought to light. After the fourth edition of this book, Caelius Rhodiginus's book came out, in which he suggests that this means not the Amazonian women, but the lower orders (*de tenuibus dicere*). As this comment is particularly feeble, how much more modest it is to do as I do, and say I don't know what I don't know!"[13]

The book gave plenty of examples of Latin fluency, sometimes of contrived *copia,*[14] of the tricks of style and diminutives Erasmus loved. But it was important not only to teach good Latin but to whet the appetite for Greek. The 1508 edition, emanating from the Aldine Academy, did not always offer Latin versions, but when Erasmus took the next edition to Froben he was conscious of the need to translate for the benefit of his northern audience, and he inserted many more Latin equivalents, and also turned the earlier Latin prose versions into verse. The Aldine edition had been so hurried, as he says in the letter already quoted of 1524,[15] that there were bound to be roughnesses: "In the *Adages* I translated verse as rapidly as prose," while the presses worked. Greek is nearly always the key to the adage; sometimes a Greek word will illuminate the meaning, as when he gives the word λαβή for *ansa,* not only a "handle," but a "hand-hold" used by wrestlers in the palaestra. Surely such a shrewd psychologist as Erasmus would know that he only stimulated a schoolboy's curiosity when he said of a phrase in Aristophanes: "I would not hesitate to translate these lines if they were as decent as they are elegant!"[16]

One of the most important functions of the *Adagia* was to supply an anthology of the Greek poets. A striking instance of this is the series of quotations from Homer in the third Thousand, introduced by the following preamble:[17]

> Antiquity held Homer in such high honour, as Macrobius testifies, that single lines of his became famous as proverbs. We have mentioned some of these here and there in the present work, especially those which we found quoted in literature. Now it seems to me that it would increase the value of the work if I selected from the whole corpus of Homeric poetry certain lines which have such a proverbial appearance that there can be no doubt that they are among the number used as adages by the ancients. There is no verse of this poet which cannot be applied to use as a proverb, but for our part we have preferred to select a few out of the many; partly so that no one could say we lacked diligence on so obvious a point, partly because for some unknown reason quotations appeal much more when each person has picked them out for himself. Thus it seemed enough to choose a small number and show the way, indicating how they should be used. Even in these cases, although we have brought out the use of the verse which sprang to mind as we were writing, there is nothing to prevent the same verse being used in various ways. I would not countenance this being done with other poets, unless it were thought allowable in the case of Virgil, whom you could rightly call the Latin Homer; but there is some divinity in Homer which makes it right and proper to borrow anything from him on any grounds, even if (as often happens with anthologies) you twist the words into a very different sense. Although we know that these cannot be appreciated unless one can enter into the meaning in Greek, we still give a translation of them, as well, in case there are people who cannot understand them.

Textual study could be dry, but not in the hands of a writer so conscious of the need for light relief. In the *Adagia* Erasmus put into practice the method he was advocating at much the same time in *De pueris instituendis*, written during his stay in Italy, 1506–09, though not published until many years afterwards.[18] The most striking of his injunctions is to create pleasure in learning: study so arranged for the child that it seems not work but a game, *ut absit laboris imaginatio, sed puer existimet omnia per lusum agi.*[19] Just so the education of Gargantua seemed "que mieulx ressembloit un passetemps de roy que l'estude d'un escholier."[20] Erasmus's treatise is full of words like *blandimentum, dulcescere, blandae illecebrae*—pleasant inducements, as he suggests learning reading from letters made of biscuit or cut in ivory. Similarly, the *Adagia* is skillfully manipulated to rest the mind; learning must be lightened by pleasure or play. It may be the pleasure of fine writing or charming pictures, like the lines of

Ennius quoted from Aulus Gellius describing the "friend for all hours," portrayed *eleganter simul et graphice;*[21] the delight in words and especially in poetry, which he quotes at length for the same reason, one feels, as Montaigne— to lighten and give color to his prose.

Or it may be the simpler forms of entertainment, sheer play. He tells tales with evident relish, and when we read *non gravabor ipsius verba inscribere* we know that something has pleased him which he wishes to share with us: stories from Aesop or Pliny, or comic interludes like the illustration to *Oleum ac operam perdidi,* which reads like a folktale even if it is from Macrobius:[22]

> Octavius had won a splendid victory at Actium. Among those who hurried to congratulate him was a man carrying a crow, which he had taught to say "Hail, victorious Caesar, hail, Emperor." Caesar was amazed at the obliging bird, and bought it for 20,000 *nummi.* A partner of the successful trainer, who had not laid hands on any of the cash, informed Caesar that he had a crow too. . . . The words it said, which he had taught it, were "Hail, Emperor, victor over Antony." Good-humouredly, the Emperor thought it sufficient to order him to share his mate's prize.
>
> When he was similarly greeted by a parrot, and a magpie, he bought those too. A certain poor cobbler was prompted by these events to teach a crow a similar salutation; wearied by the trouble it took, he often used to say to the unresponsive bird, "Oil and toil are lost on you." Finally, however, the crow did begin to say the often-dictated greeting. Hearing this as he passed, Augustus said, "I have enough greeting-birds like this in my house." A memory came to the crow of what he had heard his scolding master say, and he added, "Oil and toil lost." Caesar laughed at this, and had the bird bought at a higher price than any paid before.

Illustrations from children's games abound: the poppy-leaf which girls rub between their fingers (if it crackles, he loves me; if it doesn't, he loves me not), the finger-game still played in Italy, the joke of softening an egg to make it pass through a ring. A learned explanation of *in simpulo,* involving Cicero, Faustus Pompeius, Varro, and Pliny, ends with the suggestion, apparently Erasmus's own, that it comes from a children's game, raising "a storm in a teacup" by blowing into a small receptacle through a straw.[23]

More serious but no less entertaining are the many details of life in the past, calculated to awaken the curiosity of the Renaissance reader but also supplying a lively picture of the classical world: Greek coinage, calculation of time, status of slaves, military organization, clothes, baths, agriculture, music, painting, geographical identifications in Asia Minor—often linking mythology with fact. Even modern languages come into the picture, however remote from them

Erasmus sometimes seems to be, but it is noticeable that he often hopes to link a vernacular with Greek; what he says about London is of some interest here:

Rhodii sacrificum (2.6.43):

Lindus is a town in Rhodes, from which London in Britain may be derived: Stephanus calls this Lindonium and quotes Martianus as his authority. Rhodes and Britain are both islands, and the ancient tongue of this people (which is now called Welsh, *Walica*) shows clearly enough that it comes from the Greeks, or is at least a mixture. Even in their way of life they are not far removed from that of Greece.

All through the *Adagia* we find the constant attempt to identify the classical proverbs with those of the present day. Phrases linger on: "They left with bag and baggage," "He carries water in one hand and fire in the other" (still said in Holland, according to Erasmus); if a silence falls on the feast, it is still an omen, even if nobody says "Mercury is passing"; *suum cuique pulchrum* has its modern counterpart, "No one ever found his sweetheart ugly." Not that there are not surprises: "to play ball" does not mean consent, but arguing for argument's sake, *velut Scotista respondet Scotistice;* and "to throw cold water" is a means "to stimulate to further effort." But on the whole, things change very little. Wedding parties are as silly as they were in ancient times, the barber's shop is a center of gossip as it always was, the great men chatter through divine service as they did in Greece, the astrologers have taken the place of the ancient augurs, and the soothsayers impose themselves not only on the mob but on kings and the rulers of the earth.[24]

Are these lighter touches for the schoolboy or the scholar? No doubt they are often digressions to ease the tedium of learning. But they also have their serious purpose: to establish the continuity of history. The *Adages* were instrumental in changing the point of view toward the past, in introducing historical perspective, which is characteristic of their time. Tools for such a purpose were unperfected in Erasmus's day, and he may sometimes suggest untenable hypotheses. But the general tenor of the work was to make the past real and to see the present as an inheritance. Nowhere is this more plain than when there is a correlation to be noticed between biblical and Christian thought and the accepted notions of antiquity. For to Erasmus the study of the past was more than antiquarian speculation, it was an insight into the history of mankind which threw into prominence the coming of Christ.

These are, in a way, side issues in the *Adagia,* yet they form the essence of the book. Erasmus's whole lifework is adumbrated here, the classics are seen as a cultural force, as precursors yet on a different plane from the teaching of

Christus praeceptor noster—from the unquestioned authority of the Lord. When the *Adages* speak of Christ, it is as a teacher—and how often this has been a grievance launched against Erasmus!—but this is because the field of the *Adages* is that of education and the proverb is hallowed by its use by the Master, "Christ the true Doctor of Divinity." It was not the place for preaching or doctrinal discussion, and Erasmus reserved these for other writings. But his tone makes it clear that the teaching of Christ is different, and to be taken differently, from the precepts of men. For example, in *Lapides flere* he says that to associate feeling with stone is a hyperbole, a poetic exaggeration. But when Christ used similar terms, when he said at the entry into Jerusalem, "If men were to keep silent these stones would cry out," and "God is able of these stones to raise up children unto Abraham," there is no hyperbole. For with him all is possible.[25]

Perhaps the fact that the publication of the *Adages* and of the Greek New Testament jointly established Erasmus's fame has led critics to see him as dividing himself between the sacred and the secular and caused a critic of the calibre of Lucien Febvre to speak of "the pagan of the *Adages*."[26] But this is quite misleading. The *Adages* are essentially a part of the whole Erasmian drive toward Christian humanism.

The most striking parts of the book, those for which contemporaries looked most eagerly, were the topical parts: the comic or biting criticisms of the current state of affairs, the mischievous vignettes of public or private life, the serious and eloquent arguments on pacifism and kingship, which have become the best-known parts of the *Adagia*. Side by side with these more spectacular passages are a host of quiet asides that would be particularly savored by many readers. Often these can only be guessed at today: the unexpectedly ferocious attack on pigs seems to recall other jokes like the appearance of Janotus de Bragmardo; the demure treatment of Pythagorean rules against fish-eating has a sober connection with the colloquy *Ichthyophagia;* the aspersions of Galen on the (philosophical) sects have quite a different ring in 1528. *Artem quaevis alit terra* produces a wry sentence about the traveling journeyman, "an honest fellow if his art be honest," but what of the people who make their traveling expenses by hawking dispensations? Or the man who buys a cardinal's hat so as to have the title engraved on his tombstone? Are mitres and cardinals' hats sometimes used, like "the magistrate's purple gown," to hide an ugly tumor? The punishment for adultery was severe among the Cumani; now we are almost at the stage of giving prizes to the man who seduces most wives. The priests who need a bribe before they will administer the sacraments, the hawkers of relics, had their counterparts in ancient Greece.[27]

Considering all these different ingredients which go to make up the *Adagia,* it is clear that there are filiations connecting the book with all of Erasmus's other works. If it is not the keystone of the arch, it is at least the meeting-place of all the various elements which constitute his wide-ranging but consistent output. In this sense it is central to his work, and this is the definition we are seeking.

It is easy to see the connection between the *Adagia* and the treatises on style like the *De copia,* and the similarity of attitude with the *De pueris.* Textual criticism, so important a part of his contribution to learning, is represented here, as well as all the work on classical authors and the Fathers from which he gleaned his proverbs as the more fundamental work of editing went on. Long serious essays linked the *Adagia* with the *Institutio principis* (*Aut regem aut fatuum*), with his pacifist writings like the *Querela pacis* (*Dulce bellum inexpertis, Spartam nactus es*), and with the plea for a simplified Christianity in the *Enchiridion militis christiani* (*Sileni Alcibiadis*). Shorter comments chime with the *Colloquies,* on soldiers, on fish-eating, on pilgrimages, on banquets. The *Praise of Folly* is represented not only by a warm defense (*Ollas ostentare*) but by comedy (*Scarabeus*) and the very method of *Sileni Alcibiadis,* the paradox of holiness. Devotional works and biblical criticism have their discreet share. The *Adagia* was Erasmus's life-companion and necessarily became a running commentary on all he was doing and thinking.[28]

If this is so, what are we to say about the construction of the book on which he spent so much care, as the renumbering of adages and switching of them around, the editing and corrections show? How did he see this centerpiece as a matter of arrangement? There is a sense of order in the *Adagia,* but it is hard to put a finger on the method used. The Greek collections supplied a certain order by marshaling similar proverbs; there is occasionally a brief spurt of alphabetical order; there is often an assimilation of subjects, but never so marked as to be wearisome or constitute a catalogue. Erasmus played with the order, shifting proverbs about until he was satisfied, making cross-references, noting "I shall mention this proverb in its place," *suo loco*[29] or *alibi.* In the later sections, it is often the book he is reading which dictates a selection—Pindar, Homer, Plutarch. He takes care to open each thousand adages, often a hundred, with a long important essay. As in all his works, Erasmus is continually aware of his audience, careful to provide variety, to make the work readable in spite of its possibilities of ponderousness or diffusion, just as he left it to the last to add the touches of personal comment or homely wit which make the classical diet digestible (this we know from the manuscript of the last part of the *Adagia*).[30] This book, so long considered the most outdated of his works, was for his contemporaries the most up-to-date and topical.

Perhaps Erasmus's own metaphor in the 1500 preface is still the best description of his method:[31] "I put aside my nightly labours over a more serious work and strolled through the gardens of the classics . . . and so plucked, and as it were arranged in garlands, like flowerets of every hue, all the most ancient and famous of the adages." The result was something like those Dutch flower-pieces, where flowers that could never have bloomed together are arranged with deceptive negligence, the superb and the humble in the same bouquet.

NOTES

1. *Opus Epistolarum Des. Erasmi Roterodami*, ed. P. S. Allen et al. (Oxford, 1906–47), vol. 1, Ep. 1, pp. 73–74, and *The Correspondence of Erasmus,* trans. R. A. B. Mynors and D. F. S. Thomson (Toronto, 1974), vol. 1, Ep. 1, p. 2 (henceforth referred to as *EE* and *CWE,* respectively).

2. *Adagia in Opera Omnia* [ed. Jean Le Clerc] (Leiden, 1703), 2:166C (henceforth referred to as *Adagia*), chiliarch 1, company 1, proverb 39 (henceforth referred to as 1.1.39).

3. *EE,* vol. 1, Ep. 126, p. 291, ll. 51–58.

4. Ibid., p. 290, l. 25; p. 291, ll. 106–08.

5. Ibid., pp. 290–97.

6. *Adagia,* 1.1.68 (*LB,* 2:172F).

7. *Adagia,* 3.1.1 (*LB,* 2:713F).

8. Ibid.

9. *EE,* vol. 5, Ep. 1479, p. 516, ll. 58–61.

10. *EE,* vol. 1, Ep. 126, p. 296, ll. 230–36.

11. *Adagia,* 1.1.27, 44; 2.4.84; 1.7.96; 1.7.99.

12. Ibid., 1.5.45; 4.9.36; 1.6.39; 1.2.20; 1.5.63.

13. Ibid., 1.6.36; 2.1.45. See also *Pythagorae symbola, LB,* 2:16D–17B, where a sharp criticism of this author, dating from 1517/18, is softened by a tribute on learning of his death (1526).

14. *Adagia,* 1.1.69.

15. *EE,* vol. 5, Ep. 1479, pp. 514–21.

16. *Adagia,* 1.4.4 and 1.4.1.

17. Ibid., 3.8.1.

18. Cf. Jean-Claude Margolin, *Erasme: Declamatio de pueris statim ac liberaliter instituen-dis* (Geneva: Droz, 1966), p. 25.

19. Ibid., p. 449.

20. Rabelais, *Gargantua,* chap. 24.

21. *Adagia,* 1.2.86.

22. Ibid., 4.4.62.

23. Ibid., 4.2.47; 1.8.23; 1.9.7; 2.2.73.

24. Ibid., 4.4.90; 4.4.74; 4.4.91; 1.2.15; 3.1.99; 1.10.51; 3.6.56; 1.6.70; 3.7.65; 2.7.20.

25. Ibid., 3.10.91; 5.2.17.

26. Lucien Febvre, preface to the French translation of Johan Huizinga, *Erasme* (Paris, 1955).

27. *Adagia,* 1.1.2; 1.1.40; 1.3.92; 1.7.33; 4.9.6; 5.1.44; 4.5.25; 4.8.48, 55.

28. Ibid., 1.3.1; 4.1.1; 2.5.1; 3.3.1; 2.2.40; 3.7.1.

29. Ibid., 1.2.14.

30. The manuscript mentioned here is in the Royal Library of Copenhagen, and its shelf-mark is MS. G.K.S. 95 fol. A page from it forms the frontispiece to my book on the *Adages* (Cambridge, 1964).

31. *EE,* vol. 1, Ep. 126, p. 290, ll. 19–23.

2 The Principal Theological Thoughts in the *Enchiridion Militis Christiani*

ERNST-W. KOHLS

BAPTISM AS BEGINNING AND RESPONSIBILITY IN THE CHRISTIAN'S LIFE

Baptism is at the center of Erasmus's theological statements in his *Enchiridion,* and is understood not only as the image of the *Militia spiritualis,* but also, principally in a sacramental context, as the entire life of a Christian: "Do you not know, Christian warrior that you gave yourself completely to Christ when you experienced the mysteries of baptism—Christ, to whom you twice owe your life: once for birth and a second time for rebirth (in baptism)—to whom you therefore owe more than yourself? Don't you think about the fact that you have sworn allegiance to the will of a mild general, through which oath you are commissioned to him as if it were by gifts? Don't you think about the fact that you have promised to sacrifice your head to his annihilating threats if you are not true to your oath? What else does the sign of the cross on your forehead mean, than that you, as long as you live, will serve under his banners? What else does the anointing with sacred oil mean, than that you have entered into an eternal battle against vice? How great is the shame, how great the public curse for all mankind, when a soldier runs from his general! How can you scorn Christ, your general; are you not compelled by fear of him, since he is God? But are you not much more prevented by love from running away, since for your sake he became man?"[1]

The thought of the sanctification of Christian life in all realms of life, which results from baptism, and which can be recognized in the fact that the sacraments are based on Christian ethics in Erasmus, is intensified later in the *Enchiridion* as a result of the hermeneutic separation into *Caro* and *Spiritus.* Indeed, it serves as a basic constituent theme in all the theological writings of Erasmus.[2] In this respect, the *Enchiridion Militis Christiani* is one of the most important theological writings of Erasmus. Along with the prefaces to Erasmus's edition of the New Testament,[3] the edition of 1518[4] became the main theological work of Erasmus and was dedicated to Abbot Paul Volz (Hugshofen, Alsace).

Erasmus, by means of the image of the *Militia spiritualis,* can, in the *Enchiridion,* make visible his most important theological thoughts, since the Latin word *sacramentum* means "oath" in military language, by which both general

Translated from the German by Willard T. Daetsch (Ithaca College).

and soldier pledge mutual loyalty.[5] Baptism is to be understood in this image as "signum," as the flag under which the Christian warrior fights—i.e. leads his life.[6] The sacrament of baptism, therefore, becomes alpha and omega; and as gift and responsibility it becomes an essential motif of the Christian's life: "Baptism is the first expression of Christian philosophy which is common to all Christians," as Erasmus later defines it in the *Paraclesis.*[7]

The act of initiation which is completed by baptism is, for the Christian, the beginning of the battle against the powers of the world. The Christian, placed between God and the world, shall conquer the world. It is the task of every baptised Christian to live a godly life in this world. For Erasmus, peace with the world meant enmity toward God. Vice versa, peace and friendship with God result in an ever new battle of the Christian against the world, which always tries to draw the Christian into its power.[8]

The battle "to die to the world" (*mori mundo*), which begins with baptism, is not a battle of life but one of faith. Erasmus emphasizes that this battle is the responsibility, not only of the monks, but of every Christian who has professed the baptismal creed.[9] The battle begins precisely on the basis of baptism and faith, and ultimately it is not a matter of physical death, but death of the soul which God wants to save.[10] In the biblical sense, Erasmus values the *anima* as the *pars pro toto* for the entire person. The anima represents the point of contact for the acting God. Without God the anima and therefore the person is dead.[11] Only God can give it life, can awaken even the sick and the dead soul to a new life. Erasmus sees in Christ the epitome of the purest anima, because God was never absent from him for a single instant.[12]

The battle of the baptized Christian is not fought for protection of the body, but for saving the soul and the divine presence in it: "In worldly battle the worst defeat comes if the victor's sword separates the soul from the body. In this spiritual battle, however, the soul itself can be deprived of its life—namely can be deprived of God."[13] Eternal spiritual bliss is the goal of the *Militia spiritualis,* of which the Christian is made a part.[14] The battle is an eschatological struggle in which God himself mercifully places Christ beside the believer.[15]

GOD AND CHRIST AS THE BASES FOR LIFE

Erasmus uses the *Militia-Topos* in order to lead from the discussion of baptism to the presentation of the basis for existence of the Christian: namely God and Christ. Both stand by the Christian in the battle against the anti-God powers of the world. God is life for the Christian because God is love. God's love of man constitutes the existence and the life of the Christian.[16] God places the Christian in the battle against the powers of the world. He also determines the reward for the *Militia spiritualis:* blessed immortality. In antithetical comparison of the *Militia mundi* and the *Militia dei* Erasmus describes the rewards of this battle:

> In the world you serve not only for empty fame but also for pitiful wages. Do you want to know your reward for the *militia mundi?* Paul, standard-bearer of the *militia Christi,* names it: the wages of sin are death (Rom. 6 : 23). Who would want to enter into even the most glorious service in war if death alone were the reward? On the other hand, what rewards of victory does our army's leader place before our eyes? Not [the] three-footed (golden) stools or many mules [offered by] Homer's Achilles or Virgil's Aeneas—but he promises that which no eye has seen and no ear has heard, and which has come into our human heart (1 Cor. 2 : 9), which is already consolation for our pains during our battle: blessed immortality.... Just as the greatest reward is promised to the brave soldier, so likewise the deserter will face the most severe punishment. Heaven is held out as a reward to the brave soldier. Therefore should not the noble mind burn for the hope of so great a reward since it is he who makes the promise who can no more deceive than he can cease to exist? The battle takes place before the eyes of an all-seeing God, the entire Heavenly host is witness to our battle—should that not shame us? He whose praise means highest bliss for us will laud our excellence. Should we not, therefore, seek to achieve this praise itself even at the cost of life?[17]

In this way Erasmus has not only described God as the reason for the existence of Christian life, but also, by means of the *Militia-Topos* (in the *Enchiridion*), he describes the sovereigny of the offer of God's grace and at the same time the responsibility of man toward this offer of grace. The eschatological definiteness of these theological views of Erasmus becomes apparent by his placing at the pinnacle the reward and the promises which are assured the Christian in life after death—the *beata,* or *felix immortalitas.* The life of the Christian, newly given by baptism, which is to prove itself in the world and is to maintain the grace of baptism, reaches its goal not in the world itself, which is to be conquered, but rather in the promise of eternal life in the hereafter. God, "who cannot deceive, as he cannot cease to be" (*qui tam fallere non potest quam non esse nequit*)—as the sole embodiment of the eternal Being—guarantees this promise.[18]

We can speak about God and his concern for mankind as the sole basis for the existence of the Christian, analogous to God's incarnation in Christ. Erasmus describes this theological concept by representing Christ as the conquering general who has already won the main victory over all the powers of darkness and has supported and made easier the combat of the individual Christian against these powers.

> Do not forget, that you do not have to deal with an undefeated enemy, but rather with one who has long been battered, scattered and fully defeated—not by us, but rather by Christ, the head, by whom this enemy will without doubt once more be conquered in us. See to it only that you belong to the body (of Christ), and you will accomplish all things under this head. By yourself you are too weak, but in him you can do everything. Therefore the outcome of our battle is not unsure, for the victory does not depend on fate, but lies in the hand of God, and through him in our hand. Only he will be defeated who does not wish to conquer. The goodness of the divine Saviour has never yet deserted anyone. . . . He will fight for you, and he will give you credit for his goodness. You must give him credit for the entire victory, who as the first one free of all sin overcame the bondage of sin; to be sure, without your effort that will not be the case for you. He who says: Be comforted, I have overcome the world (John 16 :33), wanted you to have confidence, not certainty. Thus we shall finally conquer through him, if we fight according to his example. We must travel between Scylla and Charybdis so that on the one side we do not become careless and neglectful in our trust in divine grace and on the other do not lose our courage and drop our weapons in view of the difficulty of the battle.[19]

The Christian has only rearguard actions to wage in the fight against the powers of the world: Christ has already won the decisive battle for his adherents. The relationship of God to man is thereby viewed principally as an act of acceptance of man on the part of God and his justification before Him. In the image of the victory of Christ within the *Militia-Topos,* the events that accomplish justification are seen as completely a work of Christ, who gives credit to the faithful for battle with and victory over the powers of the world ("et liberalitatem suam tibi pro merito imputabit").[20] Erasmus implicitly expresses, in the image of the *Militia spiritualis,* his view of the law as one already fulfilled by Christ, and he clearly delineates the responsibility of the Christian toward the magnanimous offer of grace. The sovereigny of divine grace and the responsibility of man are not mutually exclusive, but rather mutually supportive. The will and the capability of the Christian are made possible solely through the prior accomplishment of Christ. The nature of the relationship between God and man in faith presupposes a primary and prior act of God. Also, the cooperation of man with God and Christ is already a result of a previous act of preordained grace, as Erasmus later emphasized in the *De libero arbitrio,* directed against Luther: "We can say that without limitation we are indebted to God for all that is accomplished. What free will accomplishes alone is not worth speaking about. The fact that we turn our thoughts towards salvation or that we cooperate with grace is already in itself a gift of divine grace."[21]

HOLY SCRIPTURE AND THE EXCLUSIVELY PROPAEDEUTIC FUNCTION OF ANCIENT PHILOSOPHY

As the foundation of Christian life and thought, Erasmus turns to the writings of the Old and New Testaments. Everything a Christian must know for salvation is contained in Holy Scripture. This principle of biblical authority is primary to Erasmus as well as being the primary point of departure for all works of theological thought and knowledge, because "the entire Holy Scripture is divinely inspired and of divine origin."[22]

Faith in God, Christ, and the Holy Spirit is completely based on Holy Scripture. As on the one hand faith is "the only portal to Christ,"[23] so on the other hand, "the first rule of Christian life is to hold Christ and Scripture, which was inspired by his spirit, in the highest esteem and to believe in them,—and, to be sure, not lightly, only with the tongue, and not with hesitation, as Christians commonly do, but with the entire heart; it must become totally a part of your flesh and blood, so that not one dot of an *i* is contained in Holy Scripture which might not serve for your personal salvation. It must not concern you that many people live as though heaven and hell were empty fables, merely means of frightening and enticing children. Remain all the more steadfast in your belief."[24] It is God himself who verifies the content of Scripture:

If you believe that there is a God, then you must believe that he is truthful. But nothing among those things which you hear with your ears, see with your eyes and hold in your hands is so true, sure and free of doubt as that which you read in Holy Scripture, which God himself has in truth inspired, which the Prophets have foretold, which so many martyrs have sanctified with their blood, which for so many ages the consensus of the righteous has attested. Christ himself in his human form has reasserted it in his sermons and has proved it through deed in his life. Miracles attest its content. Even the devils acknowledge and believe in it as they tremble before it (James 2:19). Finally, how uniform Holy Scripture is in its content! how self-sufficient it is! how it carries the reader along! how it can move and change the human![25]

The essential content of Holy Scripture is Christ himself. Part of the incarnation of Christ is his incorporation into Scripture. Erasmus considers it wrong to make an image of Christ in stone or wood as an object of prayer.

It is much more religious to venerate the true picture of the Heart of Christ which is presented in Holy Scripture through the art of the Holy Spirit. No Apelles could paint the contours and form of the body with a brush as well as the picture of a person's soul shines out through his speech—especially in the case of Christ, who, since he embodies the highest simplicity and truth in himself (John 14 : 6) could distinguish no difference at all between the original picture of the divine heart and the picture which emanates from his words. Just as nothing is more similar to the Father than the Son who is the Father's word, which flows from his secret heart (John 12 : 49; 17 : 8), so nothing is more similar to Christ than the word of Christ, which makes known directly the hidden being of that holiest of Hearts.[26]

Erasmus knows the significance which the word and deed of the sincere Christian have for the propagation and continuance of Christianity. But he also knows that this possibility, or oral *Traditio,* is often small and totally disfigured because of erosion.[27] In this respect, Scripture remains as norm and measure—the decisive basis of Christian belief and its constant correction. Holy Scripture, in its verification through God, in its main content—Christ—and in its definiteness through the Holy Spirit, becomes the point of intersection, the main point of the trinitarian acts of God. As much as Erasmus calls the Christian's entire "armament" a gift of God—the "armor of righteousness," "shield of belief," and "helmet of salvation"—nevertheless, the "sword of the spirit" as the word of God is the most important part of the armament with which all attacks by the forces of the world can be withstood.[28]

For Erasmus, all theological thought emanates from Scripture and it is mainly exegesis, the explanation and commentary on Holy Scripture, that is significant. It is the most important task and the real goal of all theological work to incite others to exegetical analysis of Scripture. And in the *Enchiridion* Erasmus essentially pursues this goal: to encourage those addressed to concern themselves with the study of Holy Scripture.[29] In this sense the *Enchiridion* is only a modest guidepost, a brief tract, "quickly put together" (*extemporalis scriptiuncula*),[30] which has the purpose of making itself superfluous.[31] As far as the basic meaning of Scripture is concerned, and of its exegesis, all theological thought can only be a preparatory function which through Scripture itself will always be questioned anew.

As basis and norm of Christian belief, Scripture supplies the means of interpretation itself. Through its main content, Christ, and through its main elements, which were formulated in the concept of God and in Christology (*Littera* [= *Caro*] and *Spiritus*), Scripture is to a large extent self-explanatory. For such an essentially exegetical, theological task Erasmus looks especially to the Church

Fathers for prototypes.[32] But above all he sees the theological ideal of an exegetical theology realized by Paul, whose letters every Christian should have at hand, should read every day, and should memorize.[33] Erasmus also finds this ideal in a special way in the Gospel according to John. From Paul and John—especially John 4:23-24, John 6:63, 2 Corinthians 3:6, and 1 Corinthians 2:12ff.—Erasmus derives the hermeneutical basic structure of Scripture: the separation of *Littera* (*Caro*) and *Spiritus scripturae*.[34] This perception and its practical consequences are considered by Erasmus to be the central point of all exegetical work and the most essential criterion for all Christian piety.[35]

In addition to Holy Scripture, Erasmus accepts as a further source of revelation for the Christian the writings of the ancient poets and philosophers. Basically, Erasmus emphasizes that the one who devotes himself day and night to the lessons of Holy Scripture and meditates about them in the image of the *Militia spiritualis* "is fortified and armored against all attacks by the enemies."[36] But at the same time Erasmus does not reject using the heritage of the past as basic training (*tirocinium*) "with deliberation, according to age, and, as it were, in passing."[37] In this sense—Erasmus continues—the ancient church at the time of Augustine, Basil, Cyprian, and Jerome advocated the study of antiquity.[38] Even though Erasmus might want to see the ethics of the Christian derive principally from Holy Scripture, that conviction in no way caused him to scorn entirely ancient philosophical ethics. "Even Moses did not despise the advice of Jethro, his father-in-law, who was a heathen" (Exod. 18:24).[39]

It is only in its *propaedeutic function* that Erasmus, in his *Enchiridion*, as in his earlier and later writings,[40] wants to see ancient poetry and philosophy utilized for the actual theological exegesis of Holy Scripture. For him ancient poetry and philosophy are "a marvelous preparation for an understanding of Holy Scripture."[41] Erasmus considers it a "foolhardy endeavor" to undertake to work with Holy Scripture without any knowledge of poetry and philosophy.[42]

In the eyes of Erasmus there are two reasons why such a propaedeutic use of poetry and philosophy is valid in respect to Holy Scripture. (1) To interpret poetry literally is a mistake, according to him. All poetry—including Homer's and Virgil's—can be properly interpreted only allegorically.[43] It is this necessity for an allegorical interpretation that makes poetry similar to Holy Scripture—which, for Erasmus, can also only be interpreted satisfactorily in an allegorical way.[44] (2) Especially in Platonic philosophy, Erasmus finds a structure very closely related in content and form to Holy Scripture, and for this reason he considers it very important for every Christian theologian to study Plato.[45]

So a Christian may "taste all the non-Christian literature, according to one's age and with reason, carefully and selectively, but only 'in passing' should this be done—never as a 'main effort.'"[46] According to Erasmus, the Christian should never have the study of poetry and philosophy as an end in itself, because for him the main goal is "for everything to be directed towards Christ."[47] With this as a major concept, the aphorism enunciated by Paul is valid for the area of poetry and philosophy: "for the pure all is pure, for the impure . . . , however, nothing is pure" (Titus 1:15).[48] Just as the Jews after the flight out of Egypt lived on unleavened bread—which was used only for a short time and by no means throughout the entire journey through the wilderness (Exod. 12, 34ff.)—so also the Christian can have a surfeit of "unleavened bread" (i.e. poetry and philosophy) and long for manna, which is Christ himself as the bread of life (John 6:32–35) and which will suffice until, after the end of the Christian's successful battle with life, those promises are fulfilled that will never end.[49]

With respect to Christ, this attitude toward the heritage of antiquity is merely a special case in the total relationship between Christianity and science in general; everywhere, and here too, the idea of Christ is to be used as the criterion which establishes the norm. From this conviction Erasmus advises: "You love knowledge. Well and good—if it is a case of being for the sake of Christ. But if you love it solely for the sake of knowing, then you are marching in place when you should really be making progress. If, however, you busy yourself with knowledge in order, with its help, to understand more clearly the hidden Christ in Holy Scripture, in order to love the revealed Christ, to take pleasure in him and to share him with others, then busy yourself diligently with the study of knowledge. If you have trust and hope for great reward in Christ, so, like a good merchant, dare to venture further into the area of heathen knowledge and bring back the treasure of Egypt to decorate the temple of the Lord."[50]

GOD'S ACTS AND HOLY SCRIPTURE

For Erasmus, God's acts of salvation as Holy Scripture describes them lead to a specific paradox, which human understanding can neither decipher nor understand. The basic paradox is as follows: God in his act of salvation for man has divested himself of his innate omnipotence and has accomplished only the work of goodness and love. In this special view of divine omnipotence (not of divine nature), Erasmus has seized upon the idea of κένωδιϛ developed by Origen, who referred to Paul (Phil. 2:5ff.) and attempted to utilize it in the articulation of the message of salvation: God does not frighten man with his power but puts it aside, adjusts himself to man through love, and thus pulls man to him. Erasmus sees the highpoint of divine κένωδιϛ in the incarnation, in Christ's suffering and dying on the cross (for others). Here it can be seen how

Erasmus intends to demonstrate with the idea of κένωδιζ the specific paradox of God's act of salvation, but he does not attempt to explain it through a rational principle—and thus to solve it.

With Paul (1 Cor. 1:23-24), Erasmus sees the Gospel—and with it the entire Holy Scripture—concentrated in the teaching of the cross. The cross alone guarantees, with reference to Paul again (1 Cor. 1:30), redemption (*redemptio*) and vindication (*justificatio*) to the Christian. In the paradox of the cross lies, for Erasmus, the center of God's work of salvation, which is present for each and every one personally and at all times. In its actuality as a way of salvation coming from God and intended for the needs of each individual, it becomes a life-determining and corrective force within the individual Christian life; it cannot therefore, according to Erasmus, become a one-sided application and imitation.

Erasmus wanted to express the redeeming and converting effectiveness of the cross in his description of the *Regula Christi* as *Regula Crucis*. By means of the emphasized declaration of the saving power of the cross and of its personal intention, Erasmus presented, with respect to the cross, the primacy of the *Exitus* as opposed to a one-sided and dangerous emphasis on the *Reditus*. Alongside and before love, with which Christ filled Christians by means of his suffering on the cross, Erasmus uses as a point of departure the fact that the actuality of salvation is based on the very paradox of the cross; this forms the most important aspect of the life of a Christian. On the one hand, this concept is based on the assertion that Christ can be understood only through faith (*fiducia*), and on the other hand it constitutes the entire dialectics of the individual Christian life and the totality of the church: *in the world and yet not of the world.*

The paradox of the divine act of salvation has its origin in the definition of God as *Mysterium*—because for Erasmus the character of Holy Scripture is also one of *Mysterium*. The *Mysterium* is that realm which lies behind the area accessible to perceptive cognition—the area of divine acts of salvation in the form of the *Exitus* and the *Reditus*. Man cannot penetrate into this area of the *Mysterium* of God and the origin of his divine pedagogy. Indeed, all theological work has the task of preserving these boundaries drawn by God himself. Theology, for Erasmus, must walk the tightrope between, on the one hand, not being able to penetrate into the last mystery of God and, on the other hand, having to take cognizance of its existence. Because of the Christologically oriented *littera-spiritus* structure of Scripture, it is the particular task of theology (as primarily exegetic theology) to allow for the workings of the spirit *and* the mystery. In its essential character, all written theology must be able to make itself unnecessary in the final analysis through its particular task of extracting the spiritual meaning of the written word—which Erasmus does not want to see applied one-sidedly, but in its dialectic correlation with the literal sense. Exegesis, for Erasmus, should be done so that the spirit and secret of Scripture reveal themselves—that is to say, they can dispense with human exegesis.

The heart of Erasmus's concept of Scripture is just where he says the living and real saving presence of Christ is—in the Christ-centered concern for the *sensus spiritualis*. In this personal presence of Christ in Scripture lies the reason why, for Erasmus, the ultimate concern is not a matter of knowledge but of encountering salvation—which every Christian can experience directly by personal contact with Scripture. Moreover, here is the root of the cognitive aspect of Erasmus's concept of Scripture, enabling one to combine the content of that which is to be understood with the act of understanding. At the same time this is the reason why Erasmus so passionately longed for translations of the Bible into native tongues, and also for Erasmus's conception of theology as *Theologia vitae,* and lastly why Erasmus believed that the greatest help in explaining Scripture lay in prayer and meditation.

Erasmus's understanding of Scripture depends to some extent on the *Logos* theory of Origen in its emphasis on the personal presence of Christ in salvation. On the basis of his personal and existential involvement with Scripture itself, Erasmus, to be sure, has not offered a simple repetition of Origen, but rather, from an elucidation of Scripture, has built upon, corrected, and expanded the foundations established by Origen. Since Origen, no theologian has presented such a complete, dynamic, and soteriological explanation of Scripture as Erasmus undertook in the *Enchiridion.* As a result of the constant recitation of the biblical content of Scripture in connection with the concept of God, Erasmus guarded against developing an absolute spiritualism. In the exposition of the elements of salvation in Scripture he avoided the one-sidedness of a theology of pure mystery. On the basis of his exposition of the Christological definiteness of Scripture and its soteriological centering in the word from the cross, and in its efforts with the association of the dialectical correlation of *littera* and *spiritus,* he did not succumb to a pure spiritualism that ignored the material. It has become clear that behind the design of the Christ-centered system in the *Enchiridion* stands the implicit use of the old theory of salvation defined by the *Exitus-Reditus* schema. This schema has in the works of Erasmus not only the eschatological structure of his Christ-oriented system, but—as the following passage will show—can make clear, in addition, the common thrust of Erasmus's theological messages.

THE EXITUS-REDITUS SCHEMA

In the *Enchiridion* Erasmus used the *Exitus-Reditus* schema so widely propagated in Scholasticism—above all by Thomas Aquinas. But Erasmus did not use it explicitly and definitely, certainly not in the sense of an external principle which is merely accidental to the object. Erasmus did, however, base the structure of this schema in his works on the structure of the divine story of salvation itself and in the existing essence of the divine facts of salvation as recorded in Holy Scripture, which he wanted to describe. In the work of Erasmus *Exitus-Reditus* is inseparable from his concept of Scripture and implicitly from the exegetical character of his theology. This schema, derived from the divine acts of salvation contained in Holy Scripture, is presented to the commentator as an intrinsic systematic aid. Erasmus's completely implicit use of the schema can elucidate how far, for him, the structure of the *Exitus-Reditus* is an essential structure of the divine acts of salvation as they are described in Holy Scripture, which becomes effective in the course of the exegetical efforts and thereby makes itself heard—a phenomenon that fulfills not only individual theological thinking but has already dynamically penetrated the entire course of history (of the inner-worldly occurrences).

Given these theological premises, it now becomes clear that Erasmus has by no means presented a "Theory of Piety" based only on the realm of the *Reditus.* For Erasmus the area of the *Reditus* cannot possibly be separated from that of the *Exitus.* Everything that happens within the *Reditus* proceeds from the divine *Exitus* and is completely subordinated to it. Erasmus derives this basic view from the description of God's acts of salvation in Holy Scripture itself. The theopneustics of Holy Scripture and the concept that part of the incarnation of Christ is his incorporation into Scripture form, for Erasmus, the unique value of Holy Scripture as the highest source of revelation and present the point of intersection of the Trinitarian acts of salvation. Since Holy Scripture is centrally determined by God's acts of salvation, Erasmus's main interest in the realm of the facts of salvation of the divine *Exitus* emanates completely from Scripture. Therefore it is an essential aspect of Erasmus's "Theory of Piety" that it primarily makes statements about the *Exitus:* about God and his acts of salvation. Accordingly, right at the beginning of the *Enchiridion,* Erasmus states the basis of existence for every Christian life: God and the grace he gave to man. And Erasmus joins this explanation with the other—the exposition of the basis of understanding that is given in Holy Scripture.

Insofar as the basis for existence and the basis for understanding—a concept of God and a concept of Scripture—are inextricably bound together, Erasmus can only speak about God as he is described in his acts of salvation in Holy Scripture, in his gift of grace to man, namely, in his acts of salvation for man. Not God's importance in the abstract-philosophical sense, but God's turning toward man—his going forth to man (*Exitus*) and his leading man back to God (*Reditus*) in the existential-salvation-theological sense are central topics of all theological deliberation in Erasmus's work. According to Erasmus, only through God's acts of salvation for man can God be recognized. Since his statements about God rest upon the divine acts of salvation for man, all statements about God are also at the same time statements about man.

Erasmus speaks about man basically, not in the sense of an autonomous anthropology, but in that salvation-theological sense, namely, that man finds himself subject to acts of salvation of the divine *Exitus,* whereby the life and being of man are determined as *Reditus* toward God. Erasmus sees man, because of the divine order of creation, after the Fall—saved by God's order of salvation—saved from sin by Christ's death upon the cross, and finally endowed with the Holy Spirit through baptism, through whose effect man can find the way back to God. Creation, redemption, salvation are the salvation-theological categories in which, for Erasmus, the life of man, along with the working of divine *Exitus,* runs its course. The *Reditus* of man is so basically anchored in the previous act of divine grace that even the *Cooperatio* of man with grace in the realm of *Reditus* is perfected through grace itself. God's anticipatory acts of grace, which determine salvation, are the bond that tie *Exitus* and *Reditus* together and irreversibly determine the primacy between the two realms in favor of *Exitus.*

The Erasmian recognition of the fact that God himself placed divine *Exitus* first, as Holy Scripture describes it, makes understandable that in the *Enchiridion* an all-encompassing, Trinitarian, structured concept of God can be found. In his statements on the concept of God, Erasmus turns to the realm of *Reditus,* notably in the form of "rules" derived from Scripture—of the *Regula Christi* as *Regula crucis* and of the *Regula spiritus*—and in guidelines which indicate clearly enough in their connection with the view of God, Christology, and pneumatology, how all piety is constantly and irrevocably conditioned and effected by the preceding divine acts of salvation.

CHRIST AS CENTER OF THE STORY OF SALVATION

The divine economy of salvation, as Erasmus presents it in the *Enchiridion,* has Christ as its center. Christ through his incarnation and his death on the cross has made the love of God for man known to all.[51] Christ's death on the cross, which resulted from divine love, has freed man from the guilt into which he had fallen through sins against God, because God gives man credit for the actions performed by Christ.[52] At the same time man, who through *Caro* had fallen prey to the antidivine forces of the devil and of the world, is liberated by Christ from the power of these same forces.[53] The *Redemptio* and *Justificatio* resulting from Christ's death on the cross strive toward reconciliation of man with God.

So, for Erasmus, *Christ* is the *center and at the same time the turning point within the divine story of salvation:* through Christ's love in his representative and redeeming suffering and dying, man is again led to the love of God and to God himself. In Christ the foundations have been laid for a *reconstitution* ("restitutio") of creation to its divinely ordained state. This *Restitutio*—the salvation-theological sense of this central concept of Erasmus becomes again apparent because of its position within the divine story of salvation[54]—finds its conclusion only in the *Eschaton,* but begins with the working of salvation through love, which flows to the believers from the acts of salvation through Christ, because of sanctification through the Holy Spirit. Endowment with the Spirit gives believers no habitual sanctity. Rather it effects in the emerging eschatological perfection an existential, progressive sanctification.[55]

In this sense Erasmus does not consider the believers habitually "pious."[56] He feels that piety exists not as a result of a "complete piety of the Christian,"[57] but only as a preliminary sanctification, effected through Christ's acts of salvation, which only in *Eschaton* itself achieve perfection and completion of piety in direct communion with God.[58] Within the *Reditus,* piety can never be separated from the *Exitus,* which is tied to a divine salvation-reality outside of any anthropological context. It makes piety expressible, never as a human state but as a divine goal, and only as a divinely worked sanctification. So once again at this point it is evident that for Erasmus a "Theory of Piety" means much more theologically than merely an outline of a "Studium pietatis";[59] that, in his view, "Ethics" cannot be separated from "Theology," but is essentially rooted in it and grows out of it.[60] Christ in his act of redemption forms and makes possible for Erasmus the tie between the *Exitus* and the *Reditus* within the divine economy of salvation. In this centrality of Christ, developed from Scripture, is based the much-talked-of Christocentricity of Erasmus, which obviously must always be seen against the background of Erasmus's Trinitarian view of God, just as also the divine acts of salvation are developed in the categories of creation, redemption, and sanctification.

As far as the divine economy of salvation is concerned with reconciliation between man and God, Erasmus sees this reconciliation as a redemption made possible through Christ, a redemption that once again is essentially sanctification.[61] Thus Erasmus has joined the so-called classical (or Greek) doctrine of reconciliation as it was presented most clearly by Origen, with the so-called Latin type of reconciliation as Anselm developed it after Tertullian.[62] But the most trenchant point of Erasmus's view of reconciliation lies in the "classical" doctrine of reconciliation: Christ's incarnation and his death on the cross make possible through the power of His love the redemption of man from the bonds of the devil and the antigodly forces of the world.[63]

Christ's death on the cross is a divine fight against the devil and the forces of the world, which Christ succeeds in overpowering. In his love for man, Christ assumes this fight and gives the credit for His victory to man. Christ takes man along with him into His victory and gives him the strength to take up courageously on his own part the fight against the devil and antigodly powers. The nature of this battle is eschatological: Christ has already conclusively overcome the devil and the forces of the world and has already promised the *Miles christianus* the final victory and the reward of eternal life, but this final victory and the reward of eternal life will only come to Christians in *Eschaton,* toward which the economy of God's salvation is directed. Until then, the Christian as *Miles christianus* must carry on his battle against the devil and the world: not self-assured, but confident in the helping power and love of his commander, Christ.[64]

And so it becomes apparent how the image of the *Militia spiritualis* has its rightful place within the Erasmian view of reconciliation: the theological content of this view of reconciliation and the way in which it is stated form an inner and complete unity. Each is made clear once again through the preordained continuity of the divine economy of salvation and of its structure in the *Exitus-Reditus:* it is only Christ's redeeming fight for salvation, which takes place within the *Exitus* of divine salvation, that effects and at the same time lends strength to the fight of the *Miles christianus* in the *Reditus.* For Erasmus, the essence of the divine economy of salvation in its original form can be derived from Christ as from an "archetype," because Christ, through his love of man in his incarnation, his death on the cross, and his fight for redemption against the devil, has consummated the essence of the divine economy in an exemplary way. Insofar as the love of God for man is revealed in the paradox of Christ's acts of salvation, the believers are drawn into this love and continue to live in it: through the power of divine love in Christ, the believers become imitators of the original image of Christ.

In this relationship between the original image and its imitation, Christians stand in the *Reditus.*[65] Through baptism Christians become endowed both with the spirit and with the *Lex spiritus.* The *Lex spiritus* is the inner power that governs the entire realm of the *Reditus.* It is no formal principle, certainly no nomistic concept at all. Rather, it is the result of the personal acts of salvation of Christ, and thus is the way of salvation offered by love, to which Christ is drawing the true believers. The *Lex spiritus* as *Lex caritatis* is the same as the entelechy of salvation given by Christ to the Christian, from which comes all of Christian life in its re-creating, determining, and continuing form. For Erasmus Christians are no longer *under* the law (of the letter) but *in* the law (of the spirit).[66] They receive through Christ the transforming power to fulfill voluntarily and spontaneously those aspects of the law which God had intended to be characterized by love. Christians, empowered by Christ, accomplish—not in fear but in freedom—the service of love which *Lex spiritus* as *Lex caritatis* wishes to be and at the same time helps to be.

According to Erasmus, the Old Testament law in its literal sense no longer has meaning for Christians. It is valid only in its spiritual sense as the task already completed in love by Christ. Erasmus knows the indicating and punitive function of the law; but for the Christian this can only belong to the letter of the law, because of the "Lex caritate Christi impleta."[67] No matter how positive a stand Erasmus takes in respect to the entire realm of the ceremonial law, because of love and consideration for the "weak in Christ" (1 Cor. 8 :11),[68] the entire ceremonial law of the *Lex spiritus* as *Lex caritatis* can only be preliminary, having a part in the *Usus paedagogicus* of the Old Testament law, which, for Erasmus, has as its direction Christ as the unique and perfect fulfiller of the caritative intent of the Old Testament.[69] With the fulfillment of the law brought about through the life and death of Christ—on the basis of the *Usus evangelicus* of the law within Christianity, brought to light by Christ—only the offering of love can now legitimately occur—admonitions that have only one goal, namely, to help make *Caritas* the content of the *Lex spiritus* and to make way for the dynamics of grace itself until the second coming of Christ.[70]

The Erasmian concept of the law contains (in its interpretation of the *Usus evangelicus* and the *Lex spiritus* as *Lex caritatis*) the negation of "external works," insofar as they are not understood as works of love, which the Christian may and can accomplish only on the basis of the *Lex spiritus* with the help of Christ.[71] Insofar as the *Lex spiritus* and the sacraments make effective in the Christian the divine work of the *Transfiguratio* of the believer and, correspondingly, the works of love in Christian life, Erasmus can, in this sense, come to the conclusion that, based upon the works of the Holy Spirit, the endowment with the spirit is a certainty.[72]

A one-sided view of the Erasmian negation mistakes the basic position of Erasmus in his presentation of the Christological and soteriological foundation of the *Lex spiritus* as *Lex caritas,* which Erasmus has explained not as the legal norm, but personally as the way to the ultimate, unmediated meeting with God, which way has been paved by God himself and has been made passable by Christ.[73] The *Lex caritatis* as the divine molding force and a reality that can never be manipulated by man—a reality of the individual and common life in the realm of the *Reditus*—is based, for Erasmus, entirely within the *Exitus* of the divine acts of salvation. A destruction of this correlation among statements, thought, and action is, for him, the main cause of "Judaicising," a continuous perversion of the Christian faith, which he sought to conquer.[74]

From this perspective, Erasmus had wished to express the sacraments, not only in their objective role in salvation, but simultaneously in their constantly dynamic, present, and personal effective generation of salvation, which is: baptism as the redeeming gift of the spirit and at the same time as a life-transforming rebirth into freedom and responsibility; communion as the liberating, objective remission of sins and at the same time as effect of the *Communio* and communion of love in the presentation of the γυναξις idea.[75] Erasmus had expressed with precision the correlation of the *Exitus* with the *Reditus*, for instance in connection with communion, with the words: "When you realize how you are formed in a very definite way in Christ, and live ever less for yourself, then be thankful to the spirit, who alone called such a life into being."[76] Erasmus thereby intended to express the biblical desire for the understanding of the sacrament, that the salvation factor of *Exitus* may never be separated from its form in the reality of salvation of the *Reditus* which has been ordained by God.

As an aid to the Christian during the time between the death of Christ and his second coming, between redemption and eschatological completion on Judgment Day, according to Erasmus the *Lex spiritus* as *Lex Caritatis* and the sacraments as effective signs of the grace of God determine not only the individual life of the single Christian but also further his life in the community—in church and state. Erasmus had understood both realms as being from God in their theocentric definition, and correspondingly never described them as an institution but personally as community: the Church as body of Christ and a community of love invisible in the world under the *Regula crucis,* visible under the *Lex caritatis;*[77] the state as partnership on the basis of the idea of the *Publica utilitas,*[78] intensified through the *Lex caritatis.* In both cases Erasmus had let it be known how his expressions about ecclesiastical matters and theories of government might never be separated from his theological base, but were to be understood as a result and consequence of his exposition of the *Exitus* of God's economy of salvation, just as in the theocentric-conditionality of the realms of church and state, whose mutual equality in the works of Erasmus were theologically motivated.[79] Erasmus had shown in statements concerning his theories of church and state the nature of these forms of community as transitive quantities insofar as they have their locus in the realm of the *Reditus,* in which there is no innerworldly static constancy and eternity for the individual and the community, but only the transition to the return to God himself.[80]

Totally and completely is the universal Christ-centered system, encompassing church and state, which Erasmus posited expressed by this basic eschatological view, that everything in the world subsides gradually, is formed in Christ, and finally is completed in him.[81] The true beginning of the kingdom of God, the return of Christ, the judgment of God, and eternal life with God are the signs of eschatological completion toward which Christ himself draws all the world.[82] In the extension of the *Meditatio mortis* to the *Meditatio futurae vitae,* Erasmus described a limited version of eschatological perfection which the Christian may already experience in the *Reditus* to God.[83] And so the Christian who has been led and redeemed by Christ can proceed toward his final goal, not yet in safety but nevertheless assured and confident.[84] In his description of the life of a Christian within the context of *Exitus* and *Reditus,* Erasmus had tried to explain the contradiction of "already" and "not yet" in Christian salvation.

In conclusion, Erasmus presented a theory of piety in his *Enchiridion* which, when more closely examined, proves to be a theological treatise that is comprehensive, biblically and theologically determined, and by itself firmly based. Precisely in the deterministic nature of the theological thought of the *Enchiridion* as exegesis, which derives its far-reaching systematic perspective from Scripture itself, the *Enchiridion* of Erasmus represents a masterly example of genuine and living scriptural theology, in which Erasmus was able to accomplish two things: on the one hand his ideas differentiated themselves from the philosophical tradition and on the other hand they were simultaneously used in a theologically legitimate manner that was both theoretically and practically appropriate.[85]

The *Enchiridion* clarifies the especially important and systematic basic principles of the theological thoughts of Erasmus. This was accomplished while placing limiting structures neither upon any of the multifarious abundance of theological expression nor upon the ministerial counseling ideas of the author. Large portions of this existential *Theologia vitae*[86] remove themselves from such limiting structures anyway. The development of an all-encompassing basic theological conception by Erasmus may seem surprising, in light of the reasoning faculty which was characteristic of him prior to this time.[87] However, the writings of Erasmus indeed portray his theology, directed toward a constantly renewing involvement with Scripture itself in its basic exegetical and scriptural-theological character, as well as the ensuing grandiose redemptive, theological, and systematic completeness that once again strives, both implicitly and explicitly, to nothing other than this involvement with Scripture. The insoluble entanglement of the theological and exegetical work would allow a so-called hermeneutic by Erasmus to be loosened only in the case of significant adjustments. Only in the complexity of exegetic and systematic theological consideration can the theological thought of Erasmus be appropriately portrayed.[88]

With his scriptural theology, Erasmus must be considered a true renewer and advocate of the living early Christian and medieval scriptural/theological heritage. It is in this respect that the best of his contemporary theologians, especially in light of the *Enchiridion,* saw in Erasmus the renewer and pioneer of a true theology.[89] In this same vein, Franz X. Funk has written in reference to the *Enchiridion:* "I found this book . . . so Christian, that I too could not have had even the slightest grounds to deny that it had come from some Church Father, if it had come to us under such a name."[90]

The far-reaching meaning of the interpenetration of Humanism and Reformation in the sixteenth century becomes visible precisely against the background of the theological substance of the *Enchiridion* of Erasmus. The fruitfulness of this interpenetration, as well as the boundaries in view of the abridged reform-oriented movement that was influenced by it, can be newly recognized and newly developed. This movement was inspired by such men as Bucer, Melanchthon, Oecolampadius, and last but not least, Zwingli. The reform theology of Erasmus lived on in these reformers of the humanistic camp. Alongside such followers of Erasmus as Beatus Rhenanus and Ludovicus Vives, these humanistic reformers—like the reformers of the Catholic camp—became the actual bearers of the Erasmian spirit for the following period. The modern ideas of Erasmus hearkened to a new age and found expression in this tradition, which Wilhelm Dilthey, and above all Ernst Troeltsch (especially for the Baptists), have referred to in their writings. Are these ideas really as "modern" as Dilthey himself and also Max Weber and Ernst Troeltsch believed them to be?[91] Do we not see today the relationship between concepts and representatives which allowed the latter to become radicalized? In the relationship of these ideas to the Middle Ages, we can see quite clearly the influence of fruitful and dynamic currents, but we can see also the influence of *this* epoch as well, from which Dilthey, Troeltsch, and Weber desired to separate themselves, and in which they desired to displace Erasmus by substituting Luther. It is of interest to note that Dilthey's friend Graf Yorck von Wartenburg took an opposing standpoint when he observed: "I believe that the relationship is just the opposite"; Luther would have to be "closer to the present . . . , if it is to bear a historical future."[92]

If the theological position of Erasmus as the center of his life's work is historically expressed, then the main questions arise: why did Erasmus begin the dispute with Luther, and why did Luther so totally and bluntly damn Erasmus and his ideas? One question repeats itself here and likewise addresses itself to the posture of rejection assumed by Luther in opposition to Thomas Aquinas and Origen. Reformation research has avoided this historic-systematic task for too long. The issue has a farreaching relevance for our present-day church and theological situation. One can say that the theological position and the issue of Erasmian theology have been newly disclosed to us from various sides in an unconscious manner. Therewith lies the question of the center and issue of the Reformation of Luther, based, however, on the new discovery of the theology of Erasmus.

We have allowed the view of the goals of Luther's Reformation to be obstructed, preventing true recognition of what they were. We have done this by failing to realize that—through the humanistic reformers—Erasmus had triumphed among Lutherans (Wilhelm Maurer).[93] It is not true in a technical sense that both Luther and Erasmus (as we once again realize) possessed a scriptural theology. For Luther had in any case never possessed a scriptural theology. Instead he began with the assumption that Holy Scripture is a gift of God, that the Bible has the ability to function autonomously. He defended this position in his *Invocat* sermon, "Ich habe nichts getan, das Wort Gottes hat alles gehandelt und ausgerichtet ["I have done nothing, the Word of God has transacted and conveyed everything"] (*WA*, 10, III, p. 19). Therefore Luther, in his *De servo arbitrio,* placed this concept of an autonomously functioning Scripture as a gift of God at the very beginning, and at the same time he emphasized the undesirability of questioning the dogmas contained in the Apostles' Creed— whereas Erasmus had confessed that he "didn't care of solid assertions [*assertiones*]."[94] To the extent that Erasmus had heavily emphasized the *fides* (and this may no longer be overlooked), to this same extent it must be recognized that Erasmus had always referred to the *fides activa* (like the students of Erasmus, Bucer, Calvin, and Melanchthon), whereas for Luther the important issue was the Christian faith granted by God.[95] It is this concept of *fides infusa* which Luther had presented in his summary of the dispute, *De fide infusa et acquisita* (1520).[96] Erasmus's concept of "Human Will freed by Grace"[97] was, according to Luther (whose primary assumptions rested on the Bible, filled with non-biblical and philosophical elements, and represented a qualitative encumbrance on the power of the Bible and its ability to function autonomously (the self-dynamic of Holy Scripture).

The more we recognize the important theological concepts of Erasmus, the more we must grasp the entire truth of the sixteenth century, which was soundly debated by Luther and Erasmus. We must make a decision about this dispute. Wilhelm Maurer expressed himself convincingly in his highly gifted discussion of the dispute between Erasmus and Luther in his book entitled *Revelation and Skepticism: The Outcome of the Decision Will Determine the Fate of the Western World.*[98] This decision cannot be reached through human means. Only God can grant this unto our hearts, through his Holy Scripture.

NOTES

1. Hajo and Annemarie Holborn, *Desiderius Erasmus Roterodamus: Ausgewählte Werke* (Munich, 1933), p. 24, ll. 13–26.
2. Cf. Ernst-W. Kohls, *Die Theologie des Erasmus,* 2 vols. (Basel, 1966), 1:119ff.
3. Ibid., pp. 177–90.

4. For the particular issues and the more recent edition, see Holborn and Holborn, *Ausgewählte Werke,* pp. 22–136, and Kohls, *Die Theologie des Erasmus,* 2:84ff.

5. Kohls, pp. 122–24.

6. Cf. Erasmus's presentation in the *Querela pacis* (1517) in the Leiden *Opera omnia* of Erasmus (hereafter referred to as *LB*), 4:632C–E.

7. Holborn and Holborn, *Ausgewählte Werke,* p. 142, ll. 28–34.

8. "Neque enim prorsus alia est cum illo pacis conditio, nisi, dum in hoc praesidio corporis militamus, odio capitali summaque vi cum vitiis belligeremur. . . ." Ibid., p. 24, ll. 4–7.

9. Ibid., p. 59, ll. 32–35.

10. Ibid., pp. 26ff.

11. "Neque ullum corpus tam mortuum est destitutum anima, quam mortua est anima relicta a deo." Ibid., p. 27, ll. 16–18.

12. Ibid., p. 27, ll. 24–27.

13. Ibid., p. 26, ll. 3–4.

14. Ibid., ll. 5ff.

15. Ibid., p. 27, ll. 29ff.

16. Ibid., p. 26, ll. 31–34.

17. Ibid., p. 24, ll. 34–35, 33.

18. Ibid., p. 25, ll. 28–29.

19. Ibid., p. 28, ll. 7–26.

20. ". . . Pro te [Christus] pugnabit et liberalitatem suam tibi pro merito imputabit." Ibid., ll. 7ff.

21. See Kohls, *Die Theologie des Erasmus,* 1:44ff.

22. "Omnis enim scriptura sancta divinitus est inspirata atque a deo auctore profecta." Holborn and Holborn, *Ausgewählte Werke,* p. 30, ll. 34–35.

23. Ibid., p. 56, l. 32.

24. Ibid., ll. 33–57, 5.

25. Ibid., p. 57, ll. 8–18.

26. Ibid., p. 75, ll. 15–24.

27. Ibid., p. 135, ll. 12–16.

28. Ibid., p. 36, ll. 34–37, 22.

29. Ibid., p. 134, ll. 31–32.

30. Ibid., l. 33.

31. Ibid., p. 37, ll. 20–22.

32. Ibid., p. 135, ll. 21ff.

33. "In primis autem Paulum tibi facito familiarem. Hic tibi semper habendus in sinu, nocturnus versandus in manu, versandus diurna [Horace, *Ars poetica,* 269], postremo et ad verbum ediscendus." Ibid., ll. 16–19.

34. See Kohls, *Die Theologie des Erasmus,* 1:126ff.

35. Ibid., pp. 132ff.

36. "Ergo si te totum studio scripturarum dedicabis, si in lege domini metitaberis die ac nocte, non timebis a timore nocturno sive diurno, sed ad omnem hostium insultum munitus atque exercitatus eris." Holborn and Holborn, *Ausgewählte Werke,* p. 31, ll. 31–34.

37. Ibid., p. 31, ll. 32–34, 3.

38. Ibid., p. 32, ll. 3–8.

39. Ibid., ll. 10–12. See also Kohls, *Die Theologie des Erasmus,* 1:23ff. and 62ff.

40. Cf. Kohls, 1:21ff. and 54ff.

41. Holborn and Holborn, p. 32. ll. 13–14.

42. Ibid., ll. 17–18.

43. Ibid., ll. 18–22.

44. See also Kohls, 1:132ff.

45. "E philosophis autem Platonicos te sequi malim, propterea quod cum plerisque sen-

tentiis tum ipso dicendi charactere quam proxime ad propheticam euangelicamque figuram accedunt." Holborn and Holborn, p. 32, ll. 25–28.

46. Ibid., ll. 28–31.

47. Ibid., ll. 31–32.

48. Ibid., ll. 32–33.

49. Ibid., p. 33, ll. 7–12.

50. Ibid., p. 64, ll. 14–23.

51. Cf. Kohls, 1:98ff.

52. Ibid., pp. 75ff. and 146ff.

53. Ibid., pp. 133ff.

54. Ibid., pp. 113, 123, 152ff., and 189 (and elsewhere).

55. Ibid., pp. 92ff.

56. Ibid., pp. 151ff.

57. Ibid., 2:129, n. 766.

58. Ibid., 1:150ff.

59. For the concept of "studium pietatis" and its significance, and above all for the ethics of Martin Bucer, see Karl Koch, *Studium Pietatis: Martin Bucer als Ethiker* (Neukirchen/Moers, 1962) and Kohls, *Die theologische Lebensaufgabe des Erasmus und die oberrheinischen Reformatoren* (Stuttgart, 1969). The influence of Humanism on the English Reformation has been demonstrated very well by the honored jubilarian in the following significant publication: *The English Church in the Sixteenth Century* (Ithaca, N.Y., 1963).

60. See Kohls, *Die Theologie des Erasmus,* 2:129ff., n. 769.

61. Ibid., 1:145ff.

62. See Harm Alpers, *Die Versöhnung durch Christus: Zur Typologie der Schule von Lund* (Göttingen, 1964) and Kohls, *Die Theologie des Erasmus,* 2:130, n. 771.

63. Kohls, *Die Theologie des Erasmus,* 1:84ff.

64. See the reference in note 3 of Holborn, *Ausgewählte Werke,* pp. 24, ll. 13–26.

65. For the *Exitus-Reditus* schema and its use by Erasmus, see Kohls, *Die Theologie des Erasmus,* vol. 1, especially pp. 163, 176ff., 180ff., 187ff., and elsewhere; also vol. 2, pp. 123 and 127.

66. Ibid., 1:145ff.

67. Ibid., p. 146ff.

68. Ibid., p. 149ff.

69. Ibid., p. 148ff.

70. For the difference between Erasmus and Luther on the concept of law, see Ernst-W. Kohls, *Luther oder Erasmus,* Book 1 (Basel, 1972), pp. 25ff.

71. Melanchthon's concept of law is parallel to that of Erasmus. See Wilhelm Maurer, *Der junge Melanchthon,* 2 vols. (Göttingen, 1967–69), 2:287ff. and 336ff.

72. See Kohls, *Luther oder Erasmus,* n. 72 on pp. 55ff. Finally, the understanding of Scripture is the basis of inquiry between Erasmus and Luther. The latter believed that the Word of God was a spontaneous gift, derived neither from Scripture nor theology. See ibid., pp. 125ff. See also Wilhelm Maurer, "Offenbarung und Skepsis," *Gesammelte Aufsätze,* ed. Maurer and Kohls (Göttingen, 1970), 2:366–402.

73. See Kohls, *Luther oder Erasmus,* pp. 143ff.

74. See Kohls, *Die Theologie des Erasmus,* 1:146ff.

75. Ibid., pp. 120-22, and Holborn and Holborn, *Ausgewählte Werke,* p. 73, ll. 25–35.

76. Holborn and Holborn, p. 73, ll. 25–35.

77. See Kohls, *Die Theologie des Erasmus,* 1:161ff.

78. Ibid., pp. 173ff. For the concept of "publica utilitas," see the appendix, "Zur Bedeutung und Geschichte des Begriffes 'gemeinnutz'" in my dissertation, *Die Schule bei Martin Bucer in ihrem Verhältnis zu Kirche und Obrigkeit* (Heidelberg, 1963), pp. 121-29.

For the concept of "Gemeinnutz," see the reference in Ernst Wolf, *Allgemeiner Teil des bürgerlichen Rechts* (Cologne/Bonn/ Berlin, 1973), pp. 186–88.

79. See Kohls, *Die Theologie des Erasmus,* 1 : 159 ff.

80. Ibid., pp. 175 ff.

81. See notes 77 and 78 in the pages given above.

82. See Kohls, *Die Theologie des Erasmus,* 1 : 175 ff.

83. Ibid. See the references on pp. 70, 141, 189 and elsewhere.

84. See Holborn and Holborn, p. 28, ll. 7–26.

85. See also Cornelia De Vogel, "Erasmus and His Attitude Towards Church Dogma," *Scrinium Erasmianum,* ed. J. Coppens (Leiden, 1969), 2 : 101–32, and Kohls, *Luther oder Erasmus,* p. 236, n. 15.

86. See Kohls, *Die Theologie des Erasmus,* 1 : 138 ff.

87. Naturally, scholars have established the opinion that the spiritual program of Erasmus is in reality a theology; but in reaching this conclusion, they fail to distinguish between the theology of Erasmus and that of Luther. I have devoted *Luther oder Erasmus* (Basel, 1972) to an explanation of the differences.

88. See Kohls, *Die Theologie des Erasmus,* 1 : 140 ff.

89. In this connection, see Guillaume Budé's letter to Erasmus, dated May 1, 1516: "Non enim *theologum* modo esse te arbitor, sed *eum qui verum colat.* Atque huius rei fidem apud me fecit Militia Christiana olim abs te edita." Allen, *EE,* II, Ep. 403.

90. Franz X. Funk, "Besprechung von Johannes Janssen, Geschichte des deutschen Volkes," *Theologische Quartalschrift* 63 (1880): 660–81, especially, p. 667.

91. See Ernst Troeltsch, "Protestantisches Christentum und Kirche in der Neuzeit," *Die Kultur der Gegenwart,* ed. Paul Hinneberg, 2d ed. (Berlin/Leipzig, 1909), pt. 1, sect. 4, pp. 1, 2. See also Kohls, *Vorwärts zu den Tatsachen: Zur Überwindung der heutigen Hermeneutik seit Schleiermacher, Dilthey, Harnack und Troeltsch,* 2d ed. (Basel, 1973), pp. 10–13.

92. Sigrid von Schulenburg, ed., *Briefwechsel zwischen Wilhelm Dilthey und dem Grafen Paul Yorck von Wartenburg, 1877–1897* (Halle, 1923), p. 145: letter of Grafen Yorck to Dilthey of June 8, 1892.

93. See Luther, *Luthers Werke* (Weimar, 1883–), vol. 10, pt. 3, p. 19, ll. 3–4, henceforth referred to as *WA.* See also Kohls, *Luther oder Erasmus,* especially n. 72, and pp. 148, 159 and 179.

94. "Et adeo non delector assertionibus, ut facile in Scepticorum sententiam pedibus discessurus sim, ubicumque per divinarum scriptuarum inviolabilem auctoritatem et ecclesiae decreta liceat, quibus meum sensum ubique libens submitto, sive assequor, quod praescribit, sive non assequor." Erasmus, *De libero arbitrio,* ed. Johannes von Walter, 2d ed. (Leipzig, 1935), p. 3, ll. 15–20. See also Kohls, *Die Theologie des Erasmus,* pp. 61–62, and Kohls, *Luther oder Erasmus,* pp. 160–67, especially n. 72.

95. See especially the section on the *affectus* and the *fides* in the *Ratio seu Methodus,* Holborn and Holborn, *Ausgewählte Werke,* p. 236, ll. 1–237, and p. 237, ll. 17–238.

96. Luther's disputation, *De fide infusa et acquisita* (1520), is printed in *WA,* vol. 6, p. 88, ll. 1–98. In this disputation Luther asserts the *fides infusa* and rejects completely the *fides activa* or *acquisita:* "Fides acquisita sine infusa nihil est, infusa sine acquisita omnia est." *WA,* vol. 6, p. 89, ll. 27 ff.

97. See Kohls, *Die Theologie des Erasmus,* especially 1 : 185 ff., and Kohls, "La Position théologique d'Érasme et la tradition dans le *De libero arbitrio,*" *Colloquium Erasmianum: Actes du Colloque International réuni à Mons du 26 au 29 octobre 1967 à l'occasion du cinquième centenaire de la naissance d'Erasme* (Mons, 1968), pp. 69–88.

98. Wilhelm Maurer, "Offenbarung und Skepsis," Maurer, *"Kirche und Geschichte,"* *Gesammelte Aufsätze* (Göttingen, 1970), 2 : 366–402, especially p. 402. See also Kohls, *Luther oder Erasmus,* p. 6.

3 The Logic and Rhetoric of Proverbs
in Erasmus's *Praise of Folly*

CLARENCE H. MILLER

Sir Thomas Chaloner, in the prefatory letter introducing his translation (1549) of *Moriae encomium*, wrote the first critique in English on the content and style of Erasmus's masterpiece. Concerning the content, Chaloner merely repeats some defensive remarks from Erasmus's own prefatory letter and adds, somewhat unjustly, that one important value of the work for the common people is that it will make them content with their lowly lot by showing them the miseries of high station. His remarks about style are more incisive and original. In particular, he notices one feature which a translator is more likely to perceive than a reader either of the original or of a translation—the plethora of proverbs and the difficulty of catching the peculiar flavor they lend the work:

> Likewise in all my translacion I haue not peined my selfe to render worde for woorde, nor prouerbe for prouerbe, wherof many be greke, such as haue no grace in our tounge: but rather markyng the sence, I applied it to the phrase of our englishe. And where the prouerbes woulde take no englishe, I aduentured to put englisshe prouerbes of like waight in their places, Whiche maie be thought by some cunnyng translatours a deadly sinne. But I sticke not for all that, in this foolishe booke to vse mine owne foolishe caste. And if it be misliked, I passe not greatly though I lose the praise of my Folie.[1]

Chaloner was quite aware of the effect of Erasmus's persona on the style of the work:

> For as Erasmus in all his woorkes sauoureth of a liuelie quicknesse, and spareth not sometyme in graue mattiers to sprincle his style, where he maie snache oportunitee with meerie conceited sentences: so in this booke, treatyng of suche a Theme, and vnder suche a person, he openeth all his bowget: So farfoorth as by the iudgement of many learned men, he neuer shewed more arte, nor witte, in any the grauest boke he wrote, than in this his praise of Folie. [p. 5]

Though he does not say so, Chaloner was perhaps aware that Erasmus's "bowget" or wallet was particularly well stuffed in the fall of 1509 when he wrote *The Praise of Folly:* he had just returned to England from Italy, where the year before, after months of feverish work, he had produced at the Aldine Press the first large edition of his *Adagia*.

Folly, Erasmus's most lively and penetrating persona, does indeed take advantage of her creator's well-stocked store of proverbs, sprinkling them throughout her oration with bounteous bravura and deliberate virtuosity. After one burst of proverbs, mostly Greek, she self-consciously remarks: "But I will stop propounding proverbs lest I seem to have rifled the commentaries of my friend Erasmus."[2] The density of proverbs, however we may define that most elusive term,[3] is certainly greater in the *Moria* than in any of Erasmus's other works (except, of course, the *Adagia* itself). In the approximately 24,500 words of the *Moria* there are 285 proverbs and proverbial expressions,[4] an average of one in every 86 words. The density gradually decreases: in the first part (1/1–96/15) it averages one in 78 words; in the second (96/15–155/1), one in 89; in the third (155/1–190/7), one in 111.[5]

But the distribution is by no means even throughout. We are not surprised to learn that there is a heavy concentration in the long, virtuoso proem (1/1–8/14)—one in every 45 words (35 percent of them Greek)—or in the brief epilogue, or rather nonepilogue (189/15–190/7)—one in every 23 words (all of them Greek). We might expect, and we do get, a higher frequency of proverbs in the sections on such commonplace topics as the ages of man (17/1–22/13), friendship (31/5–33/18), the necessity for self-love (35/7–37/9), prudence (46/11–53/5), or old men and women (54/17–56/21). One entire section (155/1–157/15) takes its main idea from two proverbs[6] and is developed almost exclusively by citing or paraphrasing seven other proverbs.

We might not notice, however, that (apart from the proem and epilogue) the highest percentage of Greek proverbs occurs in the last large division on Christian folly (159/8–189/14). One reason for these, and for several nonproverbial Greek words in this section,[7] is that Folly is turning the linguistic weapons of the proverbial *Graeculi-graculi* (166/3–6) against theologians who stubbornly and foolishly refused to recognize the necessity for Greek in scriptural exegesis.[8] In her survey of academic and social classes, she reserves the heaviest barrage of proverbs for dialecticians and philosophers (110/8–113/19): the treasures of traditional and often metaphorical wisdom are directed at the supersubtle spinners of abstract theories. She also tends to sprinkle her proverbs more thickly when she is refuting an imagined objection,[9] perhaps in keeping with Erasmus's own recommendation.[10]

Thus Folly is quite skillful in the distribution and deployment of her proverbs. They are part of the well-honed and brilliantly polished tools of her trade. She has chosen to play the part of the "sophist": "For it is now my pleasure to play the sophist with you for a little while, not the kind that nowadays crams boys' heads full of troublesome trifles and passes on the tradition of disputing with more than womanish persistence. Rather, I shall follow in the footsteps of those ancients who avoided the infamous title 'Sophi' (or 'wisemen') and chose instead to be called 'sophists.'"[11] In spite of her denial,[12] Folly is a dialectical sophist and a consummate rhetorician in the modern (that is, Renaissance) as well as the ancient manner. She demonstrates her dialectical sophistry and her rhetorical prowess in her artful manipulation of proverbs.

Certainly she is nothing if not shifty. Her fallacious reasoning is, of course, not limited to proverbial contexts, but proverbs are an aid in disguising sophistry even when they are not directly involved; and sometimes they themselves form part of the chain of false logic. For her sophistical prestidigitation Folly depends largely on the reader's inadvertence or forgetfulness. For her prowess in the world Folly gives more credit to Self-love and Flattery than to her other hand-maidens, but for her own sophistry the prime place must be granted to Forget-fulness. With blithe and insouciant inconsistency, Folly chooses whatever she likes from widely disparate philosophies—Platonic, Peripatetic, Epicurean, even Stoic when it suits her purposes (though generally the Stoics provide her with her favorite strawmen). Pythagorean philosophy she both accepts and rejects (15/1-3, 62/17-23). Considerable emphasis has (rightly enough) been placed on her Platonic affinities,[13] but she is not a Platonic philosopher. She specifi-cally rejects him at 39/2-5 and 39/17—40/5. She uses Plato's image of the Sileni of Alcibiades to prove an essentially skeptical or Pyrrhonist viewpoint (47/16—48/3). In exploiting the myth of the cave (91/14-18, 183/5-13), she takes diametrically opposite attitudes toward it, pinpointing for us (as it were) how the irony of the first part is both like and unlike the irony of the third part. It is not for nothing that in her second to last sentence she rewrites the proverb μισῶ μνάμονα συμπόταν as μισῶ μνάμονα ἀκροατήν.[14]

The devious devices by which Folly keeps her reader in pleasant, though sometimes perplexed, oblivion of her inconsistencies are multifarious. They run the gamut from large elements of structure to smaller techniques of style, includ-ing the liberal use of proverbs. One larger technique contributes to the dazzling, sometimes dizzying, effect of the *Moria:* Folly tends to alternate between a stepwise analysis of different points or categories and large, kaleidoscopic scenes, tableaux, or surveys which swiftly group great, confused masses of fools. Such overviews often frame or mark off the larger divisions of the work. The tableau of Folly's attendants (11/10—12/14), the description of the frolics of the gods (22/14—26/12), the list of those who are sustained by Philautia (84/8—87/13), the Lucianic Jove's-eye view of man's miseries (97/9—100/22)— these are some of the scenes in which the reader is forced to draw back from particular arguments to encompass a large, densely packed group. This vacilla-tion between stepwise analysis and the swarming groups is one of the techniques Folly uses to keep the reader off balance. She takes him down and up, as if (in cinematic terms) she were using a zoom lens, so that he is never allowed to get all the parts in the same focus.

The analogue of the swarming tableau on the level of sentence structure is the copious catalogue or list, sometimes broken off breathlessly as if to confirm the proverb "The number of fools is endless."[15] Typical of this technique is such a sentence as this: "Cuius [sc. πλούτου] arbitrio bella, paces, imperia, consilia, iudicia, comitia, connubia, pacta, foedera, leges, artes, ludicra, seria, iam spiritus me deficit: breuiter, publica priuataque omnia mortalium negocia administrantur."[16] The primary effect of such sentences is to suggest the teeming plenitude of Folly: she herself cites three times the Ciceronian proverb "Everything is full of folly."[17] Never, perhaps, did Erasmus put to better use the techniques of accumulation and elegant variation expounded in the De copia than in his Moria.

At the opposite extreme from these packed sentences are the "spontaneous," trailing, calculatingly casual sentences, often interrupted by parentheses. I choose the following example because its sophistry depends partly on the proverbs with which it opens and closes. Arguing that foolishness is necessary to bring and keep friends together, Folly seems (but only seems) to allow for some exceptions:

> De mortalibus loquor, quorum nemo sine vitiis nascitur, optimus ille est, qui minimis vrgetur: cum interim inter sapientes istos deos, aut omnino non coalescit amicitia, aut tetrica quaedam et insuauis intercedit, nec ea nisi cum paucissimis (nam cum nullis dicere religio est) propterea quod maxima pars hominum desipit, imo nullus est, qui non multis modis deliret, et non nisi inter similes cohaeret necessitudo.[18]

The two proverbs—No one is without foolish faults (that is, all men are fools) and Friendship can arise only between those who are alike—categorically clinch the point that without folly there is no friendship. Between them Folly seems to grant that wise men may engage in a certain diluted kind of friendship, but as the sentence winds to its conclusion it turns out that, as the opening denied in effect that there is such a thing as a wise man, so the conclusion asserts that (even if there were wise men) there would be no one with whom they could be friends. What Folly gives with one hand, she takes with the other.

The very density of proverbs in the Moria is one important way in which Folly manages to dazzle, not to say daze, her readers. Proverbs seem not only immediately and inevitably true (hence the frequency of hyperbole in proverbs),[19] but they are often also (strangely enough) enigmatic.[20] They not only persuade but also puzzle the reader—even more so when they are in Greek, as about 18 percent of Folly's are. A profusion of proverbs tends to distract and perplex, to prevent clear thought and discrimination. As Erasmus himself puts it, "The very density of proverbs may, by their interaction one upon another, reduce their clarity, just as nothing stands out in a picture where nothing is clearly outlined. Therefore, when painters bring together several objects in one painting, they separate them by spaces so that the shadow of one does not fall on the body of another."[21] At the same time the unrelieved glitter creates a dazzling, even blinding, surface of overwhelming plausibility.

Proverbs themselves offer plenty of inconsistencies and Folly does not hesitate to exploit them. She can cite opposing proverbs almost in one breath: "But why bother even to give you my name, as if you could not tell at a glance who I am, 'prima facie' as it were, or as if anyone who might claim I am Minerva or Sophia could not be refuted by one good look at me, even if I did not identify myself in speech, that truest mirror of the mind."[22] Where is the truth, in the external appearance ("ex vultu fronteque, quod aiunt")[23] or in the inner reality ("oratio, minime mendax animi speculum")?[24] Twice, when she wishes to stress the inner reality (in this case, folly) of women or supposed wisemen, she cites the proverb "An ape is still an ape, even if it is dressed up in royal purple."[25] Later the costumes worn by the actors in the play of life (including the royal purple) are the only reality, and hence Folly, who knows only appearances, is true prudence (48/12—49/7). At one point Nature is said to be in many respects a stepmother to mankind,[26] but when it suits Folly's argument, Nature is perfect and unfailing in her care of all creatures, including man (58/3-8).[27] The proverbial quality of admiring what is strange or exotic is attributed to fools;[28] later we learn that one essential ingredient of happiness, one provided (of course) by Folly, is not to admire what belongs to others but to be pleased with one's own qualities and achievements (35/14-19, 36/4-8).[29]

Moreover, proverbs sometimes form part of sophistical syllogisms (or enthymemes)[30] constructed by Folly. At one point she deliberately displays her sleight of hand by enveloping a scriptural quotation in an obviously false syllogism:

What should be concealed is more valuable than what is left exposed and unguarded. (Hence the Aristotelian proverb τὴν ἐπὶ θύραις ὑδρίαν.)[31]

Folly should be concealed whereas wisdom should be openly displayed. (Melior est homo qui abscondit stulticiam suam, quam homo qui abscondit sapientiam suam [*Ecclesiasticus* 41 : 18]).

Therefore folly is more valuable than wisdom (163/15—164/15).

In this syllogism, directed against those infatuated with Aristotelian logic, the use of an Aristotelian proverb to support the major is not without malice aforethought. The syllogism is also a glaring example of one of the standard fallacies discussed by Aristotle in *De sophisticis elenchis:* it argues from a proposition which is true only *secundum quid* (that is, as it applies to personal, portable property) to a conclusion *simpliciter.*[32] Would we like an example of another Aristotelian fallacy, *petitio eius quod est in principio,*[33] complete with proverbial buttresses? Folly can supply it:

The more widespread any good thing is, the better it is.[34]

But Folly is most widespread. (Hence the Ciceronian proverb "Stultorum plena sunt omnia," Otto 1701, Walther 30433a.)

Hence Folly is best of all (159/4–8).

The syllogism assumes what is to be proved, namely, that Folly is a good thing to begin with. Would we like a proverbial example of *equivocatio,*[35] the first of the Aristotelian fallacies "in dictione"? "The poets are less indebted to me, even though they are in fact professed members of my party, since they are classed as free spirits, as the proverb has it, whose whole aim is nothing more than to soothe and please the ears of fools, and to do it with sheer trifles and absurd fables."[36] Reduced to syllogistic form the argument runs:

What is free from the claims of fact and common sense is nonsense.
Poets are classed as free. (Hence the Horatian proverb "Liberi poetae et pictores," *Adagia* 2048 [*LB,* 2:727D] , Otto 1443.)
Therefore poets are nonsensical and foolish.

The ambiguous term is *free,* which means something different in the minor than what Folly makes it out to be in the major. Indeed, most of the Aristotelian fallacies "in dictione" can be reduced to some form of ambiguity, at which Folly is an expert.[37] A great deal of her sophistic reasoning (much of which, of course, does not employ proverbs directly) could be analyzed according to the categories of the Aristotelian fallacies as they were presented by Peter of Spain.

Folly is not only a sophistical dialectician but also a consummate rhetorician, both in her use of proverbs and otherwise. She is an expert in using and abusing the rules of rhetoric[38] and, in particular, the rhetoric of proverbs. Fortunately, Erasmus himself has left us a convenient summary of this subdivision of rhetoric in the prologue to his *Adagia* (*LB,* 2:1–13). After defining a proverb and attempting to distinguish it from similar rhetorical forms such as the sententia,[39] Erasmus establishes the dignity or prestige of proverbs by cataloguing the renowned writers who have collected or used them (*LB,* 2:4E–6B). Folly also is aware of the special dignity which may be associated with certain proverbs because of the famous persons who originated or used them. Apart from such unimpeachable scriptural sources as Ecclesiastes (161/4, 20-22), Jeremiah (161/13-19), and Ecclesiasticus (162/5-7), she goes out of her way to link some of her proverbs explicitly with Sophocles, Homer, Plato, Euripides, Cicero, and Aristotle.[40]

Erasmus proceeds to discuss the utility of proverbs under four main headings: (1) they are the germs of important and far-reaching philosophical and even theological ideas; (2) they are useful in persuading an audience to accept a certain point of view; (3) they ornament and beautify discourse; and (4) they help us to understand ancient authors. One of the two proverbs which Erasmus chooses to illustrate the wealth of ideas that may be derived from a proverbial gem is the Pythagorean saying that among friends all things are held in common, which virtually contains even such profound doctrines as the mystical body and the communion of Christians in the Eucharist. In the *Moria* this same Pythagorean proverb is used only as a witty and allusive way of describing thievery (99/7-10). But one of Folly's basic premises—what may be called her "naturalism"—is essentially an exfoliation of the proverbial "naturam sequi" (61/5, Walther 15922a-b). Folly also uses two other proverbs—"quae supra nos, nihil ad nos" and "arrogantia gigantum"[41] —to reinforce the idea that man should emulate the natural humility and harmonious content of flowers, insects, birds, and beasts instead of seeking to elevate himself by the pursuit of learning (57/7– 63/12). In his *Adagia* Erasmus expounds these same proverbs in a manner quite consistent with his religious and humanistic beliefs, but Folly distorts them for her own purposes by blurring the meaning of nature in order to lump men and lower creatures together in one undistinguishable concept. Similarly, Folly takes the proverbial "Sileni Alcibiadis" as the starting point of an argumentative explanation quite different from the one propounded by Erasmus himself in the *Adagia*.[42]

For purposes of persuasion, Erasmus says in his prologue to the *Adagia* that proverbs are useful, like jokes, as a last resort in refuting objections.[43] But they are primarily persuasive because their long-standing and widespread diffusion makes them unimpeachable and unprejudiced witnesses. Folly's awareness of this rhetorical function of proverbs is evidenced by the phrases with which she sometimes introduces them: "vulgi prouerbium" (4/16), "Astipulatur et vulgo iactatum prouerbium" (18/19-20), "Vulgati prouerbii non leue testimonium" (21/5), "notissimo prouerbio persuasum est" (157/23-24), "Aristotelico prouerbio teste" (176/21–177/1).

According to Erasmus, proverbs provide ornamentation partly because they embody the whole range of rhetorical figures and tropes. Folly's proverbs offer plentiful examples not only of such common figures of speech as metaphor, simile, and alliteration but also of some of the more exotic schemes, such as *homoioteleuton*.[44] She can play elegantly and almost tacitly with the figure of *etymologia*[45] in her proverbs: thus vainglory, like the proverbial Siren, draws ("trahit") fools to sacrifice their lives (45/5),[46] and bishops (ἐπίσκοποι) "in drawing money into their nets play the part of bishops [overseers] without the slightest oversight."[47] Erasmus conceives of proverbs ornamenting speech like stars in the sky or gems on a garment or tasty tidbits at a banquet (*LB*, 2:8C). Certainly Folly offers us a galaxy, an incrustation, a surfeit of proverbs. She uses them as she says ostentatious modern rhetoricians use Greek phrases, like bright bits in a mosaic.[48] Those in her audience who understand them can feel complacent; those who do not can pretend they do. She soothes the feelings of her hearers (*pathos*) and projects an image of herself as learned and widely experienced (*ethos*).

Erasmus's fourth point about the utility of proverbs is that they help us to understand many passages in ancient authors, who often allude to proverbs with elegant brevity, mentioning only a word or two in passing and relying on the reader's awareness of the whole proverb. Folly, of course, cites proverbs from such writers as Homer, Sophocles, or Euripides, not to help us understand them but to make us misunderstand them. But she herself does emulate the elegant allusiveness of the ancients. First of all, most of her proverbs are phrases or even single words, not fully predicated pronouncements. Moreover, she very rarely aids or prepares her listeners by giving any of the formulaic signals (such as "vt aiunt" or "iuxta vulgo tritum sermonem") recommended by Erasmus (*LB*, 2:13EF). She alludes to the Acarnanian pigs, the Epidaurian serpent, the Malean promontory, the Marpesian crag, the Dodonaean brass, the Tenedian axe—enough to drive a conscientious translator to desperate shifts if not to despair. She may allude to a proverb without giving a single word of it: her claim, "From me, therefore, you will hear an extemporaneous speech, unpremeditated but all the truer for that," depends on the proverbial notion that a woman's spontaneous advice is likely to be correct while her premeditated counsel is unreliable.[49] She may compose variations on an unexpressed proverbial ground:

> I ask you, can someone who hates himself love anyone else? Can he get along with anyone else if he is always at odds with himself? Can he bring pleasure to others if he is demanding and displeased with himself? No one would say so, I think, unless he were more foolish than folly herself. But if you exclude me, everyone would not only be utterly unable to put up with others; he would also be disgusted with himself, dissatisfied with everything he has, filled with self-hatred.[50]

The first three sentences give variations on the proverb "Qui sibi malus, nulli bonus" (Walther 24728a); the last sentence, three variations contrary to the proverb "suum cuique pulchrum" (*Adagia* 115 [*LB*, 2:74E], Walther 30942b).

Such allusiveness certainly renders the *Moria* difficult: from its first publication in 1511 it appeared with sidenotes (mostly to translate the Greek), and in 1515 it was provided with an elaborate commentary almost as long as the work itself and at least partly written by Erasmus himself.[51] After it was first heard or read by its ideal auditor (its namesake Thomas More), one may wonder how many have fully savored its finer bouquet—caught the wit on the wing rather than in the taxidermy of annotation. Folly's pose of virtuosity and *sprezzatura* prevents her from giving explanations. She seems to speak out of character on the single occasion when she stoops to the pedantry of annotating a proverb (23/5–11). Citing the Greek proverb δύσκολα τὰ καλά, Erasmus himself derives the excellence of proverbs from the very difficulty of using them well and claims that in using them "you must either display the highest artistry or be subject to ridicule; you must either earn extraordinary praise or else be laughed at."[52] Folly dissolves this strict disjunction between the serious and comic: through flagrant excesses she consciously makes herself the butt of laughter, but she also shows that to be laughed at as a fool is indeed the most extraordinary praise and that a fool displays the highest artistry of all because he alone knows the art of living productively and comfortably. In her use of proverbs she turns even excess and obscurity to advantage.

Concerning how proverbs should be used, Erasmus makes two main points: (1) they should be deployed with moderation and aptness, and (2) they may be modified or "accommodated" (to use Erasmus's technical exegetical term) to various senses. Folly's proverbs are always apt, but they are deliberately immoderate. For this overabundance, however, she could have cited the authority of Erasmus himself, for he allows it not only in the familiar epistle (*LB*, 2:9D) but also in the paradoxical encomium.[53] In fact, the rhetorician Menander (third century A.D.), whose treatise on epideictic oratory is one of the main sources of our knowledge of the rules for eulogies, gives as his tenth kind of speech λαλιά, a "name given to a style rather than to a topic. It is noticeable for the absence of fixed rules. Several topics of the epideictic circle might be treated in the style of the λαλιά, which was more free and easy, sometimes conversational, yet abounding in sweetness, spirited narrative, pictures, skillful turns, proverbs, quotations. . . . It may be sportive in character, praising or censuring something."[54]

Folly is quite skillful in modifying proverbs. The most obvious way to do this—a way recommended by Erasmus himself not only in his prologue (*LB*, 2:9E) but also in the main body of the *Adagia*[55] —is to use them ironically. Folly does this aptly and fairly frequently,[56] but she is far more clever in her distortion and misapplication of proverbs.[57] Erasmus's criteria in his prologue would allow for some of Folly's extensions or analogous formations,[58] but very often Folly is clearly breaking the rules. When Erasmus recommends applying a proverb to various objects or replacing a word in it with various other words, the basic meaning or moral thrust of the proverb remains constant.[59] But Folly stands proverbs on their heads. Justifying her self-praise, she argues: "Finally, I follow that well-known proverb which says that a person may very well praise himself if there happens to be no one else to praise him."[60] The Listrius commentary notes that the proverb is directed against those who speak vaingloriously about themselves—that is, it does not justify but condemns self-praise. Folly radically reverses the meaning with the adverbial fillip "recte." Concerning writers of books, Folly tells us: "It is worth your while to watch how pleased they are with themselves when they are praised by the ordinary reader. when someone points them out in a crowd with: 'There is that remarkable man.'"[61] The commentary points out that the proverbial Greek expression οὗτος ἐστιν ὁ δεινὸς ἐκεῖνος . . . (Otto 549) was applied to Demosthenes, not in praise but in ironic scorn of his vanity. If writers are pleased by such a proverb it can only be through their own remarkable ignorance.) Folly describes her handmaiden Laziness thus: "This one leaning on her elbows with her hands clapsed (consertis manibus) is Misoponia [Laziness]."[62] Although the phrase "consertis manibus" seems to apply naturally enough to the relaxed posture of Laziness, it is ironical because its true proverbial meaning is "with the greatest exertion" (Otto 1044–45). Those who do not understand such deliberate misapplications can accept Folly's proverbs as straightforward. Those who do can admire their own cleverness (and Folly's). As usual, Folly has it both ways.

Folly's proverbial parting shot is an example of blatant perversion through substitution: "The old saying was 'I hate a drinking-companion with a memory.' Up-dated, it is 'I hate a listener with a memory.'"[63] Facilely, but typically, she equates the gossip and wrangling of the tavern with the oratory of the lectern or pulpit. More subtle is the jest she creates by not making a substitution in a proverb where we would expect one. As she approaches her "nonepilogue," she apologizes for her loquacity, adding: "But also remember that Greek proverb 'Often a foolish man says something to the point'—unless, perhaps, you think it does not apply to women."[64] By not substituting μωρά γυνή for μωρὸς ἀνήρ, Folly chalks up a point for what is nowadays called women's liberation.[65]

Finally, in his prologue to the Adagia Erasmus devotes considerable attention to classifying proverbs according to their subject or origin (such as war, sailing, gods, animals).[66] If we examine the proverbs in the Moria from this point of view, we find that they do in fact present some thematic motifs and patterns. One simple design is the sixfold repetition of the proverbial tag taedium vitae,[67] which highlights one of Folly's poses and one of her major arguments: with world-weary resignation she insists that only folly can sweeten man's unalterably bitter lot and render it bearable. One category mentioned by Erasmus merely in passing (*LB*, 2:10D) seems to be especially prominent in the *Moria*: thirty-two proverbs are drawn from parts of the human body, especially the head.[68] Are we wrong to find here the humanist's regard for the human form, especially the "human face divine"? The mouth and ears, the instruments of the verbal discourse which was the center of much of the humanist program for education and reform, are especially prominent. At the other extreme is a series of proverbs which pretty clearly reflects Folly's "naturalism": forty-three proverbs refer to a large range of animals and birds.[69] One of Folly's principal arguments is precisely that man should forget the imagined superiority of his humanity and settle comfortably into the mindless contentment of the animal world. In the third part on Christian folly, we find an appropriate variation: the proverbially stupid sheep (177/1) is one of the mild animals recommended by Christ, the lamb of God. That fully ten of Folly's animal proverbs refer to the ass is clearly appropriate—Holbein's illustrations make it pretty certain that the "insolitum cultum" (2/15) worn by Folly is the fool's costume, including a hood with ass's ears.[70] Twice she alludes to Midas's ears and twice to the Cumean ass;[71] both epitomize the hypocritical and pretentious stupidity so ruthlessly exposed by Folly. The proverb ὄνος πρὸς λύραν[72] stigmatizes fumbling stupidity and incredible ineptitude. Having harped on it three times, Folly gives it a final twang by using it twice as a punning way of identifying Nicolas de Lyra.

Both as a rhetorician and as a dialectician Folly is especially fond of proverbs because they enable her to deceive and to persuade. But even more basically, they reflect the profound ambivalence of her posture and her position. Folly deals in great and mighty opposites, polarities like foolish or wise, good or bad, natural or supernatural. She assiduously avoids qualifications and refinements, keeping our attention intently but narrowly focused on one half of her disjunctions—one half at a time, that is, for she may switch from one to the other, and the cardinal point of her skill is to make such a switch without losing our credence. We are led to find opposite positions equally plausible. Nowhere in her picture of mankind is there any place for mixed characters: all old men are dotards; all old women, lascivious; all politicians, corrupt and self-serving. She is obsessed with characters driven by obsessions and does her best to make us obsessed with them too. Only the worldly fool is happy, only the otherworldly fool is happy—we are maneuvered into believing either view while Folly concentrates on it, but how can we believe both? Even paradox cannot bridge the gap, since the same paradox, "only the fool is wise," applies to both views.

Besides, paradox is itself polarized since it always implies the stereotypical notion it contravenes. "Only the fool is wise" would be no paradox if we did not implicitly believe that folly is strictly incompatible with wisdom.

Proverbs also tend to be polarized. It is not simply that they frequently contradict one another: "A stitch in time" vs. "Haste makes waste" or "A bird in the hand" vs. "A man's reach must exceed his grasp," and so on. The saying "Experience is the best teacher" would not be striking if we did not believe that being taught is basically different from experiencing. And one may well argue, as Roger Ascham does in his *Schoolmaster,* that experience is the worst teacher. To prove that childhood is foolish, Folly cites the proverb "I hate a child wise beyond his years" (18/20).[73] We nod our heads and think of precocious pests we have encountered or of such literary figures as Tom Jones's "brother" Blifil or Tom Sawyer's cousin Sidney. But Folly also cites the Platonic proverb that attributes truth to wine and children (66/15–17), and, when it suits her purpose, she refers to Christ's praise of children (178/1). Moreover, if we accept the *topos* "puer-senex," we would have to reverse Folly's proverb by changing "Odi" to "Amo."[74]

Proverbs tend to be unqualified, categorical, and extreme: they gain their intensity by narrowness of focus. So too does Folly, who loves to deal in extremities. But Erasmus, who experienced and propounded extreme views but who knew better than to love them exclusively and wholeheartedly, managed Folly's presentation of extremities in such a way as to leave his audience intensely aware of the need for some *tertium quid.* The listener who remembers the whole speech is confronted with the contradictions that Folly conveniently chooses to forget. According to Erasmus's view, the proper effect of Folly's speech should be to force the thoughtful reader to try to construct the epilogue which Folly refuses to provide. Folly hopes to confirm her audience merely as "Moriae mystae." But Erasmus leaves his audience, in a sense far deeper than Folly intended, μωροσόφοι (7/8–9).[75]

NOTES

1. *The Praise of Folie,* ed. Clarence H. Miller, Early English Text Society No. 257 (Oxford University Press, 1965), p. 6.

2. Kan, 155/20–156/1. All quotations are from my own final text (derived from a collation of all editions printed in Erasmus's lifetime), but for convenience I refer to the pages and lines in I. B. Kan's edition (The Hague, 1898). All translations are my own.

3. Erasmus himself attempts a definition in the prolegomena to the *Adagia:* Paroemia est celebre dictum, scita quapiam novitate insigne (A proverb is a well-known saying remarkable for a certain refined novelty of expression), *Opera omnia* (Leyden, 1703–06, hereafter

cited as *LB*), 2:1F–2A. But he is unable to give any clear and workable distinction between *paroemia* (or its synonyms *proverbium* and *adagium*) and the closely related *sententia*, *apophthegma*, and *scomma* (*LB*, 2:3E–4D). Adopting an empirical but rather exhaustive standard, I have accepted a saying as proverbial: (1) if it appears in Erasmus's *Adagia*; (2) if Erasmus in another work or Listrius in the commentary identifies it as such; (3) if Folly herself specifically calls it a proverb; (4) if it is so identified by such ancient authorities as Donatus or Suidas; (5) if it appears in: *Paroemiographi Graeci*, ed. E. L. Leutsch and F. G. Schneidewin (Göttingen, 1839); *Die Sprichwörter und sprichwörtlichen Redensarten der Römer*, ed. August Otto (Leipzig, 1890); *Die Sprüchwörter bei den Römischen Komikern*, ed. Wilhelm von Wyss (Zürich, 1889); *Proverbia sententiaeque Latinitatis medii aevi*, ed. Hans Walther (Göttingen, 1963–69); *A Dictionary of the Proverbs in England in the Sixteenth and Seventeenth Centuries*, ed. Morris P. Tilley (Ann Arbor, 1950); or *The Macmillan Book of Proverbs, Maxims, and Famous Phrases*, ed. Burton E. Stevenson (New York, 1968). Hereafter I cite these collections by the last name of the editor.

4. The distinction between full-fledged proverbs (complete sentences) and proverbial expressions (nouns, verbs, or nonpredicative phrases) is made by Erasmus himself (*LB*, 2:10CD).

5. On the three major parts, see my article "Some Medieval Elements and Structural Unity in Erasmus' *The Praise of Folly*," *Renaissance Quarterly* 27 (Winter 1974): 505–11. Apart from the critics mentioned there, others have also analyzed the *Moria* in terms of its three large divisions: Sister Geraldine Thompson, *Under Pretext of Praise* (Toronto, 1973), pp. 57–85; Barbara Könneker, *Wesen und Wandlung der Narrenidee im Zeitalter des Humanismus: Brant-Murner-Erasmus* (Weisbaden, 1966), pp. 283–84; and Wayne A. Rebhorn, "The Metamorphoses of Moria: Structure and Meaning in *The Praise of Folly*," *Publications of the Modern Language Association* 89 (May 1974): 463–76.

6. "Fortuna favet stultis" (Walther 9847c) and "Fortes fortuna adjuvat" (*Adagia* 145 [*LB*, 2:88B] and Otto 702).

7. ἐισαγωγὴν (163/18), νὴ τὸν δία (166/2), πενταγλωττω (167/10), συμμαχεῖν (169/3), σοφοὺς (175/6), νηπίοις . . . σοφδις (176/6).

8. Hence the witty turn of identifying Nicolas de Lyra only by allusion to the proverb ὄνος λύρας (166/16, 168/15). Folly uses the same trick against the theologians in her survey (114/1–127/12), though the Greek there is usually not proverbial. One of her deftest strokes is to call Saint Thomas Aquinas, who did not know Aristotle in Greek, ἀριστοτελικώτατος.

9. Kan, 58/2–63/21, 69/13–73/14, 92/5–94/4.

10. Postremo quod de risu scribit Fabius, maximas difficultates causarum, quae nullis argumentis dissolvi queant, joco eludi, id vel maxime praestat paroemia. (Finally, what Quintilian says about laughter—that the most difficult objections can be evaded by a joke—can be accomplished most devastatingly by proverbs.) *LB*, 2:8B.

11. 3/1–10. In Erasmus's time *sophista* meant both "rhetorician" (Charles du Fresne du Cange, *Glossarium mediae et infimae Latinitatis* [Paris, 1937–38] and R. E. Latham, *Revised Medieval Latin Word-List from British and Irish Sources* [London, 1965] and "logician" (Alexander Souter, *A Glossary of Later Latin to 600 A.D.*, Oxford, 1949). In particular, "sophister" was applied to second- or third-year students at Cambridge (*Oxford English Dictionary*).

12. Similarly, she defines and divides her subject matter by denying that it can be defined or divided (5/15–6/1). Her epilogue consists in a refusal to provide an epilogue (190/1–7). She defines the genre which she in fact follows, the paradoxical encomium, by denying (implicitly) that she does so (4/18–5/4).

13. For example, by Paul O. Kristeller in "Erasmus from an Italian Perspective," *Renaissance Quarterly* 33 (Spring 1970): 11, and by A. H. T. Levi in his introduction and notes to the Penguin edition of Betty Radice's translation (1971), pp. 21-24, 203–04.

14. "I hate a drinking-companion with a memory" becomes "I hate a listener with a memory."

15. *Ecclesiastes* 1:15, Walther 30430.

16. "His [that is, Plutus's or money's] decision governs war, peace, kingdoms, counsels, judgments, agreements, marriages, pacts, treaties, laws, arts, recreations, serious business— I'm running out of breath—in short, all the affairs, public or private, in which mortals engage" 9/8-12. The sentence is a paraphrase of the proverb "Pecuniae obediunt omnia" (*Adagia* 287, *LB*, 2:144D). For other examples, see 10/14-11/8, 19/16-19, 29/11-15, 34/19-35/5, 53/6-17, 54/17-55/9, 62/17-23, 68/11-69/10, 79/18-80/7, 96/8-14, 106/21-107/10, 117/18-118/3, but I, too, am running out of breath. A similar technique, on a somewhat larger scale, is the long series of curt sentences heaped up, often concatenated by anaphora (for example, 81/19-82/8, 86/1-87/16, 97/21-100/4, 131/1-132/10).

17. Kan, 24/14-15, 159/5-6, 162/4-5. The lists are especially effective when each element of the series is matched against its opposite (47/18-48/3, 150/3-10) or when one series is set over against another (148/15-149/12). It is noteworthy that there are fewer lists in the third part (on Christian folly), perhaps because there they are replaced by the heaped-up citations of texts.

18. "I am talking about mortal men, none of whom is born without faults (indeed, he is best who is afflicted with the fewest); as for these gods of wisdom, either they never strike up any friendship at all, or they occasionally fall into a gloomy and unpleasant sort of friendship, and even that with very few men (I hesitate to say with none at all) because most men are foolish—indeed, there is no one who does not have many foolish delusions—and, of course, friendship cannot spring up except between those who are alike" (32/10-18). The two proverbs are Otto 1918 and *Adagia* 120-21, *LB*, 2:78D-80A (also Otto 1335-36 and Walther 29641-42).

19. Erasmus himself memorably expresses this quality in his prologue to the *Adagia:* Deinde fit, nescio quo pacto, ut sententia proverbio quasi vibrata, feriat acrius auditoris animum, et aculeos quosdam cogitationum relinquat infixos. (Hence it is that, somehow or other, an idea cast in the form of a proverb pierces the mind of the hearer more deeply and leaves fixed there the barbs [as it were] of thought.) *LB*, 2:8AB. On hyperbole in proverbs, see *LB*, 2:12A.

20. *LB*, 2:3B, 8D, and 11F.

21. *LB*, 2:9C. Cf. Quintilian, *Institutio Oratoria*, 8, 5, 26.

22. "Quanquam quid vel hoc [sc. nomen meum] opus erat dicere, quasi non ipso ex vultu fronteque, quod aiunt, satis quae sim prae me feram, aut quasi si quis me Mineruam, aut Sophiam esse contendat, non statim solo possit obtutu coargui, etiam si nulla accedat oratio, minime mendax animi speculum" (6/3-8).

23. Otto 717; Walther 7422 and 34258; *Adagia* 3817 (*LB*, 2:1148A).

24. Walther 20342: "Oratio est index animi certissimus." See also Walther 28068 and 30102b.

25. Kan, 6/12-7/1, 28/15-16. *Adagia* 610-11 (*LB*, 2:264E-265A.

26. Natura, non paucis in rebus nouerca magis quam parens (35/14-15). *Adagia* 1195 (*LB*, 2:481D); Otto 1239.

27. Hence it behooves man "naturam ducem sequi" (61/5, 16). Walther 15922ab.

28. "Quandoquidem est sane et hoc nostratium voluptatum genus non inelegans, quammaxime peregrina maxime suspicere" (8/8-10). Walther 786.

29. "Tibiipsi placere." *Adagia* 115 (*LB*, 2:76B).

30. I use this somewhat slippery term merely in the sense of a syllogism, part of which is not expressed but only implied.

31. Erasmus takes the Greek proverb to mean "the waterjug is left lying in the doorway" (*Adagia* 1065 [*LB*, 2:431A] and *Ecclesiastes sive de ratione concionandi* [*LB*, 5:1047B]).

32. The Aristotelian fallacies as discussed by Peter of Spain or John Buridan were a normal part of the curriculum at the University of Paris when Erasmus was there (H. Elie, "Quelques maitres de l'universite' de Paris vers l'an 1500," *Archives d'histoire doctrinale et littéraire du moyen age* 18 [1950–51]: 199–200, 207–08, 219, 223). For the fallacy "secundum quid et simpliciter," see Peter of Spain, *Tractatus called afterwards Summule Logicales*, ed. L. M. De Rijk (Assen: Van Gorcum, 1972), pp. 157–61. The outrageous and seemingly incredible false division of "devita" into "de vita" (171/11—172/12) is actually an obvious example of one of the less common and less important fallacies "in dictione," the "fallacia accentus" (*Tractatus*, pp. 128–29).

33. *Tractatus*, pp. 166–69.

34. The saying does not occur in the usual sources, including the *Adagia*, but Stevenson (p. 992, 13) gives "bonum quo communius eo melius" as an early saying of unknown origin. Folly herself implies its proverbial status: "Quis enim ignorat, vnumquodque bonum, quo latius patet hoc esse praestantius?" Saint Ignatius Loyola wrote "bonum, quo vniuersalius, eo diuinius est" in *Societatis Iesu Constitutiones*, pt. 7, chap. 2 (Rome, 1949), p. 225.

35. *Tractatus*, pp. 98–105.

36. Kan, 105/9–13.

37. Consider, for example, her handling of such terms as εὐήθειαν (33/9–11), νήπιος (159/1, 176/5–6), prudentia (46/16–17, 47/13–15), insanus (70/2–7), to say nothing of the ambiguities of her own name.

38. Jacques Chomarat, "L' 'Éloge de la Folie' et Quintilien," *Information littéraire*, no. 2 (1972), pp. 77–82.

39. See note 3 above.

40. Kan, 16/16, 47/6, 66/16–18, 159/5, 162/3, 164/4, 176/21.

41. Kan, 50/6, 59/5–6, 62/22–23, 63/16–17. *Adagia* 569 and 2993 (*LB*, 2:250AB and 948D).

42. Kan, 47/13–50/11. *Adagia* 2201 (*LB*, 2:770C–782C).

43. See note 10 above.

44. ἢ πῖθι ἢ ἄπιθι (50/4), *Adagia* 947 (*LB*, 2:381E); alea-Malea (75/26), *Adagia* 1246 (*LB*, 2:537F).

45. On this figure, see *De copia* (*LB* 1:17BC); Ep. 2465, lines 199–220 (*Opus epistolarum Des. Erasmi Roterodami*, ed. P. S. Allen et al. [Oxford, 1906–58], 9:211); *Ecclesiastes* (*LB*, 5:923DE, 932E–933B).

46. Otto 1657. "Siren" was derived from σειρά, "chain" (*Paulys Real-Encyclopädie der classischen Altertumswissenschaft*, ed. Georg Wissowa et al., 2d ser. [Stuttgart, 1914–67], 3:289) or from σύρεω "to draw" (*Ambrosii Calepini Dictionarii Octolinguis Altera Pars* [Lyon, 1663], p. 578). Thus Mythographus Vaticanus II: "Σειρήνες igitur Graece, Latine trahitoriae dicentur" (*Scriptores rerum mythicarum Latini tres Romae nuper reperti*, ed. G. H. Bode [Celle, 1834; repr. Olms, Hildesheim, 1968], pp. 109, 233).

47. Kan, 146/12–13, "in irretiendis pecuniis, plane episcopos agunt, ὀυδ ἀλ αοσκοπιή." The Homeric tag (*Iliad* 10:515; 13:10; *Odyssey* 8:285) was proverbial (*Suidas*, ed. A. Adler [Leipzig, 1928–38], pt. 1, pp. 98, 10). "Drawing money into their nets" also carries a barb for those who were supposed to be, like Peter and Andrew, fishers of men, not money.

48. "Velut emblemata" (8/2–3). But, unlike the rhetoricians' bright phrases, Folly's proverbs are never out of place, except when she deliberately misapplies them. She is no mere fumbler.

49. Kan, 5/2–4. As a woman, Folly applies to herself the proverb "Primo crede mulieris consilio, secundo noli" (Johannes Grynaeus, *Adagia* [Frankfurt, 1656], p. 130). The proverb had wide currency before and after Erasmus's lifetime, not only in Latin but also in English, French, and Italian (Tilley W668; Stevenson, p. 2576).

50. Kan, 35/7–14. "Stultior stulticia" (more foolish than Folly herself) is also a variation on the proverbial formula "stultior stulto" (Walther 30404-30404a)–a variation nicely appropriate to the dramatic presence of Folly herself.

51. See J. Austin Gavin and Thomas M. Walsh, "The *Praise of Folly* in Context: The Commentary of Girardus Listrius," *Renaissance Quarterly* 24 (Summer 1971): 193-209.

52. *LB,* 2:9B.

53. *De copia* (*LB,* 1:110CD).

54. Theodore C. Burgess, *Epideictic Literature* (Chicago, 1902), p. 111.

55. On "Thaletes" (7/8), see *LB,* 2:889E; on "Musis bene iuuantibus" (9/1 and 70/1-2), see *LB,* 2:866A.

56. For example, "sapiens aliquis coelo delapsus" (49/8), *Adagia* 786 (*LB,* 2:329BC), Otto 287, 516); "in magnis et voluisse sat est" (75/10), Otto 1853; "vmbras volitare" (111/10), *Adagia* 1253 (*LB,* 2:506D); "e deorum consilio nobis aduenerint" (111/20), Otto 517; "Christiana ecclesia sanguine sit condita, sanguine confirmata, sanguine aucta" (151/13–14), Walther 27490.

57. The Listrius commentary sometimes, but not always, points out such distortions. See, for example, the note (*LB,* 4:588F) on 157/24-158/1, and Gavin and Walsh, pp. 203-04.

58. See, for example, "decere quod agas" (35/24—36/1, "illoto ore" (123/26), "et quidem peronatis" (172/25).

59. Thus the proverbial broken bucket may be applied to a forgetful, prodigal, avaricious, gossipy, or ungrateful person; in the proverb "The gifts of enemies are not gifts" the word *enemies* may be replaced by *paupers, flatterers,* or *poets* (*LB,* 2:9EF).

60. Kan, 2/25—3/2. Walther 33291f: Vicinum habet pravum, ipse qui se iactitat.

61. Kan, 108/1-3.

62. Kan, 12/5-6.

63. Kan, 190/4-5.

64. Kan, 189/18-190/1.

65. Translations sometimes destroy the joke by rendering μωρὸς ανὴρ simply as "a fool."

66. *LB,* 2:10C—13D.

67. Kan, 18/27, 19/22, 31/4, 54/2-3, 54/16-17, 144/17. Walther 30970a.

68. They refer to the forehead, ears, tongue, eyebrows, beard, hands, fingers, back, breast, face, mouth, lips, eye, feet. I am loath *induere leonis exuvium* and to bear the onus of demonstrating that this quantity (and others) are statistically significant.

69. Ass, ape, crow, elephant, lion, mule, goat, pig, lamb, wolf, ox, serpent, cuckoo, sow, camel, dog, bat, sheep, owl, horse, porcupine, grackle.

70. Kan, 2/17—3/1, 6/12—7/1, 7/3, 41/5, 84/16, 102/7, 139/21, 166/16, 168/15, 181/28—182/1.

71. *Adagia* 267 (*LB,* 2:138B), 612 (*LB,* 2:265C), and 266 (*LB,* 2:137EF).

72. *Adagia* 35 (*LB,* 2:164B).

73. *Adagia* 3200 (*LB,* 2:991D) and 2210 (*LB,* 2:785A). Walther 19721b. Otto 1917.

74. Ernst R. Curtius, *European Literature and the Latin Middle Ages,* trans. Willard R. Trask (New York: Harper & Row, 1963), pp. 98-101. V.-L. Saulnier ("Proverbe et Paradoxe du XVe au XVIe Siècle," in *Pensée Humaniste et Tradition Chrétienne aux XVe et XVIe Siècles,* ed. Henri Bédarida, Publications de la Société d'Études Italiennes [Paris: Boivin, 1950], pp. 87-104) traces the evolution (mainly in French writers) from accepted proverb, to proverb questioned and qualified (often through paradox), to polished, learned maxim. The *Moria* belongs to the second stage and represents "le paradoxe comme redoublement du proverbe" (pp. 97-98).

75. This word is cast in a proverbial formula (*LB,* 2:11E).

4 The *De Copia:* The Bounteous Horn

VIRGINIA W. CALLAHAN

For the Roman poets *Copia* was the goddess of Plenty, the bringer of the abundant harvest, the bearer of the bounteous horn—*beata* and *opulenta*.[1] For the two great Roman theorists of rhetoric, Cicero and Quintilian,[2] it was an easy step to transfer the metaphor from the field to the forum, from agriculture to eloquence, and to conceive of the deity as having a double attribution as *Copia* of words and subject matter. It remained for Erasmus to glorify the twofold guise of the divinity in what became one of the most popular and influential books of the Renaissance, his *De Duplici Copia Verborum ac Rerum Commentarii Duo.* It is appropriate to look again at what Erasmus referred to as his writings *ad institutionem literarum,* since so many of his scholarly efforts have engaged him in the service of those works.

Perhaps none of the works of Erasmus, except the *Adagia* and the *Colloquies,* reflect more consistently the various periods of his life than the *De Copia.* "A growing book" like the *Adages,* its genesis, development, and amplifications extended from his youth in Holland to his final years in Freiburg. Erasmus's awareness of the importance of a good Latin style is evident from his earliest letters to his friends and fellow students. D. F. S. Thomson[3] evokes, as prelude to this preoccupation, the combination of memory, "the lonely years" of his boyhood, and the "early time of quiet study." Crucial were his contact with Alexander Hegius, rector of his school at Deventer, his brief encounter with Rudolph Agricola, and his early conversion to Lorenzo Valla's *Elegantiae,* which Erasmus epitomized "for a certain schoolmaster" in 1489. The particular problems connected with the engendering of a good Latin style in one's pupils were his daily fare during the years in Paris, when much of his time was of necessity given over to tutoring.

The details of the two phases of the actual working out of the *De Copia* are available in Erasmus's letters of 1499–1500 and 1511–12. On April 29, 1499,[4] Erasmus wrote to Adolphus van Veere, the pupil of his friend James Batt: "I have begun a work that may considerably help students in acquiring Latin and will send it to you from Paris when it is finished." Although it was his original intention to dedicate the work to the young van Veere and to Batt, it was exactly thirteen years later when he was to write the dedicatory letter of the

The author wishes to thank William S. Heckscher for suggesting ways to improve this essay.

De Copia to John Colet and his boys at St. Paul's. The fate of the early manuscript of the work was a part of what might be termed "the Italian fiasco." While on his longed-for Italian journey in 1508, Erasmus left some of his papers with his friend Richard Pace in Ferrara, among them manuscripts of the *De Ratione* and the *De Copia,* and the *De Pueris Instituendis.* These Pace entrusted to a certain William Thale, who sold some of the material and gave some of it away. The *De Copia* he gave to Sixtinus, who later maintained that he thought Thale had given it to him as a gift. This early version of the *De Copia,* a dialogue between two students entitled *Brevis de Copia Praeceptio,* was ultimately printed in 1519 as an appendix to the *Formulae.*[5]

In 1509, Erasmus returned to England pinning his hopes on the generosity of the new king, Henry VIII, to whom he then thought of dedicating the *De Copia.* Although his hopes remained unfulfilled, Erasmus's presence in England at this time was an instance of the right man in the right place at the right time, for John Colet, having come into his inheritance, was seeking aid for his plans to refound the grammar school at St. Paul's, and for its use he urged Erasmus to resume work on the *De Copia.*

The Erasmus-Colet correspondence of the year 1511, which Erasmus spent at Cambridge, contains several references to the progress of the new version. On October 29[6] occurs Erasmus's pun on the word *Copia,* when he opines that he is wallowing in "Resources" (*Copia*) while he is actually minus any resources at all. By March 1512,[7] Colet was expecting Book 2 of the *Copia;* on July 15, the first edition was published by the Flemish printer Jodocus Badius in Paris, with the *De Ratione Studii.*

As for the enhancement of his "resources," Erasmus was reminding Colet a year later (July 1513)[8] that the modest sum agreed upon as payment had not been given him. However, the repayment in terms of the augmenting of his reputation and his influence was incalculable, since the work became the backbone of the grammar-school curriculum in England in the sixteenth century and was to be widely used on the Continent as well.

Not everyone shared Colet's pleasure in Erasmus having been a coworker in his pedagogical undertakings. In the spring and summer of 1516, in an amusing exchange of criticism between Erasmus and Guillaume Budé,[9] the latter expressed surprise at his friend's penchant for wasting his talents on λεπτολογήματα (trivia). Erasmus, clearly wounded, responded with typical Socratic irony that indeed all of his works seemed to him to be mere trifles, but he wondered which works Budé would wish him to avoid. Budé, eager to put things right, excused his use of λεπτολογήματα as a slip of the pen, explaining that he should have limited himself to the word συγγραμμάτια (compositions). This kind of writing, he believed, might seem to posterity to be ψσευδεπιγραφούμενα (deceptive writings). He then proceeded to single out as an example the *De Copia,* which appeared to himself and to others not to fulfill the promise of its title. Erasmus's rejoinder: "The *De Copia* which you despise (in this we are on the same side) many distinguished men have praised, averring that no work of mine is more fruitful or more skillful." The *De Copia,* Erasmus continued, was a work that needed to be done. Quintilian had only touched upon the subject, Hermogenes made him dizzy and Agricola's treatise *De Inventione Dialectica* (published after the *De Copia*) was too difficult. As for the judgment of posterity, it would be sufficient praise for him to have achieved something more careful and more exact than others.

That same summer, John Watson, a Cambridge friend recently returned from the Continent, reported:[10] "All over Italy, and most of all among learned men of the first rank, your praises are being sung. You'd hardly credit the enthusiasm shown by men of this class everywhere in devouring your *De Copia.*"

The desire of other printers for the rights to the *De Copia* was immediate. Indeed, Matthias Schürer of Strasbourg had already issued unauthorized editions before Erasmus gave his permission to print a somewhat enlarged version in 1514 together with the *Parabolae.* Erasmus's authorization of a new Strasbourg edition was the cause of some distress for Badius, who complained to Erasmus in a letter[11] in 1515 but took the loss philosophically if it was of benefit to the author.

The Schürer editions coincide with the period in Erasmus's life in which he turned from England to Germany.[12] The decision to allow the *De Copia* to be printed in Strasbourg followed upon the appreciative reception given him when he visited the city in May 1514 and was feted by the German Literary Society there, under the leadership of Jakob Wimpfeling. The Schürer and other later editions are prefaced by a complimentary letter[13] from Wimpfeling and his colleagues, and by Erasmus's no less complimentary reply.[14] From Strasbourg Erasmus proceeded up the Rhine to Schlettstadt and to Basel, where he began his association with Johannes Froben. The printing house of Froben published editins of the *De Copia* in 1517, 1519, 1521, a substantially enlarged one in 1526, and the final revision in 1534.

There are subsequent sporadic references to the *De Copia's* destiny in the different countries of Europe. In 1527 Leonard Cox, writing from Cracow,[15] informed Erasmus that he was then reading the *De Copia* with his nephew and other pupils in his household and recalled that in previous years he had lectured on the text in Hungary before a large audience. Erasmus's response[16] was to send Cox the new Froben edition of 1526, in which he had made an emendation of a word that Cox had questioned in the edition he had at hand. In 1533 Erasmus described to John Choler[17] the attack of the Parisian theologians on his writings and noted that when the shops of the booksellers were invaded "even" the *De Copia* was seized. As late as 1535, Joannes Odonus, in a long eulogistic letter[18] calculated to persuade Erasmus that he was still extravagantly admired among the Italians, assured him that it was practically de rigueur (*solenne propemodum*) for his "most fruitful" commentaries on *Copia* to be read in their schools. He added that to the students of special promise his *Adages, Colloquies, Apophthegms, Parabolae,* and *Rules for Letter-Writing* were also especially recommended.

We learn from the material compiled by Rix[19] that by 1536, the year of Erasmus's death, at least 85 editions had appeared, and that by 1824 more than 180 had come into being, as well as approximately the same number of digests. In 1528 printers in four different cities were including in their editions the brief marginal notes of Christoph Hegendorff. In 1534 Peter Brubach of Hagenau, at the behest of Melanchthon, printed along with the text the elaborate commentary of M. Veltkirchius, which became part of what might be called the standard edition in the schools of England.

It is not the purpose of this paper, which is more in the nature of a bibliographical report, to discuss the text of the *De Copia*, but some indication of the structure of the treatise should be given here. The plan is deceptively simple.

In the introductory chapters (1–10) Erasmus praises the pursuit of *Copia*, comparing a rich abundance in thought and words to a golden river; but he warns that not everyone can hope to achieve this "godlike" power of speech. His intention is not to write a big book, but to provide students with material for use in their further study. Desiring only to be helpful, he harbors no desire for glory. After acknowledging his classical antecedents, he cites particular passages in classical authors which illustrate their practice of enriching expression. Erasmus admits that a distinction between *copia* of words and of things is not always clear-cut, but expresses his confidence in it for achieving the goals of his pedagogical method. The practical advantages of the exercises are set forth: the student is promised that a mastery of them will enable him to speak and write well *ex tempore*, that he will be aided in commenting on authors, translating foreign language texts, and writing verse. Before embarking on the specific forms of verbal varying he advises the student that he must strive unceasingly for elegance and correctness in keeping with the "purity" of the language of Rome. Chapters 11–32 contain the *rationes dilatandi*, the processes by which "copy" of words could be obtained, e.g., synonymy, enallage, metaphor, tropes and schemes of speech and diction. This section of the work is climaxed by the great pyrotechnical display in Chapter 33 where Erasmus takes two sentences and transforms them into a "Protean" variety of shapes. The first: *Tuae literae me magnopere delectarunt,* personalized by a reference to a letter from Erasmus's friend Faustus Andrelinus, is written in 146 different ways: the second: *Semper dum vivam tui meminero,* poignant in its relationship to Thomas More, is given 200 variant forms. These two illustrative sentences with less numerous variations had been used by Erasmus in his first version of the *De Copia* (*Brevis de copia praeceptio*) which was published by Froben in 1519 as a concomitant of the *Familiarum colloquiorum formulae.* The rest of Book 1 (34–206) provides the student with a handbook, a set of examples illustrating the foregoing precepts. In Book 2, which is about half the size of Book 1, Erasmus offers twenty methods for acquiring a *Copia rerum,* a wealth of subject matter. There is a shift here from the minutiae of style to the amplification of topics. Processes of this kind of varying include, for example, the use of detail, the bringing in of antecedents, causes and effects, descriptions of things, persons, places and times, digressions, invention of propositions, etc. The termination of the treatise is strangely abrupt. In a final paragraph, Erasmus mentions that it was his original intention to conclude the work with an example of a theme first handled concisely and then expanded, but that he decided against it "lest it prove too heavy a burden." The theme he refers to was the *De Pueris statim ac liberaliter Instituendis* first published in Basel in 1529 and then dedicated to William, the young duke of Cleves, to whom he dedicated his *Apophthegmata* two years later.

Baldwin,[20] in his review of the curricula of the sixteenth-century grammar schools in England, showed that the *De Copia,* following Erasmus's intention, was to serve as an introduction to the more advanced classical texts on oratory, especially Cicero and Quintilian. It was used in the upper forms (by which time the student would have mastered the elements of grammar) as the chief guide in attaining the goal of grammar-school teaching, namely oral and written composition. At the same time the student would be continuing to read the best classical authors, whom he was expected to imitate and in large part to memorize. The effectiveness of this regimen, centered on the *De Copia,* would be reflected in the quality of his frequent original compositions.

On January 30, 1523, to a letter to John Botzheim Erasmus appended a catalogue of his writings indicating his wishes as to the contents of the volumes in what would ultimately be his collected works.[21] The first two volumes were to contain those pertaining *ad institutionem literarum* and in volume 1 pride of place was to be given to his *De Copia Verborum ac Rerum*. In the subsequent catalogues, the *Opera Omnia* of 1540, and the Leiden edition of 1703 this primacy was retained.

The overall contents of these two volumes is striking proof of Erasmus's willingness in every period of his life to devote his time and energy to *paideia*, the nurture of the young. By 1531 these treatises comprised a comprehensive program designed to produce the complete humanist. The professor of classical languages today might well envy the sixteenth-century schoolmasters to whom these works were available. Indeed, it would be a fascinating experience, a kind of dream experiment, for a group of graduate students in one of our classics departments today to try out the Erasmian regimen. The sequence might be as follows: a scanning of Lily's grammar revised by Erasmus for the students at St. Paul's; a quick reading of the *De Ratione Studii*, in which Erasmus outlined his system and described his method of study in action; a detailed study of the *De Copia* as the focal point; a discussion of the *De Pueris* immediately thereafter, following Erasmus's original intention; a period of practice in epistolography relying on the *De Conscribendis Epistolis;* and finally discussions of the *De Pronuntiatione* and *Ciceronianus*. Portions of the *Parabolae, Apophthegmata,* and *Adagia* would serve as supplementary material. All of this would be done in conjunction with the reading of the classical authors recommended by Erasmus, and the students would be urged to make their own "copy" books in accordance with Erasmus's suggestions. Such an experiment would atone in part for the indifference the *De Copia* met with during the nineteenth and first half of the twentieth century. That some such scheme is not an impossibility is the fact that during the year 1972–73, in the Institute of Neo-Latin Studies of the University of Amsterdam, a course on the *De Copia* was offered, comprising a review of the recent scholarly literature, reading and analysis of the text, and a discussion of the relation of Erasmus's work to Quintilian's *Institutio Oratoria*.

In 1958 J. K. Sowards,[22] in his study of the *De Copia,* remarked upon the meager bibliography then relating to a work considered of prime importance by an author so renowned. The six works he listed as dealing with it covered a span of fifty years, 1904–54; four of them were published in the 1940s, and all of them were in a sense peripheral to the work itself. Woodward,[23] writing in 1904, observed that although "the great Latinists of the 16th and 17th centuries owed to it the same debt that Erasmus, Melanchthon, and Budaeus admitted as due from themselves to Valla," the *De Copia* had received little careful attention during the past two hundred years. And while he admitted that no student of the classical Renaissance "desirous to make a first-hand acquaintance of the art of expression as understood by humanist writers," could do better than to combine a careful analysis of the *De Copia* with a reading of Cicero's *De Oratore* and Quintilian's *Institutio Oratoria,* he made no analysis himself, nor did he include any selections from the *De Copia* in the section of his book made up of translations of passages from the other educational writings.

Herbert D. Rix[24] in 1946 provided a useful but still tentative expansion of the list of the editions of the *De Copia* in Van der Haeghen's *Bibliotheca Erasmiana,*[25] together with detailed information about the several ways the text was revamped in printed form in order to make it more easily usable. Two years later George J. Engelhardt[26] entered into an investigation of the possible mediaeval sources, and Emile V. Telle[27] utilized the contents of the *De Copia* to support the supposition that the *Julius Exclusus* was an authentic Erasmian product. T. W. Baldwin, mentioned above, and R. R. Bolgar,[28] in their appraisals of the *De Copia* in larger contexts, succeeded admirably in establishing its pivotal position between classical and Renaissance rhetorical theory and application.

J. K. Sowards, on the other hand, preferred to emphasize the moral intention of the *De Copia,* singling out the many instances in which Erasmus used the discourse as an instrument for reform, potent because of the large number of boys into whom the contents were to be drilled during their pliant years. For him the work is thus essentially "a study in indirection." In this connection he suggests an analogy with the goddess Folly, whose "fatuous smile becomes the grimace of the righteous reformer." The true "res" of the title, he believes, lie in the illustrations and exempla that allow Erasmus almost subliminally to instill in the student his views on the moral issues of his time. In Erasmus's insistence from the beginning that speech must above all be "pure," Sowards finds the clue to the entire treatise, relating it to his assessment of classical learning as "a means to the education of the individual for his supreme role as a Christian man."

The neglect of the *De Copia,* wondered at by Sowards, was notably remedied in the course of the celebrations in 1969 of the 500th anniversary of the great humanist's birth. Among the historical essays published under the patronage of the University of Louvain at that time is Margaret Mann Phillips's paper on "Erasmus and the Art of Writing."[29] Because of her familiarity with the *Adages,* Phillips is particularly aware of how consistently the *De Copia* conforms to Erasmus's own method of achieving variation through an assiduous "digesting" of the thought and language of the best classical authors. In her interpretive paraphrase of the contents, she stresses Erasmus's feeling for the uniqueness of words and his gift for determining the right use of different kinds of words. What distinguishes the *De Copia,* she suggests, is the author's conviction that a mastery of the craft of writing in accordance with his precepts will "rise above imitation" and result in a style which has its own excellence. She wisely states that while a majority of Erasmus's educational works are dedicated to individual boys, the *De Copia,* despite its dedication to John Colet and the students of St. Paul's, is really dedicated to all boys. In a metaphor Erasmus would surely have approved, she describes Erasmus's free personal style as the "legitimate offspring of the marriage he was proposing in the *De Copia* between the classical and the modern mind." The treatise, she concludes, was a protest against the false *copia* that results from an indiscriminate admiration for the classics and the current Ciceronianism which frowned upon the use of any word not found in the then known text of Cicero.

One of the papers read at the birthday commemoration at the University of Tours was Giulio Vallese's "Erasme et le *Duplici Copia Verborum ac Rerum.*"[30] Vallese shares Phillips's interest in the *De Copia* as a revelation of the components of Erasmus's own method of study—namely, curiosity, a constant questioning of an author's mode of thought, energy, competitiveness with the author to be imitated, and unceasing vigilance. He sums up neatly the basic Erasmian formula: observe, memorize, imitate, have ready for use. For Vallese what chiefly characterizes the *De Copia* is Erasmus's evident desire to inculcate into the student a love of the Greek and Roman authors that will allow him to learn their secrets. Like Sowards, he dwells upon the moral utility of the work, placing it in a broad humanistic and historical framework which embraces the view of a Dante or a Petrarch that an understanding of the lofty morality of the ancient authors prepares for and integrates the Christian message. In his discussion of the contents of what Erasmus wished to be volume 1 of his collected works, Vallese makes an astute observation. Logically one might have expected that the first work in the volume would be the *De Ratione,* which Erasmus conceived of as a kind of prelude to the *De Copia.* But since Erasmus wanted the volume to begin with the *De Copia,* a work inextricably bound up with the image of John Colet, and end with his commentary on the Ovidian poem *The Nut Tree,* dedicated to the son of Sir Thomas More, Vallese contends that the volume was meant to stand as a monument to humanistic friendship, a tribute to the two Englishmen who shared and fostered his own pedagogical ideals and principles.

The 1969 Tours *Colloquia* contained, among others, Margaret Mann Phillips's paper on Erasmus and Montaigne[31] in which she speculated as to the possible impact of Erasmus's ideas on style and imitation on the thought and work of the French essayist. She feels that one can safely assume that Montaigne would at least have "tasted" the Erasmian views on style, and she is confident that he shared Erasmus's aversion to the pedantry of those who insisted on a slavish subservience to classical authors. Granting the risk of attempting a comparison between the Latin style of Erasmus and the French style of Montaigne, she nevertheless detects certain characteristics they have in common which might enable one to see in Erasmus "the precursor" of Montaigne.

Besides Phillips's and Baldwin's studies of the relationship of the *De Copia* to the works of writers in the vernacular, Eric Jacobsen[32] has suggested that in the Erasmian "duplex copia" we find "the typical formula of the development of most Renaissance poets, and more particularly of Marlowe" at whose school in Canterbury the *De Copia* was part of the curriculum.

The two long-term projects initiated as part of the 1969 anniversary of Erasmus will surely facilitate further research related to the *De Copia.* I refer, of course, to the Amsterdam edition of the Latin text which will supersede the Leiden edition, and the plan of the University of Toronto Press to make available for the first time in English all the major works in the Erasmian corpus. If one can judge from the contents of the volumes of the Amsterdam edition which have appeared thus far, the *De Copia* will probably be included in the next volume. Craig Thompson, in his review of volume 1-2 of the Amsterdam edition of the works of Erasmus,[33] which contained the *De Ratione Studii* together with three of the other educational treatises, expressed regret that the *De Copia* could not have been included. According to the prospectus of Toronto's *Collected Works of Erasmus,* volumes 23 and 24 (the *Epistolae* will be contained in volumes 1-22) will include the *Antibarbari,* the *De Copia,* the *De Ratione,* and the *Parabolae,* a grouping which would have been much to the author's liking. Through the kindness of Beatrice Corrigan, the late coordinating editor of the Toronto project, I was permitted to read Betty Knott's splendid translation of the *De Copia,* surely one of the most challenging of the works to translate. Craig Thompson has agreed to serve as editor of these volumes, which are scheduled to appear in 1978.

Mention has been made of Emile Telle's utilization of the *De Copia* to bolster the theory that the *Julius Exclusus,* a satire denouncing the militarism of the recently deceased Pope Julius II, was written by Erasmus. Telle concentrates on the coincidence of time and certain similarities in the ideational content of the two works, but does not challenge Erasmus's disavowal of the authorship of the work on the basis of style.

Another literary document of the period was brought into confrontation with the *De Copia* by Father Edward Surtz as an offshoot of his study of More's *Utopia.* In appendix B[34] of the Yale edition, More's vocabulary and diction are examined in the light of Erasmus's rules relating to the correct usage of words. Two years later, Father Surtz extended this investigation[35] by testing in painstaking detail More's adherence to Erasmus's precepts in both books of the *De Copia*. With typical modesty, he claimed that his study had "merely scratched the surface"; but on the basis of the evidence he had assembled, he reached the conclusion that, judged by Erasmus's manual of style, More's expression was "more than adequate to the thought."

In conclusion, I would like to offer a concise embodiment of what Erasmus meant by the concept of a "Double Copia." It can be seen best in an emblem of Andreas Alciatus,[36] the famous jurist and a devoted admirer of the Dutch humanist. Like all Renaissance emblems of which Alciatus was the "inventor," it has three parts: motto, picture, and poem. The motto is *Virtuti Fortuna Comes,* a sententia incorporated by Erasmus into his *Adagia.*[37] The picture depicts the caduceus, the wand of Mercury, the god of eloquence, topped by a winged cap and flanked by cornucopias. The image coincided with Alciatus's personal device (*impresa*). The multiple symbolism of the caduceus—the wand that guides, the entwining serpents with their heads in confrontation denoting wisdom and dialectic, the wings of diligence—was well suited to a professor of jurisprudence and had in fact also been used by Alciatus's teacher, Jason del Maino. The poem of the emblem reads:

> Anguibus implicitis, geminis caduceus alis,
> Inter Amaltheae cornua rectus adest.
> Pollentes sic mente viros, fandique peritos
> Indicat, ut rerum copia multa beat.

> A wand with two serpents entwined about it,
> And two wings, stands upright between the horns of Amalthea.
> Thus it indicates that a rich abundance of things
> Blesses men powerful in mind and skilled in speaking.

Alciatus often based his emblems on Erasmus's *Adagia* and other writings. What he has given us here is a graphic presentation of Erasmus's strong belief that *Copia* in the broadest sense would enrich the recipient of a humanistic *paideia,* which aimed at producing a man of character and eloquence.

NOTES

1. Plautus *Pseudolus* 2.4.46; Horace *Odes* 1.17.16; Horace *Carmen Saeculare* 59.

2. Cicero *De Oratore,* 1.12.50; 3.31.125; Quintilian *Institutio Oratoria* 1.8.8; 10.6.6.

3. D. F. S. Thomson, "The Latinity of Erasmus," in *Erasmus,* ed. T. A. Dorey (London, 1970), p. 115.

4. P. S. Allen et al., eds., *Opus Epistolarum Des. Erasmi Roterodami* (Oxford, 1906–47). vol. 1, Ep. 94, p. 233 (henceforth cited as *EE*).

5. Cf. Craig R. Thompson, ed., *The Colloquies of Erasmus* (Chicago, 1965), pp. 614–20.

6. *EE,* vol. 1, Ep. 237, p. 477.

7. Ibid., Ep. 258, p. 508.

8. Ibid., Ep. 270, p. 526.

9. Ibid., vol. 2, Epp. 403, 421, 435, 480.

10. Ibid., Ep. 450, p. 314.

11. Ibid., Ep. 346, p. 125.

12. Cf. James D. Tracy, "Erasmus Becomes a German," *Renaissance Quarterly* 21, no. 3 (1968): 281–88.

13. *EE,* vol. 2, Ep. 302, pp. 7–9.

14. Ibid., Ep. 305, pp. 17–24.

15. Ibid., vol. 7, Ep. 1803, p. 5.

16. Ibid., Ep. 1824, p. 71.

17. Ibid., vol. 10, Ep. 2868, p. 302.

18. Ibid., vol. 11, Ep. 3002, p. 96.

19. Herbert D. Rix, "The Editions of Erasmus' *De Copia,*" *Studies in Philology* 43 (1946): 595–618.

20. T. W. Baldwin, *William Shakspere's Small Latine and Lesse Greeke* (Urbana, Ill., 1944), pp. 180ff.

21. *EE,* vol. 1, Ep. 1, pp. 38–42.

22. J. K. Sowards, "Erasmus and the Apologetic Textbook," *Studies in Philology* 55, no. 2 (1958): 122–35.

23. William H. Woodward, *Desiderius Erasmus: Concerning the Aim and Method of Education* (Cambridge, 1904; reprint ed. New York, 1964).

24. Rix, together with Donald R. King, published a partial translation of the *De Copia* under the title *On Copia of Words and Ideas* (Milwaukee, 1963).

25. Ferdinand van der Haeghen, *Bibliotheca Erasmiana* (Ghent, 1893), pp. 65–70.

26. George J. Engelhardt, "Mediaeval Vestiges in the Rhetoric of Erasmus," *PMLA* 63 (1948): 739–44.

27. Emile V. Telle, "Le '*De Copia Verborum*' d'Erasme et le '*Julius Exclusus e Coelis,*'" *Revue de Littérature comparée* 22 (1948): 439–47.

28. R. R. Bolgar, *The Classical Heritage and Its Beneficiaries* (Cambridge, 1954; reprint ed. 1963), pp. 273–75, 297–98.

29. Margaret Mann Phillips, "Erasmus and the Art of Writing," *Scrinium Erasmianum,* ed. J. Coppens (Leiden, 1969), 1:335–50.

30. Giulio Vallese, "Erasme et Le *De Duplici Copia Verborum ac Rerum,*" *Colloquia Erasmiana Turonensia,* ed. Jean-Claude Margolin (Toronto, 1972), 1:233–46.

31. Margaret Mann Phillips, "Erasme et Montaigne: *De Duplici Copia Verborum ac Rerum et Essais,*" *Colloquia Erasmiana Turonensia,* pp. 492–500.

32. Eric Jacobsen, *Translation, a Traditional Craft: An Introductory Sketch with a Study of Marlowe's Elegies* (Copenhagen, 1958).

33. See *Renaissance Quarterly* 25, no. 2 (Summer 1972): 202.

34. Edward Surtz, S.J., and J. H. Hexter, eds., *Utopia,* in *The Complete Works of St. Thomas More* (New Haven, 1965), vol. 4, appendix B, pp. 579–82.

35. Edward Surtz, S.J., "Aspects of More's Latin Style in *Utopia,*" *Studies in the Renaissance* 14 (1967): 93–109.

36. Alciatus, *Emblemata* (Padua, 1621), p. 507. The cornucopias are missing in the 1531 Augsburg edition with which Alciatus was dissatisfied; they are present in the 1534 and later editions.

37. Erasmus, *Adagia,* 4.10.47 (i.e. *LB,* 2:1035F).

5 *Apologiae:* Erasmus's Defenses of Folly

MYRON P. GILMORE

In September 1514, Martin Dorp, a young philosopher at the University of Louvain who was about to take his doctor's degree in theology, wrote a letter to Erasmus, recalling their former intimacy and asserting that, although Erasmus now had so many friends and admirers throughout Christendom, none had a warmer affection for him than the writer.[1] This very affection permitted him to speak frankly in warning Erasmus that many, even among former friends, have been offended and scandalized by *The Praise of Folly*.[2] Furthermore, although Dorp wished to compliment Erasmus on his edition of the *Letters of St. Jerome,* he warned him of the dangers of undertaking the edition and translation of the Greek *New Testament*.[3] According to the testimony of Johann Reuchlin, Dorp was instigated to make these criticisms by his professors of theology at Louvain.[4]

The objections to *The Praise of Folly* presented by Dorp show that he completely misunderstood Erasmus's purpose. Erasmus, he charges, has been too severe in his condemnation of all the professions and impious to allow Folly to identify herself with Christ and the Christian religion. In the conclusion of this part of the letter, Dorp begs his friend to devote himself to writing an "Encomium of Wisdom!"[5]

Erasmus did not reply to this letter until the following May when he returned from England. He then wrote Dorp a lengthy explanation and justification of the *Folly* as well as a defense of the relevance of Greek to theological studies.[6]

Erasmus begins his apology by saying that he himself almost regrets that he ever published the work. It has brought him fame but also enmity, and this he regrets because, although many writers in the past have found an outlet for their emotion in attacking individuals, he has always tried to be indulgent and can indeed boast that he has no enemy whom he would not wish to bring back to friendship if he could.[7] He asserts that his aim in the *Folly* has been exactly the same as in his other works. In the *Enchiridion* he presented the form of a Christian life; in *Folly* there are the same ideas as in the *Enchiridion* but under the form of a joke, "sub specie lusus." Salutary advice has often been presented under a pleasing guise.[8] He explains how lightly he assumed the character of Folly during a period of illness spent in the country house of More, when he was without books. He intended to divert himself, and his host and friends were pleased with the enterprise and urged him to continue it.[9]

On the charge of severity he begs Dorp to notice that he does not mention the name of any particular person, and even when he speaks of the self-love which is characteristic of national cultures, he assigns qualities to the Spaniards, English, and Italians which they will hardly be displeased to hear.[10] Everyone takes pleasure in hearing of the follies of monarchs, priests, wives, husbands, so long as they are not individualized.[11] On the severity of Folly against theologians, how can Dorp believe that the whole order of theologians is disturbed because some foolish or bad theologians are attacked?[12] Erasmus himself has the highest respect for true theology and is indeed enrolled in the order and wishes no other title. He has only sought to condemn those who pervert the profession.[13] On the charge of impiety, Erasmus protests that there is surely no danger in anyone's imagining that Christ and the apostles were fools in a literal sense. The folly attributed to them is the folly which triumphs over all the wisdom in the world. And in showing a folly which is wise, Erasmus points out that he has shown an insanity which is sane and a madness which retains its senses.[14] He cites the language of Saint Paul on the "folly of the Cross."[15] Finally he urges his friend Martin to improve his understanding of theology by beginning the study of Greek and gently repudiates the pathetic suggestion of Dorp that Erasmus should follow *The Praise of Folly* with an "Encomium of Wisdom."[16]

This letter, in a version somewhat expanded from the one that was probably sent, was printed at the end of the edition of the *Moriae encomium* published by Froben in 1516, and thereafter in most early editions of the work after that date.[17] Erasmus's defense was taken up and reinforced by his dear friend More, who on 21 October 1515 sent Martin Dorp a long letter—really a treatise—in response to his reply to Erasmus, justifying the *Folly* and the necessity of Greek studies for an understanding of the Christian tradition.[18] This letter, together with the earlier one of Erasmus, has recently been described as the clearest manifesto of humanist theology.[19]

It is to be noticed that neither Erasmus nor More enter into great detail in their defense of *Folly* in these well-known letters. Erasmus protests that he is animated by the desire to do good to everyone and to present the pattern of Christian living. He has not slandered individuals and he has been severe only toward the bad theologians, monks, merchants, and rulers whom he has attacked. His conception of the *furor divinus* of true Christianity is Platonic and Pauline and in no way impious.

Of the same character was the defense included in the *Commentary* added in the name of Gerard Lister to the Aldine and Froben editions of 1515. These notes were also frequently reprinted. Interspersed with the explanations of classical references are assertions that Folly is not attacking good rulers or good prelates, and no one should be offended.[20]

At the same time, in the new edition of the *Adages* by Froben in 1515, was added the adage "Ollas ostentare," "To make a show of kitchen pots," in which Erasmus describes his indulgence in joking and the composition of *The Praise of Folly* in seven days without benefit of a library. Here again he protests that he had no intention of harming anyone; his criticism is gentle, not offensive; his critics (who are few) have not understood that it is Folly and not Erasmus who is speaking.[21] These rather diffident and complaisant justifications were replaced later in his life by much more polemical defenses written in the period when Erasmus was under attack by Luther and his followers on the one hand, and by conservative representatives of the Roman tradition on the other.

Among the latter were the French Carthusian, Petrus Sutor, and the Spanish theologian, Jacobus Stunica, both of whom wrote violent attacks questioning Erasmus's orthodoxy, primarily directed against his edition and translation of the *New Testament* and the *Paraphrases,* but also including an indictment of the *Moria.* In a series of counterattacks against both opponents, Erasmus spiritedly defended himself, especially against the charge of blasphemy for having put a defense of Christianity into the mouth of Folly.[22] The most serious critiques of the *Moria,* however, came in 1529 and 1531 from the pen of Alberto Pio, prince of Carpi, and nephew of Giovanni Pico della Mirandola, who devoted the last years of his life to a particularly bitter and comprehensive attack on Erasmus. As early as 1525 Erasmus had heard from Italian friends that Alberto was talking against him in the Roman curia. In October of that year he wrote a courteous but firm letter to the prince, repudiating the charge that he had been in any way responsible for the Lutheran revolution, and asserting on the contrary that he had struggled against those abuses which were the true cause of that revolution. He affirms his allegiance to the Roman church.[23]

The Prince of Carpi spent the winter composing a rather severe reply to this letter. In it he charges that Erasmus has supplied much ammunition to the Lutherans and especially indicts the *Folly* and the *Paraphrases.* This document circulated in manuscript form and was finally printed, in spite of Erasmus's efforts to stop it, in January of 1529.[24] Erasmus immediately composed a response which he describes as having been written in haste in the space of ten days. Since it consists of more than eighty octavo pages, it is probable that Erasmus had prepared some of the material in anticipation of the appearance of Alberto's attack.

The Erasmian *Responsio* was printed by Froben in March 1529.[25] It contains a refutation of all the charges made by Alberto, but a particularly prominent section is devoted to the *Folly* since Erasmus says that he has often heard in letters from Rome that Alberto is in nothing more zealous than in accusing the *Folly.*[26] Erasmus begins by reflecting that he remembers no other book to have been published with greater applause, not only from the young but from princes and prelates of the church. He has heard from friends that Pope Leo took particular delight in it. Erasmus says he recognizes his fate in that the *Folly* has now come into Alberto's hands but without the defense "in which I replied to Dorp who first of all complained about it and began the celebrity of its reputation." From the *Letter to Dorp* Erasmus repeats the dubious statement that he really did not wish the work to be published. Many charges of ineptness have been made; many libelous statements, but no one has attributed such impiety to the *Folly* as Alberto has. No one has ever lost a hair of his head over this work, and Alberto has smeared his pages with lies, either those that came into his own mind or those he has gathered from others.[27]

First, in refuting Alberto, Erasmus confesses that there are certain things in the *Folly* which are included for no other purpose than to incite the reader to laughter:

> Such things offend no one unless some gloomy and captious individuals who are so far from the graces that they neither know how to make a joke or to bear that others do so. In fact Folly condemns no walk of life nor repudiates any discipline: what is sinful in individuals is brought out not by a reprimand but by the enticement of a joke. . . . Everyone knows that I do not criticize disciplines or institutions or arts but only indicate what is amiss in each category. For it is the chief point of this argument that I taught that no one of the race of mankind is free from folly. Therefore the vices of mortals—not men themselves—are exposed to ridicule through a joke.[28]

Erasmus recalls that Plato approved this kind of correction in drinking matches and that the Germans today bring wandering fools into their banquets to reprimand the guests. No one can be offended because it is a fool who speaks, and no one of the company is spared. But in demonstrating what ought to be avoided in any situation, does Folly teach nothing serious, nothing solid, nothing to be sought for in life? On the contrary, she arranges it so that the things which are to be sought in life may be pursued more happily. Who could possibly take the jokes of Folly so seriously as to believe that there is indeed no felicity for mankind? Erasmus quotes from Alberto's critique: "I confess that there are many things in the life of man at which we laugh, but he is too wicked a judge of human affairs who condemns all things without discrimination." "But," replies Erasmus:

> does Folly condemn anything which ought to be approved? Rightly do you philosophize that human affairs are so tempered between actual and potential, that is between perfect and imperfect, that nothing can be so absolute

as not to have some admixture of vice. Since this is so, it is necessary to fight more stoutly against vice. You add that I have spared neither sacred rites, nor religion, nor even Christ himself. Who has dared suggest to you this mass of lies? I condemn superstition not sacred rites, and I further the cause of religion when I maintain that hypocritical religion is to be avoided. . . . Whoever turns over my writings will easily perceive unless blinded by hate that I bear no impious feeling toward Christ. . . . I believe that you, Prince Alberto, are a Christian man endowed with piety and therefore I will speak more frankly to you what I think, that you will more easily find those who slander divine things in Italy among the men of your own class, and in that much praised city of Rome than among us.[29]

But what do you call deriding divine things? Do they deride divine things who condemn the superstitious cult of saints? Does he seem to you to deride the Aristotelian philosophy who condemns those who interpret wrongly an Aristotle they have not understood?[30]

To Alberto's charge that Erasmus has murdered the Christian religion by saying that it is founded on Folly, Erasmus replies that Alberto has distorted his words and furthermore has not understood that when Paul speaks of the "folly of the Cross" and attributes folly to God, and denies that there are any wise men among the disciples, he is distinguishing between the wisdom of the world and evangelical wisdom. Erasmus recalls that Christ embraced children and invited the apostles to imitate their example, and that he inveighed with great severity against scribes and pharisees. In defending the description of Christ and the Christian religion with which the *Folly* concludes, Erasmus repudiates Alberto's accusation that he has distorted texts of Scripture.[31]

At the end of the section on the *Folly* in the *Responsio*, Erasmus cannot resist some satiric comment on both the Italians and Alberto. He says, "Among the Italians I do not know whether any of them are so weak in the faith that they fall away from Christ on account of a humorous book. With us even the women are more constant, than to decline from faith because of jokes of this kind, nor has anyone up to now in these regions ascribed these jokes to impiety, as you do."[32] Erasmus recalls that the *Folly* has circulated for so many years through the hands of all and, translated into French, found high favor in the halls of princes, and nobody shuddered over her except a few pseudo-monks, who had been treated differently than they wished. If in accusing the *Folly* Alberto had been animated by a zeal for religion, Erasmus must approve his motive although condemning his judgment. The latter would be acceptable to no one, except to those who would reject the Gospel itself if it were brought forward in the name of Erasmus. For such people hatred and a warped mind vitiate all judgment.[33]

In general, although with a far more polemical tone, Erasmus in this *Responsio* follows the same arguments he had developed in the *Letter to Martin Dorp* fifteen years before. Erasmus in the *persona* of Folly does not condemn individuals but only the vices of the various professions and categories of mankind. He is neither severe nor impious and defends himself from the latter charge by invoking the Pauline conception of the folly of the Cross, distinguishing between an evangelical wisdom which is folly in the eyes of the world and a worldly wisdom which can be seen as madness.

This was not the end of the controversy. The Prince of Carpi had lost his principality by changing his allegiance from the imperial to the French cause. Although he continued in high favor with Clement VII at the papal court, he was one of the victims of the Sack of Rome in 1527. By the time Erasmus's *Responsio* was published in March 1529, he had taken refuge in Paris, where he was received with great favor by Francis I. He was greatly offended by the contemptuous tone of Erasmus's defense and by the vehemence with which he repudiated the charge of having prepared the way for Luther. The prince immediately decided to use his enforced leisure to prepare a more comprehensive indictment of Erasmus. To this project he devoted the remaining months of his life until his death in January of 1531. The work was posthumously published in Paris on 9 March 1531, two years after it had been begun. In a preface the printer Badius Ascensius explained that Alberto had labored continuously to his last day for the Catholic faith. His purposes had been to prove conclusively his charges against Erasmus and to persuade him to recant and retract his errors. Alberto's secretary, the Italian humanist Francisco Florido Sabino, helped to see the book through the press after Alberto's death and may indeed, as Erasmus believed, have been responsible for writing some of the text.[34]

The full title of this rare book is *Alberti Pii Carporum illustrissimi et viri longe doctissimi praeter praefationem et operis conclusionem tres et viginti libri in locos lucubrationum variarum D. Erasmi Roterodami quos censet ab eo recognoscendos et retractandos.* It is a massive tome of 252 folios and begins with a recapitulation of the history of the controversy. Erasmus's original letter of 1525 and Alberto's *Responsio* of 1526, published in 1529, are reprinted as an introduction. Book 1 consists of the text of Erasmus's reply to Alberto in 1529 with extensive marginalia by Alberto creating the effect of a dialogue between the participants. Book 2 is Alberto's *praefatio,* in which he justifies his enterprise and explains how he has studied Erasmus's works in order to make his examination as complete as possible. In this preface he confesses that in an earlier period he had read only a few of Erasmus's works "not because I despised you but because I had no leisure. Some ten years before, I had read the *Adages* which I judge most useful for the study of literature. Then

I read the *Praise of Folly* which I found at first lively and elegant but which subsequently so disgusted me as to turn me away from your other writings. . . . After your last attack, however, I have tried to get hold of as many as possible although the reading thereof is made difficult because of your many digressions."[35] Book 3, the first of the twenty-three books in which the work is presented, is entirely devoted to an indictment of the *Folly* which had so disgusted the Prince.

Erasmus's reply, again hastily executed, was published by Froben in June of 1531.[36] It was a savage invective and, although friends remonstrated with him for attacking an opponent who was dead, Erasmus felt that the false and distorted character of Alberto's accusations justified his refutation. Since Alberto's examination and condemnation of the *Folly* was much more complete than what he had presented in the *Responsio paraenetica* of 1529, Erasmus in this *Apologia* gave a correspondingly fuller reply than he had in his previous work.

Erasmus opens his attack by complaining that Alberto does not understand the character of Folly in spite of his careful description of her and seems to expect that she will speak about everything with wisdom. She condemns the disciplines, beginning with the grammarians whose miserable labors are converted into pleasure through the agency of Folly.

Among the grammarians Erasmus had mentioned Aldus Manutius as one who had produced five editions of a grammar. Alberto, who had been a pupil and subsequently a friend and patron of Aldus, accuses Erasmus of ingratitude and maintains that without the aid he received from the Aldine Press, Erasmus would never have perfected his knowledge of Latin and Greek. Erasmus replies:

> Aldus himself if he were alive would not hear this without laughing. On the learning of Aldus I shall not expatiate. I loved him when he was alive and I shall not harm him now that he is dead. This one thing however I can truly say that when I came into Italy, I wrote better Greek and Latin than I now know. I had brought a mass of work with me from England to Venice, together with a bundle of books, especially in Greek, in which I had made notes. I begged, I confess, that this work should be published in the celebrated press. Aldus received it eagerly. I lived in the house of Aldus for almost eight months and the work was written and published at the same time in a few months. How could there have been any time left over for learning Greek and Latin? So great was the press of work as hardly to leave time for scratching one's ears.[37]

Erasmus then continues, in a characteristic digression, to describe—certainly not entirely disingenuously nor accurately—his life in the Aldine Press. He gives an account of how his proofs were corrected by the reader Serafino but also by Aldus himself, who was eager to read his work. He admits that Aldus aided him by furnishing him with manuscripts but asserts that the same was done by other scholars, among whom he names Janus Lascaris, Marcus Musurus, Baptista Egnatius, and Urbanus Regius. He did receive his board and lodging in the house of Andrea Asulano, the father-in-law of Aldus, and from the skimpy diet he there received, he claims, began his trouble with kidney stone. He was relieved by invitations from Janus Lascaris to eat at this house, but when he grew weak from the unaccustomed diet at the Asulano table, he asked Aldus that he be allowed to prepare his own food in his bedroom, and this request was granted.

Erasmus indignantly repudiates the conclusion of Alberto that he was the servant of Aldus during this period, and asserts that he never played such a role even in the households of cardinals in Rome. He recalls that Aldus confessed that he had learned much from Erasmus and that he sought to retain him throughout the winter so that he might improve his own knowledge of rhetoric. This whole digression on his Italian experience concludes: "I owe nothing of my knowledge of literature to Italy, would that I owed it all. There were there those from whom I might have learned, but such there were also in England, in France and in Germany." And rather sadly, "But in Italy for the sake of seeing which I had made so much effort, there was no time."[38]

This passage certainly shows how strongly Erasmus felt at this time about accusations that he owed his mastery of classical languages, and especially Greek, to Italy, and in particular to his experience in the Aldine household in Venice. The tone of this account is no doubt partly to be explained by his passionate desire to refute all of Alberto's charges. He was well aware that Alberto had been a close associate of Aldus, and furthermore that he was a close friend of Girolamo Aleandro, who had been a roommate of Erasmus's in Venice but was now regarded by Erasmus as his worst enemy in the Roman curia. It must also be remembered that this passage was written in the spring of 1531 when the controversy over the *Ciceronianus* which Erasmus had published in 1528 was still raging.[39]

After Folly's attack on the grammarians, which is the occasion of Erasmus's digression on his experiences in Italy, come her criticisms of the poets, the lawyers, and the dialecticians, and here Erasmus limits himself to a brief, sharp, and not very original or significant response to the objections of Alberto.[40] On theologians Alberto condemns Folly and Erasmus because of the proposal to send the theologians into battle against the Turks and Saracens and thus get rid of them. Erasmus triumphantly replies that here the words of Folly have been distorted. What she actually says is, "In my judgment the Christians would be wiser if, instead of those unwieldy battalions of soldiers with whom they have been warring without any help from Mars, they would send against the Turks and Saracens those brawling Scotists, and stubborn Occamists, and invincible Albertists, together with the whole band of Sophists." Folly, Erasmus emphasizes, speaks only of sophists and this has nothing to do with pious and sober theologians. This kind of quibbling in the intepretation of his own text reflects the haste and desperation in which he wrote the *Apologia*.[41]

After the theologians, Folly takes up the monks and Erasmus wearily reiterates that she is not attacking the institutions of monasticism itself but its abuses. He feels that on no other subject has Alberto been so calumnious as on this. As proof, he offers that Folly speaks of "the great part of the monks who are so intent on their ceremonies," the use of *part* indicating that she did not speak of the whole body of monks.[42] On the question of philosopher-kings, Erasmus similarly accuses Alberto of having substituted the word *philosopher* for Folly's *philosophaster*, "a bad philosopher," thus making it mistakenly appear that Folly condemns the Platonic philosopher-king.[43]

Because Folly speaks of the life of man as a "fabula" and declares that his happiness depends not on facts but on opinions, Alberto accuses her of academic skepticism and even praises Luther, his hated enemy, for having called Erasmus a skeptic, an ironic turn which Erasmus could appreciate as worthy of Folly herself. Alberto's accusation that Erasmus was a skeptic was repeated elsewhere in his attacks on Erasmus, and his condemnation and fear of the skeptical tradition may have been stimulated by his reaction to the *De vanitate doctrinae Gentium* which had been published in 1520 by his cousin Gianfrancesco Pico della Mirandola. This was the first work to make available in print the ideas of Sextus Empiricus, and it may well have reinforced Alberto's inclination to take his stand on the necessity of maintaining unchangeable dogmatic truth.[44]

There follows a lengthy passage on the much discussed contrast between apostolic poverty and the riches of contemporary popes and prelates. Erasmus asserts that in condemning the latter he, speaking through Folly, does not mean that holders of ecclesiastical office should not live in dignity but that their wealth should be devoted to charity and not used for luxury and war.[45]

Coming to the heart of his argument that Erasmus "Lutherizes," Alberto recalls that Folly condemns pontifical indulgences and that this is one of the dogmas of Luther denounced in the Bull of Leo X. Erasmus replies that if he has to defend everything Folly says, he admits that she does speak in a pagan fashion about the gods and praises many things which should be censured, such as flattery and drunkenness and finally herself. But he declares:

> On this subject I do not refuse to put myself in peril with Folly. And I begin
> by stating that on no point are the theologians more just to Luther than in

the condemnation of indulgences, so much so that the Parisian theologians omitted this article and only stated that he wrote many false things about indulgences without saying what they were. And I myself heard the Carmelite theologian of Louvain who promulgated the Bull of Leo, say to the people, 'We do not give much importance to indulgences.' . . . What theologians think about indulgences, such as we have seen them applied, is well enough known. But those indulgences which the *Decretals* and old diplomas mention were nothing but a relaxation of penitence granted by men, which they intended to be moderate, and granted only in necessary cases, such as the building of a basilica where none existed before. Afterwards appear those who relax the pain of purgatory and bid the angels of God to convey souls bought for a price directly to heaven. The Dominicans, indeed, hawking these among the populace in a too complacent and impudent not to say blasphemous manner, excited Luther to propose some propositions for disputation. To these, Prierias so responded that the fire was kindled. And long before *Moria,* many attacked pontifical concessions at least in part. But Folly does not touch these in any way. She attacks only fictitious concessions and calls them fictitious either as clandestine and not properly conceded or received otherwise than they ought to be. For the Pontiff conceded them to those who have confessed and are contrite, but the common people think innocence is achieved with the payment of money, although they have no idea of the necessity of a changed life. The whole tenor of the speech of Folly argues this conclusion and these are her very words quoted by Pio for calumny: 'Take for example some merchant, soldier, or judge who believes he has only to give up one single tiny coin from his pile of plunder to purify once and for all the Lernean morass he has made of his life. All his perjury, lust, drunkenness, quarrels, killings, frauds, perfidy, and treachery he believes can somehow be paid off by agreement, and paid off in such a way that he's now free to start afresh on a new round of sin.' From which it is clear that Folly does not simply condemn indulgences but only those which are proposed or received otherwise than they ought to be.[46]

The remaining paragraphs of Erasmus's *Apologia* are devoted to the distinction between what is superstitious and what is genuine in the invocation of saints and the cult of the Virgin.[47]

Finally, on the theme of the folly of Christianity in the eyes of the world, Erasmus reiterates that "if Alberto had been able to distinguish the fools of this world from the fools in God and the wise of this world from the wise in God, he would confess that the doctrine of Folly is entirely Christian.[48] In a resounding conclusion, Erasmus proclaims that Pio has not been able to prove any of the charges he has promised to demonstrate. His assertions are all lies, in which he claims that there is no book of Erasmus that has not attacked the sacred traditions of the Fathers, the institution of monasticism, theologians and priests, the dignity of prelates and pontiffs, the authority of the sacraments, the customs of the church, good works, the dogmas established by the church, the cult of saints, the veneration of the Virgin, and some of the canonical Scriptures. Alberto is revealed as a man who has learned no theology, is not familiar with the Scriptures or the Church Fathers, has never seriously reflected on piety, and has not even read the works he attacks.[49]

Sixteen years separated Erasmus's final defense of *Folly* against the attacks of Alberto Pio from the gentle and ironic remonstrance explaining to Martin Dorp in 1515 the true meaning of the message of Folly. Erasmus had come far from the position that he had no enemy of whom he would not like to make a friend if he could.

The *Apologia ad Albertum Pium* was written in haste and shows in places the results of careless composition. Erasmus was so eager to refute his opponent at every point that he more than once resorted to quibbles or was not quite fair in his analysis of what Folly had actually said. Furthermore, he made liberal use of personal invective and introduced a highly colored version of his own experience at the Aldine Academy many years before.

Nevertheless, the effort to reply to his opponent in such detail compelled Erasmus to distinguish, more sharply than he had previously done, the ambiguities in Folly's oration, and to separate those passages where she was speaking frivolously from those in which her message was serious. There is much repetition, especially on the issue of the difference between the abuses and the true uses of institutions and doctrines. However, there were certain subjects, such as skepticism, superstition, and indulgences, with which Erasmus had to deal in a context that he could not have foreseen in 1509 when he was writing the first version of *The Praise of Folly*. The passages in the *Apologia* in which he expounds his views on these subjects give us a more detailed understanding of his attitude in the last years of his life toward the great religious revolution of his age.

NOTES

1. P. S. Allen, ed., *Opus Epistolarum Des. Erasmi Roterodami,* 12 vols. (Oxford, 1906–58), vol. 2, Ep. 304. Hereafter cited as Allen, followed by the volume, letter number, and lines or page, if relevant.

2. Ibid., 2, 304, ll. 15–16.

3. Ibid., 304, ll. 81-140.

4. L. Geiger, ed., *Johann Reuchlins Briefwechsel* (Tübingen, 1975), p. 198. Cited in ibid, 2, p. 11.

5. Allen, 2, 304, ll. 15-80.

6. Ibid., p. 337.

7. Ibid., ll. 26-71.

8. Ibid., ll. 86-120.

9. Ibid., ll. 120-58.

10. Ibid., ll. 175-80.

11. Ibid., ll. 245-48.

12. Ibid., ll. 264-66.

13. Ibid., ll. 349-55.

14. Ibid., ll. 476-86.

15. Ibid., 2, l. 497.

16. Ibid., ll. 609-59.

17. Ibid., p. 91. There is a recent English translation in Erasmus, *Praise of Folly and Letter to Martin Dorp, 1515 . . .* , translated by Betty Radice with introduction and notes by A. H. T. Levi (Harmondsworth: Penguin, 1971) pp. 211-52. The letter was not reproduced in the early Italian editions. See F. Van der Haeghen, *Bibliotheca Erasmiana,* 2d reprint (The Hague, 1961), E851, E857, E867.

18. E. F. Rogers, *The Correspondence of Sir Thomas More* (Princeton, 1947), pp. 27-74.

19. S. I. Camporeale, *Da Lorenzo Valla a Tommaso More: Lo Statuto Umanistico della Teologia* (Pistoia, 1973), no. 4, pp. 9-103.

20. It seems clear that Erasmus collaborated in the composition of these notes. See Allen, 2, p. 407. Examples of the justification of Folly in *LB,* 4, col. 403, n. 17, and col. 481, n. 9.

21. M. M. Phillips, *The 'Adages' of Erasmus* (Cambridge, 1964), pp. 96 and 355-57, which contain a translation.

22. On Stunica, see Allen, 4, p. 622, and on Sutor, Allen, 6, p. 132. Erasmus's reply to Stunica in 1522 on the charge of blasphemy is in *LB,* 9, col. 360, and to Sutor in 1526 in *LB,* 9, cols. 805, 806.

23. On Erasmus and Alberto, see M. P. Gilmore, "Erasmus and Alberto Pio, Prince of Carpi," in *Action and Conviction in Early Modern Europe: Essays in Memory of E. H. Harbison,* ed. T. K. Rabb and J. E. Seigel (Princeton, 1969), pp. 299-318.

24. Ibid., p. 305.

25. Reprinted in Erasmus, *Opera omnia,* ed. Jean Le Clerc, 10 vols. (Leiden, 1703-06; and anastatic reprint, Hildesheim, 1962), vol. 9, cols 1094-1122. Hereafter cited as *LB* with volume and column numbers.

26. *LB,* 9, 1111F.

27. Ibid., 1109F-10B.

28. Ibid., 1110 B-C.

29. Ibid., 1110 C-F.

30. Ibid., 1111 A.

31. Ibid., 1111 B-D.

32. Ibid., 1111E.

33. Ibid., 1111F.

34. On the circumstances of the publication, see M. P. Gilmore, "Italian Reactions to Erasmian Humanism," *Itinerarium Italicum: Essays Presented to Paul Kristeller* (Leiden, 1975), pp. 69-74, and on Florido, pp. 109-10.

35. Alberto Pio, . . . *tres et viginti libri in locus lucubrationum variarum D. Erasmi . . .* (Paris, 1531), fols. 68^v-69^r. It is probable that when Alberto wrote the *Responsio paraenetica* in 1526 (published in 1529) he used one of the Italian editions of the *Moria*

which lacked the letter to Dorp and the Lister *Commentary,* as well as material Erasmus had added in 1515. After he was established in Paris in 1529, however, he probably used one of the more available Swiss or French editions. This passage certainly confirms that he gave a second reading to the *Moria* which filled him with disgust.

36. Its title is *Apologia adversus rhapsodias calumniosarum querimoniarum Alberti Pii quondam Carporum principis quem et senem et moribundum et ad quiduis potius accommodum homines quidam male ausplicati ad hanc illiberalem fabulam agendam subornarunt.* It is printed in *Opera omnia, LB,* 9 cols. 1123–96 under the title *Apologia brevis ad viginti quatuor libros Alberti Pii quondam Carporum principis.* Citations will be given to this edition.

37. *LB,* 9, cols. 1136F-37A-B.

38. Ibid., 1137B-E.

39. The Colloquy *Opulentia sordida,* "Penny Pinching," which also contains an unfavorable account of Erasmus's stay in the household of Asulano, was published in September 1531, and was perhaps written at the same time as this *Apologia.* Cf. Craig R. Thompson, *The Colloquies of Erasmus* (Chicago, 1965), introductory note to "Penny Pinching," pp. 488–90. The repudiation of any debt to Italy is found not only in the *Ciceronianus* but also in the *Responsio ad Petrum Cursium, LB,* 9, 1755 E.

40. Ibid., 1137F.

41. Ibid., 1138B–C.

42. Ibid., 1138E–F; 1139A.

43. Ibid., 1139C-D.

44. Ibid., 1139E.

45. Ibid., 1139F; 1140A-F; 1141A-B.

46. Ibid., 1141C-F: 1142A/Eng. trans. from *The Praise of Folly* by Betty Radice (Harmondsworth: Penguin, 1971), p. 128.

47. *LB,* 9, 1142B-C.

48. Ibid., 1142D-E.

49. Ibid., 1142F; 1143A.

6 Erasmus's Annotations and Colet's Commentaries on Paul: A Comparison of Some Theological Themes

CATHERINE A. L. JARROTT

As interest in Erasmus's theology increases, scholars are paying more and more attention to his annotations on the New Testament. Before 1970, very little had been done on this aspect of his work;[1] now, several studies have begun to explore this largely uncharted and surprisingly fruitful terrain.[2] Several key ideas emerging from his annotations on Paul's letters (Romans in particular) offer a challenging similarity to central concepts in John Colet's commentaries on Paul, at least in those portions that have come down to us.[3] The similarity is challenging not merely because it suggests another chapter in the ongoing discussion about Colet's influence on Erasmus,[4] but, more important, because it throws a spotlight on two significant themes of pre-Reformation theology: the fulfillment of the promises of the Old Testament in the Gospel of the New, and the practical consequences of this fulfillment in the spiritual transformation of every believing Christian.

In exploring these themes through the annotations of Erasmus and the commentaries of Colet, I do not intend to retrace the steps already taken by others. Much valuable information about Erasmus's methodology in the annotations and their relation to the *Paraphrases*, which he was doing at the same time, can be found in Rabil.[5] Both Rabil and Payne have effectively covered the data regarding the inception, chronology, and facts of publication of the annotations through various editions.[6] Lupton, Jayne, and Duhamel have discussed the conditions prevailing at Oxford when Colet lectured on Paul in the Divinity School;[7] Lupton has summarized the sketchy information we have about Colet's manuscripts, and Jayne has added some interesting conjectures.[8] Such information is the necessary background of the present study. My concern here is to see how a key idea emerges in the work of both authors, and what its implications are.

To examine the theme of promise-and-fulfillment, a good place to start is at the beginning of Romans, with Erasmus's first notation on Paul's calling. The very word he chooses, *vocatus* (κλητός) excludes the works of the law and human merit, and asserts instead the grace of the Gospel, which is given to all. Paul's calling has a divine origin; it does not arise from the ceremonies and precepts of the Mosaic Law, in which the Jews put their trust, nor from the human wisdom which dazzled the Greeks, but from God. The aim of the Epistle to the Romans, then, is to unite Jews and Greeks equally in Christ by removing the arrogance of both: the Jews' fidelity to the Mosaic Law, and the Greeks' dependence upon philosophy.[9]

Erasmus calls attention to the vocabulary that Paul uses in order to stress the divine rather than the human: *gratiam, vocationem, electionem,* etc. In fact, these words are deliberately chosen by Paul to erode his hearers' confidence in the works of man and transfer their attention to the God who is calling them, because it is only by listening to that call that they can be saved—just as Paul himself responded when he was called.[10]

This note establishes the context in which Erasmus is reading Paul. Theology does not begin with propositions but with human experience—specifically, man's response to God's call. It does not end in the formulation of dogma, but in a life formed by Christ and directed to religious ends.[11] The individual—Paul, or the new Christians in Rome to whom he is writing—recapitulates in his own experience of conversion the calling out of God to his people and their transformation under his guidance—to the Jews first, as the historical bearers of the message, and now to the Gentiles as the full inheritors of the promises made to the Jews. The relation of Jew to pagan in salvation history is thus an essential element in the process of God's making himself known to us.[12]

The next note on *segregatus* (ἀφωρισμένος) continues this emphasis on the difference between Paul's present calling and his former life as a Jew, yet finds a certain continuity in the notion of separateness. The Jews had separate sects and factions; Paul himself was a Pharisee. But now his separateness signifies the transition to a new way of being and acting. Paul's conversion is both a cessation and a commencement; it includes the former and transfigures it.[13] Erasmus's explanation of this point presents a triad of contrasts that carry the theme throughout his annotations on Romans: "from Moses to Christ, from the letter to the spirit, from confidence in works to grace."[14]

These fundamental contrasts also govern Erasmus's treatment of a word that was to become the focus of bitter controversy a little later: *praedestinatus* (ὁρισθέντος). Here in verse 4 it refers to Christ as Second Person of the Trinity, in contrast to *factus* (γενομένου) in verse 3, which refers to Christ in his human nature. First Erasmus examines the meaning of the word, with the help of Chrysostom, Origen, Jerome, and even Aquinas, whom he praises. Turning directly to the text again, he settles on *declarare:* the flesh (σάρκα) declared that he was man; power and the spirit of sanctification declare that he is the Son of God and God.[15] This revelation was announced by figures, types, and prophecies in the Old Testament, and then finally by the Resurrection in the New. Incidentally, this particular note is a good example of Erasmus's method in action: he starts with the grammatical meaning, turns to the Fathers, then occasionally to a more recent commentator (more often Valla than Aquinas), then, in light of this broadened perspective, back to the text again.

The opposition of contraries continues in the note on *in virtute* in this same verse (ἐνδυνάμει). Saul is contrasted to Paul, the servant of the Mosaic Law to the servant of the Gospel, flesh to spirit. To the flesh he then opposes the power of God and the Holy Spirit: namely, power to weakness, holiness to uncleanness.[16] But Erasmus does not let his rhetorical analysis lead him too far into abstractions. He concludes his excursus on Christology by bringing it all right back to the human condition and the divine purpose, summarizing Chrysostom with a concise parallel: from David Christ received the flesh in order that he might be able to die; from his Father, the power in order that he might make us immortal.[17]

In note 21 on verse 9, Erasmus shows how Paul wants to stress the newness and difference of Christian worship compared to the Mosaic observance. Paul refers to his own experience to show this difference. He had been urged by the Jews to force the Gentiles into observance of the Mosaic Law. But he has passed from Moses to Christ, to a worship that no longer requires the sacrifice of animals but honors the same God in another way—namely, by the preaching of the Gospel of His Son, a spiritual form of cult and therefore far more pleasing to God.[18]

This transition from old to new cannot be accomplished without faith that God will fulfill the promises that he has made. In his note on Romans 1:17, Erasmus discusses the meaning of faith. No Latin word corresponds exactly to the Greek πίστις. In Latin, to have faith in someone means to believe what he says. The Greek can mean this too, but πίστος can also mean "he who does not deceive" (*qui non fallit*). The sacred texts often misuse these words, for they frequently say *fides* when they mean *fiducia*, or trust in God, which does not differ much from hope. Sometimes the word *faith* embraces both the assent to matters narrated and promises made, and also trust inspired by God's goodness and the consequent expectation that he will fulfill those promises.[19]

This is the faith that man should have in God. But there is also the faith that is said to be *of* God, which he shows us in his promises: God is faithful, trustworthy (πίστος) because he does not deceive; man is said to be faithful when he believes, but this usage, though common, goes beyond the strict meaning of the word.[20] "The phrase under consideration, 'through faith for faith,' has this same double significance. For God at appointed times began to reveal his nature and to fulfill his promises; and likewise man's understanding of and trust in God increased by steps. Few believed in prophets until God actually revealed to their eyes what he had promised."[21]

Colet's definition of faith reflects his limited understanding of etymology.[22] In *Edmund's Romans,* his first treatise on this epistle,[23] he says that according to Latin writers[24] *fides* properly means "'an abiding by, and true fulfillment of, our promises and agreements'; so called because what is said is *done (fiat)*."[25] In showing the transition from pagan to Christian usage, he emphasizes the part played by the believer: "The word is also used at times in those [Latin] writers for a belief in that which is not seen. And in this sense it is adopted by our divines . . . to have faith is to believe."[26] The relation between faith in this sense and hope is close,[27] but it is clear that the faith of which Colet speaks is never entirely fiducial; it is based on an intellectual assent to specifically revealed truths, of which the Apostles' Creed is a summary.[28]

For Colet as for Erasmus, Abraham is the preeminent type of this faith because he believed that God would fulfill what he had promised to him. For Abraham, it was this faith that justified—not the observance of circumcision, a rite that was introduced later: "In this chapter St. Paul shows that Abraham was counted righteous from his faith, by God's grace alone, before he was circumcised; and that circumcision followed, as a sign of his faith. He was thus the father, alike of the circumcised and of the faithful; while yet the justification of them all is by faith."[29] Erasmus's note on Romans 15:5 points out that the Gospel is Abraham's final vindication, because it shows that God has accomplished what he said he would do.[30]

Both Erasmus and Colet emphasize the fact that for the Christian, faith means belief in the entire New Testament dispensation. Colet sometimes uses the word *sacrament* in a general sense to include the whole plan of salvation in which we must believe: "ineffabile misterium et sacramentum."[31]

Colet uses several metaphors to describe the fulfillment in the New Testament of that which was promised in the Old. In his discussion of 1 Corinthians 10: 1–11, he begins by pointing first to the familiar types that Paul enumerates: the sea and the cloud prefigure the "rebirth of men in Christ of water and the Holy Ghost";[32] the manna and the water flowing from the rock symbolize the body and blood of Christ. Faced with these "great realities," the Corinthians have even less excuse than the Israelites for falling into sin. If they do, their "table" is turned into a "trap" for them, as David warned in Psalm 68; in other words, they have rejected what should have nourished them. Colet develops this metaphor by further comparing the Old Testament to a table on which the dishes are covered and sealed; "the setting aside of the covers is in the New Testament, with the revealing of the rich banquet of truth and an invitation to eat." Christ then becomes the "Master of the Feast" (*architriclinus*). Through the ministry of Moses he piled the table high, present but unseen as ruler of the banquet. In the New Testament, "he himself struck off the covers, offering himself, Truth itself, for the plentiful banqueting of his chosen guests."[33] The Scriptures, then, are a "splendid table" (*lauta mensa*) in contrast to the tables—i.e. books—of the pagans, where "no Christian man ought to seat himself." To expect substantial nourishment from that source, or to place any confidence in it, would be tantamount to becoming, in Paul's words, "a partner with demons."[34]

Another set of metaphors which Colet applies to the fulfillment of the promise comes from his favorite author, the pseudo-Dionysius.[35] God is seen as pure light, an "unmixed ray" (*simplex radius*), too bright for the eyes of man. In earlier ages, this light was broken up into different colors and a variety of shadows, so that men's eyes could become gradually accustomed to it. These colors and shadows were the ministry of Moses (who was privileged to see the unclouded light on Sinai) and the Levitical priesthood, through whom the light was mediated. The people could then look upon it through the "painted flowers of the Mosaic Law."[36] Again, the world before Christ is seen as a "blank canvas" (Lupton's translation for *nuda tabula*) on which the image of God's truth is faintly outlined and then gradually grows brighter until it is illuminated by Christ himself, the image of the Father. "On this canvas of the world the work of God has so proceeded; from the shadow to the image, from the image to the reality."[37]

The development of the parallel between Adam and Christ raises the whole question of the nature and transmission of Original Sin, and calls forth Erasmus's longest note on Romans. Discussing the celebrated pericope of 5:12-14, he tries to put our relation to the sinfulness of Adam into its whole Pauline perspective, instead of assuming, with Augustine and the tradition of the Latin church, that the passage is concerned only with Original Sin, not personal sin. Erasmus's translation of 5:12 reads as follows: "Propterea, quemadmodum per unum hominem peccatum in mundum introiit, ac per peccatum mors, et sic in omnes homines mors pervasit, quatenus omnes peccaverunt."[38] He explains that both sin and death come to us through Adam, and we repeat the connected sequence in our own lives. The most significant change from the Vulgate here is *quatenus* for *in quo* (ἐφ᾿ ᾧ). As several scholars have pointed out, Erasmus means by this connective to indicate that we sin in imitation of Adam.[39]

This interpretation fits the whole context of Paul's letter to the Romans, which Erasmus proceeds to summarize here. In the first chapter, Paul reproaches the Gentiles because they have degenerated into every kind of sin, even beyond the limits of natural law and the dictates of human reason; in the second chapter, he reprimands the Jews because they did not observe their law; in the third he holds Gentiles and Jews equally guilty and needful of grace; in the fourth he teaches that neither Jews nor Gentiles can be saved by their own works, but through faith, in imitation of Abraham, for the promise made to him extends to all who believe as he did; in the fifth, Paul teaches remission of sin, and righteousness extending to all through the gratuitous love of God, who by the blood of his only-begotten Son has washed away the sins of all.[40]

So far there is nothing, says Erasmus, that does not fit in with the context of personal sin. Chrysostom states specifically that Paul is concerned in this chapter with the way in which those who have been baptized ought to live their lives, that is, to abstain from sin lest they rescind that peace with God which has been restored to them. Lyonnet has observed that Erasmus's thinking here is close to that of the Greek patristic tradition, particularly to Cyril of Alexandria,[41] though Erasmus does not mention Cyril by name.

By thus stressing the entire context of this troublesome passage, Erasmus opens the possibility that Paul's purpose here was not to discuss Original Sin.[42] Augustine, on the other hand, made use of this verse for a polemic purpose, when he was fighting the Pelagians.[43] Further, by emphasizing the time between Adam and the Mosaic Law, Paul wants to show that the reign of sin and death in the world was pervasive even before the Mosaic Law was introduced to define transgressions. This point is important in regard to both the nature of sin and the traditional parallelism between Adam and Christ.

To clarify the meaning of sin in this context, Erasmus turns to Chrysostom's question: if death draws its roots from sin, how can death reign from Adam [i.e. before the Law] to Moses (verse 14), since Paul has just said (verse 13) that sin is not imputed when there is no law?[44] The answer must be that the sin in question was not the violation of a law, but that sin committed through the disobedience of Adam. It was this act that contaminated everything, introducing the reign of death even for all those who lived before the Law.[45] Paul is talking here about a force hostile to God, separating man from God, bringing spiritual as well as physical death.[46] The power of sin introduced into the world by the disobedience of Adam is exercised by the individual who sins in imitation of his transgression, and produces the effect of death in the sinner, understood in the sense of privation of salvation. This power of sin spreads to all of Adam's posterity, "since there is no one who does not imitate the example of his first parent."[47]

Far from weakening the traditional parallel between Adam and Christ in the exegesis of this passage, Erasmus's interpretation strengthens it by emphasizing what man is saved from by means of the Redemption. Furthermore, as chapter 5 continues, it becomes apparent that Paul's objective is to describe this work of Christ, to which the parallel of Adam is distinctly subordinate. Even if we grant the parallel, it is obvious that the one is not equal to the other. The relation of Adam to Christ is that of figure, or type, to its fulfillment.[48] Just as Adam gave an example of transgressing the law of God to those who wanted to do this, so

Christ gave an example of following the will of the Father to those who wanted to imitate him. As Adam was the *princeps* of sinning and dying, so Christ was the *dux et auctor* of innocence and immortality. According to kind (*genus*) we can say that there was a similitude; according to species, there was a contrariety (*repugnantiam*). From Adam the genus (human race) extended to all, including Christ. The "species" deriving from Adam was sin and death; from Christ, the "species" is innocence and life.[49]

Colet also treats the reign of sin and death before Christ as a contagion affecting the whole world.[50] But in the same breath he contrasts this sinful state with the redeemed world, the power of sin with the power of grace. It is not a contrast of equivalents. He makes this point briefly in his first treatise on Romans: "There is a likeness between the two in many ways: seeing that, as sin came from one Adam unto death; so grace comes from one Christ unto life. But there is this difference between the gift and the fault: namely, that, however much sin grew unto death, so much the more did grace grow unto life; that more abundant and more powerful grace might overcome death."[51] Again in the second treatise, in his summary treatment of chapter five, this is the point he chooses to emphasize:

> If sin had this power of destruction, even the sin of one man, so much the greater ought to be the power and force of grace to give life to men. . . . For it requires more power to take away accomplished evil than to begin it. So it happens that men, seized and drawn to God by his love and grace, will be sustained, if they have hope, and maintained in a life-giving direction by that same all-powerful grace more forcefully and firmly than the power of sin could pull them toward destruction. . . . For undoubtedly virtue is a much more life-giving thing than sin is deadening."[52]

To Colet the world of the Christian is not a vale of tears but a grace-filled, love-filled existence of endless opportunity for spiritual growth.[53]

For Erasmus, too, the present Christian reality is also a grace-filled world. His treatment of the contrasts in Romans 5:18–21 is characteristically philological at the outset but, as so often happens in his notes, his careful examination of the Greek text adds a new dimension to the meaning of the words. The word in question here is the Vulgate *superabundavit*, verse 20: "ubi autem abundavit delictum, superabundavit gratia," which Erasmus translates as *magis exuberavit*. He explains the change by pointing out that the Greek ὑπερεπερίσσευσεν does not mean simply an overflowing, like a liquid that spills over from a full jar; it means instead that there is an abundance *supra modum*, in a higher way, for ὑπέρ in Greek enlarges.[54] The new kind of life offered to man by Christ, in contrast to the life he derives from Adam, is qualitatively different—a difference in kind, not just in degree. Both Colet and Erasmus make a closer examination of what precisely this difference is.

In what sense is the "new life" of the redeemed Christian truly new? One way to answer this question is to distinguish it from the kind of life that preceded it. The Christian fulfillment of the promises made to the Jews means the abrogation of the Mosaic Law. Many of Erasmus's annotations stress this point, as we have noted above, but in his note on Romans 10:4 he explains more fully why it is no longer possible for the old law to apply. It has not simply been replaced; it has been consummated, for its purpose has been achieved. Therefore Erasmus changes the Vulgate "finis enim legis Christus" to "perfectio legis," explaining that the Greek word used here, τέλος, conveys this idea of consummation or completed purpose, better translated by the Latin *perfectionem*. This translation distinguishes the fulfillment in question from the kind of ending that would be a destruction. He cites Augustine as support for this reading.[55]

Both Erasmus and Colet see the rite of circumcision as a good example of a Mosaic precept which has been abrogated in this way, and they both interpret Paul's comments on it allegorically with Origen as their guide. Erasmus's note on Romans 4:11 points up the distinction between *signum* and *signaculum*. *Signum* (σημεῖον) means a sign which stands for something else; so the circumcision of the flesh is a type, or prefiguring, of "Christian circumcision," which is not the removal of flesh from the body, but rather of all harmful lusts from the heart.[56] *Signaculum* (σφραγιδα), on the other hand, means sealing something to be put aside for later use—for example, the mystery to be revealed. Both words signify the righteousness which Abraham had by faith while he was still uncircumcised, but the latter conveys the idea that Abraham's righteousness is an example of that justice promised to all believers by faith, without circumcision.[57]

Colet has a similar comment in his interpretation of the passage. Abraham had "the invisible, no less than the visible, circumcision. He had at once both the reality, and the token of that reality."[58] The rest of this chapter in *Edmund's Romans* explains the symbolism at some length.[59]

One cannot speak of Abraham's faith without mentioning his righteousness; the justification of the believer also marks the difference between the old life and the new. As Payne has demonstrated,[60] Erasmus recognizes two kinds of righteousness: that achieved by the Jews through the observance of the Mosaic Law, and that which is accomplished in the Christian through faith. Just as the Old Law was abrogated by the law of the Gospel, so the dependence on ceremonies and external observance gives way to faith. One main reason for Erasmus's dislike of the proliferation of ceremonies in the church of his own day was that they tended to obscure the essential relationship between Christ and the believer, reducing him again to a Judaic dependence upon externals.[61] On the contrary, the Christian's justification goes deeper than even the observance of the moral law; the "new life" open to him by faith is different in kind[62] from that which he led before, because the Incarnation makes the divine life available to him in a new way.

This is the point that Erasmus makes in his celebrated note on the familiar *Gloria in excelsis,* Luke 2:14. He changes the Vulgate *in hominibus bonae voluntatis* to read *in hominibus bona voluntas,* meaning God's good will toward men, now freely extended to all humanity.[63] The barrier of sin is removed ("jam non amplius interstitium est coelum") and a new kind of union between God and man is possible. He tries to express it in the word *refocillatio,* or "revivifying."[64] It is this new life, not just the following of the moral law, that will bring to man the peace that the angels proclaim.

Therefore in Romans 5:1, he changes the Vulgate *habeamus pacem,* "let us have peace," to *habemus pacem,* "we have peace," explaining that Paul is speaking to those who have been justified. This reading fits the context better, as Paul goes on to discuss faith, hope, and love; Ambrose also prefers *habemus,* arguing that it is faith, not law, which makes us at peace with God.[65] Erasmus concludes that the other reading is also possible, for Paul is exhorting those already justified not to slip back into a condition that would again create an impediment between God and man.

There has been some dispute as to Erasmus's stand on the *sola fide* question. Bainton holds that Erasmus agreed with Luther that genuine merit does not exist, but he thought God would be willing to accept "congruous merit."[66] Payne's analysis of this point indicates a certain ambiguity and the need for careful definition in context. In both the *Paraphrases* and the annotations, *sola fide* is usually set over against the ceremonial "righteousness" of the Old Testament, but Erasmus later broadened the latter to include other legalistic works, namely, those lacking in faith and charity.[67] In his note on 1 Corinthians 13:2, Erasmus shows by many examples drawn from both sacred and secular literature that one can say *solus* without necessarily meaning to exclude everything else; therefore he who says that man is justified *sola fide* is not excluding charity, or the works of charity, but human philosophy, and the ceremonies and works of the law.[68] Paul's letters are full of his insistence that man is justified by faith and not by works, and yet he never separates faith and love, and continually exhorts his hearers to the works of charity.[69]

Colet presents a variety of definitions of justification, most of which stress all three of the theological virtues and indicate that he is more interested in right action than in theological precision. In his treatise on the sacraments, *justitia* is "faith in God through Christ, and love of God and neighbor";[70]

in a letter to the Abbot of Winchcombe, he says that justice is confidence in God;[71] in *Romans,* the emphasis is on love.[72] When he speaks of Abraham in *Edmund's Romans,* the stress seems to be on fiducial faith,[73] but in commenting on the same passage (Rom. 4) in the later treatise, he stresses belief in the principal articles of faith.[74] Hope is required if one is to believe that God's promises will be fulfilled in his own case, but the indispensable foundation of all of this is love.[75]

The real change wrought by God's love in man's soul and the response he makes to God (*amare redamare*) are thus essential movements in the decisive event of justification. For Colet it must be more than the fact that one's sins are no longer imputed to him. An active response on his part is required: "When we say that men are attracted, called, justified, and glorified by grace, we mean only that men return love to a loving God. Man's justification consists in this love and return of love."[76]

Like Erasmus, Colet stresses the newness of the life enjoyed by the justified; the comparisons he uses to get this point across are, if anything, stronger. In *Romans* he suggests that the justified sinner is like an actor who has discarded his former role so completely that he is henceforth no longer recognizable in that part.[77]

On the *sola fide* question, Colet agrees with Erasmus that the observance of the law has no saving power; justification comes from God alone.[78] But there is a necessary sequence between justification and good works. Justification comes to man on God's initiative as a totally free and unmerited gift; but once justified, a man must perform good works in order to be saved, and if they are informed by charity, they are meritorious. Colet takes this stand in a number of places in his works. His comment on Romans 2:13 interprets "doers of the word" to mean not just those who comply with outward observances, "but those alone who carry out the mind and spirit of the law, and live according to its spiritual meaning."[79]

He further develops this point in *Corinthians.* Starting with a reference to Romans 10:8-10, he emphasizes faith first as the "necessary beginning," but "not by itself enough for righteousness, which stands above faith in love continually doing good acts."[80] *Justitia* stands above faith in the sense that it is more inclusive, and what it includes is the love that generates good works. To show that these are necessary for salvation, he goes on to paraphrase James 2:14-26. When these works are informed by charity, they proceed from the doer himself as well as from God, and hence can be properly described as meritorious.[81] The believer acting thus can even be called a "co-worker and cooperator with the Spirit of Christ" in contrast to the man without charity, who is nothing but a "dead instrument" in the hands of God.[82]

Thus, for both Colet and Erasmus the new life of the justified is not a static condition but a way of acting. Both authors use the same phrase, "philosophy of Christ," to describe what should be the guiding principle of the Christian life. Erasmus's insistence on this point is well known.[83] Colet's earlier use of the same phrase to make a similar point has not, as far as I know, been pointed out. In chapter 4 of *Edmund's Romans,* probably written as early as 1496,[84] Colet urges the imitation of Christ and states that the Christian who follows in the steps of Jesus will practice the three theological virtues. He goes on to contrast the active good life of such a Christian with mere lip-service: "This sect and school of philosophy of Christ is one not so much in words, as in deed, in works, in life itself; and a justifying faith implies in its very meaning an imitation of Christ, and fellow-working with Him; being elsewhere [Gal. 5:6] called by St. Paul, *faith which worketh by love.*"[85]

On what levels, philosophically and spiritually, are Colet and Erasmus speaking when they tell us to imitate Christ? Morally, the meaning is clear enough: we are to practice the virtues he exemplified in his life. In this way we will be freed from servitude to sin and empty ceremonies, and we can fulfill the law of the Gospel that shall bring us to salvation.[86] Colet especially enjoins patience, humility, and obedience—"feminine virtues," he calls them, because the soul is "female" before God.[87] Moreover, these are the, virtues which render us most responsive to the divine power, enabling us to be re-formed by God: "And just as primal matter, in order to be formed, is naked, that there may be nothing in it to counteract the formation; so it is needful that man should strip off all his own powers, and patiently subject himself in every way to God, if he would be enlightened by inspiration to understand things divine, lest, if he do anything of himself, he hinder the divine working and reforming of himself."[88]

This comparison of the soul to prime matter and the action of God to its form, or organizing principle, introduces another level of meaning which is basic in Colet's thought. In spite of his expressed dislike of Aquinas, Colet was the heir of the scholastic tradition, and he uses the concept of matter and form as the philosophical foundation of this part of his soteriology:

> The agent disposes into a form. The object, being formed, at length acts *per se.* All right action of a perfect object is by its own form, and from the form action is derived. Now man is, as it were, unformed matter, and destitute of spiritual form, but he is apt for the Spirit to form him. Of his own nature, man is deprived of the divine. But the cause transforming this carnal man into a spirit and an efficient cause is the Spirit of God Himself, who moulds the matter (as it may be called) by His power, so that at length man may become what he is capable of being, may be transformed at the free

choice of the moulding Spirit (who imparts to each as He will), no otherwise than soft wax by the shaping and moulding of a hand, into some spiritual and divine shape; and it is for this that the Spirit works.[89]

This transformation into a higher kind of life is an actuality for Colet, not just a pious wish, and it is certainly more than a merely human effort to copy the moral virtues of Christ.[90] Since this new form is a unifying principle, its loss through sin or neglect means a spiritual disintegration.[91] The Eucharist is a means of maintaining this form and thereby becoming united with its source. Christ does not enter into the diversity of those whom he nourishes; instead, "they are formed anew by the stronger Christ into one, and it is their good fortune to pass from themselves into that by which they are fed."[92]

Colet does not hesitate to affirm that the redeemed Christian's participation in the divine life can make him godlike: "For it was the will of the good God that man should be saved; and that cannot be unless men be made godlike and re-fashioned to a divine condition, and become gods by being made like unto God, that they may represent God."[93] The Incarnation makes this possible: "God, made man, was the means whereby men were to be made gods."[94] Again, love is at the center: "for love is the source of begetting; holy love, of begetting holiness; and the love of God, of godliness."[95]

Erasmus does not, as far as I know, use the same scholastic analogy of matter and form, but he does speak of the formative power of God's Spirit, even to the extent of mitigating the pains and problems of old age by providing a supra-human aim, the anticipation of eternal life. Therefore we are told that our youth is renewed like an eagle, and we can flourish like the lily in the sight of God. Just as the Divine Spirit, inhabiting our own, overflows into it and transforms it into itself, so our own spirit, unaltered, overflows upon the body as its dwelling and transforms it, in so far as it can.[96] When Erasmus adopts Origen's tripartite division of man in the *Enchiridion,* "spirit" is that part which unites us to God.[97]

In another way, the Scriptures can exert a transforming power upon the man who is properly disposed. Like Colet, Erasmus emphasizes receptivity, the willingness to set aside one's own prideful thoughts and be instructed. Taking a hint from Jerome, he uses a word from the Septuagint, θεοδίδακτος, to describe this condition. Changing the Vulgate *docibiles Dei* (John 6 :45) to *docti a Deo,* he explains that the Greek διδάκτος means a readiness or fitness to be taught.[98] An interesting example from Homer is quoted here: he uses αὐτοδίδακτον to describe a harp that is played by divine impulse (*afflatu numinis*), not by human art. Furthermore, *docti a Deo* suits the context better, since Christ has just said (verse 44), "No one can come to me unless the Father who sent me draws him." θεοδίδακτον conveys this idea of being drawn by the Father's inspiration (*afflatu Patris*).[99]

If a man comes to the Scriptures with this disposition, and if he loves what he reads there, he will be transformed, for the presence of Christ is in these words. They are "the living image of His holy mind and the speaking, healing, dying, rising Christ himself, and thus they render Him so fully present that you would see less if you gazed upon Him with your very eyes."[100] The spiritual nourishment to be gained from this contact is itself a kind of communion.[101] To be transformed into that which he is learning should be the theologian's aim.[102]

Like Colet, Erasmus specifies love as the ultimate begetter of this transformation. Discussing the idea, in Psalm 1, that the proof of our love of God is that we fulfill his law, Erasmus broadens the concept of "law" to include "universam Scripturam divinam." He goes on to say that to love something is a necessary condition of our human nature; that we become what we love; hence the lover of Scripture will be transfigured into God.[103]

Both Colet and Erasmus use the same word to indicate the reciprocal nature of this transforming love: *redamare.* Both stress the divine initiative enabling man's response, which remains free. "Because we are loved, we give love back to God," says Colet, and makes this the cornerstone of his definition of justification.[104] Erasmus stresses the same dynamic connection in his interpretation of Romans 8:45. The Vulgate reads "Quis ergo nos separabit a caritate Christi?" Erasmus recommends that *ergo* be dropped on the ground that it implies a new turn in Paul's thought, as though he were suddenly rapt by his feelings into making this exclamation as a result of all the arguments for faith which preceded it. But the whole passage is more coherent if *ergo* is omitted, for then *quis nos separabit* follows as a direct consequence of Christ's resurrection and intercession for us; ἀγάπη is both an active and a responsive love.[105]

In summary, then, this analysis has tried to point out and pull together some elements of the Christian message which seem most significant for both Colet and Erasmus: the relation of promise-and-fulfillment between the Old Testament and the New; and the nature of the redeemed Christian's new life in a grace-filled world. Much more could, and should, be said about both topics, but several conclusions, however tentative, can be drawn. First, both authors try to grasp Paul's teaching as a whole, putting it into context and interpreting it as the biblical text requires, instead of using bits and pieces of it to prove some extraneous point. "I have tried, insofar as I could, with the help of divine grace, to express Paul's true meaning," said Colet in his conclusion to *Romans.*[106] Defending himself against his detractors, Erasmus protests that he does not want to do any violence to Holy Scripture; instead he wants diligently to weigh what Paul means, looking closely to see exactly what he is talking about, where he begins, where he is going, and whether the particular discourse fits in with the mystery he wants to reveal to his hearers.[107] Second, both men's humanistic desire to proceed *ad fontes* results in a coherent, biblical vision of Christianity which could have done much to reform the church of their day, had not the stormy factionalism of the Reformation swept it aside.

Finally, this study suggests that there are dimensions in both authors that have not been sufficiently explored. The old image of Colet as the "gloomy Dean," more puritan than humanistic, has to be revised.[108] As for Erasmus, even this brief sketch of a few elements in his exegesis of Paul shows that the *philosophia Christi* cannot be fully understood apart from the *Annotations.*

NOTES

1. See A. Bludau, "Die Beiden Ersten Erasmus-Ausgaben des Neuen Testaments und ihre Gegner," *Biblische Studien* 7 (Freiburg, 1902): 48–58; C. A. L. Jarrott, "Erasmus' 'In Principio Erat Sermo': A Controversial Translation," *Studies in Philology* 61 (January 1964): 35–40; Marvin Anderson, "Erasmus the Exegete," *Concordia Theological Monthly* 40 (December 1969): 722–33.

2. See especially Georges Chantraine, "Le Musterion selon Érasme," *Recherches de Science Religieuse* 58 (July–Sept. 1970): 351–82; also John B. Payne, "Erasmus: Interpreter of Romans," *Sixteenth Century Studies and Essays,* vol. 2, ed. Carl S. Meyer (Foundation for Reformation Research, 1971), pp. 1–35; and Jarrott, "Erasmus' Biblical Humanism," *Studies in the Renaissance* 17 (1970): 119–52.

3. There are three separate works: *Ioannis Coleti enarratio in epistolam S. Pauli ad Romanos: An Exposition of St. Paul's Epistle to the Romans,* ed. and trans. J. H. Lupton (London, 1873; reprint, Gregg Press, 1965), hereafter referred to as *Romans; Epistolae B. Pauli ad Romanos Expositio Literalis; Exposition of St. Paul's Epistle to the Romans,* in *Ioannis Coleti Opuscula Quaedam Theologica,* ed. and trans. J. H. Lupton (London 1876; reprint Gregg Press, 1966), hereafter referred to as *Edmund's Romans* because of the youth to whom it was addressed, and to distinguish it from the later treatise above; *Ioannis Coleti in primam epistolam S. Pauli ad Corinthios: An Exposition of St. Paul's First Epistle to the Corinthians,* ed. and trans. J. H. Lupton (London, 1874; Gregg Press reprint); hereafter referred to as *Corinthians.*

4. For bibliography and summaries of recent opinions, see Roland H. Bainton, *Erasmus of Christendom* (London: Collins, 1970), pp. 74–83 and n. 27 (p. 83); James D. Tracy, *Erasmus, The Growth of a Mind* (Geneva: Librairie Droz, 1972), p. 84 and n. 4.

5. Albert Rabil, *Erasmus and the New Testament: The Mind of a Christian Humanist* (San Antonio, Tex.: Trinity University Press, 1972), pp. 99–113.

6. Ibid., pp. 83–97; Payne, "Erasmus," pp. 3–9.

7. Lupton, Introduction to *Romans,* pp. xiv–xxvi; Sears Jayne, *John Colet and Marsilio Ficino* (Oxford, 1963), pp. 22–26, 35–38; P. Albert Duhamel, "The Oxford Lectures of John Colet," *Journal of the History of Ideas* 14 (1953): 493–510.

8. Lupton, *Life of John Colet, D.D.* (London, 1887), pp. 62–63; Jayne, pp. 26–34.

9. Erasmus, *Opera Omnia,* vol. 6 (Leiden, 1705), 553E (hereafter cited as *LB*): "Nam id potissimum agit in hac Epistola divus Paulus, ut utrisque detrahat supercilium, & Judaeis

adimat Mosaicae legis fiduciam, & Graecis philosophiae praesidium, atque ita utrosque ex aequo conjungat in Christo."

10. Ibid., 554B. See also Chantraine, "Le Musterion selon Érasme," p. 368.

11. Rabil, *Erasmus and the New Testament*, p. 141.

12. Chantraine, p. 367.

13. Ibid., p. 368.

14. "Coepit igitur Paulus esse in Evangelio, quod fuerat in Judaismo, sed alio pacto. Illic supercilii titulus erat, hic mire separatus erat a Mose ad Christum, a littera ad spiritum, a fiducia operum ad gratiam." *LB,* 6:554C.

15. "Caro declaravit hominem, virtus & Spiritus sanctificationis declarat Filium Dei ac Deum." *LB,* 6:555D. Cf. Authorized Version (AV): "And declared to be the Son of God with power, according to the spirit of holiness. . . ."

16. "Miro autem consilio Paulus contraria contrariis opposuit. Primum enim *Paulum* opposuit Saulo, *servum Jesu Christi* Mosaicae Legis servituti, *vocatum Apostolum* iis qui se ingerebant, *segregatum in Evangelium* Pharisaismo, quem ante profitebatur. . . . Deinde Christi geminam in eadem hypostasi naturam mira verborum emphasi discribit, de homine dicit, *factus est:* ut intelligas aliquid accessisse quod non erat: de divinitate dicit, *declaratus est.* Illic addit, *secundum carnem:* cujus comites sunt infirmitas & impuritas. . . . Proinde carni opposuit virtutem Dei, & Spiritum sanctificationis, hoc est, potentiam imbecillitati, & sanctificationem immunditiae. Assumpsit igitur nostram carnem, & ostendit suam potentiam. . . ." *LB,* 6:555F-56B.

17. ". . . quemadmodum interpretatur Chrysostomus: a David accepit ut mori posset, a Patre ut nos redderet immortales." Ibid.

18. "Subindicat enim Paulus religionis et cultus rationem esse novandam, urgentibus Judaeis, ut ad Mosaicae Legis ceremonias pertraherentur Ethnici. Proinde quanquam ipse Paulus a Mose provectus ad Christum, jam non immolaret pecudes, tamen eumdem Deum alio ritu colebat, nempe praedicando filii Evangelio, qui cultus spiritualis esset, et ob id Deo longe gratissimus." *LB,* 6:560C.

19. "Nonnunquam haec omnia complectitur fidei vocabulum, assensum illum et in narratis et in promissis, et fiduciam ex illius omnipotente bonitate conceptam, non sine spe, hoc est, expectatione promissorum." *LB,* 6:562F. Cf. also Payne's discussion of this passage, "Erasmus," pp. 21–22, and Rabil, *Erasmus and the New Testament,* pp. 143–44.

20. "Caeterum et Dei *fides* dicitur, quam ille praestat in promissis: unde Deus *fidus* sive *fidelis,* hoc est πιστος dicitur, eo quod non fallit: sed homo fidelis dicitur, qui credit promittenti, praeter usum Latini sermonis, et tamen sic frequenter loquuntur Sacrae Litterae." *LB,* 6:562F.

21. "Ad utrumque pertinet quod hic dicit, Ex fide in fidem. Quemadmodum enim Deus statis temporibus aperire coepit qualis esset, et praestare quae promiserat: ita crevit per gradus hominibus erga Deum cognitio et fiducia. . . ." Ibid. The translation is Rabil's, pp. 143–44. Both Rabil and Payne discuss at some length Erasmus's use of *fides* and *fiducia* in the *Paraphrases.*

22. There is some question about Colet's knowledge of Greek. In a letter written in June 1516 to Erasmus (Ep. 423, in P. S. Allen, *Erasmi Epistolae* [Oxford, 1906–58] vol. 2), after the publication of the first edition of his New Testament, Colet laments that he does not know Greek but indicates his willingness to learn it. By September of that same year, Thomas More told Erasmus that Colet was now working hard at Greek (Allen, Ep. 468). This was more than ten years after he had lectured on Paul at Oxford, but some Greek words are scattered through his commentaries. See the summary of information on this point in P. Bernard O'Kelly, *John Colet's Commentary on I Corinthians, An Edition of the Latin Text, with Translation, Notes, and Introduction,* (Ph.D. diss., Harvard University, 1960), pp. 66–68.

23. *Epistolae B. Pauli ad Romanos Expositio Literalis;* see n. 3 above. It must have been written before his other treatise on Romans (called *Enarratio*) because the latter recapitulates chapters 1–5 very briefly and starts with chapter 6, where the *Expositio* leaves off. Jayne (*John Colet and Marsilio Ficino*) discusses the chronology at length and sees a significant difference in style and method between the two treatises, pp. 26–27. Lupton first assumed (1873) that the manuscript of the *Expositio* in the library of Corpus Christi College, Cambridge, was the same as that in the University Library (MS Gg. iv. 26), though incomplete (see his preface to the *Enarratio,* p. vi). Later, when he edited the *Expositio* in 1876, he acknowledged his mistake (preface to *Opuscula Quaedam Theologica,* p. vii), but the error was perpetuated in James's *Catalogue of the Corpus Christi Library* (see my article, "Bibliographical Note on Corpus MS. 355, *John Colet in Romanos et in Genesim,*" *Transactions of the Cambridge Bibliographical Society,* vol. 5 [1970]).

24. Lupton suggests that he means Cicero here, having found a similar definition in *De Officiis,* 1.7.

25. Chap. 3, p. 92; Lupton's translation.

26. Ibid., pp. 92–93.

27. "Spes est expectatio hominum sibi omnium a Deo. Quod expectatum fuit, qui hominibus presens esset omnia, omnipotens fuit Jesus Christus, *gentium expectatio.*" *Corinthians,* 7:205.

28. *Edmund's Romans,* 3:93. Cf. "Non est faciendum solum ut expectemus futurum aliquid, sed etiam quum is venerit qui venturus erat, credamus venisse, et eundem peramemus, ut per illum Deo credere, a quo expectavimus, et Deum amare possimus." *Corinthians,* 7:205.

29. *Corinthians,* 4:117.

30. *LB,* 6:664C-D.

31. *Romans,* 4:141; cf. Erasmus, n. 40 on Rom. 11:33 (*LB,* 6:627F).

32. *Corinthians,* 10:235.

33. Ibid., p. 238; the translation is O'Kelly's. In the margin of the manuscript, little drawings illustrate the covered and open dishes.

34. 1 Cor. 10:20; *Corinthians,* 10:238–39, O'Kelly's translation. This passage should not be taken to mean that Colet was opposed to the reading of pagan authors under any circumstances. On the contrary, in the Statutes for St. Paul's School, he includes the best ancient authors, "both Latin and Greek," in the curriculum (Lupton, *Life,* appendix A, p. 279). His stricture here should be understood in the context of the metaphors he is using, which are concerned with specifically spiritual nourishment and are used to point up the difference between what is divine and what is merely human.

35. Although the belief that Dionysius was a disciple of Paul had been effectively demolished by Valla, Colet apparently continued to believe in Dionysius's apostolic connections, and revered him as our closest link to Paul himself. He wrote two books of commentary on the Dionysian hierarchies: *Super Opera Dionysii: Two Treatises on the Hierarchies of Dionysius,* ed. and trans. J. H. Lupton (London, 1869; Gregg Press reprint, 1966).

36. *De Ecclesiastica Hierarchia,* in *Super Opera Dionysii,* 1:233.

37. Ibid., p. 104. There follows, appropriately enough, a discourse on the various senses of Scripture, particularly the allegorical.

38. *LB,* 6:584B-86A.

39. Payne, "Erasmus," pp. 12–15; Rabil, *Erasmus and the New Testament,* pp. 147–48; Stanislas Lyonnet, "Le Péché Originel et l'Exégèse de Rom. V. 12–14," *Verbum Salutis* 10 (Paris: Beauchesne, 1957): 531–33.

40. "Siquidem primo capite gentibus exprobat, quod praeter naturae legem ac philosophiae cognitionem degenerarint in omne scelerum genus: in secundo reprehendit Judaeos, quod legem qua gloriabantur non observarent: in tertio colligit et gentes et Judaeos pariter

obnoxios egere gratia Dei: in quarto docet nec Gentes nec Judaeos servari ex suis operibus, sed per fidem: et Abrahae factam promissionem ad omnes pertinere, qui illum fide referunt: in quinto docet remissionem peccatorum, ac justitiae, hoc est, innocentiae donum, omnibus contingere per gratuitam Dei charitatem, qui sanguine Unigeniti sui omnium peccata abluit." *LB*, 6:587B–C.

41. Lyonnet, "Le Péché Originel," p. 533.

42. "Primum illud in confesso est, totius huius disputationis exordium aliunde profectum quam a peccato originali, ac disputationis summam alium habere exitum." *LB*, 6:587B.

43. *LB*, 6:589F. Erasmus defends himself at some length here from the charge of being a Pelagian himself.

44. Ibid., 588B–C; *Patrologiae Graecae*, 60, col. 475.

45. "Etenim si ex peccato mors radicem traxit, quum autem non est lex, non imputatur peccatum, quomodo mors superabat? Unde perspicuum est, quod non hoc peccatum violare legis, sed illud per inobedientiam Adae commissum, erat quod omnia contaminabat." Ibid.

46. Lyonnet, p. 524. Erasmus speaks of the "death of gehenna" in his effort to make this distinction (*LB*, 6:587E).

47. ". . . dum nemo non imitatur primi parentis exemplum." *LB*, 7:793B; Cf. also *LB*, 6:587E; Payne, "Erasmus," p. 14, and Lyonnet: ". . . les enfants d'Adam par leurs péchés personnels, loin de renier en quelque sorte le péché de leur père, le ratifient bien plutôt en faisant leur sa revolte" (p. 533).

48. Rom. 5:14, "qui est forma futuri" (Vulgate). Erasmus's version: "qui typum gerit illius futuri." *LB*, 6:592A. Cf. Colet, "Erat primus Adam minister Dei in propagatione carnis ad mortem; secundus Adam minister Dei in propagatione spiritus ad vitam. Primum Adam vocat Paulus in epistola ad Romanos 'formam futuri;' cujus gratia in plures abundavit ex multis delictis in justificationem, ut justi conregnent in vita per unum, Jesum Christum, per cujus obedientiam homines justificantur." *De Sacramentis Ecclesiae*, ed. J. H. Lupton (London, 1867; Gregg Press reprint, 1966), pp. 54–55.

49. "Forma igitur et typus erat Christi Adam. Quanquam ea figura in diversum recidit et analogia potius est quam similitudo. Nam ut ille princeps peccandi et moriendi, ita hic dux et auctor innocentiae et immortalitatis. Proinde eleganter scripsit Origenes, et hunc sequutus Ambrosius, *juxta genus constare similitudine, juxta speciem repugnantiam esse.* Ut ab Adam quiddam dimanavit in omnes, ita et a Christo, hic genus est. Caeterum ab illo mors et peccatum, ab hoc innocentia et vita, hic species est." *LB*, 6:591E.

50. ". . . ita enim ab Adam deinceps magis atque magis invaluit morbus, et lues ac feda contagio mali ita alte pervasit, ut humanis viribus nulla potuit esse curacio." *Romans*, 6:147; see also 7:150.

51. *Edmund's Romans*, 5:149.

52. *Romans*, 5:142; my translation.

53. This is a constant theme; see especially *Romans*, 13:96–103; *Corinthians*, vol. 13; *De Caelesti Hierarchia* (in *Super Opera Dionysii*), vol. 2; *De Ecclesiastica Hierarchia*, vol. 1. Colet's emphasis on man's misery and impotence without grace has led some interpreters of his thought to overlook the positive elements of his theology. See, for example, Eugene Rice, "John Colet and the Annihilation of the Natural," *Harvard Theological Review* 45 (1952): 141–63.

54. "Caeterum quod Latinus Interpres dixit *superabundavit*, Graece est ὑπερεπερίσσευσεν, quod non perinde valet quasi dicas, sic abundare liquorem, ut effundatur quod superfluum est, sed quasi dicas vehementer ac supra modum abundare. Auget enim ὑπερ apud Graecos non aliter atque quam *per* apud nos." *LB*, 6:592E.

55. "τέλος hoc loco *consummationem* ac *perfectionem* sonat, non *interitum:* . . . Nam Graeci quod absolutum et omnibus, quae solent requiri, perfectum est, τέλειον appellant. Summa igitur legis est Christus. . . ." *LB*, 6:617E.

56. "Siquidem jam tum carnalis illa circumcisio typum gerebat Christianae circumcisionis, quae non aufert pelliculam a glande sed amputat omnes noxias cupiditates a corde." *LB*, 6:579C.

57. "Eadem enim res dicitur σημεῖον, quatenus declarat justitiam ex fide quae erat in Abraham ante circumcisionem, et σφραγίς, quatenus exemplo Abrahae omnibus credentibus promittebatur justicia ex fide sine circumcisione." Ibid.

58. "Abraam patriarcha justus erat et spiritu et carne, et apud Deum et apud homines; circumcisus in occulto, et circumcisus in aperto. Habuit simul et veritatem, et signum veritatis." *Edmund's Romans*, 4:248; Lupton's translation, p. 118.

59. "Itaque fidelis et Christianus apud Deum, prius quam circumcisus, gratus Deo, gratae suae fidei rude signaculum accepit in corpore, quandam apud homines fidei testationem. Nudata mente Deo, nudatur corpus; ut hoc illud testificetur." Ibid., p. 249. Cf. *Romans*, vol. 4; *De Sacramentis*, p. 74.

60. Payne, "Erasmus," pp. 18–20.

61. Note 26 on Eph. 2:13–15; *LB*, 6:839.

62. This difference does not mean that man's nature is totally destroyed; for Erasmus (in contrast to Luther) grace builds on nature. Cf. Rabil, *Erasmus and the New Testament*, pp. 170–71.

63. *LB*, 6:234A; n. 16, 231F–33F.

64. "Pax est ipse filius Dei. Ego enim, inquit, sum pax. Haec igitur pax, nempe filius Dei, in terra facta est. Et in hominibus bona voluntas, seu beneplacitum, hoc est, refocillatio Dei." *LB*, 6:232D. See a fuller discussion of this point in my article, "Erasmus' Biblical Humanism," pp. 132–35. Cf. Erasmus's note on Rom. 4:9: "Justitiam autem hic appellat non universam virtutem, sed innocentiam, quae contingit gratuita condonatione peccatorum." *LB*, vol. 6.

65. *LB*, 6:582D on Rom. 5:1; cf. Payne, p. 24.

66. Roland Bainton, *Erasmus of Christendom*, pp. 188–89.

67. Payne, p. 19.

68. "Itaque qui dicit homines sola fide justificari, non protinus excludit charitatem, neque charitatis opera, sed philosophiam humanam, aut ceremonias operaque legalia, aut vitam actam ante baptismum, aut aliud simile, quod ex sermonis tenore colligitur." *LB*, 6:725D.

69. "Hoc genere sermonum omnes Paulinae scatent epistolae. Qui tamen nusquam separat charitatem a fide purificante, ac toties hortatur ad opera charitatis." Ibid. Cf. also n. 85 below.

70. *De Sacramentis:* "Justitia autem est fides Deo per Christum, et caritas Dei et proximi" (p. 79).

71. "Credens & confidens deo justus est. Confidens creaturis quibusquunque impiis & iniustus est. Unde justicia deo confidentia est." Letter to the Abbot of Winchcombe, MS Gg. iv. 26, Cambridge University Library.

72. "Haec in Deo graciosa dileccio et caritas erga homines ipsa vocacio et justificacio et magnificacio est; nec quicquid aliud tot verbis dicimus, quam unum quiddam; scilicet amorem Dei erga homines eos quos vult amare." Chap. 5, p. 143.

73. Chap. 4, pp. 247–48.

74. *Romans*, 4:141: ". . . justificacionem non esse operancium sub lege, sed fidem Abraae imitancium. . . . Ita eciam in hoc quoque tempore qui confidit Deo, et credit illum tum posse, tum voluisse, tum egisse cum suo filio quod egit; videlicet quia incarnatus, mortuus, resuscitatus erat, pro humani generis redempcione et reconciliacione Deo; qui, inquam, illud ineffabile misterium et sacramentum credit firmiter et jugiter colit, eo solo habet satis quo justificetur, salvusque fiat."

75. "Sed hic notandum est, quod haec gracia nichil est aliud quam Dei amor erga homines; eos videlicet quos vult amare, amandoque inspirare spiritu suo sancto; qui ipse est amor et Dei amor; *qui* (ut apud Ioannem evangelistam ait salvator) *ubi vult spirat.* Amiti autem

et inspirati a Deo vocati sunt; ut accepto amore amantem Deum redament, et eundem amore desiderat et exspectent. Haec expectacio et spes ex amore est." Ibid., 5:143.

76. "Item cum homines gracia attractos, vocatos, justificatos, et magnificatos dicimus, nichil significamus aliud quam homines amantem Deum redamare. In quo amore et redamore consistit hominis justificacio." Ibid.

77. ". . . utque deposita persona peccatrice ac solita consuetudine peccandi omnino abolita, homines ii qui vocati sunt, quales fuerunt deinceps non appareant, sed sint quasi simul mortui cum Christo; qui quodammodo crucifixerunt veterem hominem pristinamque illam vitam peccabundam, ut perinde omnino ac mortui et sepulti postea in peccatis personaque peccatrice nusquam extent nec agnoscantur; sed in novam condicionem renovati, et cum Christo resurgente in novam vitam exorti, exhibeant se semper et perpetuo novos, longe a pristino eorum statu differentes. . . ." Ibid., 6:144; see Lupton's note, p. 14.

78. *Edmund's Romans*, 4:251: "Verum coram Deo, qui scrutator est cordis, talibus carnis observantiis non justificatur aliquid sed fide. Operantibus corporaliter merces est debita; sed justificatio gratis credentibus. Nam per graciam credunt homines, et per gratiam credentes justificantur. Opus autem carnis corporisque, sine justicia fidei, in spiritu nihil est."

79. Ibid., 2:219; Lupton, p. 76.

80. "Et bene inquit *ad iusticiam* et *ad salutem*, ut ostendat illuc tendere fidem, et inchoamentum esse necessarium, quo ad iustitiam salutemque eatur; non tamen ipsam fidem per se ad iustitiam satis esse, quae consistit supra fidem, ex amore in continua actione bonorum." Chap. 7, p. 198.

81. Chap. 13, p. 260.

82. Ibid., p. 261. For a fuller treatment of this topic, especially in relation to Colet's use of Dionysius, see my article on "John Colet and Justification," in *Sixteenth Century Journal* 7 (April 1976), pp. 59-72.

83. See, for example, *Paraclesis*, pp. 139 ff. and *Enchiridion*, pp. 5-9, in *Ausgewählte Werke*, ed. Hajo and Annemarie Holborn (Munich: Beck 1933).

84. Jayne, *John Colet and Marsilio Ficino*, p. 77.

85. "Haec secta Christi et philosophatio non tantum est verbis quam re, operibus, et vita ipsa. Et fides justificans importat in suo significatu imitationem Christi, et cooperationem cum illo, quam alibi vocat Paulus *fidem quae per dilectionem operatur*," trans. Lupton, p. 118. Cf. *Corinthians*, 7:199; Erasmus on Gal. 5:6: ". . . ad Galatas describit fidem quae per charitatem operatur: opera charitatis, fidei tribuenda sunt. Qui convenit ergo charitatem a fide separare, hoc est, radicem a ramis." *LB*, 6:724D.

86. Rabil has a good discussion of this point in the section called "The Nature and Work of Christ and the Christian Believer," with ample references to the *Paraphrases; Erasmus and the New Testament*, pp. 146-55. Cf. also Payne, "Erasmus," pp. 25-33, who holds that Erasmus was more interested in the "ethical demand made upon the follower of Christ" than in Paul's soteriology.

87. *Corinthians*, 2:176; 11:241. Cf. Erasmus, n. 11 on Rom. 1:5, *LB*, 6:558D.

88. *Romans* 9-10:165; trans. Lupton, p. 43.

89. *Corinthians*, 13:257; trans. O'Kelly, pp. 332-33. Lupton points out (p. 138) how close this passage is to Pico's *Heptaplus*.

90. "Quod quamdiu tenet, quasi nova tum forma effigiatus ad imaginem Dei expressius, non tam homo quam Deus videtur esse." *Romans*, 12:176.

91. "Tenet autem, vel tenetur potius (nam superioris amplecti et tenere est) quamdiu sua ipsius anima corpus cohibet, et sursum in obsiquela sibi sustentat. Quod si neglexerit, sique corpus effluere in libidines siverit, e vestigio tunc simul a sustinente spiritu negligetur ipsa et deseretur, totusque homo deorsum pronus et preceps ad terram et mortem miserrime corruet." Ibid.

92. *Corinthians*, 10:237; trans. O'Kelly, p. 290.

93. "Voluit enim bonus Deus salvetur homo; quod quidem esse non potest certe nisi

homines deificentur, reformenturque in divinum statum, diique fiant assimilati Deo, ut Deum referant." *De Ecc. Hier.,* 1 :201; trans. Lupton, p. 54.

94. "Deus homo factus medium erat quo homines dii fierent; cujus deitate deificantur omnes." *De Corpore Christi Mystico,* in *Opuscula Quaedam Theologica,* p. 190; trans. Lupton, p. 40. Cf. *Romans,* 12 :63.

95. "Amor enim principium gignendi est; et sanctus amor sanctitatis, et Dei amor deitatis." *De Ecc. Hier,* vol. 2, pt. 2, 206; trans. Lupton, p. 62.

96. "Quemadmodum enim divinus Spiritus, nostrum in habitans spiritum, in eum redundat, et ut est potentior, eum in sese veluti transformat: ita noster spiritus immutatus redundat in corpus domicilium utique suum, idque quoad licet in sese transformat." *Enarratio Psalmi Beatus Vir, LB,* 5 : 192A.

97. "Spiritum vero, qua divinae naturae similitudinem exprimimus, in qua conditor optimus de suae mentis archetypo aeternam illam honesti legem insculpsit digito, hoc est Spiritu suo. Hac Deo conglutinamur unumque cum eo reddimur." *Enchiridion,* ed. Holborn, p. 52. Cf. Colet: "Hoc divinum vinculum ecclesiae in Christo Jesu vel spiritus ipse est Dei in Christo, vel ejus virtus conglutinans . . . ." *De Corpore,* p. 190.

98. "Cujus sententiae [Valla's] et ipse subscribo: διδακτικὸς enim dicitur, qui est appositus ad docendum, interprete Hieronymo. Unde Paulus inter caeteras dotes vult Episcopum esse διδακτικὸν, hoc est, idoneum ad docendum, ut suo commonstrabimus loco. Docilis autem est is, qui facile discit." *LB,* 6 : 365F–66E.

99. "Ut consentiat cum eo quod praecessit, *nisi Pater qui misit me traxerit eum.* Hoc nimirum est esse θεοδίδακτον, trahi Patris afflatu." Ibid. Cf. Erasmus's similar use of *afflatu* in his note on John 7 : 39: "Agit enim non de substantia Spiritus Sancti, verum de illo munere et afflatu, quo Apostoli subito mutati sunt in alios viros." *LB,* 6 : 371F–72D.

100. *Paraclesis,* trans. John C. Olin, in *Desiderius Erasmus: Christian Humanism and the Reformation: Selected Writings* (New York: Harper Torchbooks, 1965), p. 106; cf. Holborn, p. 149. See also prefatory dedication to Leo X, *Novum Instrumentum* (Basel, 1516); Allen, *EE,* vol. 2, Ep. 384, 184–87.

101. *LB,* 7 : 379C.

102. "Hic primus et unicus tibi sit scopus, hoc votum, hoc unum age, ut muteris, ut rapiaris, ut affleris, ut transformeris in ea, quae discis." *Ratio Verae Theologiae,* ed. Holborn, p. 180. Georges Chantraine shows at some length how this "connaissance transformante" is at the heart of Erasmus's theology: "Théologie et vie spirituelle; un aspect de la méthode théologique selon Érasme," *Nouvelle Revue Théologique* 91 (October 1969): 823–30; also *"Mystère" et "Philosophie du Christ" selon Érasme* (Bibliothèque de la Faculté de Philosophie et Lettres de Namur, fasc. 49, 1971).

103. "Sic natura conditus est hominis animus, aliquid amet necesse est: vacare non potest. Caeterum, cujusmodi sunt qui amat, ejusmodi et ipse efficitur. Si Divinas amat litteras, rapitur, afficitur, transfiguratur in Deum." *Enarratio Psalmi Beatus Vir, LB,* 5 : 180.

104. ". . . quia amamur, Deum redamamus. . . ." *Romans,* 5 : 143. See above, nn. 75–76. Cf. also *Corinthians,* 13 : 256.

105. "Sin conjunctim legas, melius cohaererent, sublata conjunctione, quum Deus et Christus sit talis erga nos, *quis nos separabit a charitate? Charitas* autem hic active videtur accipi, ἀγάπη, nempe qua nos dilexit Deus, et ad redamandum provocavit." *LB,* 6 : 608B.

106. "Quod velim lector boni consulat, beneque de nobis sensiat, qui de Paulo voluimus bene sentire, conatique sumus, quoad potuimus, divina gracia adjuti, veros illius sensus exprimere." Ibid., 16 : 227.

107. N. 17 on Rom. 5 : 14; *LB,* 6 : 591D.

108. See Rice, "John Colet"; H. C. Porter, "The Gloomy Dean and the Law," *Essays in Modern Church History in Memory of Norman Sykes,* ed. G. Bennett and J. Walsh (Oxford, 1966), pp. 18–43.

7 Erasmus's *Paraphrases of the New Testament*

ALBERT RABIL, JR.

GENERAL ORIENTATION TO THE PARAPHRASES

Known until he was nearly fifty through the *Adages* and *Praise of Folly* as the leading man of letters in Europe, Erasmus established himself as a "Christian Humanist" with the publication of his *Novum Instrumentum* in 1516, containing a Greek text of the New Testament, a Latin translation, and notes on the text, together with several tracts designed to introduce his work to the learned world. This was followed in 1517 by the appearance of the first of his "paraphrases" of the New Testament, that on Romans. Thereafter, work on the text of the New Testament and on the paraphrases proceeded in tandem.

The New Testament was published in revised editions (now entitled *Novum Testamentum*) in 1519, 1522, 1527, and 1535. After the paraphrase of Romans, Erasmus published paraphrases of the remainder of the Pauline Epistles: Corinthians in January 1519; Galatians in May 1519. Romans, Corinthians, and Galatians were published in a collected edition in January 1520. Paraphrases of Timothy, Titus, and Philemon appeared during this same month. Colossians, Philippians, and Thessalonians were not published separately, but appeared for the first time in a collected edition of the Pauline (and other) Epistles in March 1521.

Erasmus turned his attention next to the other canonical Epistles. Peter and Jude were published in June 1520; Hebrews in January 1521. John and James probably did not appear in separate editions but were published for the first time in the collected edition of March 1521, mentioned above.

The Gospels and Acts were paraphrased only after all the paraphrases of the Epistles had been published. Matthew appeared in March 1522; John in February 1523; Luke in August 1523; Mark in December 1523; and Acts in February 1524. The first collected edition of all the paraphrases of the New Testament (excluding Revelation, on which Erasmus never wrote a paraphrase) appeared in March 1524.

A close study of this publishing history suggests that Erasmus did not conceive the idea of writing paraphrases of the entire New Testament at once. There is a hiatus of one year between the paraphrases of Romans and Corinthians, though after completing the paraphrase of Corinthians, Erasmus worked steadily until all the Epistles had been paraphrased. Then there was a gap of another six months before he began work on Matthew, the impetus for which was the urging of his friend, Cardinal Matthew Schiner. He seems to have intended to stop with Matthew, for there is another one-year lapse before he published his paraphrase of the Gospel of John. After completing John, however, he decided to paraphrase Mark, Luke, and Acts, and began work on these immediately. Thus, Erasmus began with the notion of paraphrasing Romans only (perhaps the fulfillment of his intention to write a commentary on Romans as far back as 1504) and did not intend to complete paraphrases of all the books of the New Testament until 1522.

The publishing history of Erasmus's work on the New Testament is intimately related to his association with the Froben Press in Basel.[1] Erasmus left Cambridge in June 1514, after a three-year stay. His destination was Basel and the Froben Press. He arrived in September and was warmly welcomed into Froben's house. The two began an immediate collaboration. Erasmus had revised his *Adages* in England as long ago as 1512; Froben published the third edition early in 1515. Erasmus also brought with him from England much work he had done on the New Testament text and notes. These he intended Aldus rather than Froben to publish, for no sooner had he arrived in Basel than he announced his intention of going to Italy. But, detained by the new edition of the *Adages* and the circle of learned men associated with the Froben Press, he remained longer than he intended. When Aldus died in February 1515, John Froben promised to match any other offer Erasmus might receive for his New Testament manuscript. The result was that Froben published Erasmus's New Testament and annotations.

The earlier paraphrases were not published first by Froben, but rather by Thierry Martens of Louvain in a small edition, always followed within a month or so by a larger edition from the Froben Press. For example, Martens published Romans in November 1517; Froben published his first edition of this paraphrase in January 1518 (and separately again in November 1518 and April 1519). The one exception to this pattern were the shorter Pauline Epistles (Timothy, Titus, and Philemon). These were published by Hillen in Antwerp in January 1520, presumably in order to prevent that publisher from bringing out an attack on Erasmus by Edward Lee.[2] Froben published an edition of these Epistles in March 1520. Thereafter all the revised editions of the paraphrases were published first by Froben: the separate editions of the Gospels and Acts, the collected edition of the Epistles and Acts in 1532, and the complete editions of the paraphrases in 1524 and 1534.

All of the earlier paraphrases were dedicated to high church officials. Romans, Ephesians, Peter and Jude, and James were dedicated to cardinals (Grimani, Campeggio, Wolsey, and Matthew Schiner, respectively); Corinthians, Timothy,

Titus and Philemon, Galatians, and Hebrews were dedicated to bishops (Erard de la Marck, Philip of Burgundy, Antony de la Marck, and Sylvester Gigli, respectively). The paraphrases of the Gospels and Acts, on the other hand, were dedicated to the most powerful figures in European life: Matthew to Charles V, Holy Roman Emperor, 1519-55; John to Ferdinand of Austria (1503-64), emperor of the Holy Roman Empire from 1556; Luke to Henry VIII, king of England, 1509-47; Mark to Francis I, king of France, 1515-47; and Acts to Clement VII, pope from 1523 to 1534.[3]

There are two explanations, I believe, for the changes in the rank of persons to whom the paraphrases were dedicated. First, while the text, translation, and notes on the New Testament embroiled Erasmus in conflict from the first edition to the last (a large part of his later writings are answers to these attacks), the paraphrases were relatively well received,[4] and he could therefore present them to his patrons as the consensus of Christian Europe on the nature of Christian existence. This in turn increased his own enthusiasm for them. He writes in 1518: "It must however be admitted that our paraphrase (of Romans) is applauded by everyone. It is some satisfaction to have produced even a single book which pleases such surly critics. I only wish that I had confined myself to like fields, in which much more credit was to be had with much less labor."[5] The relatively noncontroversial character of the paraphrases made them a good medium through which to communicate his ideas of Christian humanism to the rulers he wished to educate.

Related to but distinguishable from this motivation is the fact that with the publication of his works on the New Testament, Erasmus came to see himself as a "Christian humanist" whose role it was to lead a religious reform in Europe. As he had made clear in *The Education of a Christian Prince* (1516) and *The Complaint of Peace* (1517), written during the same period when his New Testament was being published for the first time, the reform of the Christian life should begin in the circle closest to the center, Christ, and emanate outward.[6] Leaders should both set an example and establish policies commensurate with a Christian existence. Therefore, to dedicate his paraphrases to princes of the world and the church (he had dedicated his New Testament to Pope Leo X),[7] was to suggest that they should lead in the new age of Christian humanism. The dedications, as well as the paraphrases themselves, then, attest to Erasmus's serious intention of bringing about religious reform through his work on the New Testament. His scholarly work was not "academic" in the sense of "for its own sake." Its definite purpose was to change people's lives through scholarship.

Erasmus was the only writer in his generation to entitle his works "paraphrases" instead of "commentaries." How are we to understand the distinction between the two? In a letter to Thomas More accompanying the first edition of the *Paraphrase of Romans,* he writes: "I send you the book of Paraphrase, rightly so entitled."[8] Before publication, he had used the word *commentary* rather than *paraphrase.* He never states that he consciously changed his plans.[9] And he does not comment on the distinction between the two until he had been engaged in the writing of paraphrases for some time. In 1522 he writes: "For a paraphrase is not a translation but a certain freer kind of continuous commentary with the integrity of the persons speaking maintained."[10] And in 1523: "However, I do not wish that anyone grant more to this paraphrase than would have been granted to a commentary, as if I had written a commentary—although a paraphrase also is a kind of commentary."[11]

There were perhaps two reasons why paraphrases were congenial to Erasmus. First, he could show that his "philosophy of Christ" was the heart of Christian truth, the core of the New Testament. Second, his own views were so blended with the "paraphrase" that the two were difficult to extricate, providing in this way a certain camouflage for Erasmus's views. Given the happy reception of his paraphrases in contrast to the controversy in which his explicit translation and annotations on the New Testament embroiled him, the camouflage might well have proved welcome.

Although his annotations on the text of the New Testament were written "not for the multitude, but for scholars and students of theology,"[12] the paraphrases were intended for a wider audience. They were written, therefore, in a clear and free-flowing popular style. In spite of appearances, however, they were not hastily or haphazardly produced but were set down only after much thought and labor, as Erasmus testifies more than once.[13] In contrast to the annotations, he does not refer to the Fathers upon whom he relies for his interpretations. His exegesis, however, is often dependent upon theirs.[14]

For the most part the paraphrase of each verse is brief. This is especially true of the earlier paraphrases of the apostolic epistles, where in only two cases are the paraphrases extensive enough to require a column in the Le Clerc edition.[15] There are, however, several others of more than average length in these letters.[16] The Gospels, and especially Luke's, contain many more lengthy paraphrases.[17] There is one in Luke which, like a number of the annotations, is virtually long enough to be a short treatise in its own right.[18] There are a number of other paraphrases in the Gospels (none in Acts) which are of more than usual length.[19]

Erasmus's paraphrases usually follow closely his own translation. Occasionally, however, the paraphrase gives his preferred interpretation, while the translation, particularly in 1516, adheres more closely to the Vulgate. On the other hand, sometimes his paraphrase will retain a Vulgate reading and/or translation which he has rejected in his own translation.[20] Finally, whereas in his translation Erasmus is often forced to make a decision concerning the possible variant meanings of the Greek text, in his paraphrase he will sometimes combine two differing senses.[21]

PARAPHRASES OF LETTERS TRADITIONALLY ASCRIBED TO PAUL

Since I have made a close textual study of the letters traditionally ascribed to Paul (Romans, Corinthians, Galatians, Ephesians, Colossians, Philippians, Thessalonians, Timothy, Titus, and Philemon), the remainder of this essay will focus on these letters. It is an interesting question why Erasmus began with the Pauline Epistles when he decided to write paraphrases of the New Testament.[22] In the first instance, he seems to have been drawn particularly to Paul by John Colet. When Erasmus made his first visit to England in 1499, he met John Colet in Oxford where the latter was at the time lecturing on Romans and Corinthians. Erasmus took a great interest in Colet's work, urging him later to publish his lectures. Either before or immediately after he had returned to Paris from his first English visit, Erasmus wrote commentaries (now lost) on Paul. Shortly after this, he met Jean Vitrier, who introduced him to Origen and to Origen's allegorical method of scriptural interpretation. In his life of Vitrier, Erasmus testifies that Paul was Vitrier's favorite in Scripture, and that he had memorized Paul's letters.[23] In the *Enchiridion,* which Erasmus wrote between 1501 and 1503 under the strong and immediate influence of Vitrier and Origen, he exhorts the dissolute knight to whom he addresses his book: "Above all, however, make Paul your intimate friend, Him you should always cling to, 'meditating upon him day and night' until you commit to memory every word."[24] It is also clear that this appropriation of Paul had to do with his perceived affinity with Origen: he was, in Erasmus's view, the best of the allegorizers.[25]

Perhaps a more adequate answer can be gained by asking of those who influenced Erasmus: why did Colet and Vitrier choose Paul to comment upon and memorize? In one respect they, and especially Colet, were breaking new ground; for during the Middle Ages historical exegesis of the Bible was confined largely to the Old Testament, and in the Old Testament to the historical and prophetic books.[26] An obvious reason for the relative neglect of the New Testament was that Greek was not as well known as Hebrew. Moreover, knowledge of Hebrew was acquired explicitly for the purpose of studying Scripture, whereas knowledge of Greek could be employed to study profane authors, as it often was. Related to this was the fear that the language used by the heretical Greeks must contain heretical views. A number of humanists, notably Reuchlin, were accused of heresy on precisely this ground.[27] Erasmus often finds himself defending the study of the Greek (as opposed to Latin) Fathers.[28] Paul in particular, among medieval thinkers, was regarded as the property of the dialecticians rather than of the exegetes. Beryl Smalley writes in this regard:

> The eleventh- and early twelfth-century masters were inclined to identify exegesis with theology. . . . We find the theological questioning but not the biblical scholarship. It is no accident that the two favorite books for commentators were the Psalter and the Pauline Epistles, their creative energy being centered in the latter; St. Paul provided the richest nourishment to the theologian and logician.[29]

An obvious reason for the humanists' attention to Paul was their interest in purifying the sources of the Christian tradition from the corruptions of scholastic theology.[30]

As is true with virtually all his writings, Erasmus emended the paraphrases in successive editions. The pattern of changes in the Pauline letters is interesting.[31] In Romans and Galatians, most of the significant changes were made in 1532 (41 of 43 and 15 of 18, respectively). In all the other Pauline letters in which significant changes occurred, all were made in 1524 (24 in Corinthians, 3 in Philippians, 3 in Colossians, 5 in I Timothy, 2 in Titus). Analysis of these changes yields some interesting conclusions.

Fully half of the significant changes in Romans and Galatians show some accommodation to the views of the Protestant Reformers.[32] Twelve changes in Romans make a more explicit connection of righteousness to faith in Christ; eight speak of the "justifying faith" of the Gospel and emphasize the gift of grace.[33]

Six changes in Galatians reveal the same pattern (added portions are italicized):[34]

3:9   . . . abandon faith in *the works and* ceremonies of the law. . . .

3:14   Why, however, did God want this to happen? Clearly in order that the curse *brought by the law* might be removed and that the blessing *through faith* formerly promised to Abraham might take its place.

4:14   I have preached nothing other to you than Jesus Christ was crucified *for you.* . . .

4:14   . . . when we promised immortality *on the basis of this faith.* [Earlier editions read: "on the basis of these things."]

5:2   For it is granted to faith alone, not to the merits *of works.*

It is incorrect to speak here of an "influence" of the Reformers on Erasmus, if that means that his views were changed by them. He remained consistently himself while accommodating himself to their special emphases. He had asserted his belief in this possibility as far back as 1524, in the colloquy *Examination Concerning Faith;* and virtually at the same time as he was revising these paraphrases in the direction noted, he was composing *On Mending the Peace of the Church,* reasserting his stubborn belief in the possibility of unifying all Christians. Erasmus believed that his view of Christianity was encompassing enough to include the emphases of the Reformers.

That these changes were an accommodation rather than a systematic revision is further suggested by the nature of some of the changes themselves. In a long annotation to Romans 1:17 written in 1527 (triggered, no doubt, by disagreement between Catholics and Protestants), Erasmus points out that in Scripture faith (*pistis*) has at least two senses: "belief" and "trust." Accordingly, in his paraphrase Erasmus uses both *fides* and *fiducia* to interpret *pistis.* But strictly speaking, *fides,* like "faith" in English, may mean either "belief" or "trust," while *fiducia* means only "trust" or "confidence." In some instances of its use in the paraphrases of Romans and Galatians *fides* seems to have the meaning of belief,[35] whereas in others it is not clear how Erasmus intends its meaning. It is probable that often he does not have in mind a precise sense for the word but that either or both connotations may be present. In 1532 he seems to indicate that both meanings are present in Romans 3:22 when he adds *ac fiduciam* to *per fidem.* In 1521 he changes one case of *fides* to *fiducia* as the merit on account of which Abraham was considered justified.[36] In his paraphrase of Galatians 2:15–16 he uses both *fides* and *fiducia* to describe the gate of salvation.[37]

The interchangeability of these two terms precludes the idea of *sola fides* in Erasmus's thought[38] and suggests that for him (as for Origen, Ambrosiaster, and Chrysostom among the Fathers, whom he often cites in his annotations), faith is not an entirely free gift but a merit in which free will has a role.[39] Nevertheless, in one passage Erasmus makes a startling change in the direction of asserting predestination. The paraphrase of Romans 9:16 ("So it depends not upon man's will or exercise, but upon God's mercy") read in the 1517 edition: "And yet some part of it depends on our own will and effort, although this part is so minor that it seems like nothing at all in comparison with the free kindness of God." But in 1532 this sentence was dropped out and in its place Erasmus wrote: "However, it does not follow that God is unjust to anyone, but that he is merciful toward many."[40] Why Erasmus made this one change (while leaving other passages untouched) is not clear unless to demonstrate the possibility of accommodation, to soften the antagonisms. Previous generations of interpreters might have found in these examples instances of Erasmus's fundamental ambivalence. It seems much more plausible to me that he was trying to find—haltingly but seriously—a middle path between opposites that would not be reconciled.

The alterations in the other Pauline letters, made in 1524, are of a very different character.[41] Only three of the thirty-seven changes in these letters show concerns similar to those predominantly present in Romans and Galatians:

> 1 Cor. 12:1 Now your former error is not imputed to you.
>
> 1 Cor. 12:31 [The spirit] both gives his gifts and maintains them.
>
> Colossians 4:3 . . . that he through faith opening men's hearts.

The overwhelming majority of the other changes stress aspects of Erasmus's "philosophy of Christ." Here are a few examples (if only a portion of the quoted passage was added, that portion is italicized):

> 1 Cor. 2:6 [When we were among you] you were proud of human wisdom, ignorant of divine wisdom; we taught more simple things, but things necessary to salvation. We have the more hidden wisdom of Christ, but we speak of this among the perfect. Therefore, be diligent so that you might be perfect, so that you might partake of the mysteries [of God.]
>
> 1 Cor. 2:13 It is fitting for a spiritual person to have a spiritual philosophy with his *mind purged through faith and his desires corrected by love.*
>
> 1 Cor. 10:28 . . . by no means would [Christians imitate carnal things] if they execrated our religion with their minds as much as with words.
>
> 2 Cor. 5:16 In vain, therefore, do some glory in the fact that they are Christ's countrymen or because they are his kinsmen, or because they were familiar acquaintances while he was in the flesh. For since his flesh was given only for a time, while afterwards his spirit was sent, he wishes to be known according to the spirit, and counts him the nearest of kin who has the greatest faith in his promises. Let no man esteem us less who are later apostles because we did not know Christ while he was in his mortal body on earth. For even if we had so known him, now we would forego that knowledge as a hindrance to the spirit, and since he has now become spiritual, we would love him spiritually.
>
> 2 Cor. 5:17 Away therefore with these words: This man is a Greek, this man a barbarian, this man a Jew, this man a worshiper of idols, this man a spoiler of holy places. The man has forsaken what he was and by the workmanship of Christ changed into a new creature as unlike he was as any beast is unlike a man.
>
> Col. 2:12 For when sinful desires are killed, perfect quietness of mind follows.
>
> 1 Tim. 1:19 He who does not have a sincere conscience cannot have

a sincere faith. *For how can a thing be called sincere which is dead? Or how can a thing endure which lacks life and spirit?*

Titus 3:9 *But these are such curious things. But what benefit is there in questioning* why the Jews think such great care must be expended over the blood of a weasel?

The occasion for these revisions was the publication by Froben of the first collected edition of all the paraphrases of Erasmus on the New Testament. Erasmus made these changes to reinforce the intention of the paraphrases, namely, to be an instrument of reform in the direction of his "philosophy of Christ." As in the case of the later revisions of Romans and Galatians, however, his emendations were relatively slight, not systematically carried out, though intentionally done with a given thrust. The themes of Erasmus's "philosophy of Christ" shine through clearly in the paraphrases of the Pauline Epistles, though there is room here for only a brief outline of his ideas and approach to the Christian religion as reflected in them.[42]

Erasmus views the religion of the Jews as a religion of law and law in this context as wholly of the flesh. "When I say the law," he paraphrases Galatians 5:4, "I mean that crass and carnal part of the Mosaic law which is the only thing the Jews hold onto doggedly."[43] This "crass and carnal" part of the law is most often related by Erasmus to a religion of ceremonies or formal observances. Many times in the paraphrases of Paul he repeats, as if it were a formula, that the observation of circumcision, special feast days, the new moon, special foods, and all the rest is a substitute for holiness rather than the reality.[44] Nothing good can ever come out of such a religion. The degree of its perversity is suggested by its equation with the seeking of personal advantage through religion. Even some who preach the Gospel, he says on Philippians 3:18, do so for riches; those who preach feast days, circumcision, special foods, etc., do so in order that they may live at ease through other men's fastings.[45] This leads him to a sharp dichotomy between Judaism and Christianity. Either, he says on Galatians 5:2, "you must be Jews completely and give up Christ, or Christians completely and reject Judaism."[46]

Viewed in this context, Erasmus is asserting that only by becoming a Christian can one transcend "crass and carnal" religion. Christianity promises something else: a religion of the spirit. There is not only the crass aspect of the law which we call the letter, he says on Galatians 5:16, but "a different heavenly aspect which we call the spirit."[47] For the spiritual law, external things do not matter;[48] what does matter is the transformation of one's inner self. This transformation has been made possible through Christ, who has overcome the power of the law and taken away the sting of death which it brings.[49] Christ thus stands over against Moses as the bringer of a new dispensation.[50]

The sign of this new dispensation is baptism. Time and again in the paraphrases when there is no mention of baptism in the text, Erasmus says that Christians are joined to Christ through baptism.[51] But baptism is truly a spiritual sign rather than a fleshly one. For no value is to be placed on the act itself, only on that to which it points as a sign—namely, a new life in Christ. If one is baptized and does not lead this new life, one is not really baptized in Christ and, conversely, if one is not baptized and lives in Christ, then one is still a true Christian.[52]

What is the new life to which baptism in Christ points? It is the life of the spirit. This life is preeminently one that is free from sin. Erasmus stresses throughout the paraphrases that God in Christ has restored us to innocence.[53] This is one of the strong points of contrast between him and the Protestant Reformers. For since we are restored to innocence through Christ, our lives can (and indeed must) reflect this innocence. No Reformer could have written "be diligent so that you might be perfect."[54] But Erasmus could, and he meant to place the responsibility for Christian existence squarely on the shoulders of each Christian. The gifts that God gives us are gifts of the spirit, he says, "but *through our effort and prayer* the spirit both preserves and augments his gifts."[55]

What are the gifts of the spirit? The marks of a Christian life? The perfection of the Christian? Erasmus describes these in a variety of ways, each of them based on an "imitation of Christ," our Savior and example.

To imitate Christ means first to suffer in the world as Christ suffered.

> But a Christian, who seeks true and eternal glory, must seek it in the same way Christ entered into it. The way to true glory is through [suffering] false ignominy, the entry into immortal advantage is through the loss of transitory things. We ought not to strive for glory but to deserve glory.[56]

Indeed, there is nothing better than suffering to testify to our trust in God. "Whenever you are hammered by afflictions," he writes on 2 Corinthians 12:9 at the same time my [God's] glory is illustrated, for while you are guarded by my help you cannot be overcome, however much you are cast down."[57]

To imitate Christ means also to lead a pure life. Erasmus sums this up best in his paraphrase of 1 Corinthians 3:12:

> I for my part proposed Christ as the mark at which you are to aim; if someone teaches by his example—living innocently, deserving well even of his enemies, not trusting in riches, despising honors, cursing voluptuous agreements as a plague, referring all things to the glory of Christ, hoping for no gift by right of deeds except immortality, even choosing death if this should mean meeting Christ—he adds a worthy building to his foundation, Christ.[58]

This is the surest way to bring others closer to the Gospel. "For no man sooner persuades other men to follow his doctrine than he who does what he asks other men to do."[59] On Philippians 4:9, Erasmus has Paul say that he has not only taught but exemplified before them in his own life what he has taught.[60]

Finally, the idea of the "fool for Christ" which appears in the *Praise of Folly* and other works has a prominent place in the life of the Christian as portrayed in the paraphrases. Time and again he returns to the theme that learning and worldly wisdom are not important. God reveals to the lowly what he withholds from the great and wise.[61] Knowledge which does not have as its aim the strengthening of faith is useless. No Christian seeks knowledge for its own sake, but only for the sake of imitating Christ.[62]

Just as a Christian leads a spiritual life in this world, so the reward he seeks is spiritual and not earthly:

> For things seen here [in this world], aside from the fact that they are neither truly good nor truly bad—of which sort are wealth, honor, pleasure, life, injury, disgrace, torments and death—are also not of long duration, whereas things seen with the eyes of faith are both true and eternal.[63]

Suffering in the world, imitating Christ, in short, living for the spirit rather than for the flesh, assure this eternal reward, immortality or resurrection (Erasmus uses the words interchangeably). The emphasis in the paraphrases is much stronger on the nature of the Christian life and the exhortation to lead it than on the reward promised. And there can be little doubt that Erasmus' primary orientation was toward the renewal of Christian existence here and now.

The paraphrases, as I stated at the beginning, were no academic exercise for Erasmus. They were an instrument of Christian reform. To read the paraphrases today in this light is to recover something of what they meant to Erasmus and to the generation that had received them with enthusiasm.

NOTES

1. For notes and further details on what follows, see Albert Rabil, *Erasmus and the New Testament* (San Antonio: Trinity University Press, 1972), pp. 89–91 and nn. 147–52 (hereafter cited as Rabil, followed by page numbers.

2. See *Erasmi Epistolae*, ed. P. S. Allen, H. M. Allen, and H. W. Garrod, 12 vols. (Oxford, 1906-58), 3:123, introduction to epistle 1043 (hereafter cited as *EE*, followed by volume and page numbers).

3. The letters of dedication may be found in *EE* as follows: Romans, 3:136ff.; Corinthians, 3:480ff.; Galatians, 3:560ff.; shorter Pauline epistles, 4:123ff.; Ephesians, 4:

180ff.; Peter and Jude, 4:283ff.; James 4:416ff.; John 4:434ff.; Hebrews, 4:436ff.; Matthew, 5:4ff.; John, 5:163ff.; Luke, 5:312ff.; Mark, 5:352ff.; Acts, 5:389ff.

4. *EE.* 3:249, ll. 78-83. The translation is that of F. M. Nichols, *The Epistles of Erasmus,* 3 vols. London, 1901-18), 3:305 (hereafter cited as Nichols, followed by volume and page numbers). The popularity of the paraphrases is further suggested by the fact that they were translated into several European languages. The Epistles were translated into German in 1523 and the Gospels and Epistles into German in 1530. A Bohemian translation of Matthew appeared in 1542 and a French translation of the Epistles in 1543. An English translation of the entire paraphrases was prepared by a number of persons under the editorship of Nicholas Udall and published in 1548 and again in 1551. On this, see Rabil, 128, n. 65. There is no modern translation of any of the paraphrases. But see below, n. 32.

5. To be sure, the paraphrases were subject to criticism, within the context of critiques of Erasmus's text, translation, and annotations of the New Testament, launched as early as 1519 and continuing into the 1530s. Had it been a question of the paraphrases alone, however, it is safe to say that the critiques would never have been launched. This conclusion is buttressed by the fact that when, in 1524 and 1532, Erasmus made changes in the paraphrases, he moved in the direction of accommodation of the Reformation emphasis on justifying faith apart from works of the law, as suggested later in this article.

6. In two passages in works written in 1518 Erasmus speaks of the social order as three concentric circles with Christ as their center. In the first circle is the ecclesiastical order, in the second the political order, and in the third the common people. The more power (and therefore responsibility for others) one has in the world, the more one should be like Christ. The first passage is in a letter prefaced to a new edition of the *Enchiridion* (*EE,* 3:368-71, ll. 231-371; trans. J. C. Olin, *Christian Humanism and the Reformation* (New York: Harper & Row, 1965), pp. 118-23. The second is in his treatise on theological method, *Ratio verae theologiae,* published in 1518 and included in the second edition (1519) of the *Novum Testamentum.* A critical text of this treatise may be found in Annemarie and Hajo Holborn, *Desiderius Erasmus Roterodamus Ausgewählte Werke* (Munich: C. H. Beck, 1933), pp. 202-04 (hereafter cited as Holborn and Holborn, followed by page numbers).

7. For the letter of dedication, see *EE,* 2:181-87.

8. Ibid., 3:153, l. 2; Nichols, 3:166.

9. See Rabil, 134, n. 87.

10. *EE,* 5:47, ll. 37-39.

11. Ibid., 172, ll. 395-97. For further discussion of this distinction, see Rabil, 135, n. 89.

12. *Erasmi Opera Omnia,* ed. Jean Le Clerc, 10 vols. (Leiden, 1703-06), *Contra Moros.,* vol. 6, *** recto (hereafter cited as *LB,* followed by volume and page numbers).

13. *EE,* 3:707, ll. 14-16; 714, ll. 7-9; 717, ll. 3-4.

14. For example, his discussion of free will follows the interpretation of Chrysostom and Ambrosiaster, whose views agreed with his own, as he notes in the annotations.

15. 1 Cor. 8:7 (*LB,* 7:885F-86F) and 1 Tim. 2:3 (1040B-41A). In the first, Erasmus uses the occasion to point out that idolatry is to be abolished but that Christians are to bear with weaker persons in weaning them from their pasts. The second is an encomium on peace and a critique of war, both themes close to Erasmus's heart.

16. See, for example, in *LB,* 7, the paraphrases of 1 Cor. 1:1-2 (859B-E); Gal. 1:19 (945E-46C); 2:10 (948F-49D); 1 Tim. 1:2 (1035A-E); 3:2 (1043D-44B); 1 Peter 1:2 (1083A-D); James 1:27 (1124F-25D); 1 John 1:1 (1141A-42B); 1:9 (1144D-45B); and 2:21 (1149C-50B).

17. There are four column-length (or longer) paraphrases in Matthew (*LB,* 7): 1:1 (1A-3F); 2:1 (8A-9A); 3:12 (15F-16F); and 28.19 (145B-46B). There are five in Mark: 1:1

(157B-58B); 1:9 (160D-161D); 1:14 (162F-63F); 2:12 (171E-74C); and 6:9 (201E-02E). There are thirteen in Luke: 1:5 (283A-84D); 4:4 (319C-20B); 4:12 (322B-23D); 4:21 (325E-26E); 4:41 (332A-33A); 7:15 (352E-54C); 10:37 (377D-78D); 15:7 (405B-06B); 19:4 (427D-28D); 19:40 (434A-35D); 23:34 (462A-63A); and 24:27 (469A-84F). There are two in John: 1:1 (497A-98E); 1:14 (503E-04E). The largest number of these occur at the beginning of each of the Gospels.

18. *LB*, 7, Luke 24:27 (469A-84F). The verse reads: "And beginning with Moses and all the prophets, he interpreted to them in all the Scriptures the things concerning himself." Erasmus uses the occasion to cite and comment upon many passages in the Old Testament which prophesy Christ. Cf. paraphrase of 2 Tim. 3:16 (1064E-F).

19. See, for example, in *LB*, 7, the paraphrases of Matt. 2:22 (12A-E); 5:12 (26D-27B); 5:30 (31E-32D); Mark 1:5 (159B-F); 1:45 (168D-69B); 4:29 (190A-91A); 4:41 (192C-93A); 5:43 (199A-F); 8:6 (216D-17B); Luke 1:2 (281F-82D); 1:35 (290A-E); 2:47 (306B-F); 4:14 (323D-24C); 5:7 (335A-E); 5:14 (337E-38D); 5:45 (349D-50C); 7:50 (359B-F); 19:26 (431F-32E); John 14:31 (631B-14A).

20. For example, in Romans 9:25 the phrase "and her who had not obtained mercy, one who has obtained mercy," is present in the Vulgate but was not in the Greek manuscripts used by Erasmus or in the patristic interpreters. Erasmus omits the phrase in his own text and translation of the verse but retains it in his paraphrase.

21. For example, in the paraphrase of Romans 8:19, Erasmus combines two senses of creation (*ktisis*): one that thinks of it as the sensible world (represented among the Fathers by Chrysostom), the other that understands it as including especially the world endowed with intelligence, the angels (represented by Origen and Pelagius, among others). In answer to a criticism by Beda concerning his interpretation of creation, Erasmus states that when he included angels as part of its meaning he was following the opinion of Jerome, namely, pseudo-Jerome (Pelagius), but he does not inform Beda that he has any doubts concerning the authenticity of the work traditionally ascribed to Jerome. *Responsio ad notata per n. Beddam in Paraphras. in Paulum* (1526), *LB*, 9:471A-C.

22. This discussion draws freely upon a longer treatment of the same question in Rabil, pp. 128ff.

23. Allen, *EE*, 4:508-09, 11, 44-47, 52-54; trans. Olin *Christian Humanism and the Reformation*, p. 167.

24. Holborn, p. 135; *The Enchiridion of Erasmus*, trans. Raymond Himelick (Bloomington: Indiana University Press, 1963), p. 199 (hereafter cited as Himelick, followed by page numbers). The quoted phrase is from Horace *Ars Poetica* 269.

25. "In unveiling the hidden sense, however, one ought not to follow conjectures or his own mind but acquire a method and, so to speak, a kind of technique. . . . After Christ, the apostle Paul opened up certain allegorical fountains; and following him, Origen easily holds the leadership in this aspect of theology." Holborn, p. 71; Himelick, p. 107.

26. See Beryl Smalley, *The Study of the Bible in the Middle Ages* (Oxford: Blackwell, 1952; reprinted in paperback by the University of Notre Dame Press, 1964), pp. 361-62 (hereafter referred to as Smalley, followed by page numbers).

27. See W. Schwarz, *Principles and Problems of Biblical Translation* (Cambridge: University Press, 1955), pp. 92, 93, and 93 n. 4.

28. See, for example, Allen, *EE*, 3:321, ll. 342-49.

29. Smalley, pp. 76-77.

30. For other possible reasons, see Rabil, p. 132. There were a few historical commentaries on Paul during the High Middle Ages, notably that of Nicholas of Lyra, to which Erasmus refers in his annotations. There were many medieval dogmatic commentaries on Paul, but with the exception of Thomas Aquinas these were either ignored by or unknown to Erasmus.

31. There were no significant changes in Ephesians, 1 and 2 Thessalonians, 2 Timothy, and Philemon.

32. A critical translation of the paraphrases of Romans and Galatians has been completed by John B. Payne, Albert Rabil, Jr., and Warren S. Smith, Jr., and will be published in the near future by the University of Toronto Press as part of the Collected Works of Erasmus. This work will also contain a translation of most of the annotations on these two letters.

33. These are listed and discussed in Rabil, pp. 136–39.

34. All translations from the paraphrases are my own.

3:9 Proinde qui diffisi Legis ceremoniis *atque operibus*. . . . (*LB,* 7:953C)

3:14 Cur autem id fieri voluit Deus? nimirum ut sublata exsecratione, *quam invebebat Lex,* benedictio *per fidem* succederet quondam Abrahae promissa. (*LB,* 7:954A)

4:14: Nihil aliud praedicavi vobis, quam Jesum Christum *pro vobis* crucifixum. . . . (*LB,* 7:958B)

4:14 . . . cum *ex ejus fide* immortalitatem polliceremur. (*LB,* 7:958B)

5:2: . . . nam soli fidei datur, non meritis *operum.* (*LB,* 7:961B)

35. See paraphrases in *LB,* 7 of Romans 1:5 (779C), 3:1 (785B), and 3:2 (785C); Gal. 1:2–3 (944F), and 2:10 (949C).

36. Romans 4:3 (*LB,* 7:788C). For one other instance of a change from *fides* to *fiducia,* see Romans 10:12 (*LB,* 7:811E). It is not at all clear why in these two cases alone Erasmus chose in 1521 to make this change, since he must have been able to discover many other instances in his paraphrases in which *fides* has or could have the meaning of *fiducia.*

37. *LB,* 7:950D–E.

38. In the paraphrase of Romans 3:1 (*LB,* 7:785B), Erasmus goes so far as to place "the pious life and innocent habits" ahead of "faith in Christ" as the basis of salvation. The order reveals where his emphasis lies. In response to a criticism by Beda of his addition "of works" to Galatians 5:2 (see above, n. 34), he replies that he is not rejecting all merits of faith working through love, but only the merits of works which precede faith and love, especially the ceremonies of the law. *Responsio ad Notata per N. Beddam in Paraphras. in Paulum* (1526), *LB,* 9, 476C. See also *Supputatio Errorum N. Beddae* (1527), ibid., 690D–E.

39. See paraphrases in *LB,* 7, of Romans 4:5 (788E–F), 4:14 (790A), and 4:16 (790C–D).

40. The 1517 edition reads: "Imo nonnihil est in voluntate conatuque nostro situm, licet hoc ita sit exiguum, ut ad dei gratuitam, beneficentiam nihil esse videatur." This was replaced in 1532 by: "Nec tamen hinc consequitur, Deum in quenquam esse injurium, sed in multos misericordem" (*LB,* 7:807F).

41. Because the various editions of the paraphrases have never been collated, I shall quote here the Latin text of all the passages added in 1524. If only a portion of the quoted passage was added, that portion is italicized. All references are to *LB,* 7.

1 Cor. 2:2: "Hominem praedicavi, sed a Deo unctum, et a Prophetis promissum ad redimendum genus humanum" (864C).

1 Cor. 2:6: "Vobis humana sapientia tumidis, sed divinae sapientiae rudibus, proposuimus simpliciora, sed ad salutem necessaria. Habemus et reconditiora de Christo, verum ea loquimur inter perfectos. Ergo curate ut perfecti sitis, quo mysteriorum sitis capaces" (864E).

1 Cor. 2:7: Hujus secretiora non objicimus vulgo, sed in occulto communicamus idoneis" (865A).

1 Cor. 2:13: Audotor enim spiritualis, spirituali Philosophiae congruit, *purgato per fidem intellectu, et castigato per caritatem affectu*" (865F).

1 Cor. 2:15: "Ut enim homo non judicat divina, ita carnalis homo non judicat spiritualem" (866B).

1 Cor. 6:2: "Vos enim estis lux mundi, quae coarguat impiorum errores. Hoc quo pacto fiat, si in vobis ipsis sint tenebrae? sitque quod redargutione sit dignum?" (875A).

1 Cor. 6:7: "atque adeo gravem jacturam inferatis Evangelio" (876A).

1 Cor. 10:21: "vel cum ingenti offensione infirmorum" (893C-D).

1 Cor. 10:28: "Quantumvis *verbotenus* abominantur Deos nostros Christiani, tamen non abhorrent ab immolatitiis carnibus, *haudquaquam facturi si nostram religionem tam exsecratentur animis quam verbis*" (894B).

1 Cor. 11:8: "Prius conditum est quod erat perfectius, idque contra vulgarem naturae ordinem: mox quod erat imperfectius. Quod enim in homine est ratio, id maritus est in matrimonio: quod in homine affectus, id mulier est . . . in conjugio" (895C-D).

1 Cor. 11:9: "atque in generationis adjumentum, ubi pro forma et actu est vir, mulier pro materia" (895D).

1 Cor. 11:16: "externa sunt ista, nec perinde faciunt ad Evangelicam pietatem" (896B).

1 Cor. 12:1: "Nunc non imputatur pristinus error" (898B).

1 Cor. 12:13: "sive mares, sive foeminae, sive conjugati, sive coelibes, sive potentes, sive humiles" (899A).

1 Cor. 12:31: "et quod dedit tuendum augendumque" (900D).

1 Cor. 13:8: "etiam quum post hanc vitam sublata erit oficii necessitas, manebit tamen animorum caritas. Atque hic interim" (901C).

1 Cor. 14:2: "Frustra igitur loquitur in Ecclesia, qui a nemine auditur. Non auditur autem qui non intelligitur: porro non intelligitur sermo spiritualis, nisi retrusiorem sensum accipias, quem illis verbis nobis significavit coelestis Spiritus. Id vero nullus hominum potest, nisi ex peculiari dono Spiritus" (902B).

1 Cor. 15:34: "Nec animadvertunt facilius esse restituere quòd collapsum est, quam quod non est, ex nihilo condere" (909C).

2 Cor. 4:17-18: "(quod genus sunt lucrum, honos, voluptas, vita, damnum, ignominia, cruciatus, mors)" (923A).

2 Cor. 5:16: "Frustra igitur gloriantur quidam, quod gentem habent cum Christo communem, quod illi sanguinis propinquitate juncti sunt, quod cum eo corporalem habuerint consuetudinem. Caro ad tempus exhibita est. Nunc sublato corpore, ac misso Spiritu, juxta spiritum vult agnosci, eumque sibi proximo gradu cognatum ducit, qui maxime fidit ipsius promissis. Nec est quod nos posteriores. Apostolos quisquam hoc nomine minoris faciat, quod Christum mortali corpore in terris versantem non novimus, quando etiam si contigisset novisse, nunc eam notitiam, quae obstabat spiritui, deposuissemus, et spiritualem factum, spiritualiter amaremus" (924F-25A).

2 Cor. 5:17: "Absint igitur illae voces hominum, hic Graecus est, hic Barbarus, hic Judaeus, hic modo cultor simulacrorum, hic sacrilegus. Desiit esse quod erat, et Christi opificio versus est in novam creaturam tam sui dissimilis, ut nulla bestia sit homini magis dissimilis" (925A-B).

2 Cor. 6:13: "quum hactenus paterna caritate vos sim complexus (non haec exprobro velut hostibus, sed ut apud filios carissimos commemoro) par est ut animi magnitudine patri respondeatis. Audete contemnere . . . frigidas Judaeorum ceremonias" (926D). (Earlier editions had only: "ut filiis loquor, animi magnitudine patri respondeatis.")

2 Cor. 12:9: "Etenim quum per homines humiles et imbelles adversus Satanam ac mundum omni saevitiae genere frementem perstat et efflorescit Evangelium, palam sit hoc negotium, non humanis praesidiis, sed virtute Numinis geri. Porro quo majoribus malis affligimur, hoc illustrior sit Dei gloria, per nos agentis exserentisque vim suam" (938D-E).

Phil. 2:17: "Vestro, quos ad Evangelium conversos gratissimam victimam obtulerim Christo; meo, qui peracto tali sacrificio, sim et ipse totus immolandus" (997D).

Phil. 2 : 30: "periclitanti, ut unus quodammodo vos omnes mihi referret" (998D).

Phil. 3 : 4–5: "quae semper juncta fuit tribui Judae, unde . . . Reges et Levitae" ((999C).

Col. 2 : 9: "Veritas palam exhibita est omnibus sensibus, non est quod jam typos, aut ambiguas pollicitationes spectetis" (1010A–B).

Col. 2 : 12: "Mortificatis enim affectibus sequitur altissima quies mentis" (1010D).

Col. 4 : 3 : "illo referante per fidem pectora hominum" (1014E).

1 Tim. 1 : 19: "Qui enim sincerum dici potest, quod mortuum est? Aut qui durabile est, quod vita spirituque vacat?" (1039B).

1 Tim. 2 : 2: "Per Ethnicos quoque magistratus Deus largitur nobis publicam tranquillitatem: per est igitur et pro his gratias agere, ac nobis incertum est an ille simulacrorum impius cultor, brevi sit amplexurus Evangelium. Omnium itaque salutem optat Christiana caritas" (1039F–40A).

1 Tim. 4 : 14: "non ambitus aut hominum favor, sed divinus Spiritus per ora Prophetarum significans Dei voluntatem" (1048E).

1 Tim. 5 : 4: "ut bis peccent quae non tantum Deo rebelles sunt, sed et ad communem naturae sensum obsurduerunt, quo commoventur etiam illi, qui Deum ignorant" (1049F).

1 Tim. 6 : 11: "et huius gratia proximum" (1055A–B).

Titus 1 : 8: "ac bonorum hominum amantem" (1069B).

Titus 3 : 9: "sed haec curiosa tantum. At quid prodest quaerere" (1074B).

42. The following outline and notes are based on all the traditional Pauline letters except Romans. For a detailed study of the content of the *Paraphrase of Romans*, see Rabil, chaps. 5–6. See also John Payne, "Erasmus: Interpreter of Romans," in Carl S. Meyer, ed., *Sixteenth Century Essays and Studies* (St. Louis, Mo.: Foundation for Reformation Research, 1971), 2 : 1–35.

43. "Cum Legem dico, crassam illam atque carnalem Mosaicae Legis partem intelligo, quam solam mordicus tenent Judaei. . . ." (*LB*, 7 : 961E). See also Titus 1 : 15, *LB*, 7 : 1070B–C.

44. See, for example, in *LB*, 7, Gal. 4 : 10 (957E); 5 : 3 (961C–D); Phil. 3 : 18 (1000F–01A); 1 Tim. 1 : 5 (1036E–F); 4 : 3 (1047B–C).

45. *LB*, 7 : 1000F–01A). See also 1 Cor. 3 : 12 (868A); 1 Thess. 2 : 6 (1019E–F); 2 : 8 (1020A).

46. "Aut plane Judaei sitis oportet, abdicato Christo: aut plane Christiani sitis oportet, rejecto Judaismo" (*LB*, 7 : 961B).

47. "Etenim quemadmodum in uno homine corpus est crassum ac grave, animus coelestis et immortalis, utque in eadem Lege crassum quiddam est, quam dicimus litteram, atque e diverso coeleste quiddam, quod spiritum appellamus" (*LB*, 7 : 964A). The passage quoted was added to the original paraphrase in 1521.

48. *LB*, 7, 1 Cor. 11 : 16 (896B) [passage added, 1524] .

49. Ibid., 1 Cor. 15 : 56 (911D).

50. On the contrast between Moses and Christ, see in *LB*, 7, 2 Cor. 3 : 6 (919F–20A); Gal. 1 : 4 (945A); 2 : 16 (950D); Eph. 1 : 12 (974C); 2 : 10 (977B); 2 : 14 (977E); 2 : 21–22 (978D–E); Phil. 3 : 9 (999F); Col. 1 : 25–26 (1008C–D); 2 : 11 (1010B–D); 1 Thess. 2 : 12 (1030A); 1 Tim. 3 : 15 (1046B); Titus 1 : 1 (1067A–B).

51. See, for example, in *LB*, 7, 1 Cor. 6 : 19 (877F–78A); 12 : 13 (899A–B); Gal. 5 : 3 (961C); 5 : 24 (964D); 6 : 14 (966E–F); Eph. 2 : 1-2 (975F–76B); 2 : 10 (977A); 4 : 22-24 (983D); Col. 2 : 12 (1010D).

52. 1 Cor. 6 : 9-10: (*LB*, 7, 876C). See also 1 Cor. 10 : 12 (892D); Gal. 5 : 21 (964C).

53. See, for example, in *LB*, 7, 1 Cor. 1 : 30 (863F–64A); 10 : 21 (893C–D); Gal. 1 : 2 (944F); 3 : 11 (953E); 3 : 13 (953F); Eph. 1 : 1 (972E–F); Eph. 1 : 2 (972F–73A); 2 : 1-2 (975F–76B).

54. 1 Cor. 2 : 6, *LB*, 7, 864E: "Ergo curate ut perfecti sitis, . . ."

55. 1 Cor. 12:31, *LB,* 7, 900D: "Dona sunt Spiritus, ne quid nobis hinc arrogemus, sed is ad dandum et quod dedit tuendum augendumque nostro conatu nostrisque precibus solet evocari" (emphasis added in translation).

56. Phil. 2:8, *LB,* 7:996D: "At Christianus, qui veram et aeternam gloriam quaerit, hac via debet ad illam contendere, qua Christus ingressus est. Per falsam ignominiam iter est ad veram gloriam, per momentaria dispendia aditus est ad immortalia compendia. Gloriam captare non oportet, sed promereri."

57. "Quod afflictionibus tunderis, simul et ad meam gloriam illustrandam pertinent, dum meo praesidio tutus vinci non potes, quantislibet procellis" (*LB,* 7:938D). See also 1 Tim. 1:2 (1035A–B); 2:3 (1040F–41A); 2 Tim. 2:10 (1061A); 2:11 (1061A–B).

58. "Ego Christum vobis scopum proposui, si quis hujus exemplo doceat, innocenter vivendum, bene merendum et de inimicis, non fiedendum opibus, adspernandos honores, voluptates foedas ut pestem exsecrandas, omnia ad Christi referre gloriam, praeter immortalitatem nullum sperare praemium recte factorum, mortem etiam optandam, si pro Christo sit obeunda, is structuram addit Christo fundamento dignam." (*LB,* 7:868A). See also Col. 3:15 (1013D): "What the Christian should exemplify is peace and concord, the cessation of pride, wrath, and contention."

59. Titus 2:7, *LB,* 7:1071B: "Neque enim quisquam facilius persuadet, quam qui constanter id facit, quod faciendum esse docet."

60. *LB,* 7:1002C. See Col. 4:5 (1015A–B).

61. *LB,* 7, 1 Cor. 2:10–12 (865C–E).

62. *LB,* 7, Titus 3:9 (1074B).

63. 2 Cor. 4:17–18, *LB,* 7:923A–B: "Nam quae hic cernuntur, praeterquam quod nec vera sunt bona, nec vera sunt mala (quod genus sunt lucrum, honos, voluptas, vita, damnum, ignominia, cruciatus, mors) ne diuturna quidem sunt, cum ea quae cernuntur oculis fidei, sint ut vera, ita et aeterna" (passage in parentheses added in 1524).

8 As Bones to the Body: The Scope of *Inventio* in the *Colloquies* of Erasmus.

SISTER M. GERALDINE THOMPSON, C.S.J.

Everyone, Erasmus says, rhymes off the five duties incumbent on the orator or writer—and then proceeds to rhyme them off himself: *inventio, dispositio, elocutio, memoria, pronunciatio.* In a sentence or so for each, he also defines their proper functions and significance. About *inventio* he says that it supplies the matter for the speech (or, in Erasmus's context, the sermon or homily); but more—it embraces also both the disposition or ordering of the matter and the style. And it is to the work what bones are to the living body; unless they are firm, all else will collapse.[1]

To make my own *dispositio* fitting, then, for this survey of Erasmus's invention in the *Colloquies,* I propose to rely largely on Erasmus's paragraph, and order what I have to say under two headings: (1) *inventio* in its primary function: the selection of certain themes around which to make the colloquies revolve and the rejection of others; and (2) *inventio* as determining the form of what is to be written, the ordering of the parts, and even in some measure establishing the broad lines of style.

I

I once listened to a drawing master instructing a group of students engaged in sketching what was then called "still life." "See the shape of what is there," he said, "yes, of course; but see too the shape of what is not there—of the spaces between the gloves and the guitar, between the guitar and the shoe-polish. The shape of what is not there will help you see the shape of what is."

The analogy is less than perfect, of course, but it has its points. On a cursory reading of the *Colloquies* one's first thought is surely that they canvas every virtue and every vice. But this is not so. Many aspects of human life find no place in the *Colloquies,* though in this great "field of folk" there are garrulous fellows who seem to have heard all the gossip that is going and who are eager to regale their cronies with it.

Some thirty of the fifty-four colloquies are about wrong-doing or wrong-thinking. But the greatest of all sins, pride, is never shown in its overwhelming abundance, though there is plenty of vanity about. The abbot, for instance, is vain; and in *The Godly Feast* we have a momentary and generalized glance at a tyrant-king exultant in his power, but he is not real. What we miss is that species of pride that cares nothing for praise or popularity, for it has moved far beyond such caring. And so we have to conclude that Milton's Satan has no counterpart in the dialogues, that men live and die in the Erasmian neighborhoods, and sometimes very foolishly, but not as Marlowe's Faustus died, or Golding's builder-monk, or even Eliot's Becket, who came to the very edge of such fearful thinking. We also miss despair, that final sin that doubts the mercy of God. It was surely a part of Spenser's *inventio* not many years later, when he called into being his Cave of Despair and allowed round after round of tortured thinking to drive a wretched knight to suicide; but Erasmus does not let his reader enter into such thoughts. And a third absence: although one colloquy tells of a great shipwreck, the ship's complement does not include any Lord Jim who will wear out the rest of his life reliving that moment of infinite dimension that proffered no middle way between heroism and cowardice.

Among the virtues extolled in the colloquies there are fewer lacunae. The four moral virtues are certainly there, and the three theological; the seven corporal works of mercy and the eight beatitudes in some measure, and of course, the Ten Commandments. But, although the virtues themselves are presented, perhaps one might say that their interaction does not much interest the Erasmian townsfolk. Faith, for instance, is certainly presented often enough and sometimes is operative by its very absence,[2] but the relation of faith to good works, a hot topic in these early 1520s surely, and one that was to engage Erasmus mightily in the end, is hardly mentioned, though the percipient reader may indeed note that Eusebius of *The Godly Feast,* himself the very heart of faith, does leave his own dinner party early to go on an errand of mercy.[3] Again, chastity is presented, sometimes positively and sometimes negatively, and Erasmus lets his reader see it against its opposite, promiscuity; but never does he show it, as Shakespeare does, balanced measure for measure against charity as the human predicament works itself out. And in some places Truth is presented in all its unalloyed splendor, and kindness is extolled in others; but that nice sensitivity that tempers or withholds a true but unpalatable fact in the interests of charity is beyond the scope of the colloquies, though Erasmus's *Moria* had known all about it and had tossed off some wry observations on the subject.[4]

These absentee themes, with their provocative shapes, fall, it seems to me, into two classes: there are the dread moments of temptation and sin or of racking decisions, and there are some precise distinctions between what is right and what is only half right. And it is the consideration of these crusts of life omitted in the *Colloquies* which brings us right into the heart of the *inventio* or *res* of the writing. It lies in the author's purpose.

The effect of Erasmus's tremendous moral purpose on his fictional writing is something I have already hounded to death elsewhere,[5] and I hesitate to disinter an old ghost. But a writer's *habitus* of mind is surely the determinant of his creative imagination, constantly ordering his fancy to its own ends. It is unlikely that Erasmus ever forgot that the double thrust of all creative writing is toward the *prodesse* and *delectare* of Horace's counsel,[6] but with him the first term would take precedence over the second. The very delightfulness of the colloquies, for instance, he calls a "bait"—something devised to màke the reader receptive to the message given, the lesson taught. So it is as educator and moralist that we have to see the author of the book.

It is a book for boys. Not for the canonists of Paris these silhouettes of adult life, not for Martin Dorp or even Thomas More. Erasmus speaks of writing them to "allure the young" through pleasant places into a "zeal to the refinement of Latin speech and to godliness . . . [and] a taste for excellence."[7] Surely, he would reason, a certain surefootedness among the basic virtues and vices should be acquired by the boy before he is asked to contemplate the finer distinctions or even the agonies of great temptation. And surely too, he would argue, the ability to reason and judge is impaired, perhaps even paralyzed, in the fume and fret of passionate pride or wasting despair. Erasmus must have wanted his young readers to see life steadily before they had to see it whole, and to see it with emotional freedom.

As educational pieces the *Colloquies* are much in line with his ideas of education expressed in his tracts and treatises,[8] for they provide vicarious experience; and if this is not *exercitatio*, it is at least a good surrogate for it. This is the third term in Erasmus's triad of terms for what constitutes man's attainment of "felicity." He is born with the first—the *natura* that is in some measure bent toward "honest things," wisdom and goodness; and this is not just the perquisite of the specially endowed, but the dower of all normal men, who differ from birds and butterflies in this very potential or tendency.[10] *Ratio*, the second term, is related to the actual provision of precepts by the teacher. Sometimes Erasmus uses it to mean the teaching or the things taught, or the process by which the mind takes unto itself new being; but usually it is the mind itself with its potential realized so that it is able to reason and make judgments and choices.[11] And the *Colloquies* often devolve into a direct bit of teaching,[12] as well as being, as they always are, proxied experience. Until this experience or drill is brought to bear on the child's mind, the educating process is not complete, Erasmus would say, for what is known with advertence and deliberation must be made habit.[13] If *exercitatio* is to be applied to the knowledge of verb forms or long division it is, one supposes, in the form of drill and more drill; but if—and it is here that Erasmus's greatest interest lies—the precept concerns the promotion of sound moral attitudes and an ability to meet the circumstances and situations of life with common sense and integrity, the *exercitatio* is less easily provided, for one cannot maneuver life into fittingly moral situations. Thus the colloquies. A boon to the educator.

The follies Erasmus proffers are chiefly, therefore, the follies that an ordinary man adopts or sees others adopting every day. True, there are great cosmic vices of which his people are aware, and his wise men mourn for the sins of Christendom. But the world is just a lot of men and the sins of the world are written in minuscule in the individual lives of Tom, Dick, and Harry—or of Antony, Lucretia, and Pampirus. Eutrapelus lists the sins of the great as he lectures the new mother:

> King Christian of Denmark . . . is in exile. Francis, King of France, is a 'guest' of the Spaniards. . . . Charles is preparing to extend the boundaries of his realm. Ferdinand has his hands full in Germany. Bankruptcy threatens every court. The peasants raise dangerous riots and are not swayed from their purpose, despite so many massacres. The commons are bent on anarchy; the Church is shaken to its very foundations by menacing factions; on every side the seamless coat of Jesus is torn to shreds. The vineyard of the Lord is now laid waste not by a single boar but at one and the same time the authority of priests (together with their tithes), the dignity of theologians, the splendour of monks is imperilled; confession totters; vows reel; pontifical ordinances crumble; the Eucharist is called in question. . . . [260]

Greed, extravagance, irresponsibility, ungodly materialism: they are the perquisites of the nations and the nations' rulers; but the small folk know them too. If Charles is greedy for land, young clerics are greedy for the best livings; if kings are vain, so is the abbot who talks to the learned woman; royal self-indulgence may impoverish courts, but Arnold and Cornelius, who have been rollicking off on a pilgrimage, reflect in retrospect that the pilgrim may also be self-indulgent and irresponsible; and of course the old men who chat in the stage coach provide a scaling for degrees of pleasure-seeking and idleness. As for war, men supposedly committed to the things of God propagate it in one colloquy (*Charon*), and in another (*The Funeral*) banish peace from the last hours of a dying man. War is, of course, the chief object of the scorching satire in the long colloquy *Julius Secundus Exclusus.*

Of the various follies that surface again and again in the *Colloquies*, many can be seen as particular expressions of two fundamental character flaws, superstition and hypocrisy. The first, it will be noticed, differs from the second in that it is folly rather than vice and is symptomatic of wrong thinking rather than bad will. And it is with the sins of the intellect that Erasmus is usually concerned.

After all, these are the faults that respond to good teaching: the man who can be taught to think through a projected action to its true essence *may* be amenable to the right reason shown him. Not so the one whose wrong-doing is deliberate and knowing.

Superstition (in the *Colloquies*) shows itself, for instance, in the two pilgrimage colloquies: these expeditions are sometimes irresponsible, sometimes the result of rash promises, and usually accompanied by other spurious devotions—to certain places, things, times, words. The absurd prayers and promises the shipwrecked crew shout to the lord of the storm in another colloquy are of the same nature; and the dying man dressed in Franciscan garb in an effort to beguile the Almighty into thinking him a devout and mortified son of Saint Francis provides further illustration. And there are others.

In all of this we see God and the things of God shrunk to human dimensions—and of the worst kind: heaven is sold for bargain prices, not to the one who loves his God with all his heart and mind, nor even to one who, like Ben Adam, loves well his fellow men, but to the one who knows the right words. And it is not true holiness, but magic, Erasmus would say, that lies in certain formulated words, in places, in things, in rituals.

In another sense one might see in this the confounding of signs and things. And, familiar as he was with the Augustinian distinctions, Erasmus must have been very conscious of the ways in which a thing can be a sign[14] and, less happily, of the way in which a sign can lose its representational quality and cease to be a sign, arrogating to itself a spurious thingness.[15]

It is to be remembered that, in the examples Saint Augustine gives of real things having sign value, the realness, the thing *as thing,* is prior to the expanded essence, the sign quality. Thus, he speaks of the tree of Mambra as being a tree first, then the sign of vision. And Erasmus, writing in his later years, and outside of the fictional frame, follows this pattern: the calf killed by Abraham for his guests, he says, was just a calf sacrificed to provide food for an honored guest, but then, and only then, it is seen as a sign—the sign of the supreme deserts of God and of Abraham's recognition of this (*LB,* 5, 1036D–F).

In the *Colloquies* the superstitious signs (for they *are* signs and, rightly ordered, might have been godly and good) have long since parted from their original significance and have become a kind of negotiable currency in themselves, an inflation of sorts. Such, for instance, is the religious habit in which poor George is dressed up to die. The first Franciscan had clothed himself as simply and poorly as he could in clothing that would have fulfilled Erasmus's own prescriptions for the function of dress:[16] it protected him from cold, safeguarded decency, and, later on, marked him as one of a special group. That third function made of the thing (the dress) a sign, of course; but isolated from the commitment that originally gave it significance, it is neither a true sign nor a true thing: it is masquerade, sham.

The promised candle is another no-thing, for it neither lights up a dark place, as a candle should, nor symbolizes the light of faith, as an emblem should, since the panicky fellow promising it (in *The Shipwreck*) has lost sight of both meanings. And there are many other examples of lost significance in the *Colloquies*. Relics, formula-prayers, ritual, ceremony, even the sacraments— Erasmus can distrust them all, or at least can be apprehensive of them, unless they are allied to the sincerely good and Christian life. Too easily they may become easy substitutes for good living and the love of God.

Hypocrisy, the other moral preoccupation, although it is less of the intellect than of the will, and so is unlike the follies of superstition, is not unrelated to the sign-thing confusion. For the hypocrite also uses things—words, postures, clothing—as signs that bespeak some desirable quality, some worth or wealth or knowledge, that he does not have. All satirists love to pillory the hypocrite, and Erasmus is no exception. Hypocrisy is always the concomitant of some other character flaw and so is double-edged. Thus, for instance, the abbot who entertains the learned lady, even if he were not wearing the dress of, and pretending to be, a humble monk or man of God, would be less than admirable by reason of his discourtesy and vanity. And the deceitful exterior makes the other two faults more odious. But the abbot is not like the pilgrims or the bargaining folk in the boat: he *has* awareness, and is less likely, one thinks, to benefit from Erasmus's good teaching. There are plenty of hypocrites in the *Colloquies*: young clergymen who pretend to zeal for the salvation of souls, especially souls in a rich parish, preachers who "instil into the ears of princes a love of war, who proclaim in their evangelical sermons that war is just, holy and right." Polyphemus, who carries a New Testament around with him and is a bit of a hypocrite himself, says "Hypocrisy is for monks"; and it seems to be fairly true according to Erasmus's way of thinking. The monk or priest or nun is a tempting target for the satiric pen, since he or she bears the exterior marks of religious purpose, and any shortcoming of that person readily takes on the added iniquity of deception.

Counseling the young bride or young mother, in the *Christiani Matrimonii*, Erasmus says:

> What you pour into these susceptible minds is of the greatest importance, for nothing sticks better throughout the whole of life than what in these early years is drunk in . . .
>
> [*LB*, 5, 713B]

and he goes on to quote Horace's couplet:

> Once steeped when new, the jar
> Its fragrance long will keep.[17]

Into the presentation of the varied facets of sixteenth-century life, then, Erasmus would put all the energy of his prolific invention. All the examples are not of foolish thinking and unseemly behavior: much that is admirable in man is shown too. Men of faith, reasonable, sincere, and well-intentioned men, mingle with the foolish ones in these pages and are shown in actions that are earnest of their good will and Christian attitude: Eusebius, for instance, who gathers his friends together to dine with him and points out to them God's constant and loving instruction of man through the prodigalities of nature; Eutrapelus, who visits the young Fabulla and gently scolds her for her adherence to custom; and Reuchlin, the Hebraist, who knew his scholarly work was not at all injurious to Christian faith and so pursued his studies in the face of censure. And many others.

II

One of Erasmus's most revered models, Quintilian, cites Cicero as authority for saying that the *dispositio*, like the subject matter, is embraced by the *inventio*. Erasmus, as we have seen, thinks so too. But I am not so sure that he would agree with a later dictum of Quintilian's that eloquence surely belongs to the orator, but that invention and arrangement are within the reach of any man of good sense.[18] Erasmus perhaps would not consider the distribution of parts and the ordering of their progression within the competence of any but the ablest writers. The *dispositio*, he says, not only makes the speech fittingly elegant and pleasing to the ear, but even helps the receptivity of the listener and the memory of the speaker; for, "when a thing is said in a suitable way, it is easier to comprehend it, and so easier to remember it." Erasmus would put all the dialogue that narrates or bespeaks the attitudes he has chosen to elucidate into the best possible order, for only thus will they persuade the reader and have the being they are meant to have.

One might enumerate perhaps some twenty or thirty ways in which Erasmus's *Colloquies* show his care in constructing them. Shall I count the ways? To avoid this embarrassment of riches I propose to deal with only two aspects of the "disposition," though, with luck and a bit of skulduggery, I hope some of the other aspects will also find therein a place, for I shall, of course, amplify as a good Erasmian should. First, I want to mention the dialogue form: it is a given, of course, in a book entitled *Colloquies*, but Erasmus's dialogues are of a special kind and their particularity merits a small consideration. Secondly, I want to look at the actual ordering or placing of the parts; true, within the gamut of fifty or more dialogues this arrangement is so various as to resist any firm presentation of a least-common-denominator. But one can always posit a careful positioning so that the early parts fulfil an exordium's function as the *captatio benevolentiae audientium,* then move away from surface brightness into serious argument, and finally recapture the light conversational touch, with, often enough, the triumphant prevailing of truth. And there is, almost always, sufficient reference to the life of grace to put Erasmus in the tradition of those who see the moral life as weighted with the promise of eternal happiness.

All Erasmus's fiction is either declamation or dialogue. The dialogue of the *Colloquies* is not so uniformly Socratic as one might think. Its subject matter is comparable to Socrates', concerned with thought and behavior, but in the Socratic dialogues the main speaker is sometimes countered by those holding other opinions and expressing them with some cogency, and truth emerges through a kind of ironic questioning. Only occasionally does Erasmus allow a second-best attitude to find place: he is too intent on driving home to his inexperienced and immature reader the unassailably right viewpoint to let it appear adulterated with counterclaims.[19] Thus purpose is seen dominating the arrangement even as it was seen to govern choice of subject matter.

Nor are the colloquies quite dramatic, though some of them—notably *The Well-to-do Beggars* and *The Shipwreck*—would require only a small injection of plot-line to make them so. This much of drama does find a place in most of the colloquies, however: they take their being in what we might call a "composition of place," and sometimes of time. We know, for instance, that Eutrapelus is visiting Fabulla at her home, that the beggars stand at the rectory door, then in the stove-room of the inn, and eventually in the dining room; we know that the old men meet at some sort of bus terminal and continue their talk in a chartered stagecoach; and we know Sophronius meets Lucretia in or near a brothel.

For the most part there is only one kind of plot and denouement: one man, wiser than his friend, convinces the other of some right way of thinking, or if both are possessed of right reason, they confirm each other in their rightness by proffering examples of it. Occasionally there is something more: the well-to-do beggars, for instance, do at least win through to a good meal; but actually Erasmus is not much interested in this victory; if he had been, the colloquy would surely have ended there. Quite the contrary: his real interest focuses on the table talk that ensues and the emerging ideas about monks and their clothes.

Far from wanting to engage the reader in dramatic situations, Erasmus seems to want to remove him from any active involvement in decision or choice. The ones who talk are either onlookers at other people's activity, or, if they speak of their own experience, it is well placed in the past and so remote from present involvement that it can be viewed dispassionately. Indeed, Erasmus's interest in the spectator had shown itself in his earliest fiction: a pertinent passage in *The Praise of Folly* brings the spectator to the reader's awareness (p. 38). Moria has been noting the anomalies in the castings for the play of life and in the parts some players had deliberately arrogated to themselves; and she envisions some wise man "from the sky" coming down and witnessing the incongruities. For a moment the reader takes on the mind of that percipient stranger, for it is his problem, not the maneuvering of the cast, that interests Moria. What should the wise man do about what he sees? Is it wiser to let the play play itself out, or should one interrupt—cry havoc and let loose the dogs of unrest and ill-will? Moria has no answer; but she does see that the stranger from some other world is the one who is emotionally free, not embroiled in the conflicts contingent on power play and vanity and greed. And in this person the reader, too, is able to judge with cool reason. The speakers in the colloquies have not the sky-man's power to change the casting or sequences of the play, but they are like him in his nonparticipation, and through empathy with him, the reader may build up in himself a resolute attitude toward the anomalies he sees about him.

Thus, in the *Colloquies* we do not enter directly, for instance, into the dying man's last moments; we listen to someone who has witnessed them—they are two removes from us. So, too, with the hurly-burly of the storm: for Adolph it is now just a memory. We do live through the rejection of the two Franciscans at the parish house, but the real business of that colloquy begins only when the two are restored to tranquillity and are happily sharing supper and opinions with the innkeeper and his wife; Sophronius is already converted when we meet him, and Lucretia is encountered in a moment of quiet; the old men no longer feel the temptations of youth; and the Echo has no human feelings at all.

Too plotless to be dramatic and too one-sided to be Socratic, the colloquies look more to Lucian as model than to any other. That Erasmus and his friend Thomas More had spent some youthful hours translating and imitating Lucian is a well-known fact. And in the colloquies Erasmus actually recasts some of the Lucian situations.[20] If Erasmus had been a first-century pagan or Lucian a Christian in the sixteenth, the colloquies would have been very similar indeed to Lucian's Dialogues. But the Lucianic influence has been amply detailed by C. R. Thompson and needs no further articulation.[21]

For the actual *dispositio* or ordering of parts, I should like to take a cue from Erasmus himself and make use of an *exemplum*. One could choose a colloquy almost at random and never fail to find illustration of Erasmus's care and competence in his distribution of parts. I should like to look at *The Young Man and the Harlot*, a colloquy whose sensational title belies its content. In it a young man, once a prodigal son but now having returned to his father's house, revisits the haunts of his unregenerate days to seek out one of the old crowd, one whom he must think worth reclaiming and ready for his counseling. I think this collo-quy is more concerned with the power of persuasion than it is with Lucretia's sins, for the author shows us the young man's persuasive talk *actually working* and effectively bringing about a change—and this in the most unfavorable cir-cumstances and where the folly is one that is least amenable to reason. It was right that he should make the spokesman for rectified reason belong to a former habitué of the place because, first, only as such could he have persuaded the girl to listen at all, and second, he has the voice of both experience and reason: *ratio* and *exercitatio* join in the effort to persuade this girl, and incidentally whatever readers happen to overhear.

The opening lines are lively, and one is reminded of what Erasmus tells the young preacher about his initial attack: let it be less formal than the exordium of a piece of oratory, retaining, however, something of the *captatio benevo-lentiae,* so that it will "do the good offices of the exordium and produce atten-tion, docility and good will" in the listener (*Ecclesiastes, LB,* 5, 862C). Here the young readers must have chuckled over Sophronius's rather awkward attempts to convince Lucretia of his new role; he is affectionate but less warm, one suspects, than heretofore; and Lucretia uses the easy familiarity and the honeyed words of her profession.[22]

Even within these twenty or thirty lines of near-stichomythia, Erasmus is preparing the reader for the longer, soberer speeches of the middle part. From the beginning both speakers are aware of the omnipresent God. When So-phronius begins to warm to his subject, Lucretia's interruptions become gradu-ally less frequent, so that there is no definable place where the sparring gives way to Sophronius's persuasion. One cannot but notice, too (and record it at the risk of being pedantic), that Erasmus, consciously or unconsciously, has his young man use Quintilian's four modes of amplifying an argument.[23] He starts with simple reasoning (*ratiocinatio*): Lucretia's way of life cannot bring happi-ness, for it grieves her friends, alienates her family, pleases her enemies; she cannot make friends in such a calling, and her clients will abandon her when her beauty fades, as fade it will, hastened by the excesses of her life; she must, then, be pursuing this calling only for money, but money is available from other sources and so she has no reason at all to cling to such a life.

As the arguments fall relentlessly like hammer blows on the girl's untenable convictions, we see them as forming a *congeries;* and at least once the congeries takes on a cumulative effect that might be called *incrementum.*

> You used to think obeying your mother burdensome; now you're at the
> beck and call of an utterly repulsive bawd. You were fed up with parental

reproofs, here you must often endure beatings by drunken, maddened whoremongers. To do some of the housework at home in return for bed and board, disgusted you; here what commotions, what late hours you put up with! [p. 156]

That same paragraph shows, too, that Sophronius knows how to incorporate some *comparatio* into his exhortation. But his creator lets the reader see another kind of comparison. It hovers about the imagery of money. For what greater contrast could there be than that between the woman who sells herself for money, and the one who surrenders for love alone?

The only dramatic movement in this colloquy is the action in the mind of Lucretia. Her turning toward new attitudes Erasmus records in carefully graded responses to Sophronius. There is first the scornful "Save your sermon for another occasion," then some small concessions: "It was my fate"; "almost everything you say is true, but . . ."; "then where am I to go?" and then the final capitulation, "Well, Sophronius, I trust myself entirely to you.

One or two digressions break the sweep of the argument and must have made it still more palatable for boys. One of them is the amusing self-reference: Sophronius has taken Erasmus's New Testament to Rome with him, a preservative. And one is a carefully placed and purposeful incidental: Lucretia gives alms to mendicants, but it seems they are also her clients, and so she gets back what she gives. This side-swiping at clerics and monks is one of Erasmus's *idées fixes*, almost an obsession; and readers must take it with a grain of salt. But here the function is, I think, to establish a neighborhood for vice and show it as widespread and prolific in generating further vice. There is hardly a colloquy in which we cannot spot this self-fertilization: here Lucretia shows profligacy and dishonesty growing together and given a boost through their germination under the religious dress; other colloquies show warmongering united to hypocrisy (*Charon*), vanity dragging along behind illiteracy (*The Abbot and the Learned Lady*), quack science joined to greed and lust (*The Alchemist*), the polygamist (in the *Old Men's Chat*) is also a gambler and cheat, and Pamphagus, who hunts a benefice, is also improvident and irresponsible. This device shows the reader, one supposes, that follies, like troubles, come not as single spies but in companies.

Similar to this strategy is the Erasmian way of presenting vice in unlovely settings and virtue in the sweetness of garden and rural delightfulness. The inhospitable pastor, for instance, in the *Beggars* is full of animal talk—wolves, dogs, apes—while Pamphilus, pleading his case (for a chaste marriage) to Maria must be surrounded with the elements of his imagery; fragrant roses, grapes, vines, elm trees; and the garden in which Eusebius entertains his godly friends is celebrated as a typical *locus amoenus*. In *The Young Man and the Harlot*, the actual setting does not seem to be redolent of either sweetness or foulness, but the same effect is achieved—a kind of "landscape of the mind"—in the imagery Sophronius uses about Lucretia's life: "dirty, vile, diseased . . . filth a sewer . . . dung heap."

The long speeches become shorter as the colloquy draws to a close: the young man is winning both his point and Lucretia, and he make plans for her immediate removal from this district; the interchange of question and response is again in quick alternation. But this is the only attempt to round off the pattern of the dialogue. In some of the colloquies there is a more conscious effort to bring unity and finish to the rise and fall of action: the *Well-to-do Beggars,* for instance, begins with the pastor's fear that the beggars will want to preach in his church, and ends with the innkeeper's eager anticipation of their possible sermon; and the *Old Men's Chat* begins with the old men disparaging the idle hired coachmen and ends with the coachmen disparaging the old men. But Erasmus himself would not, I think, be dissatisfied with the movement or pattern of the *Young Man* . . . ; its conclusion shows a thumping victory for the power of the spoken word, the persuasive word, and the conversion of Lucretia to sounder thinking would be dramatic dénouement enough.

The colloquies, we have seen, fulfil a function as *exercitatio.* In many instances they also contribute to the advancement of the *ratio* by precept as well, for the counsels of the right-thinking speaker are given not only to the fictional listener but to the real one too. All through the central part of this colloquy Sophronius is teaching Lucretia, feeding her the precepts that should promote good behavior. And this is good. But I should like to say again that the important lesson does not come by precept in this colloquy but by vicarious experience: the reader experiences (aesthetically) the power of the word. One man, with the right word, and with good will and energy, has persuaded a foolish girl into wanting the good life; and if one—maybe many.

Erasmus will not tie his Sophronius, however, to human logic. All the Erasmian people, however foolish or bad, are still in some measure dwellers in the City of God and retain some modicum of belief in an afterlife. At least minimally, their behavior is cognizant of faith and charity (which are beyond reason), and of hope (which sublimates reason in a way, for who, Erasmus would say, would barter eternal life for transitory pleasure?). The young man's talk begins in human logic, as we saw: vice brings its own punishment, the loss of friends, of love, even of outward beauty, for "the bloom of beauty . . . will soon fade," the more speedily as a result of the excesses.

But even in Sophronius's human logic Lucretia divines some "holiness," and he takes heart from this and moves into the explicitly religious. He has been on pilgrimage—some pilgrimages, we now see, are admissible, especially when the pilgrim is armed with Erasmus's translation of the New Testament—and his own change of heart is somehow bound up with those moments of faith and charity. In this colloquy, more than in most, this love of God does come through to the reader. And this is as close to the anagogical reading as Erasmus usually comes.[24] The soul's response to the love of God is not, with him, something to trust to the reader's ability to find arcane meanings in the seemingly mundane. The idea of man's pursuit of divine love here or hereafter is introduced, not allegorically, but as part of the literal level, after or together with the moral message. That moral lesson, for the Christian, is, Erasmus would say, anchored in the life of grace—and is incomplete otherwise. This is something he teaches in all his educational works.

Yet, in this colloquy there is a hint of something not quite allegory, not quite anagogy, but cognate to them.[25] One might call it an enlargement of theme and character. Sophronius is certainly the word, the good, human, regenerative word. One wants to ask, then: is he also the incarnate Word, the *Logos?* At first the analogy seems blasphemous, for Sophronius has once been a sinner like Lucretia and can hardly be proxy to the sinless Christ. But perhaps he can. For Christ did take on, in some mysterious or metaphorical way, man's burden of sin in order to pay his ransom, to *be* his ransom. And certainly Sophronius does pursue his lost sheep with Christ-like persistence, with love, and what is more, with power—even to having the wherewithal to care for the girl during the time of her readjustment.

In any case, whether or not Erasmus intends the reader to take such a meaning, there is little doubt that he is saying something about the self-perpetuating quality in repentance. It was a kindly priest's rueful recollection of his own sinful past that confirmed Sophronius in his high resolves, and Sophronius, thus converted, who used the same kindly persuasion on Lucretia. And behind Sophronius too, of course, or under his arm, is the regenerative word of Erasmus intermediating between the Word of God and the word of God.[26] Thus, if the characters and actions are not quite symbolic, it might be safely said (and not just about this colloquy but about others too) that they are highly expansible—a vice or virtue narrowed into the particular individual who bespeaks it, but then, within the individual, enlarging itself so that it has universal dimension.

When Richard DeMolen was seeking for some approach to the *Colloquies* suitable to this book, the idea of the "meaning of the colloquies" was suggested and approved. I have tried to keep this in mind as I wrote; and if I have not quite succeeded, I should at least like to say this: the colloquies are really all about meaning, because meaning is what preoccupies the author of them. The meaning of life, the meaning of signs, the meaning of words, the meaning of holiness, the meaning of the Church, of redemption, of wisdom—he would like to awaken his readers to thinking about meaning and being less concerned with unthinking action, action that pays tribute to a sign that is no longer a sign of anything and to custom which has wrenched itself away from the first cause of the accepted form or custom. The whole of *The Godly Feast* is about meaning—the meaning of the frescoes, the natural beauty of the house and garden, the scriptural passages, and even the meaning of art. The more biting colloquies are almost all concerned with the sickening loss of meaning: holiday trips that are meant to be holy, fasting that is just a stunt, candles that illuminate nothing, dress that clothes the hollow men. The whole gamut of satire is geared to the failure of significance. And the meaning of the colloquies *is* meaning.

And since purpose is everything to Erasmus, the *inventio* sees clearly the kind of virtues and iniquities and follies it wants to present, and sees, too, that they must be presented simply and clearly with singleness of purpose, as befits the reading of young students and always bearing in mind that the writer, the fictional figures, and the readers who will be entertained with the bait are all children of two worlds: a fallen Christendom and a world of divine grace and presence.

NOTES

1. *Nunc per Oratoria singula officia decurremus, sed ita ut memineris nos non Patronum forensem, sed Divini verbi praeconem instruere. Sunt autem ab omnibus decantata: inventio, dispositio, elocutio, memoria, ac pronunciatio. Inventio, quae res suppeditat, tametsi re vera complectitur et elocutionem et ordinem, hoc est in oratione, quod ossa in corpore animantis, quae nisi solida sint, caetera omnia collabuntur.* Erasmus *Opera Omnia* (Leiden, 1703–06), 5:861F (*Ecclesiastes, sive De ratione Concionandi*). Subsequent references will be to this edition unless otherwise stated, and will be designated as *LB* followed by volume and column numbers. Erasmus, it might be noted, is not alone in his conviction. A reference to Cato in the *Ars Rhetorica* of Julius Victor speaks of ". . . Catonis praeceptum paene divinum qui ait: rem tene, verba sequentur." See Carl F. von Halm, *Rhetores Latini Minores* (Leipzig, 1863), p. 374.

2. It is faith that is wanting in the two pilgrimage colloquies, for instance, and in the two accounts of funerals.

3. *The Colloquies of Erasmus,* trans. Craig R. Thompson (Chicago, 1965), p. 78. Subsequent references to the colloquies will be to this edition, and the page number bracketed into the text.

4. *Moriae encomium declamatio* (1509), trans. H. H. Hudson as *The Praise of Folly,* Princeton, N.J., 1941, 1947, and New York, 1967, pp. 35–36 and 18.

5. *Under Pretext of Praise* (Toronto: University of Toronto Press, 1973), pp. 29–50.

6. The *prodesse* would include, of course, both intellectual and moral inprovement. But many texts could be adduced to show that Erasmus thought the two so tightly inclusive of each other as to be hardly separable. His use, for instance, of the term *honestae res* as the true end of man's striving catches up both truth and goodness; and virtue is incomplete, he says, if man is unknowing. See *LB*, 1:491E and 496F; and 10:1723D; This is the burden, too, of most of the *Antibarbari*.

7. From *The Usefulness of Colloquies,* Erasmus's apologia for the colloquies (*Colloquies,* ed. Thompson, p. 625). Even the later editions show Erasmus still mindful of the youthful reader. The 1524 edition carried a dedicatory letter to his godson, Erasmius Froben, a boy at that time about eight; and still later, in the 1529 edition, the inclusion of the colloquy *The Art of Learning,* with its semifictional Erasmius as interlocutor, bespeaks renewed awareness of the boy as reader, though, of course, there is much for the adult mind too. (See ibid., pp. 459–61).

8. Especially *De Pueris Instituendis, LB,* 1:496D–497B, and *Christiani Matrimonii Institutio, LB,* 5:710C–E and passim.

9. Quintilian, whose ideas Erasmus greatly reveres, puts more weight on the *natura* and differences in natural ability than does Erasmus. See *Institutio Oratoria,* vol. 1, proem, p. 26. This perhaps makes Erasmus's emphases more deliberative and significant. Erasmus grants that there are poorly endowed children, but somehow—educatio superat omnia (*LB,* 5:710C)!

10. *LB,* 1:496D–E: "Quemadmodum autem canis nascitur ad venatum, avis ad volatum . . . ita homo nascitur ad philosophiam et honestas actiones." See too, *LB,* 1:491E.

11. "Ratio praeceptis judicat quid expetendum, quid fugiendum." *LB,* 5:710D; and compare with *LB,* 1:497A.

12. As, for instance, when Eutrapelus, urging Fabulla to nurse her own child, simply delivers to her a simplified version of what Erasmus had written on that subject in the first pages of the marriage tract; and Conrad teaches the innkeeper directly; Sophronius, the harlot; and the butcher, the fish merchant.

13. "Usus ducit in habitum id quod praescriptum est." *LB,* 5:710D.

14. Augustine's *De Doctrina Christiana,* Book 3, sect. 4, no. 29 and following, would have been well known to Erasmus. He himself speaks of signs and things, though less explicitly than Saint Augustine, in his tract on homiletics, *LB,* 1:521A–B, and in *The Godly Feast* (*Colloquies,* ed. Thompson, pp. 51–54, 58, 59).

15. One of the simplest examples that comes to my mind of a sign's proneness to lose significance and become only "thing" is the "emblem" of the Sacred Heart. It represents, of course, the human love of Christ for men and, as such, is the object of admirable devotion. Some years ago Catholic bishops became aware that the heart, pictured so often in a disembodied form, had come to mean, for some, simply the honoring of the physical organ—a thing isolated from its original sign-value; and at the hierarchical behest, pastors cautioned their congregations against what was thus becoming an abuse.

16. See *The Well-to-do Beggars,* in which Conrad gives the three functions of dress listed above. In *The Soldier and the Carthusian,* the monk gives only two uses, though the third is later implied (*Colloquies,* ed. Thompson, pp. 210 and 130 respectively).

17. Horace *Epistles* 1.2.67–68. The translation is by Thompson. The lines appear in *The New Mother:* they are spoken by Eutrapelus to Fabulla (See *Colloquies,* ed. Thompson, p. 273).

18. *Institutio Oratoria,* vol. 8, proem, p. 14. Cicero is again cited.

19. Notable exceptions include *The Godly Feast,* where slightly different interpretations of scriptural passages are given equal consideration; *A Fish Diet,* where the respective merits of fishmongering and butchering are both entertained; and, in *The Old Men's Chat,* Eusebius makes a fair case for accepting a benefice, though Erasmus usually scorns this.

20. *Charon,* for instance, and *The Imposture,* and *Pseudocheus and Philetymus.*

21. C. R. Thompson, *Translations of Lucian by Erasmus and More* (Ithaca, 1958); his editorial comment in his edition of the colloquies, especially pp. 230, 390, 412; and his edition of More's *Translations of Lucian,* Yale Edition of the *Complete Works of St. Thomas More,* vol. 3, pt. 1 (New Haven, 1974), introduction. See also Martha Heep, "Die *Colloquia Familiaria* des Erasmus und Lucian," Hermaea 18 (1927): 1–74; and my *Under Pretext of Praise,* pp. 22–24.

22. And the translation loses nothing of the original flavor.

23. *Institutio Oratoria,* 8:4, 3. Erasmus refers to the four modes in *De Copia* (*LB,* 1:83F–84F), but he himself treats amplification as one department of Enlargement, for which larger category he provides many modes.

24. Lucretia's welcoming cry, "Euge, mi lepidissime Sophroni!" becomes simply, "Welcome Sophronius darling!" Her follow-up "Quid rei est, meum Corculum?" evolves as "What's the matter, sweetheart?"—and so on. Throughout the whole colloquy the offhand, sometimes slangy idiom is preserved: "How come?" translates *unde,* and *O Bone* comes out as "Chum"; Sophronius, Lucretia complains, was once the *nugator omnium nugacissimus,* and Thompson has her call him the "wildest playboy of them all." (*LB,* 1:718E–F and 719D; *Colloquies,* ed. Thompson, pp. 154 and 156).

25. My feeling that there may be a deeper way of reading this colloquy comes, perhaps, through association rather than logic. I am reminded when I read it of a play I saw many many years ago, in which Sir John Martin-Harvey was a "king's messenger" in a play of that title. His leading lady (his wife) was simply called "the harlot." Both messenger and harlot were passengers on a ship, and the story line was one of love and redemption—the conversion just a little subtler and more sophisticated than is Lucretia's. The end of that play left the audience in little doubt as to the true identity of the mysterious stranger. But he was a little like Sophronius, and the harlot a little like Lucretia—unless half a lifetime has blurred the memory or distorted it.

26. Erasmus does recognize the relation of man's word to that of God—not, perhaps, as explicitly as some later theologians were to do, but enough to warrant the suggestion that the young man is both *sermo* and *Verbum.* See, for instance, the *Ecclesiastes* in *LB,* 5:772E–F.

9 The *Ratio Verae Theologiae* (1518)

GEORGES G. CHANTRAINE, S.J.

Erasmus's *Novum Testamentum* (1516) is a monument of history. It is a landmark in the history of biblical exegesis from the Middle Ages to modern times. Moreover, it is a symbol of the "return to the sources" that is so characteristic of the Renaissance; and it attests, consequently, to the indispensable role of philology in scholarly pursuits. Such generalizations constitute the prevailing opinion.

Curiously enough, however, there was very little support for this opinion from scholars who had worked either on the text of the *Novum Testamentum* or on the commentary until a few years ago. Indeed, neither the annotations nor the prefaces to the various editions had been subjected to critical examination. Stimulated, however, by the outburst of Erasmian studies, some scholars have recently begun to question the annotations and to scrutinize the prefaces to the *Apologiae,* the *Paraclesis,* and the *Methodus* of the *Ratio.* Among the first were Jean-Pierre Massaut,[1] who produced a judicious and nuanced study on Erasmus's esteem for Saint Thomas Aquinas; Georges Chantraine,[2] who discussed the notion of "mystery" and the influence of Saint Paul on Erasmus; and Albert Rabil, Jr.,[3] who examined the annotations on Saint Paul's Epistle to the Romans in order to uncover the methodology of Erasmus. Moreover, in a forthcoming study, André Godin tries to measure, using the annotations, the influence of Origen on Erasmus. As for Erasmus's prefaces, the following authors have written about them from different perspectives: M. Hoffmann[4] enquired into the epistemology of Erasmus's *Ratio.* Gerhard B. Winkler[5] discussed the "theological aesthetics" that he found in the work of Erasmus. G. Chantraine[6] tried to show, according to the *Ratio* and the letter of Erasmus to Paul Volz (August 14, 1518), that true theology, which is the philosophy of Christ, has "mystery" for its central object. In spite of different perspectives, all of these authors recognize the theological nature of the Erasmian method.[7] I shall consider this point in greater detail below.

What, then, is the theological method of Erasmus? As I perceive it, the major ideas are as follows: (1) let him who practices reading Scripture have a pure heart; (2) let him learn Hebrew, Greek, Latin, and be formed in liberal disciplines,

Translated from the French by Louise M. Kamenjar.

especially grammar and rhetoric; (3) let him perceive some of the dogmatic complexities inherent in the various texts of Scripture, and yet let him bring everything, many-sided though it be, back to Christ as the center; (4) let him practice with sobriety spiritual exegesis; and (5) let him, finally, pursue his work methodically and not abuse dialectics. Such are, in substance, the counsels that Erasmus addressed to the beginner in theology—elementary counsels, perhaps, but not at all rudimentary. Rather, they are fundamental; for a higher theology could not be constructed on any other foundation.

At the heart of Scripture, as its sanctuary, lies the mystery. The Holy Spirit alone is able to penetrate it; submissiveness to the Holy Spirit alone prepares one to understand Scripture. To be submissive is to have one's heart pure and one's soul at peace, to have the mind thirsting after understanding alone; it is to venerate the mysteries without succumbing to "impious curiosity"; it is to have no other purpose, no other wish, no other action than to be entranced, inspired, transformed by what one is comprehending. The interior teacher (*doctor*), who is the Holy Spirit, thus elevates, for the person who is submissive to his action, the capacity for comprehending. The understanding of Scripture, which Saint Paul calls prophecy, is knowledge that is capable of transforming.

For this reason it is important not to abuse dialectics and to temper its excesses. Indeed, not only can dialectics serve to conquer passion, but it essentially governs knowledge that is very rational. Theological knowledge, however, is of another order: "Theology derives its name from divine prophecy, not from human conjecture. And a good part of theology is inspired, which does not affect one unless his will has been purified."[8] Theological knowledge must submit dialectics, then, to its own process, to its own rationality. It must then possess its own instrument of knowledge, its *organon*, which, without confusion, one would know how to identify with Aristotle's.

What, then, is the instrument and how can one make use of it? That is the question of the *Ratio*. It is already clear that it must be adapted to the rationale of Scripture. The method must correspond not to human logic but to spiritual advancement: the *Ratio* is the Holy Spirit's, not man's. It is, so to speak, the a priori of theology, according to Erasmus. The unity of knowledge and reality is thus presented directly.[9] That is why it is important to distinguish it from a discursive knowledge, where the unity of knowledge and reality is intended, without being expressed.

Rendered submissive to the prophetic Holy Spirit, human reason receives at the outset inspired Scripture. In an effort to understand Scripture in its spiritual sense, human reason strives in the first place to understand it literally in Hebrew, Greek, and Latin. If one wants to apply himself seriously to theology and if one has some talent in that area, he must learn these three languages. Such knowledge is humble in itself. It has the humility of the incarnate Word. Scripture is, indeed, "like the humanity of the Word of God. In it is the Word of God who speaks to us even today. That is why, finally, the cult and adoration of the Word implies respect for the literal sense of Scripture: in it is the Word of God who is made known."[10]

Likewise, in Scripture that is taken literally, we hear the "appropriate language" of the Holy Spirit, which is "theological."[11] How can one read Scripture in the original without perceiving at the outset the warmth and breath of it? The mystery lies within the writing. That is why he who would interpret Scripture without knowing the languages would risk profaning it: no one can have access to the mystery without understanding the form through which it is revealed.

That is to say, one must perceive not only the indispensable character of the languages themselves, but the necessity for grammar and rhetoric. It is a question, indeed, of familiarizing oneself with the "style" of the Holy Spirit.[12] This is an additional reason for using dialectics only with sobriety. On the other hand, the chief reason for beginning with the school of the ancients is to study the figures of speech and the nature of rhetoric.[13] However, one should study the classics only for a short time and with care: the purpose is, indeed, to treat Scripture in an allegorical manner, as true theology asks.[14] The profane disciplines can awaken the mind to beauty and instill a sense of taste.[15] They do not reveal the actual beauty of Scripture, however, nor the intimate force of its language. The allegories of the ancients are not those of Scripture; the eloquence of Cicero is not that of Christ: "less florid in color" perhaps, but Christ's is "very much more efficacious,"[16] owing to the power of "incantation," to the "strength of its harmony which creates enthusiasm."[17] Grammar, poetry, rhetoric, then, have only propaedeutical value.

From this observation, it follows that Erasmian aesthetics is neither gratuitous nor formal. It is not aestheticism: it is theological. It has for its object the Word of God incarnate. Hence comes the apprenticeship of the sacred languages, the respect for the literal, and also the establishment of the text as exactly as possible.[18] Hence comes the interest in "space" and biblical times.[19] Finally, hence comes the classification of Scripture on the basis of "commonplaces" and the memorization of the New Testament along with that in the Old Testament which is in agreement with the New.[20] It is important, indeed, to understand, in terms of "space" and time, the realities of which Scripture speaks and to instruct those who are beginning theology in these matters. Even if Erasmus does not insist on the spatial aspect of knowledge, he nevertheless does not neglect it. He says enough about it, correctly at least, so as not to unbalance theology. For his part, he is more preoccupied with another cause of imbalance: the disdain for the liberal arts, so common among professional theologians. Erasmus intends to give the arts their place among the theological disciplines.

With the aid of these disciplines, the mind can approach the mystery of the Word incarnate without, however, realizing it. This approach is a necessary but insufficient preparation. In order to realize it, it is necessary to know Christ: his doctrine and his history. Christ's doctrine consists, not only of the teachings that he proclaimed during his public life, but the law which the heavenly teacher instituted on earth and gave to the chosen people.[21] His history does not extend only from his birth to his death, it embraces also the history of the two Testaments; it encloses him as in a circle.[22] It is in the light of such a doctrine and such a history that the candidate in theology should read the whole of Scripture. From it, he will derive understanding, which, let us recall, is spiritual.

In order to discern the doctrine of Christ in Scripture, one must discover more than the literal sense which is found in the narration; it is necessary to associate the words with the person who is speaking and the history with Christ's Act of Atonement. It is necessary, indeed, to consider how the words proceed from the person of Christ and how the latter is interior to his words. For Christ expresses himself on some occasions as pastor or head, at other times as member of the body or fold, "conveying in him the sentiment of his members."[23] It is equally necessary to consider the difference in time: the time of shadows and figures in the Old Testament; the time of light and truth in the New. For the Act of Atonement of Christ has, in history, produced a new era, irreducible to that which had preceded and prepared for it.[24] The contents of Scripture have, then, varied according to times, persons, and things. However, it is not impossible to bring Scripture back to unity—unity not at all abstract and ideal, but concrete and real. It is the image of Christ attracting to him all men through the three circles of his church: priests, princes, the faithful.[25] In one such unity, at the center of which the young theologian is situated, he can perceive the internal coherence of the dogmas: the Christological concentration of the dogmas.

This concrete and real unity is to be found in the life of Christ, or more precisely, in his redeeming Act of Atonement. This act Erasmus designates by a term he had not used in the *Methodus: fabula—action* which, as in a drama, responds to a plan, and is led to a happy ending while unraveling a cruel conflict.[26] The idea of *fabula* is "synthetic: it united the idea of universal symbolism and that of history as destiny."[27] It permits, thus, the uniting of the abstract universality of language and the concrete particularity of history, preserving both the universal and the singular. It is suited, then, to a reflection on the incarnate Word of God as mediator between God and man and as the center of the history of God with man. However, Erasmus utilizes this concept without noting all its possibilities.

This *fabula,* this *action,* is redeeming: it is turned toward us; it is motivated by our salvation. Christ acts *for us!*[28] It is an action which is not fleeting and transitory. It is a tradition of Christ himself, which this *action* effects and from which it draws its source and its vigor. Christ is indeed given to them. He himself is delivered unto death, as his Father has delivered him. But by this tradition he delivers his doctrine. The latter is also perfect: it is absolute like its action; it is so by reason of this action. Between action and doctrine, the circularity is then perfect. That is why the tradition of Christ depends on no single philosophical or religious tradition. Indeed, by its fullness, it overflows and integrates the philosophical and religious traditions. It overflows, then, for in no other tradition does one find his fulfillment, his absoluteness, his circularity. This tradition integrates all, purifying the philosophical tradition of the Greeks of its errors and fulfilling the religious tradition of Israel.[29] It thus establishes true philosophy while restoring human nature; it sets up a cult in spirit and truth while manifesting in its truth the mystery of the "divine counsel."

What, then, is this mystery? It is the ineffable charity of the Father. It is at work in the varied actions of Christ. On account of it, "it has become everything to everyone, moreover, without being in anything unlike itself."[30] This charity is, indeed, the principle and the source of the identity of the Word through which it suffers no dissimilarity with itself, and the principle of its "essential difference" according to which the Word changes condition, becomes man—a man—and is humbled. It is through it that Christ unites in his person the divine and the human nature, without confusing them.[31] It is through it, again, that he realizes his apostolic mission: it is, indeed, while becoming everything to everyone that he has attracted all men to himself and reunited them in him when they were separated by different religions.[32] Briefly, it is through charity that Christ, in order to give himself, accommodates himself to the advancement of each and every man, and so given, attracts them to his Father in the unity which is His with his Father. Charity unites, then, *traditio Christi, accomodatio Christi,* and *attractio Crucis.* It is at the heart of the redeeming *Action.* Better: it *is* the heart of it.[33]

Such is the mystery which is revealed in the allegorical language of Holy Scripture. It is, indeed, manifested in history or in the literal sense, and at the same time hidden under the veil of allegory. It is adapted to the internal dispositions of our minds: mystery invites our minds to pass from the visible to the invisible and to look into history for the truth already prophetically announced. It adapts itself, thus, to the language of the pagan and the Jew. Through this adaptation, it gives us the joy of discovery, along with testing the sluggishness and idleness of our minds. On the other hand, it puts in the hearts of those who scrutinize it with piety the hope of finding it without being exposed to the profane and the impious.[34]

Allegorical exegesis responds to allegorical language and derives its rules from it. It also consists of two levels of understanding: the literal or historical sense and the mystical or spiritual sense. The latter can be subdivided into allegory, tropology, and anagoge, following a quadripartite formula that Erasmus did not wish to imitate.[35] To pass from the historical to the spiritual, or from the literal to the mysterious, is not to abandon or reject history in order to imagine an allegorical explanation (it would be *allegorismus*);[36] rather, it is to recognize the Holy Spirit who animates history and reveals in it the mystery that is found in the literal meaning. This is why the historical and literal sense is the foundation of the spiritual or mystical sense. On the other hand, this spiritual or mystical sense is the principle of understanding the historical or literal sense: in the spiritual sense is found the meaning of the literal. That is why, what would appear to be absurd, if taken literally, cannot be considered in a literal or historical sense. In this case, as Erasmus says, following a long tradition, there is no literal sense; there is only an allegorical sense.[37]

If, in conclusion, one wanted to have a synthetic view of the *Ratio,* one should look upon the theological method as flowing from the ineffable charity of God the Father, who is mystery itself. God gives himself through his Son Jesus Christ. In giving himself, He gives so that one may come to know Him. Likewise no one knows Him without giving himself in return: knowledge is transforming. Moreover, God gives himself to the point of being totally given, delivered, and, consequently, of appearing as a gift. That is why what is given in a manner that is appropriate to God must constitute and does constitute, indeed, the object of knowledge. It is not a means of surmounting the gift by imposing a form of human rationality: knowledge itself is revealed. Hence comes the necessity of a new *organon,* which is not from Aristotle (or from any other philosopher). Neither is it a means of knowing what is given, except in the gift itself. Such is the necessity for literal exegesis, along with the discipline and the purification that it imposes on reason and the heart. But this necessity does not result from a rational urgency; it proceeds from the superabundance of what is given in the gift; it is required by the spiritual sense itself and finds in it its own rationality.

NOTES

1. Massaut, "Erasme et saint Thomas," in *Colloquia Erasmiana Turonensia,* ed. J.-C. Margolin (Paris: Vrin, 1972), 2 : 581–611.
2. Chantraine, "Le mustèrion paulinien selon les annotations d'Erasme," in *Recherches de Science religieuse* 58 (1970): 351–82.

3. Rabil, *Erasmus and the New Testament: The Mind of a Christian Humanist* (San Antonio, Tex.: Trinity University Press, 1972), pp. 115–27.

4. Hoffmann, *Erkenntnis und Verwirklichung der wahren Theologie nach Erasmus von Rotterdam,* Beiträge zur Historischen Theologie, no. 44.

5. Winkler, *Erasmus von Rotterdam und die Einleitungsschriften zum Neuen Testament: Formale Strukturen und Theologischer Sinn,* Reformationsgeschichtliche Studien und Texte, no. 108 (Munster: Aschendorff, 1974).

6. Chantraine, *'Mystère' et 'Philosophie du Christ' selon Erasme* (a study of the letter to Paul Volz and of the *Ratio verae theologiae* [1518]), Bibliothèque de la Faculté de Philosophie et Lettres de Namur, no. 49 (Gembloux: Duculot, 1971).

7. To these authors it is advisable to add the following. Marjorie O. Boyle, *Erasmus on Language and Method in Theology* (Toronto: University of Toronto Press, 1978), includes a major chapter on the *Ratio verae theologiae.* Moreover, one should not overlook John B. Payne, "Towards the Hermeneutics of Erasmus," in *Scrinium Erasmianum,* ed. Coppens (Leiden: E. J. Brill, 1969), 2:13–49. Finally, we should mention J. W. Aldridge, *The Hermeneutic of Erasmus* (Richmond, Va.: John Knox, 1966).

8. *Desiderius Erasmus Roterodamus: Ausgewählte Werke,* ed. Hajo and Annemarie Holborn (Munich, 1933), p. 305, ll. 14–17, which I shall cite henceforth in this manner: Holborn and Holborn, p. 305, ll. 14–17.

9. This has not been seen by M. Hoffmann in *Erkenntnis und Verwirklichung.* . . .

10. Chantraine, *'Mystère' et 'Philosophie,* p. 241.

11. Holborn and Holborn, p. 158, ll. 28–31.

12. Ibid., p. 155, ll. 9–12; p. 190, ll. 25–27; p. 191, ll. 1–2.

13. With considerable detail and vigor, Marjorie Boyle has demonstrated how Erasmus himself relied on these points of the ancients. See note 7.

14. Holborn and Holborn, p. 154, ll. 17–18; p. 187, ll. 17–18 and 20–22.

15. In this respect, the thesis of Winkler is very suggestive.

16. Holborn and Holborn, p. 139, ll. 9–12.

17. Ibid., ll. 30–31.

18. Ibid., p. 181, l. 15 to p. 184, l. 2.

19. Ibid., p. 184, l. 23 to p. 186, l. 34.

20. Ibid., p. 291, l. 13 to p. 293, l. 10; p. 293, l. 19 to p. 294, l. 35.

21. Ibid., p. 193, ll. 24–30.

22. Ibid., p. 209, ll. 1–3.

23. Ibid., p. 197, l. 5 to p. 198, l. 32; p. 197, ll. 14–15.

24. Ibid., p. 198, l. 33 to p. 201, l. 33.

25. Ibid., p. 202, l. 1 to p. 204, l. 9. Marjorie Boyle (see n. 7) has carefully analyzed the cosmographical and urban dimensions of the image of the circle, without putting into perspective Christ's exegetical role.

26. Ibid., p. 209, ll. 1–5; *Adversus Epistolam Lutheri* (*LB,* 10 :1542D).

27. Chantraine, *'Mystère' et 'Philosophie,* p. 275.

28. Ibid., pp. 280–82.

29. Ibid., pp. 285–87.

30. Holborn and Holborn, p. 211, ll. 30–31.

31. Ibid., p. 211, l. 32 to p. 212, l. 2. See also p. 215, l. 32 to p. 216, l. 30.

32. Chaintraine, *'Mystère' et 'Philosophie,* pp. 301–34.

33. Ibid., pp. 304–07.

34. Holborn and Holborn, p. 259, l. 33 to p. 260, l. 10.

35. Ibid., p. 284, ll. 2–10.

36. Ibid., p. 282, l. 9.

37. Ibid., p. 274, l. 28 to p. 275, l. 1.

10 *De Libero Arbitrio* (1524): Erasmus on Piety, Theology, and the Lutheran Dogma

B. A. GERRISH

I had rather be a pious theologian with Jerome than an invincible one with Scotus.[1]

The papal bull *Exsurge Domine* reached Luther by 10 October 1520. His books containing certain specified errors were to be burned, and he himself had sixty days in which to recant.[2] On 10 December, as the days of grace ran out, the pope had his answer. In reprisal for the burning of Luther's books, a bonfire was ignited just outside Wittenberg, and the papal constitutions, the canon law, and books of scholastic theology were commited to the flames. Luther himself then threw in the papal bull. "As they did to me," he explained in the words of Samson, "so have I done to them."[3]

Forty-one propositions were condemned in the bull as "respectively heretical, or scandalous, or false, or offensive to pious ears, or seductive of simple minds, and opposed to catholic truth." Among them was Thesis 13 from Luther's Heidelberg Disputation (1518): "Freedom of choice, after the fall, is a reality in name only (*res est de solo titulo*); and in 'doing what is in it,' it sins mortally."[4] That the language of the thesis was none too happy—or, rather, deliberately provocative—appears from the accompanying "explanations."[5] But *Exsurge Domine* did not occupy itself with Luther's refinements; it merely cited, in Article 36, the thesis itself. For his part, Luther sharpened the offense. In his *Assertion of All the Articles of M. Luther Condemned by the Latest Bull of Leo X* (1520), he ironically "revoked" Article 36:

I was wrong when I said that freedom of choice before grace is a reality in name only. I ought to have said simply: Freedom of choice is a fiction or a name with no reality (*figmentum in rebus seu titulus sine re*). For to purpose anything either evil or good is in no one's control, but (as Wycliffe's article condemned at Constance rightly teaches) everything happens by absolute necessity.[6]

The German version (or *vernacula assertio*, as Luther called it) concluded more modestly: "I wish that little word 'freewill' had never been invented. It is not found in Scripture and should more aptly be called 'selfwill.'"[7] Understandably, his adversaries preferred to deplore the more shocking Latin version, especially

since Luther there embraced an earlier heretic. Moreover, they took due notice
of his declaration that the article on freedom of choice was "the best of them
all and the very essence of our case (*omnium optimus et rerum nostrarum
summa*)"; beside it, the questions of the papacy, of councils, and of indulgences
were mere trifles.[8]

The reason why Luther singled out Article 36 is clear from his defense of it
in the *Assertion*. It was his bulwark against the new Pelagians who taught that
a man could prepare himself for grace by morally good deeds, performed by
his natural powers under the general impulse of divine providence. To be sure,
the attempt had been made, as Luther noted, to mitigate the appearance of
anticipating God and wresting his grace from him. Not that the works were
held to be strictly meritorious (*de condigno*); rather, merit of congruity (*de
congruo*) was assigned them by God, who does not refuse anyone who does
what is in him. Luther remained unimpressed. "The same impious mentality
persists, by which grace is believed to be given, not freely, but on account of
our works. . . . The same Pelagius has held the field triumphantly."[9]

Indeed, the new Pelagianism was worse than the old; for whereas Pelagius
denied the necessity for grace, the new theology put grace at the disposal of
men. Such a scheme is contradicted by Scripture and experience alike. When
the will of fallen man "does what is in it," it sins mortally. Why? Because what
is in a man, since the fall, is more aptly called "self-will" than "free will": an
aggressive, all-consuming, self-seeking will, which Luther considered to be the
fundamental spring of human action (apart from grace).[10] Self-will seeks its
own, not only in what is base, but also in what is good and noble—even in religion and in God himself. The best works of such a man are not base; but insofar
as they are infected with his self-will, they remain radically defective. To appeal
to the fallen will is therefore a fearful mistake; for the will can only arouse
itself to further acts of self-seeking, or else fall into the misery of despair.

Whether Luther's driving concern for the grace of God was wisely defended
by the dogma of absolute necessity may well be doubted. But our interest is
in Erasmus's response to Luther and whether it implies, as Luther believed,
that the humanist had taken up the cause of the Pelagians. Luther concludes
his discussion of Article 36 with a challenge and a wish. He sees no sign that
anyone is disposed to take up the real issue and join battle with him. He can
only express the wish that some new Ezra might appear, equipped with the
biblical languages, to recover the Scriptures.[11] Erasmus never fulfilled the
wish—not, at least, as Luther intended it. But he did take up the challenge;
and Luther was later to announce (with some exaggeration): "I heartily praise
and commend you for this: that you alone, unlike all the rest, have attacked
the real thing, that is, the essential issue."[12]

I

On 8 October 1520, just two days before the bull reached Luther, his books had been ceremoniously burned in Louvain, where Erasmus then resided. The very next day, Nicholas Egmond, a Carmelite friar and a theologian at the university, was preaching in St. Peter's Church when he noticed Erasmus in the congregation, deserted his theme ("charity," so Erasmus recalled), and publicly denounced him as a Lutheran. At a meeting arranged, at Erasmus's request, by the rector of the university, Egmond could find no stronger argument to support his accusation than the fact that Erasmus had not written against Luther. "Why then," was the response, "by the same reckoning I shall take you for a Lutheran, too, for you do not write anything against him either!"[13]

In a series of important letters during the years 1519–20, Erasmus had taken up a cautious and balanced stance toward what he variously called "the Lutheran tragedy," "the Lutheran malady," or simply "the Lutheran affair."[14] He explained that he did not personally know Luther and could not be held responsible for Luther's books, which, since he had only leafed through them, he could neither defend nor condemn. But the enemies of learning had used the Lutheran affair to attack *him* too, alleging a connection between scholarship and heresy. One source of the affair (not the only one) was thus *odium bonarum literarum.*[15] This is how Erasmus summed up his position in a letter to Luther himself: "As for me, I remain impartial, as far as I may, in order to be more useful to the renascence of learning."[16]

The Erasmian program was a different one from Luther's, and Erasmus preferred to be a spectator, rather than an actor, in the tragedy.[17] Still, he could not ignore the Lutheran movement, not only because of the attempt to discredit him by association with it, but also because the revival of learning was, after all, harnessed to the cause of church reform. Erasmus had written against ecclesiastical abuses long before he learned of Luther's existence, and he more than once admitted that he had, in a sense, "precipitated a great part of it all."[18] Hence the programmatic letters of 1519–20 insist upon the crying need for reform, the irreproachable character of Luther, and the requirement of gentleness in dealing with him.

But at the very beginning of the Lutheran affair, Erasmus suspected that the indiscretion was not all on the side of Luther's opponents, whom he urged to oppose Luther with the pen and not with slander and uproar. There was the further problem of Luther's own temperament, which, by its natural vehemence and impatience, could turn reform into disorder and division. Besides, Luther made a public issue out of matters that should have been handled more discreetly. Luther, too, could be bad for the cause of learning, and Erasmus constantly recalls the advice he gave Froben not to print Luther's books. In short, the danger (for *bonae literae*) was that the Lutheran affair would become the Lutheran uproar (*tumultus*).[19]

It was a policy of mediation, therefore, that Erasmus pursued, culminating in his activities at Cologne during the last few days of October and the early days of November.[20] But already by the month of December a note of bitterness and disillusionment obtruded. In a world that thirsted for the pure and living waters of the evangelists and apostles, Luther had appeared as perhaps the man of the hour. But the offensiveness of his writings did not reflect the gentleness of the apostolic spirit.[21] By spring the following year, there was little optimism left for the Cologne policy of mediation, though Erasmus did not abandon it. Luther's burning of the decretals, his *Babylonian Captivity,* and the extravagant *Assertions* had "rendered the malady, so it seems, incurable."[22] As Luther's enemies helped him, so he was helping them.[23] He put the sword into their hands.[24]

Erasmus's fears thus proved to have been prophetic: the Lutheran affair was a disruptive one (*seditiosa res*), and Luther's medicine was worse than the disease.[25] And yet, as the action shifted from Cologne to Worms, Erasmus could not bring himself to oppose Luther totally. A certain "scrupulousness" (*religio quaedam*) held him back, and he played the part of Gamaliel (Acts 5:33-39), lest he be found opposing God.[26] Though he did deem it proper to muzzle both Luther and his opponents, he continued to warn against excessive severity.[27] Much the same advice was given by him to Adrian VI two years after Worms. Harsh measures had been tried before, against the Wycliffites, with no great success. While recommending censorship and the restraint of novelties, which promote disruption more than piety, Erasmus urged amnesty for past offenses; for this is the way God deals with us every day, forgetting our trespasses. The sources of the malady should then be investigated and remedied. To this end, as at Cologne, he proposed a commission of cool-headed and highly respected men.[28]

The constant complaint of Erasmus was that no one seemed willing to oppose Luther with the pen, to refute him rather than to defame or crush him.[29] His friends agreed, and they thought the pen should be Erasmus's. To begin with, he protested that he lacked time or talent to oblige them.[30] He did once decide to write, but for concord, not against Luther; and even this plan was set aside because tempers had waxed too hot.[31] Finally, as the pressure to write continued unremittingly,[32] Erasmus yielded. Now, it may seem natural enough that he chose as his theme the question of freedom and necessity. After all, Luther's adversaries had agreed with him, if in nothing else, at least in judging that his doctrine of necessity was the heart of the matter. Duke George singled it out as "the most fertile spring of the Lutheran errors."[33] The fact is, however, that the question of freedom and necessity had a quite different status in Erasmus's mind than it had either for Luther or for Duke George.

Erasmus was being summoned by friends and patrons to dispose of a heretic.[34] In his reply to von Hutten's *Expostulation,* however, he insists that he made no mention of a "heresy," but spoke rather of "tragedy," "dissension," "uproar." The issue, he explains, does not concern the articles of faith but matters commonly debated in the schools. (His list includes the question whether freedom of choice contributes to salvation.) Such matters warrant neither the taking of another's life nor the sacrifice of one's own. For his part, Erasmus is not willing to be a martyr for Luther or his paradoxes; and he does not think that paradoxes are cause enough for throwing the whole world into an uproar.[35] The same point was made in a letter written about the same time to Zwingli, to whom Erasmus dedicated his writing against von Hutten.

The first Lutherans to die for their faith had recently been burned in Brussels (1 July 1523), and Erasmus had martyrdom on his mind. He marvels at the constancy of one who could lay down his life, not for an article of faith, but for the paradoxes of Luther. "For these," he admits, "I myself would not care to die, since I do not understand them." The enigmas propounded by Luther are then specified: that all the works of the saints are sins, that freedom of choice is an empty name, that a man is justified by faith alone. Erasmus comments: "I do not see what fruit it would yield to argue over what Luther may mean by these [enigmas]." And this is what he claims for himself: "I think I have taught nearly everything Luther teaches, only not so harshly, and I have refrained from certain enigmas and paradoxes."[36] Erasmus once wrote that the world had been lulled to sleep by endless talk about matters which, even if true, were not of much help for "evangelical vigor."[37] Now, it seemed, Luther had woken the world up only to vex it with some fruitless questions of his own.

Erasmus never did quite oblige his patrons, then, since he did not regard the issue as one of heresy.[38] But his estimate of the issue was poles apart from Luther's appraisal too, since he thought it not worth an altercation, much less a martyrdom. What *was* it worth then? A polite discussion. The theme so dear to Luther and so abhorrent to Duke George suited Erasmus's purposes very well: it sufficed to establish his distance from Luther but by no means demanded a total severance of relations. It enabled Erasmus to be as he had always been toward Luther: not vacillating but firmly ambivalent. While denying the allegation that he was a Lutheran, he wished to remain on speaking terms with Wittenberg.[39] Even before he had focused on freedom of choice as his theme, he had intended a work *On Settling the Lutheran Affair* that would take the actual literary form of a fictitious conversation, a *collatio* more than a *disputatio*. A series of three dialogues between Thrasymachus (Luther or a Lutheran), Eubulus (a papalist), and Philalethes (Erasmus or an Erasmian) was to deal, in order, with Luther's manner of proceeding, with some of his doctrines, and with Erasmus's counsel for assuaging the uproar.[40] Erasmus did not carry through his original design.[41] But perhaps there are echoes of it in a letter to Laurinus, which may be said to stand midway between the original design and the final product: it contains an imaginary dialogue with a Lutheran, and it moves toward preoccupation with the problem of free choice.[42]

II

Publication of the book continued to be delayed until long after Erasmus had finally agreed to write it.[43] But he did eventually bring himself to the point of squandering five precious days on the irksome task, and—most likely, in the winter of 1523—he was able to send a first draft to Louis Baer for his expert theological counsel. (Baer responded with a memorandum on the distinction between *necessitas consequentiae* and *necessitas consequentis*.)[44] Another copy of the first draft went to King Henry VIII. If a taste of the work met with his majesty's approval (and that of other learned men), Erasmus would finish it and have it printed. But not in Basel! "For here, I suppose, there is no printer who would venture to print anything that reflects in the slightest upon Luther, though you may write whatever you please against the Pope."[45]

Rankled by a well-intentioned but overbearing letter from Luther, which offered him a truce, Erasmus professed that he had still not written against Luther, but added that nothing would please him more than if Luther were to write against him.[46] In the end, he decided to make the first move. The word was out: it was known well enough that he had been preparing a book against Luther. And Erasmus judged that, in any case, he had treated his subject with such moderation that not even Luther could be displeased. Better to publish what he had written than to encourage suspicions that it was something worse![47] By the end of August 1524 the book was—at last!—in the press.[48] In September, Erasmus distributed copies to key personages in Rome, England, and Saxony.[49] The *Discourse on Free Choice* had been printed—and, to be sure, in Basel.[50] "The die is cast," Erasmus announced rather dramatically. "The little book on free choice has gone out into the light of day."[51]

The book gathers up many themes from the correspondence of 1518–24, often with verbal echoes. In particular, it is one of Luther's *doctrines* that is under discussion (I a 3). (No mention is made of any Lutheran *heresy*.) Nonetheless, this one "dogma" is a culpable exaggeration, a "paradox" (in a derogatory sense)[52] (I a 10, I b 6): namely, Wycliffe's claim that all things—both before and after grace, good things and bad alike, and even things in-different—happen by pure necessity. Although it makes us mere instruments of God, like tools in a craftsman's hand, Luther expressly approves this opinion in his *Assertion* (II b 7-8; cf. I a 1). The issue, then, is whether the human will can be considered "free" in the sense of possessing ability to choose between alternatives.[53] More exactly, as Erasmus's definition of *liberum arbitrium* indicates, the issue is whether a man has freedom of choice in the matter of his salvation: "Now, by *liberum arbitrium* I mean, in this place, a capacity of the human will by which a man is able to apply himself to the things that lead to eternal salvation, or else to turn away from them" (I b 10).

The central structure of the treatise is given by the remark (I b 10) that there are many passages in Scripture which seem plainly to establish freedom of choice (discussed in sec. II), others which seem entirely to take it away (discussed in sec. III). Since the whole of Scripture is inspired by the selfsame Spirit and therefore cannot contradict itself, the problem is to arrive at a har-monizing interpretation, which can be shown to possess superior probability, first, because it is supported by weightier and more numerous texts and, second, because the alternatives have undesirable or even absurd consequences (I b 10, IV 1, IV 17). Plainly, the discussion is to be exegetical: if the labyrinth of free choice confronts us in the Scriptures (I a 1), then the method appropriate for dealing with it will be through the clash of texts and arguments (I a 3). This also suits the refusal of the partner in the discussion to listen to anything but the canonical Scriptures—as well as the readiness of Erasmus himself to econo-mize his efforts (I b 1). And yet it should not be overlooked that no previous writer has totally abolished freedom of choice, except Mani, Wycliffe, and perhaps Laurentius Valla (I a 6, I b 2, IV 16). To point this out is not to sur-render the unique authority of Scripture, but simply to give due weight to the overwhelming consensus among its interpreters (I b 3, IV 17). Of course, the majority is not necessarily right; but it is more likely to be right than the private judgment of an individual or two (I b 2), just as a philosopher has the advantage over a fool or a council over a conventicle (I b 5).

The central argument of Erasmus can readily be picked out. Looking in the Bible for proofs of free choice, he remarks, is like looking for water in the ocean (II a 17). The Bible is filled with imperatives, exhortations, promises, accusa-tions, threats, all of which make no sense on the supposition that everything happens by necessity (II b 1-2, III a 13, III b 6, etc.).[54] Indeed, Scripture hardly speaks of anything else but conversion, zeal, effort for improvement (II a 16). The metaphors of running a race, fighting the good fight, toiling for the harvest, cannot be reconciled with the notion that the will is not active, but passive (II b 4). For two reasons, the Lutheran dogma must be overwhelmed by this ocean of texts.

First, man's freedom of choice (together with his knowledge of the good) is the condition of human responsibility—of blame and praise, reward and merit (II b 1-2, III a 6, III a 10, IV 3, IV 11, IV 16). "Had the will not been free, sin could not have been imputed; for it ceases to be sin where it is not voluntary" (II a 7). This holds good not only for Adam but for his entire progeny: in no man can freedom of choice be wholly extinguished, not even when habituation to sin makes it appear otherwise (II a 8). Second, man's freedom of choice is the condition of the divine justice and mercy (IV 7). For if the will were not endowed with freedom of choice, then God would be responsible for evil actions as well as for good (II b 5, IV 12). And what kind of justice or mercy would inflict anger upon any who had not done wrong of their own accord, but had no choice to be other than they were (II b 3, IV 4, IV 13, IV 16)?[55] Those whom God hates or loves he surely hates or loves for just reasons (III a 12).

From among the many questions that may occur to the reader of the *Discourse,* two may be taken as worthy of a closer look. Where, as he goes about refuting the Lutheran dogma, does Erasmus himself seem to stand on the old problem of divine grace and human freedom? And why, in the introductory and concluding reflections (sec. I and sec. IV), does he so carefully frame his subject between apparent admissions of its relative unimportance? Pursuit of these two questions will show that Erasmus was no Pelagian (as Luther thought) and not quite a semi-Pelagian (as others have thought); further, that the message of the book concerns the relation of theology to piety at least as much as the relation of grace to freedom. In this second respect, in particular, the *Discourse* marks the culmination of those thoughts on the Lutheran affair that Erasmus recorded in his correspondence between 1518 and 1524.

III

In the course of the treatise, and especially in the first part of sec. 1 and the conclusion, Erasmus outlines the alternative views on grace and freedom. By the fall of man, the will was so depraved it could not recover by its own resources, but lost its liberty and was obliged to be the servant of sin. All Christians agree, as Erasmus sees it, that sin is forgiven by God's grace and the will in some measure made free. But he notes a difference, from this point on, between the Pelagians and the orthodox. In the Pelagian view, the will is then able to gain eternal life without the help of further grace, salvation being ascribed to God simply in the sense that it was he who created and restored the will. (Erasmus does not ask *how*, according to the Pelagians, God restores the will.) In the orthodox view, it is only with the help of further grace, continually sustaining man's effort, that the will is able to persevere in the right condition. And even then, in this view, the inclination to sin is not eradicated—not because grace could not do so, but because it would not be good for us if it did (II a 3; cf. II a 9, III c 5, IV 10).

Among non-Pelagians, however, differences remain. They all insist on the need for continuous divine aid, but they entertain various opinions about the manner in which divine aid is given. Some hold that in his fallen state a man is able, without any divine action beyond God's providential concurrence with the creature (the *influxus naturalis*),[56] to perform deeds that prepare him for grace and move God to mercy (II a 11). This party is identified by Erasmus as the followers of Scotus, who, he says, are "rather favorably disposed" to freedom of choice.[57] "They believe its capacity is sufficient that, even before the reception of forgiving grace, a man is able by his natural capacities to perform what they call 'morally good' works, through which they merit sanctifying grace—not strictly, but by congruity" (II a 9). Another party argues, by contrast, that there can be no preparation for sanctifying grace without special grace (*gratia peculiaris;* II a 11). Their view is diametrically opposed to that of the Scotists, since they contend that morally good works, if they do not proceed from faith and love of God, are as detestable to him as criminal acts like adultery and murder (II a 10). Here Erasmus must have in mind "St. Augustine and his followers," whom he goes on to name in the same paragraph.[58] Augustine denies that a man in sin can turn himself to amendment of his life or do anything that would contribute to his salvation unless he is stimulated by the gratuitous gift of God (as *gratia operans*).[59]

Now, Pelagius seems to attribute too much to freedom of choice, and even Scotus allows it a great deal (IV 16; cf. IV 7). For their part, the Augustinians attribute most to grace and almost nothing to freedom of choice—yet without quite abolishing it! Their opinion therefore differs from two final options, which it is Erasmus's intention to contest.[60] According to Andreas von Carlstadt, the sinful will is "free" only to do evil, so that grace alone performs good works—not through or with, but *in* our "freedom of choice," the will remaining like wax in a modeler's hand. According to Luther, the will is free neither for good nor for evil, whether before or after grace, since everything happens by pure necessity and "freedom of choice" is an empty name.

There are, then, five opinions in all: those of Pelagius, Scotus, Augustine, Carlstadt, and Luther. The first is disqualified because unorthodox. The last two are the opinions Erasmus is writing against. They are distinguished as *durior* (Carlstadt's view) and *durissima* (Luther's):[61] that is, as "harsher" and "harshest" in comparison with the Augustinian view, which is the one Erasmus designates "likely enough." The reason why the Augustinian view earns this cautious endorsement (*satis probabilis*) is because it leaves a man his zeal and effort but nothing to ascribe to his own powers (II a 12). How, we must now ask, does Erasmus understand this "Augustinian" formula?

The fallen will, he assumes, is unable to restore itself (*sese revocare ad meliorem frugem*), and in this sense its liberty is lost (II a 3). It is ineffectual with respect to eternal salvation, unless grace is added (II a 5). But it does not follow that man has no freedom to will the good at all. We do not wholly lack either the capacity or the use of free choice (III c 1; cf. II a 14). In particular, when the offer of assisting grace comes, a man retains the freedom to accept or reject it. Erasmus's central thought, then, seems to be that freedom of choice is inalienable: it includes the freedom to speak or be silent, to sit or to stand—and also to attend to the things, such as sacred books and sermons, by which God awakens the sinner and makes him a "candidate" for the final, sanctifying grace. The distinction between this view and the view of the Scotists, it appears, is that what to them was preparation for special grace is for Erasmus a free response to it (II a 11).[62] The greatest of all the commandments—to turn to the Lord—is not only possible but easy to fulfill (II a 17).

Of course, unlike Adam's will (before the Fall), our will is not poised in perfect equilibrium, so to say, but biased toward evil.[63] And yet our freedom of choice, though impaired, is never extinguished (II a 7-8). Hence, at that crucial moment when the assistance of grace is offered, it is possible for us freely to embrace it or to turn our hearts away and close our eyes to the light (II b 6, IV 8-10). Assistance and necessity are, indeed, mutually exclusive notions (II b 5), while grace understood as aid and sin as weakness are correlative and logically presuppose freedom. For we do not call "weak" someone who can do nothing, nor do we say someone is "helping" if in fact he does it all (III c 12).[64] Grace and freedom belong together (III a 16-17; III c 13): this is the guarantee that grace shall be grace, inviting without compelling (III c 3; cf. II a 11).[65]

Erasmus's "moderate" solution is therefore a both/and. The two seemingly contradictory sets of scriptural texts are easily reconciled if we simply join human effort and divine grace. The knotty problem of grace and freedom is then unraveled (III a 17; cf. II b 6). Man's effort and God's aid are united. Not, however, in equal proportions! That would be a quite false inference from the concept of grace as aid. "I like the opinion of those who attribute something to freedom of choice, but most to grace." Room is then left for good works and merits, but it is not enough to boast about (IV 16). In a sense, it can even be said that we owe the whole work to God, without whom we bring nothing to completion (IV 7). But more exactly, we owe *wholly* to God the beginning and the end, while the middle—the continuance—depends *chiefly* on him.

> It is because of this proportion that a man should ascribe his salvation wholly to grace, since what the free choice does here is precious little (*per-pusillum*); and the very fact that it can act at all is of God's grace, who first created the will with freedom to choose, then freed it, too, and healed it. [IV 8][66]

All is of grace, though stage 2 is not of grace in quite the same sense as stages 1 and 3. For there is, in the middle stage, a minimum that Erasmus apparently attributes to the grace of nature (III c 4), which many people do not understand to be grace at all (II a 11). If this sounds, in the end, dubiously Augustinian, it must at least be admitted that the intent to go as far as possible with Augustine is clear.[67] The initiative of God's grace is strongly affirmed (*qui nos aversos vocavit*) (III c 5), and the total scheme can be stated in language almost as paradoxical as Luther's:

> The mercy of God goes before our will, accompanies it in its endeavour, gives a happy issue. Yet all the while, it is we who will, who run, who reach the goal—but in such wise that even this which is ours we ascribe to God, for we are wholly his. [III a 4]

And so, Erasmus can readily demand (III c 5), in the words of that favorite Augustinian text (1 Cor. 4 : 7): "What have you that you did not receive?"

Still, Erasmus did find *some* Augustinian notions extreme and distasteful, and he could make them sound even more extreme than they actually were (I a 10).[68] At times, he speaks as though it were more a matter of courtesy than of dogmatic accuracy to ascribe *everything* to God.[69] Similarly, on the other side, he puts in a good word for the *intention* of the rival Scotist party: they did, at least, invite a man to exert himself, like Cornelius (Acts 10), in the hope of obtaining salvation (IV 7).[70] And he showed how their funda-mental notion could be reconciled with the primacy of grace—by recalling that a man does not possess his natural powers *ex sese* (III c 4).

Small wonder that the scholars continue to differ about Erasmus's real sym-pathies! The problem becomes still more complex if his subsequent affirmations on the subject are added to those of the *Discourse*.[71] The options seem to be either to admit a certain oscillation in his thinking,[72] or else to move him toward one or other of the two poles, the Augustinian-Thomistic[73] or the semi-Pelagian.[74] A much fuller investigation is called for than is possible here. But I may at least risk a tentative statement on the direction in which, I believe, the evidence points.

I cannot see that Erasmus fully appreciated the notion of operative grace.[75] But if this casts doubts upon his right to be classified with the Augustinians and Thomists, it does not follow that he must therefore belong with the semi-Pelagians. If I have correctly located the point at which Erasmus, for all his wariness, does take a firm stand, then his kinsmen are not so much the medieval semi-Pelagians, whom Luther attacked, as the Lutheran synergists, who were, of course, Erasmus's stepchildren. Not meritorious preparation for grace, but the natural freedom to consent to grace is the minimum of free choice that he will not surrender.[76] On occasion, he does suggest the possibility of uniting the two schemes: it would not be improper, he thinks, to subsume the free response to prevenient grace under the scholastic terminology of *merita de congruo*.[77] Insofar as that is his proposal, he makes of the terminology something not quite "semi-Pelagian" (in the customary sense).

Is this, then, all that needs to be said about Erasmus's *real* view? Surely not. His view on grace and freedom was also that there are *several* views on grace and freedom. He was later to complain, in his response to Luther's attack, that an *opinio probabilis* is not the *opinio sola, certa, et indubitata*.[78] And he would have registered no surprise had he been able to foreknow that, after his death, the Lutherans were to be divided over their synergist controversy, Dominicans and Jesuits were to debate efficacious grace, and Calvinist was to fall out with Calvinist over effectual calling. This would merely have confirmed his persuasion that the relationship of grace and freedom, within limits, is a matter of opinion.

IV

In the very first paragraph of the *Discourse on Free Choice* Erasmus judged that his theme had marvelously occupied the talents of philosophers and theologians, both ancient and modern, but with more toil than fruit (I a 1). It remained, for him, a school question, and he could not concede that it had the importance assigned it by his adversaries (I b 4), who even contended it was the chief point (*caput*) of the entire teaching of the Gospel (I b 8). To him, it was a *quaestio disputata*. Hence, although the goal of the inquiry was of course to try whether the truth could be made more evident, he proposed nothing more conclusive than a civil conversation; and he wanted to avoid anything as unseemly as a contentious debate or gladiatorial combat (I a 1–3, I b 9). Any issue which carries one beyond the inviolable authority of Scripture or the pronouncements of the church calls for tentativeness and reserve rather than fanatical addiction to one's own opinion.

Unlike Luther, then, whose *Assertion* had rekindled the old debate, Erasmus disowned any taste for "assertions" about such matters. He was willing to remain a skeptic (I a 4). In fact, he admitted that he had not entirely made up his mind about all the various options, except that he did think that was *some* capacity of free choice. On this, Luther's *Assertion* had not yet (*nondum!*) persuaded him otherwise (I a 5). He believed he had understood Luther, but granted he could be wrong; and he therefore played the debater, not the judge; the inquirer, not the dogmatist (I a 6).

It is not true, however, as Luther and others after him have alleged,[79] that Erasmus considered the entire issue of free choice to be trivial—although he may have expressed himself incautiously. What he intended was to circumscribe the points that mattered and could be stated definitively, leaving in an outer circle, so to say, points open to debate. (Luther believed that the inner circle could only be secure if certain questions in the outer circle were first settled.) For Erasmus, the practical criterion of what mattered was *pietas.* Hence the first of the summarizing conclusions (at the end of the *Discourse*) is this: "It is of no advantage to piety to investigate [the matter] more deeply than necessary, especially in the presence of laymen" (IV 17).[80]

Erasmus offers a list of affirmations concerning free choice that can be made on the basis of the Scriptures. In essence, they simply set out the obligation of human effort and the availability of divine mercy. This, he judges, is enough for Christian piety without intrusion upon such remote—not to say superfluous— questions as whether God knows anything contingently (that is, whether he can foreknow contingent events), whether our will is of any avail in what concerns salvation or whether it is only passive under the action of grace, whether the good or evil we do is done by us (or rather *to* us) by pure necessity. It is not piety but *irreligiosa curiositas* that pries into such questions (I a 8).

The paradox of Wycliffe and Luther—that "whatever is done by us happens, not by freedom of choice, but by pure necessity"—is classed among those matters which, even if we supposed them true, could not usefully be made public before the whole world.[81] To the same class belongs Augustine's assertion that God works in us both good and bad and rewards his own good works in us and punishes the bad.[82] To proclaim such an utterance among the masses would be to throw open the window to impiety: the faint-hearted would weary of the struggle against the flesh, the wicked would not endeavor to mend his ways. And who could induce himself to love with his whole heart a God who prepares the flames to punish in his victims his own evil deeds (I a 10)?

Erasmus certainly found Luther's dogma a challenge to his credulity. Presumably, he included it among those new hyperparadoxes which had not yet been verified by so much as the curing of a lame horse (I b 6). But his fundamental concern was for the moral and religious consequences of the paradox—in short, for *pietas,* understood as a matter both of good conduct and of a proper

attitude toward the Deity.[83] Luther's denial that confession is a binding obligation was, to Erasmus, a similar case in point: even had the denial been correct,
Erasmus would have feared to make it public, since compulsory confession
restrained the impulse to scandalous sins (*flagitia*).

> There are some diseases of the body which it is a lesser evil to endure than
> to cure. . . . Paul knows the difference between what is "allowed" and what
> is "expedient" [1 Cor. 6 :12]. It is allowed to speak the truth, but it is not
> expedient to do so in front of anyone, any time, or in any way. [I a 9]

Luther's critique of the penitential praxis and his denial of free choice were
thus subject to the same objection: they undermined religious endeavor. Indeed,
when judged by the norm of *pietas,* the dualism of Mani was perhaps less injurious (*minus inutile ad pietatem*): it at least left grounds for imploring the
Creator's help against the powers of darkness, whereas Wycliffe's pure necessity
left room neither for prayer nor for effort (I b 2).

Did not Paul himself, however, lay claim to a wisdom that he uttered among
the more mature (1 Cor. 2.6)? Matters noxious to the masses, like wine to the
fevered, could perhaps have been discussed among the learned or in schools of
theology, though even there only with sobriety (I a 11). Without some such
allowance, Erasmus's exploration of free choice in the *Dialogue* would have lost
its justification. But it can hardly be doubted that he was more interested in
preserving the inner circle than in arguing about the outer, for there was always
the risk that a discussion among scholars might become a public performance
for the multitude. And that would be not just useless but pernicious. Erasmus
accordingly ends his preface with the remark:

> For this reason, I should prefer it if, rather than either refuting or affirming
> Luther's dogma, we could be persuaded not to fritter away time and talents
> in labyrinths of this kind. It would justly be thought that I had been too
> wordy in this preface were it not almost more to the point than the disputa-
> tion itself. [I a 11]

If Erasmus had left out the little word *almost,* we might well wonder, with
Luther, why he went ahead and disputed anyway. Even with the *almost,* we may
still nurse a few lingering doubts, which the ending of the introduction only
confirms:

> Half my book is already done. For if I carry my intended point—that it is
> better not to quarrel too fussily over matters of this sort, especially before
> the common people—then the argument for which I now gird myself is not
> needed. . . . [I b 10]

In the conclusion of the *Discourse,* Erasmus returns to the introductory theme of dogma and piety. But resumption of the theme is not mere repetition. The test of *pietas* is now employed, not simply to draw a firm line between fundamental affirmations and theological opinions, but to display the point of the opinions themselves. The reference to *pietas,* we may say, is not just a limit, but a hermeneutic principle. The two extremes, between which Erasmus looks for a "moderate" position, have each been supported by one-sided appropriation of the Scriptures; but the inner reason for the divergence he thinks he can trace back, behind the proofs, to different religious concerns.

Considering men's negligence in the pursuit of piety and the risk that they may be infected with despair of salvation, the one side has been betrayed into overemphasis on freedom of choice. The other side, noting what a plague upon genuine piety is man's confidence in human powers and merits (which he even presumes to offer for sale), has either diminished freedom of choice or wholly exterminated it. Either way, the attempted cure is another disease (IV 1; cf. II a 9-10). In the correction of morals, the saying holds good: "To straighten a bent stick, bend it in the opposite direction." But in dogmatics (*in dogmatibus*), a balanced statement is desirable. "The Scylla of arrogance was not to be evaded by being carried into the Charybdis of despair or indolence.[84] The dislocated limb should not have been remedied by bending it back in the opposite direction, but by resetting it where it belongs" (IV 16).

The claim of Erasmus in the *Discourse on Free Choice* is that he has preserved Luther's religious concerns (*quae Lutherus pie quidem et Christiäne disseruit*) without the troublesome paradoxes. It is hardly true, though often repeated,[85] that Erasmus failed to appreciate Luther's concerns, despite his own belief that he had understood him. At least, he knew it was Luther's wish to transfer confidence from human merits and capacities solely to God and his promises (IV 17; cf. IV 8).[86] And he could gladly exclaim: "Surely, it is a pious and winsome opinion that takes from us all conceit, transfers all our boasting and confidence to Christ, drives from us the fear of men and of demons, makes us mistrustful of our own resources, and gives us strength and courage in God." These are thoughts Erasmus applauds—short of exaggeration (*usque ad hyperbolas*) (IV 2).[87] And exaggeration is what it is if anyone asserts that there is no merit, that the works even of the pious are sins, that everything we do or will must be traced to absolute necessity (IV 3).

In Erasmus's judgment, Luther was forced to such extremes by the demands of polemic: at one time, Luther did allow something to freedom of choice, but he was driven in the heat of argument to abolish it entirely (IV 7). Perhaps he also took a certain natural delight to hyperboles. In any case, he countered one extreme with another: the traffic in merits with the denial of merit, and so on with satisfactions, papal power, monastic vows, and the rest. There may be a place for an occasional use of hyperbolical language—for reassuring the timid that "God does everything" or admonishing the proud that "man can do nothing but sin." But "from the clash of such exaggerations the thunder and lightning are generated that now shake the world" (IV 15-16).

What Erasmus offers in his conclusion is a genetic account of the Lutheran dogma. He uncovers the root religious concern (and unambiguously approves it). The expression of this concern in harsh and exaggerated language he explains as an understandable byproduct of controversy—though Erasmus hints that Luther did seem to *like* hyperbole, too. Even the exaggerations may be warranted if taken functionally as belonging more to exhortation than dogmatics. But the language remains defective insofar as it loses the (equally legitimate) interests of the rival party. Luther's view is rejected for the sake of piety. But it is also interpreted as itself an expression of authentic piety.

Erasmus may not have solved one of the knottiest problems in the history of theology. But he did, in the course of exploring it, offer some absorbing insights into the nature of theology itself—what to look for in it and how to improve it. The Lutheran dogma thus became the occasion for a characteristic Erasmian reflection on theology and piety.[88] In the end, Erasmus's verdict upon Luther was that he did not overcome the "sophistic theology," but merely offered another version of it.[89] But it would be a mistake to conclude that while Luther stood for scholastic theology, the Erasmian renewal of theology was more closely linked with religion. The twofold irony of the debate on freedom of choice is that Luther *began* by sharing the Erasmian concern for a practical theology and Erasmus *ended* (in his *Hyperaspistes*) by trying to show himself better at scholastic theology than Luther. If we overlook the dual gap between intention and execution, we may justly conclude that what divided them was less a difference over the need for anchoring *theologia* in *pietas* than a difference over the requirements of *pietas* itself.

This is not to exclude the possibility of generous overlapping between the two conceptions of religion. Still, a difference remains. For Erasmus, the *prime* requirement was for strength to supply what was lacking in the will's best efforts. For Luther, the moment of the will's highest endeavor was the moment of greatest anguish because it marked the end of a tragic mistake. The issue over freedom of choice, whether or not it is the chief point of the Gospel, is at least an index to two different modes of being religious. That there *is* freedom of choice was, to Erasmus, a point on which there could be no yielding. Luther admitted that he would not want free choice even if he could have it.[90]

NOTES

1. Erasmus, *Methodus*, in *Desiderius Erasmus Roterodamus: Ausgewählte Werke*, ed. Hajo and Annemarie Holborn (Munich: C. H. Beck, 1933), p. 162. All translations are mine.

2. The text of the bull is in Carl Mirbt and Kurt Aland, eds., *Quellen zur Geschichte des Papsttums und des römischen Katholizismus*, vol. 1 (6th ed., Tubingen: J. C. B. Mohr [Paul Siebeck], 1967), pp. 504-13. On the arrival of the bull, see Luther to George Spalatin, 11 Oct. 1520: *W.A.* (=Weimarer Ausgabe, 1883ff.), *Briefwechsel*, no. 341, and the editor's comments (2.193-95). *W.A.* will be cited by volume, page, and (where appropriate) line.

3. *Warum des Papstes und seiner Jünger Bücher . . . verbrannt sind* (1520): *W.A.*, 7.182.7 and 12. The citation from Judges 15:11 concludes the work.

4. *W.A.*, 1.354.5.

5. Ibid., 1.365.21ff.

6. Ibid., 7.146.3-8.

7. *Grund und Ursach aller Artikel . . .* (1521): *W.A.*, 7.448.25/449.24.

8. *W.A.*, 7.148.14. The German has "chief article" (*hewbt artickell*): *W.A.*, 7.448.7/449.7.

9. Ibid., 7.142-49; esp. 146.20, 26.

10. In the remainder of this paragraph, I have used some themes from Luther's *Römerbriefvorlesung* (1515-16) to interpret the thirteenth Heidelberg thesis and the concept of *Eigenwille* in *Grund und Ursach*. See esp. *W.A.*, 56.258.23-259.7, 304.25-305.20, 325. 1-21, 355.28-357.26, 390.23-394.5.

11. *W.A.*, 7.148.35ff. Note the explicit statement that grace was the real issue.

12. *De servo arbitrio* (1525): *W.A.*, 18.786.26. In actual fact, others took up the *summa caussae* before Erasmus, who was himself partially dependent on John Fisher's *Confutatio assertionis Lutheranae* (1523). For some recent comments on Erasmus's relation to Fisher, see Bernhard Lohse, "Marginalien zum Streit zwischen Erasmus und Luther," *Luther. Zeitschrift der Luther-Gesellschaft* 46, no. 1 (1975): 5-24; esp. 13-15.

13. Erasmus to Godescalc Rosemondt (the rector), 18 Oct. 1520: *EE* (=*Erasmi Epistolae*), 1153.15 (4.362); to Thomas More, November (?) 1520: *EE*, 1162.220-24 (4.389). I cite the epistles in the edition of P. S. and H. M. Allen and H. W. Garrod, *Opus Epistolarum Des. Erasmi Roterodami*, 12 vols. (Oxford: Clarendon Press, 1906-58), by number and line. The volume and page, where given, are added in parentheses.

14. See esp. *EE*, 939 (to Frederick the Wise), 967 (to Cardinal Wolsey), 1033 (to Albert of Brandenburg), 1143 (to Pope Leo X), and 1167 (to Lorenzo Campeggio). Many of the themes of these programmatic (or apologetic) letters can be found scattered throughout Erasmus's correspondence in the period. It is not feasible to list the extensive secondary literature on the relation of Erasmus and Luther. I have probably learned most from Zickendraht, Augustijn, and (on Erasmus, but not on Luther!) Humbertclaude: Karl Zickendraht, *Der Streit zwischen Erasmus und Luther über die Willensfreiheit* (Leipzig: J. C. Hinrichs, 1909); C. Augustijn, *Erasmus en de Reformatie. Een onderzoek naar de houding die Erasmus ten opzichte van de Reformatie heeft aangenomen* (Amsterdam: H. J. Paris, 1962); H. Humbertclaude, *Erasme et Luther. Leur Polémique sur le libre arbitre*, Études de Theologie et d'Histoire (Paris: Bloud, 1909).

15. Used in the *Axiomata* (see n. 20), the phrase occurs also in the correspondence: e.g. to Gerard Geldenhauer, 9 Sept. 1520: *EE*, 1141.25 (4.340). The real target of the opposition was not Luther, but the Muses: to Christopher Hegendorfer, 13 Dec. 1520: *EE*, 1168.30-31 (4.412-13).

16. To Luther, 30 May 1519: *EE*, 980.37 (3.606).

17. To John Reuchlin, 8 Nov. 1520: *EE*, 1155.8 (4.371). With the words *Lutheri causam*

a tua bonarumque literarum causa seiungere (p. 372, 1. 18), cf. to Philip Melanchthon, 6 Sept. 1524; *EE*, 1496.50 (5.546).

18. To Pope Adrian VI, 22 Mar. 1523 (?): *EE*, 1352.91 (5.259).

19. In addition to the letters already cited, see to John Lang, 17 Oct. 1518 (?): *EE*, 872 (3.408-10); 30 May 1519 (?): *EE*, 983 (3.609). The Roman monarchy is the plague of Christendom (872.16-18), and Erasmus does not see who could attempt to abolish it without uproar (983.14). "Sed tamen haud scio an expediat hoc ulcus aperte tangere" (872.19). Cf. to Spalatin, 6 July 1520: *EE*, 1119.27-41 (4.298).

20. The monuments of these activities are Erasmus's "three Reformation tracts" (as Ferguson calls them): the *Acta academiae lovaniensis*, the *Axiomata*, and the *Consilium:* Wallace K. Ferguson, ed., *Erasmi Opuscula: A Supplement to the Opera Omnia* (The Hague: Martinus Nijhoff, 1933), pp. 304-61.

21. To Campeggio, 6 Dec. 1520: *EE*, 1167.137-41, 155-58 (4.403-04). For Erasmus's sense of *kairos*, cf. also *Axiomata*, ll. 37-38, and *Consilium*, ll. 114-16: Ferguson, *Erasmi Opuscula*, pp. 337, 359.

22. To Louis Baer, 14 May 1521: *EE*, 1203.24 (4.494).

23. To Aloisius Marlian, 25 Mar. 1521: *EE*, 1195.33 (4.459).

24. To Richard Pace, 5 July 1521: *EE*, 1218.2 (4.540).

25. To Jodocus Jonas, 10 May 1521: *EE*, 1202.31-37, 48, 128-33 (4.487, 489). Luther is disruptive because of his manner (ll. 47-50), his radicalism (ll. 215-26), and his divulging to cobblers what should be confined to scholars (ll. 56-65). Note also the reference to his "paradoxes" (l. 51).

26. To Marlian, 25 Mar. 1521: *EE*, 1195.128 (4.462). Despite the sentiments expressed to Jonas (n. 25 above), Erasmus could still wonder, even after publication of *De libero arbitrio*, whether perhaps God intended to heal the church by Luther's "bitter and drastic remedy": *EE*, 1495.7-11, 1497.1, 1523.137-41, 1526.132-39. In any case, he did not want the good in Luther to perish with him: e.g. *EE*, 1313.12-17.

27. To Alexander Schweiss, 13 Mar. 1521: *EE*, 1192.55-78 (4.454-55).

28. To Adrian VI, 22 Mar. 1523: *EE*, 1352.147-91 (5.260-61). The development of Erasmus's relations with Luther has been variously interpreted: it has been held that at the end of 1520 he was a committed advocate of Luther (Kalkoff); that a break had already been occasioned by the Leipzig Disputation of the previous year (Krodel); that his attitude had been two-sided from the first, but a crisis occurred in 1520 (Augustijn). I cannot here discuss the problem, and I do not need to: it is sufficient to indicate certain Erasmian principles that remained constant as the circumstances changed. With the earlier letters already cited, cf. the retrospective apology to Duke George, 12 Dec. 1524: *EE*, 1526. That Erasmus was publicly understood to have turned against Luther after 1520 has been carefully documented by Heinz Holeczek, "Die Haltung des Erasmus zu Luther nach dem Scheitern seiner Vermittlungspolitik 1520/21," *Archiv für Reformationsgeschichte* 64 (1973): 85-112.

29. See, e.g., to Schweiss, 13 Mar. 1521: *EE*, 1192.19 (4.453).

30. *EE*, 1217.138-46, 1225.239-41, 1263.43-50, 1313.50-54.

31. To Willibald Pirckheimer, 30 Mar. 1522: *EE*, 1268.79 (5.35); to Peter Barbirius, 17 Apr. 1523: *EE*, 1358.3 (5.276).

32. *EE*, 1408.21-23, 1411. 23-24, 1415.54-55, 1416.24. Duke George was particularly biting (*EE*, 1340). Even after Erasmus had determined to write, George blamed him for writing too late (*EE*, 1448.33-56).

3. Felician Gess, ed., *Akten und Briefe zur Kirchenpolitik Herzog Georgs von Sachsen*, 2 vols. (Leipzig: B. G. Teubner, 1905-17), vol. 1, no. 508, p. 509. This was George's response to King Henry VIII's letter to the Saxon princes (20 Jan. 1523), in which Zickendraht saw a key document for understanding Erasmus's choice of theme (see note 14

[pp. 16–17]). Zickendraht's thesis, that the *Diatribe* "betrays its intellectual derivation from England" (p. 17), though a similar view was maintained by Freitag in his introduction to Luther's *De servo arbitrio* (in *W.A.*, 18), has generally been judged an overstatement. See the critical remarks of Johannes von Walter in his edition of Erasmus's book: *Quellenschriften zur Geschichte des Protestantismus*, no. 8 (Leipzig: A. Deichert, 1910), p. x. Henry does seem to have been especially influential on Erasmus's decision to write (*EE*, 1408.21, 1415.54), but not necessarily on the theme chosen.

34. *EE*, 1324.23, 1367.25 ff., 1448.54.

35. *Spongia adversus aspergines Hutteri* (1523): *LB* (=*Desiderii Erasmi Roterodami Opera Omnia*, ed. Jean LeClerc, 10 vols. [Leiden, 1703–06]), 10: 1654A, 1663A⁼B, 1672C. Erasmus means that he made no mention of heresy in his letter to Laurinus (see n. 42 below), which provoked Hutten's outburst; but the denial can be generalized, and elsewhere Erasmus states expressly that nowhere in his writings does he call Luther's doctrine a "heresy": *Adversus calumniosissimam epistolam Martini Lutheri* (1534), *LB*, 10: 1537D.

36. To Ulrich Zwingli, 31 Aug. 1523: *EE*, 1384.2–14, 89 (5.327, 330).

37. To George, 3 Sept. 1522: *EE*, 1313.21–28 (5.126). The list of soporifics is revealing: "Mundus indormiebat opinionibus scholasticis, constitutiunculis humanis, nec aliud audiebat quam de indulgentiis, de compositionibus, de potestate Pontificis Romani" (ll. 22–24).

38. Not every error is a heresy: *EE*, 939.81, 1033.234–43, 1202.253. See further n. 41 and n. 88.

39. In his correspondence with Melanchthon after the printing of *De libero arbitrio*, Erasmus expresses the wish that he could visit Wittenberg in person (*EE*, 1496.15) and denies that the "salt" detected in his book by Melanchthon was intended for Luther (*EE*, 1523.125). But he makes it plain that he does not want the gentle reply Melanchthon assured him he could expect from Luther (*EE*, 1523.120–24). In other words, he was counting on the very vehemence he professed to deplore. It is possible to exaggerate Erasmus's virtue, which (in his own phrase) was not *sine certo consilio*. But this is not to doubt his sincerity in moving the issue onto the academic plain. On this strategy, see esp. Augustijn, *Erasmus en de Reformatie*, pp. 210, 296.

40. Mention is made of the plan to John Glapion, 21 Apr. (?) 1522: *EE*, 1275.20 (5.48), and the details of it are in the *Catalogus lucubrationum* contained in the letter to John Botzheim, 30 Jan. 1523: *EE* (1.34–36). Cf. *Spongia*: *LB*, 10: 1651B.

41. Thompson offers the conjecture that the *Inquisitio* may be an abbreviated version of one of the planned dialogues: Craig R. Thompson, ed., *Inquisitio de Fide: A Colloquy by Desiderius Erasmus Roterodamus 1524*, Yale Studies in Religion, no. 15 (New Haven: Yale University Press, 1950), p. 37. Thompson's interpretation of the *Inquisitio* strongly supports the conclusion that, for Erasmus, the Lutheran affair was not a matter of heresy. See esp. pp. 2–3, 38–43.

42. To Marcus Laurinus, 1 Feb. 1523: *EE*, 1342.733–1021 (5.221–27). Echoes of this letter can be heard unmistakably in *De libero arbitrio*. One reason why Erasmus had become preoccupied with this theme is plain from ll. 926–58: the Lutherans had attacked *his* views on freedom of choice. On Erasmus's alleged pelagianizing, see *EE*, 1225.282, 1275.27.

43. To Henry, 4 Sept. 1523: *EE*, 1385.11 ("Molior aliquid adversus nova dogmata"); to John Faber, 21 Nov. 1523: *EE*, 1397.14 ("Si suppetent vires, addetur libellus De libero arbitrio"); to Paul Bombasius, 19 Jan. 1524: *EE*, 1411.24 ("Aggressus sum negotium"). As the letter to Bombasius indicates, the procrastination was partly out of fear that he might only add to the uproar. Cf. to Theodoric Hezius (?), 16 Sept. 1523: *EE*, 1386.22 (5.331).

44. To Baer, Feb. 1524 (?): *EE*, 1419 (5.399–400); from Baer, Feb. 1524 (?): *EE*, 1420 (5.400–02).

45. To Henry, Mar. 1524 (?): *EE*, 1430.12–20 (5.417).

46. From Luther, 15 Apr. (?) 1524: *EE,* 1443.67 (5.447); to Luther, 8 May 1524: *EE,* 1445.16, 21-22 (5.451-52).

47. To Pirckheimer, 21 July 1524: *EE,* 1466.58-60 (5.496); to Barbirius, 26 July 1524 (?): *EE,* 1470.46 (5.506).

48. To Haio Hermann, 31 Aug. 1524: *EE,* 1479.182-85 (5.521). Note that Erasmus anticipated a sharp reaction from the extremists in the Lutheran camp, if not from Luther himself.

49. See the remarks of the editor on *EE,* 1481-98 (5.525).

50. *De libero arbitrio* διατριβή *sive collatio per Desiderium Erasmum Roterodamum.* Although the book was published during September 1524 also in Antwerp and Cologne, the primacy of the Basel edition (by Froben) was maintained by Walter (n. 33), pp. xiii-xvii). It was promptly translated into German—from the recondite language of the scholars to which Erasmus's intent naturally assigned it! I use the text, edited by Winfried Lesowsky, together with *Hyperaspistes I* in the *Ausgewählte Schriften,* vol. 4 (Darmstadt: Wissenschaftliche Buchgesellschaft, 1969), which follows the definitive edition of Walter. My references are to the divisions in Lesowsky (taken from Walter), which I give, as far as possible, in parentheses in the main body of the essay. I cite both books of *Hyperaspistes* (1526-27), Erasmus's reply to Luther's *De servo arbitrio,* from *LB,* vol. 10.

51. To Henry, 6 Sept. 1524: *EE,* 1493.4 (5.541).

52. Since even the Apostles taught paradoxes, they are not excluded on principle (I, b 6). But Luther's paradoxes are virtually "enigmas" (IV, 16), and all Christendom is in uproar because of them (IV, 17). One such paradox must generate a system of supportive paradoxes, such as an exaggerated doctrine of original sin (IV, 13-14).

53. On the meaning of *liberum arbitrium,* which I have translated "free choice" or "freedom of choice," see esp. III, b 4: "Porro voluntas huc aut illo versatilis dicitur arbitrium." Cf. the phrases *voluntas, qua eligimus aut refugimus* (II, a 3), *eligendi potestas* (II, a 7), *utroque volubilis* (ibid.), and *voluntas huc et illuc flexilis* (II, a 18).

54. Erasmus does not deny that God, in the Scriptures, does sometimes force a man's judgment, altering his volition or even depriving him of reason; as, for example, when he caused Balaam to bless those he meant to curse (Num. 23.11). But this is not how God acts *as a rule* (III, a 8; III, b 7).

55. As often in Erasmus, the abstract argument is accompanied by lively analogies drawn from human relationships: the king and the commander, the lord and his servant (IV, 5).

56. Since he speaks of this common grace as *insita,* Erasmus seems to lump together what Thomas distinguishes as the form by which a created thing acts and the motion imparted to it by the Prime Mover: *S.T.* (=*Summa theologiae*) IaIIae, Q. 109, Art. 1, etc.

57. If *proniores in favorem liberi arbitrii* is intended as a specific comparison with the Pelagians, then we would have to agree with Lesowsky—see note 50 (p. 49, n. 74)—that this is an error on Erasmus's part. I have preferred to take the phrase as a more general comparison, a placing of the Scotists on the total spectrum. They are then in antithesis to the Augustinians, later to be described as *propensiores in favorem gratiae* (II, a 10).

58. In *Hyperaspistes I* (*LB,* 10:1327C), Erasmus includes Thomas in this group. It is, presumably, the same party that he subsequently describes in the *Discourse* as farthest removed from the Pelagians (II, a 12).

59. Besides the *gratia naturalis,* Erasmus distinguishes three kinds of grace in II, a 11: (1) *gratia peculiaris, exstimulans,* or *operans* (granted, some think, to everyone at some time in his life); (2) *gratia gratum faciens, provehens,* or *cooperans* (presumably the same as *gratia, quae peccatum abolet:* II, a 9); and (3) *gratia consummans.* But although he can speak of receiving the first without the third, he acknowledges the accepted view that, if we leave aside *gratia naturalis,* there is only one grace, divided in name according to the di-

versity of its operations in us. For *gratia naturalis* and *gratia exstimulans* (or *praeveniens*), see the interpretation (borrowed from Jerome) of the Parable of the Prodigal Son (III, c 11).

60. The identity of the final two opinions is clear enough; it is made explicit in *Hyperaspistes I (LB*, 10:1327C-D).

61. The difference between Carlstadt and Luther is restated in II, a 15. Though not so bad as Luther's, even Carlstadt's view goes too far (*praeter casam:* II, a 12), and Erasmus had a profound dislike for Carlstadt's impersonal metaphors (the potter's clay, the craftsman's axe: II, a 12, also IV, 11 and IV, 16).

62. Whether Erasmus interpreted the Scotists fairly, or whether he assimilated their view to that of Gabriel Biel, Luther's *bête noire*, depends on the status of *gratia gratis data* in the Scotist system; and this has been a matter of debate among the scholars. On the relations among the Thomist, "old Franciscan," and Scotist doctrines of grace, see Reinhold Seeberg, *Lehrbuch der Dogmengeschichte*, 5th ed., 4 vols. (Graz: Akademische Druck und Verlagsanstalt, 1953-54), 3:444-86 and 664-67, which takes account of the work of Minges. For Biel, see Heiko A. Oberman, *The Harvest of Medieval Theology: Gabriel Biel and Late Medieval Nominalism* (Cambridge, Mass.: Harvard University Press, 1963), pp. 135-39.

63. At one point (III, b 2), Erasmus finds the inclination to sin only "in most men." Cf. the qualifying *ferme* in the sentence: "Sunt enim ferme mortalium ingenia . . . proclivia ad scelera . . ." (I, a 10). Elsewhere (II, a 5), he recognizes the existence (along with the *lex naturae*) of a contrary bias toward virtue, though—without grace—it remains *inefficax ad salutem aeternam*. In general, Erasmus seems to think that, before grace, we are *more* inclined to evil than to good (II, a 8). Cf. also III, b 4.

64. On sin as weakness, see further II, a 4 (where *ad honesta inefficax* presumably means "lethargic" rather than totally "impotent"), II, a 5, II, a 8 (sin is like an injury or disease), III, b 1, and III, b 4; on grace as help, see II, a 6, III, c 13. Luther's central thought on sin was rather that sin vitiates the motivation.

65. Once again, the analogies are striking: the sheep and the branch (III, c 3), the child and the apple (III, c 3, IV, 9-10). But the credit should go mainly to Augustine: *In Joann. evang. tract.* xxvi.5.

66. See also III, a 4, III, c 4, III, c 12, IV, 7, IV, 10. The *posse consentire et cooperari* is a *munus dei* (III, c 4; cf. IV, 7). God's unchangeable will does not work in us the *velle* itself (IV, 3). (Erasmus, accordingly, is glad to avail himself of Ambrose's interpretation of Phil. 2:13: III, c 6.) But is the *munus* a gift of nature or of special grace? This, of course, is the crucial question. The answer to it, I think, is given in III, c 11-12: the ability to apply oneself to prevenient grace is among the *dotes naturae*. (Erasmus would thus endorse the notion, reported in II, a 11, that repentance is possible to those who "apply the remnant of free choice, with all their might, to the assistance of the Deity, who invites, as it were, but does not compel them to betterment.") Man's freedom to respond to prevenient grace, it appears, is a particular instance of the natural freedom of choice. Hence one must assume that when Erasmus speaks of the "freeing" or "healing" of the will (as in IV, 8) he is implicitly denying, not the natural freedom of the will to say yes or no to grace, but its ability either (1) to control the offer of grace, without which a man does not perceive the right path, or (2) to achieve, without grace, the goal that grace presents.

67. The three stages correspond, of course, to the three types of grace (n. 59); and the distinction between *initium, progressus,* and *summa* (IV, 8) indicates what Erasmus intends by the word *summa* in III, c 1 and III, c 4: the "completion" or "consummation" of the entire movement. Cf. also the distinction between *cogitare, velle,* and *perficere* (in III, c 4).

68. Cf. the remarks on pagan virtues (II, a 10) and *peccatum alienum* (IV, 13-14).

69. We attribute the whole to him because our contribution is minimal (III, c 1; cf. III, c 12). "God does not want a man to claim anything for himself, even though there were something he could claim deservedly" (III, c 8).

70. The additional phrase *adiutus auxilio dei,* in a similar passage in III, b 3, perhaps moves the thought out of the Scotist orbit.

71. Besides *Hyperaspistes,* there is the important letter to Thomas More, 30 Mar. 1527: *EE,* 1804 (7.5–14). Naturally, these sources would require an essay to themselves.

72. Walter concludes: " . . . über ein Schwanken zwischen Thomas, Alexander und Duns Scotus ist er nicht hinausgekommen" (n. 33), p. xxx. McSorley places Erasmus "between Neo-Semi-Pelagianism and Augustine": Harry J. McSorley, *Luther: Right or Wrong? An Ecumenical-Theological Study of Luther's Major Work, The Bondage of the Will* (New York: Newman Press, and Minneapolis: Augsburg Publishing House, 1969), pp. 288–93. According to Levi, Erasmus was caught in a "dilemma" and—given the limits of the sixteenth-century discussion—*could* not incorporate Pico's theme of man's natural moral endeavor into a non-Pelagian theory of grace: Anthony Levi, *Pagan Virtue and the Humanism of the Northern Renaissance* (London: Society for Renaissance Studies, 1974).

73. Kohls argues that Erasmus's notion of a "will made free by grace" aligns him with Thomas: Ernst-Wilhelm Kohls, "Die theologische Position und der Traditionszusammenhang des Erasmus mit dem Mittelalter in 'De libero arbitrio,'" in Karlmann Beyschlag et al., eds., *Humanitas-Christianitas. Walther v. Loewenich zum 65. Geburtstag* (Witten: Luther-Verlag, 1968), pp. 32–46. Winsome though this line of interpretation may be, my remarks above (in n. 66) will betray the fact that I am not persuaded by it. When Kohls speaks of grace as simply the offer of grace, and of freedom as simply the freedom to decide, it must be replied (1) that for Thomas the turning of the will is the effect of grace as *gratia gratum faciens* and *operans* (*S.T.* IaIIae, Q. 113, Art. 3), and (2) that for Erasmus freedom of choice is the gift of grace as *gratia naturalis.*

74. "Erasmus trat aus dem Bannkreis der von ihm bekämpften scholastischen Theologie mit ihrer Lehre vom meritum de congruo et de condigno nicht heraus." So Max Richter concluded: *Desiderius Erasmus und seine Stellung zu Luther auf Grund ihrer Schriften, Quellen und Darstellungen aus der Geschichte der Reformationsjahrhunderts,* vol. 3 (Leipzig: M. Heinsius Nachfolger, 1907), p. 61. Whatever the ambiguities of the *Discourse,* Humbertclaude—who thought that the Augustinian tendency of the work against Luther may have been merely prudential—detected an increasing sympathy for the Scotist view after 1524 (pp. 220ff.). In this he is followed by John B. Payne, *Erasmus: His Theology of the Sacraments* (Richmond, Va.: John Knox Press, 1970), esp. p. 264, n. 18, and p. 265, n. 20. But I am not sure that Payne allows sufficient weight to the Pauline veto of merits *de congruo,* of which Erasmus writes to More (*nisi refragaretur Paulus: EE,* 1804.93).

75. Contrast, for instance, the remarks against Carlstadt in IV, 11, with Thomas, *S.T.* IaIIae, Q. 111, Art. 2. Cf. also *Hyperaspistes I, LB,* 10:1331E. Erasmus's position in fact resembles a view that Augustine retracted: *De praedest.* iii.7. Cf. *Hyperaspistes II, LB,* 10:1528F, 1532A.

76. Erasmus employs the expressions συνεργὸς *gratiae* (III, c 5) and *gratiae* δός ερδ ἑυ (IV, 7), the Greek cognates from which the concept of "synergism" is derived (cf. 1 Cor. 3:9). The Formula of Concord (1577) expressly distinguishes the questions of preparation for, and acceptance of, grace in the preamble to the Epitome, art. II. Cf. the corresponding distinction between the errors of semi-Pelagianism and synergism (Epit., art. II, secs. 10–11; Sol. Decl., art. II, secs. 76–77).

77. This, I take it, is the intent of III, c 12. Cf. *Hyperaspistes II, LB,* 10:1533F–1534A, etc.

78. *Hyperaspistes II, LB,* 10:1340A. In *Hyperaspistes I,* Erasmus insisted that the Scotist view was a legitimate *opinio,* left open by the church (*LB,* 10:1323D, 1327D). He makes no mention of the pronouncements of the Second Council of Orange (529).

79. *W.A.,* 18.609.15ff.

80. "Das problem der Willensfreiheit gehört auch und vor allem in das Gebiet der Frömmigkeit. . . ." Erasmus viewed it as *Seelsorger* and *Pädagog.* Karl Heinz Oelrich, *Der späte Erasmus und die Reformation,* Reformationsgeschichtliche Studien und Texte, no. 86 (Munster: Aschendorf, 1961), pp. 128, 133.

81. In I, a 9, Erasmus distinguishes between (1) matters God wants to remain wholly un-known to us (like the date for the Last Judgment), (2) matters we may explore only as far as reticence toward God permits (such as the distinction of Persons in the Trinity), (3) matters God wants us to know thoroughly (namely, the precepts of the good life), and (4) matters which, even if true and knowable, it would not be expedient to expose to common ears (e.g., that a council had erred). It will be noted that moral matters receive top priority. The belief that some matters ought not to be divulged to the laity is a constant theme in Erasmus's correspondence, sometimes accompanied by disavowal of Plato's "noble lie": *EE,* 872.19, 1033.91, 1167, 167–72, 1195.105–19, 1202.56–62, 123–28, 1523.84–87.

82. It is uncertain what passage from Augustine Erasmus has in mind (if any). See Lesowsky (n. 50).

83. The selfsame concern underlies Erasmus's reflections on trinitarian speculation (though this is an instance of Class 2 matters, see n. 81): "At the high price of unity, we love less while wanting to know more than enough" (I, a 9).

84. The same figure occurs in Allen, *EE,* 1342, 959–63 and (with the priorities reversed) 1804, 96–99.

85. By Walter (n. 33 above), p. xxxii, and McSorley, *Luther,* p. 284, for example.

86. He also understood the doctrine of sin as radical defect (II, a 10) and presumably could have answered the question he sets aside in IV, 14: why the Lutherans taught the impossibility of keeping the Commandments.

87. Cf. the honorific title bestowed on Luther in *Hyperaspistes II: doctor hyperbolicus* (*LB,* 10:1345D).

88. Zickendraht's judgment that "the shell [of the *Discourse*] is more authentic than the kernel" (*Der Streit zwischen Erasmus und Luther,* p. 26) is of one piece with his claim that Erasmus was led to deal dogmatically with his theme (i.e., as a question of truth) only by external pressure (see n. 33 above). "It is plainly the main purpose of the *Diatribe* . . . to permit validity to [*Glaubenslehren*] only as subservient aids for a pattern of ethical exis-tence." Erasmus's case is not against *necessitas absoluta,* but against the overestimate of dogmatic formulations exhibited by the Lutheran movement (pp. 26–27). This is an in-triguing interpretation of the *libellus.* But, surely, Erasmus *did* want to object to the Lu-theran dogma; and he did so, in part, because he thought it was *false* (absurd as well as dangerous). Hence he argued against it with the norm of Scripture in the *Discourse* and, in *Hyperaspistes I,* with the authority of the church—finally asserting bluntly that to doubt free choice was considered by him to be heretical (*LB,* 10:1259D).

89. "Neque tu sophisticam theologiam sustulisti, sed mutasti." *Hyperaspistes I: LB,* 10:1277B.

90. *W.A.,* 18.783.17.

11 Erasmus's *Ciceronianus:* A Comical Colloquy

EMILE V. TELLE

LE RIDICULE TUE

I

Erasmus's *Ciceronianus* (March 1528) hit the world of the Republic of Letters like a bombshell. Forthwith it fired the reactions of his contemporaries into an uproar similar to that brought about, some eighteen years before, by *The Praise of Folly,* even though the overt target did not seem to be the most irritable of the human species, to wit the theologians, with whom the Rotterdamer had been fighting pitched battles since the publication of the *Novum Instrumentum* (1516).[1] Owing to the fame of the great humanist and his Latin style, the *Ciceronianus* did not fail to delight, dismay, disturb, or fluster those fellow scholars whose overwhelming preoccupation lay with the purity and efficacy of Latin.

There can be little doubt that Erasmus's main intent (though unavowed) was to vindicate his own kind of practical stylistics, which the conservative theologians and Luther as well had branded as imprecise, ambiguous, spellbinding—in other words, un-Ciceronian and therefore apt to foment ideas or strengthen leanings they deemed favorable to new evangelisms—evangelisms that frowned upon an authoritarian approach to the Bible, and especially the Epistles of Saint Paul.

In this essay, I shall not deal with the unexpectedness nor the novelty and seriousness of this dialogue. This has already been done.[2] I merely want to bring out its stark comedy.

Beyond any doubt, the *Ciceronianus* is, besides the matrimonial colloquies published in August 1523, the best and most forceful colloquy Erasmus ever wrote. (He had not produced a farce of this length since the *Julius exclusus e coelis* [1513; published 1517], which we may safely attribute to him.) Numerous studies have appeared in the last fifteen years on the many facets of the Dutchman's genius and activities: but his gifts as a budding playwright of "comédies de caractère" deserve our attention too,[3] and it is fitting that I should broach the subject on the occasion of the publication of a volume meant to honor the able and witty translator of Erasmus's comedies; I mean, of course, the *Colloquies.* May I remind my reader that the *Ciceronianus* was printed again in March 1529 by Froben and Herwagen at Basel, bound with a new edition of the *Colloquia.* After that edition, it never became part of or associated with the

211

Colloquies, because it made too bulky a volume (over a thousand pages).[4] However, it is indeed a colloquy.[5]

II

The play opens on a street scene in Padua (?). Bulephorus (bearer of good advice, who is about seventy) is taking a walk in the company of Hypologus (his "yes-man"). They notice a man who looks like—indeed, who is—dear Nosoponus (sickly one) whom they have not seen for some time. He is an old acquaintance from way back, when they were in school.

Poor fellow! He is not what he used to be. He was once so nicely plumpish and frisky. He is now the very shadow of himself: A shadow forsooth—.

Thus we shall meet with the hero of the comedy before he actually arrives on stage; that is to say, the Ciceronian, the man who fell prey to an ill-conceived Ciceronianism. Both Bulephorus and Hypologus bandy quips about their old friend and his sickness. What's ailing him? Is it hydropisia? No. It is a deeper affliction. A new type of leprosy? Tuberculosis? Liver trouble? Hard to say. For this new type of fever does not raise the temperature of the body. As yet it has no name (And we know that naming a disease is the first step toward a possible cure—). It does not have a Latin name; in Greek, however, it is called *Zelodouleia,* in other words, a frenzy caused by an overpowering and enslaving desire to imitate and to emulate. The patient has been suffering for the last seven years. Obviously it is a mental disorder, Bulephorus assures Hypologus, which may best be treated by the doctor (Bulephorus assumes that he himself has the qualities of a psychiatrist) pretending that he too is afflicted with the same trouble. Both Hypologus and his friend shall therefore play the game in order not to arouse any violent antagonism in Nosoponus, who now draws near.

The second scene reveals a Nosoponus whose candid sincerity and youthful enthusiasm keep him from detecting the trick being perpetrated upon him by his well-intentioned friends. He, pregnant with his scholarly endeavors, is anxious to be fooled; he opens himself up disarmingly to a searching questionnaire and confesses without any compunction that he will not rest and be satisfied until he achieves the goal attained by Christopher Longolius when he was acclaimed by the Italian Ciceronians themselves as the true Ciceronian and granted Roman citizenship. However, premature death (in 1522) had deprived Longolius and the world of humanism of the exquisite fruits of his talent. He, Nosoponus, expects to fulfill the promises Longolius could not carry out and even outdo him:

> Would that I die should I not reach this aim, rather than be counted among the saints! which in these "theological" times, was an utterance smacking of blasphemy. . . .[6]

Bulephorus (of course!) is in full agreement with this rather pagan wish: tongue in cheek, he corroborates by saying that immortality is better achieved through Ciceronianism than Christian virtues: "How do you plan to attain this goal?" Nosoponus, whose gullibility is beyond reproach, goes about explaining his method in detail. And this is the gem of the comedy.

Our patient has not put his hand or set his eyes on any book not written by Cicero for the last seven years. Moreover, to avoid any accidental mistake or even temptation on his part, he locked all non-Ciceronian literature in a strong box. The only volumes to be seen in his library are Cicero's. A picture of the great orator is hung above the lintel of every door in his home, including the door to his chapel (obviously he did not care to place it inside—with the other saints), since Cicero's name is to be found with the apostles' in his calendar. In and on his mind, even during his sleep and before his eyes, Cicero is at all times present.

This is the cadre of his study. "Now, tell us about your actual work," Bulephorus asks in feigned wonderment.

Nosoponus first went through a period of purification and probation which took as much time as was required to read all of the orator's lucubrations. After this ordeal, he made an alphabetical lexicon of all the vocabulary in these books (without computer, of course): the result is a volume two robust men could hardly carry on their backs!

A second one, heftier and bigger than the first, contains all the stylistic expressions and devices used by Cicero. There is even a third opus, which enables our Ciceronian to check on all the rhythms of the sentences, according to their beginnings and their endings, the cadences, the inner clauses, etc., etc., so that none of Cicero's periodic measures, traits, and features may escape the scholar.

Bulephorus, overwhelmed by the ponderous size of volume one, asks: "How is it that it be bigger than all the works of the Roman?" Nosoponus wonders at the lack of gumption on the part of his friend. The volume is enormous in size because, for each word, Nosoponus went to the trouble of stringing out all the exceptions used for each vocable, and each and every case is illustrated in each context, with reference to page and line number. An asterisk is added to point out whether the word appears at the beginning or end of the line, or in the middle—nothing is left to chance.

Such a stupendous masterpiece is to be used first by consulting the index, and with such reverence (*tanta religione!*) that no word is to be chosen unless it can be found in the index, but also according to the case, as illustrated by Cicero. For example: *nasutus* may be used; the comparative and superlative, never to be located in Cicero's works, are to be shunned: *lego,* yes: *legor,* no!; *lectio,* yes, but not the diminutive *lectiuncula.* What is only Cicero's is underscored in red;

the rest, in black. Nosoponus's indexes cannot therefore be misused or im-
peached. Cicero's Latin is the only trustworthy coinage; the rest is false money
or counterfeit, including Terence or any other classical author. No exception is
to be made: *Cicero unus!* Do not let us minimize the importance, value, and
size of these indexes, which an elephant could hardly carry.

Such is Erasmus's sketch for the full portrait of Nosoponus, as a man wholly
and blindly addicted to his mania and totally immune to any criticism when it
comes to his faith in practice: (1) in writing and (2) in speech. In order to speak
well, one must first and foremost speak to paper, that is, in writing. Obviously!
Nosoponus writes only at night, in the most profound silence of nocturnal
quiet—provided those nights are not distraught by stormy winds. "So wrote, of
yore, men anxious to chisel something worthy of immortal fame," Bulephorus
adds unperturbed. Our man has located his study in the inner recesses of his
house: the walls are thick; the doors and windows double, made soundproof
with plaster and pitch; no outside light, no noise can penetrate this sanctuary,
unless the din be unusual, such as that caused by quarreling women or a
blacksmith hammering away. Of course, Hypologus insists, thus outbidding
Nosoponus:

> "It's why I do not allow anyone to sleep in a room next to my library.
> People sometimes snore or talk in their sleep when dreaming. They sneeze
> also."
> Mice often hinder my writing at night," concurs Hypologus. There is no
> room even for a fly in my house."
> Wisely and happily devised, Nosoponus," agrees Bulephorus. "But those
> cares of the mind which beset in spite of this silence, are they not far more
> troublesome than the bellows or hammer of a smith? Indeed," underwrites
> Bulephorus, "haven't you ever been disturbed by love, hatred, fear,
> jealousy?"[7]

But Nosoponus has managed to cast away all passions of the mind or any greed
for worldly possessions:

> This quest is so sacred that the heart must be cleansed of all vain cares,
> just as it is required for the most arcane pursuits, such as magic, astrology,
> alchemy. . . . With taut concentration, I have thus imposed this discipline on
> myself. That is the main reason why I decided to live in celibacy. Not that
> I do not know how holy a state marriage is, but one cannot help that wife,
> children, relatives are the source of much worry and care.
> [Bulephorus:] You are a wise fellow, Nosoponus. For, in my case, should

I consecrate my nights to Cicero, my wife would break down my door, tear up my books, burn my papers. To cap it all, while I am busy with the Roman orator, she would call for an alternate to take care of her. Thus, while I would be striving to become another Cicero, she would bring forth some offspring unlike Bulephorus.[8]

Nosoponus skirted all those pitfalls, and, at the same time, turned away from all mundane ambitions. No public office, no prebend, no ecclesiastical dignities did he covet. He would not even have anything to do with the consulate or the papacy, were it offered to him. "He who truly loves cannot but love one person," chimes in Hypologus sententiously, in true Platonic form.[9]

Nosoponus eats lightly on the nights of his labors. No fat. No poetical fury when it comes to Ciceronian pursuits. The Ciceronian travail is a matter for sobriety: "As for me," Hypologus sheepishly confesses, "I cannot think well on an empty stomach." Nosoponus's diet on such nights, in contrast, consists of ten Corinth raisins, plus three coriander seeds dipped in sugar. Cold nights are conducive to his work. He then burns a type of firewood which is smokeless, and astrological tables tell him which evenings are more propitious for his labors.

A single letter, even on the most trifling subject (asking, for instance, for a book to be returned), requires several nights to compose, sometimes ten: writing, rewriting, correcting the corrections with the help of his dictionaries. The final product does not sound at all like the original draft. The addressee, in the meantime, is waiting for his letter, which will be an extremely well-written epistle (and the sender will also wait for his book).

Now we come to the art of speaking. Nosoponus makes a point never to speak Latin. Why is that? Casual conversation may spoil the purity of one's language. For daily use on trifling subjects, French or Flemish are sufficient for him. On occasions when the use of Latin is unavoidable, he has ready-made sentences he has learned by heart, thus giving the impression of spontaneity: "In this conversation of ours, now," Nosoponus states without mincing words, "I am aware of the stylistic shortcomings of your speech as much as I am of mine. Hence, to repair the damage a month's study might be needed."[10] When our Ciceronian has time to meditate, he goes over his phrases and sentences, polishes them up, and recites them to himself aloud.

Here ends the first act of the play, quite lively as we have seen, and not unworthy of Molière. I am thinking especially of the introductory scenes in *Le Tartuffe,* where the main character does not enter the stage until we have heard all we need to know about him, and even more.

III

As a comedy, the second act of the *Ciceronianus* is not to be compared with the first, inasmuch as bantering is no longer dominant and the tables are turned. Bulephorus now holds the floor. He lectures to Nosoponus, hoping to show him that the absolute perfection he attributes to the great orator is more a question of personal taste and untimely infatuation than one of dogmatic definitions in favor of this or that author. However, the stubborn attitude of Nosoponus cannot be mollified but is only hardened by all the skillful maieutics set to work by Bulephorus. The patient who is unable to laugh at himself is past recovery: a sure sign of insanity!

> Forsooth, I believe it is better to write three letters in Ciceronian style than a hundred volumes in a manner as exquisite as you may think, but different from Cicero's.[11]

No argument, no inducement will budge Nosoponus, who will find no defects in Cicero, whose failings he condones or overlooks, even in poetry: it is a religion with him, a superstition, a sort of literary Pharisaism. So the character of Nosoponus, intractable and adamant, is a source of constant amusement and laughter for the reader, who, when the play is over, has come to think of him as another Misanthrope whose very obsession and straightforwardness may endear him to us.

The last act of the comedy consists of a catalog of authors from antiquity to those contemporary with Erasmus, the purpose of which is to harp upon the nonreality of the ideally true Ciceronian: none of those authors could be dubbed Ciceronian, as Nosoponus understands the term. This honor roll, though long and tedious for the modern reader only, does not lack humor, since Bulephorus-Erasmus, with as much naive obstinacy as Nosoponus, wishes to drive home his point to such exhaustive length that Cicero himself, given the test, and coming back to life (of course), would be neither the Ciceronian nor even the Cicero Nosoponus dreamed him to be.

IV

The comical element is not confined to the character-caricature of the Ciceronian. As is Erasmus' wont, the text is sprinkled with anecdotes, humorous or sarcastic, which relieve the monotonously academic demonstration of Bulephorus's counterattack in the second part of the colloquy:

> The worst students are usually those who brag of their having been alumni of such and such university, under so and so as a teacher. The worst Ciceronians are those who boast of their addiction to Ciceronianism.

I knew doctors held in especially bad repute who wanted to be known as former pupils of a famous physician, in order to boost their fees. And when asked why did they prescribe a medicine, they would say: "Are you more learned than this celebrated doctor whose advice I am following?"[12]

Hypologus, not to be left outwitted, adds a tall tale concerning Erasmus himself: an individual had once seen the Rotterdamer tie a piece of wood to a quill that the famous scholar had found too short to write with. Thereupon, "monkeywise," he affixed sticks to all his pens, in order to be able to write in the Erasmian style (*erasmico more*)!

Continuing in this vein, Hypologus narrates at length the case of a poor painter unable to produce a truthful likeness of their friend Murius. He would spend his time and take refuge in "parerga" (i.e. unessential details): a hat, a scar, a few hairs on the right eyebrow. Seeing that his subject had shaved his beard, he painted a new chin, then retouched the chin when the beard began to grow again, adding a few pimples around the lips when the model had had a fever, etc.,[13] There are other amusing traits and innuendoes that could not escape his contemporaries but would pass unnoticed by today's readers not familiar with the period.

Erasmus, whose aversion to monasticism was well known in his lifetime, tells us that the Ciceronian does not handle a book that is not Cicero's, just as a Carthusian never touches or eats meat. Moreover, the author of the *Colloquia,* who was quite fond of diminutives and who did not shrink from coining them when needed, has Nosoponus state that *lectio* may be used, since it is to be found in the works of Cicero, but not *lectiuncula,* the joke being at Erasmus's expense.[14]

Nosoponus, who preaches "Cicero unus," inadvertently quotes Virgil, Ovid, and Horace. He raises the question of marriage versus celibacy—a moot question at all times, but a burning issue in the century of the Reformation. Moreover, he poses the subsidiary one: should the lay scholar marry? Bulephorus solved the problem long ago, we are led to understand, by risking the perils of matrimony.[15]

The play presents details amusing for the 1528 reader: the quest for pure and perfect Ciceronianism has nothing to do with the *furor poeticus,* in favor then with the vogue of Neoplatonism; nothing to do with Bacchic fury, of course, since sobriety and ascetic self-denials and privations are, as with monkdom, the sine qua non for those pursuits.[16]

Erasmus has Bulephorus (his alter ego) declare that Erasmus is nothing but a polygraph, using much ink, blackening paper. He always writes in a hurry, never giving birth but aborting. Never was he able to impose on himself the task of correcting anything that he has dashed forth without even sitting down.[17]

For example, Erasmus errs when he states that Charles V sent a letter to Codrus Urceus in 1500. Charles V was born in 1500, the very year Urceus died.[18]

Nosoponus never uses Latin in everyday conversation: this is a dig at the most famous Italian Ciceronians, such as Bonamico, Egnazio, Giulio Camillo, Romulus Amazeus, Fondulus, Sadoleto, who, contrary to the habits of German humanists, refused to use Latin as an ordinary instrument of communication—with their house servants, for instance, or their dogs.[19]

V

In 1528, the ailing Erasmus was around sixty, turning out books that leave us marveling at the intellectual vigor and nimbleness of a man who was at his best and most efficient when making fun of the foibles of man and his *ridicules.*

The *Ciceronianus,* considered in one aspect, is an addendum as well as an antidote to the *Encomium Moriae:* it is an attempt, a medical and literary therapeutic try, at curing a form of mild insanity that usually affects scholars whose intelligence or misdirected industry got away with them—who, no longer being able to cope with futile endeavors, glory and wallow in them, and above all relish their pangs.[20]

The title of the dialogue is in itself ambiguous, hence comical to the 1528 reader. If he left aside the subtitle ("the best style of writing"), *Ciceronianus* might well apply to Nosoponus himself, who is the prototype of an "all-out" insane Ciceronian. If he kept in mind both title and subtitle together, it might point to Erasmus himself and to his Latinity.

One of the unforeseen consequences of the *Ciceronianus* was that, by scoffing so successfully at the foolishness of overzealous Ciceronians, Erasmus unwittingly brought into disrepute the good Ciceronians as well, and dealt a body-blow to the prestige of Latin,[21] whose exclusiveness as the language to be used for matters held to be seriously treated—theology, philosophy, medicine, jurisprudence—was thereafter impaired. The rise of the vernacular tongues as scientific tools was swiftly thrown into high gear because of the sudden religious revolution. The reformers, especially those of the "Left," realized at once that the main and lasting support they were going to get was to be had from the popular forces at work in the sixteenth century—forces mainly propelled by the invention of printing at the service of a new, laicized political and social outlook, and not from scholars alone or exclusively, as had usually been the case in previous centuries.

In other words, a reformation merely of Latin would not and could not have been the religious upheaval of the Renaissance as we know it. Latin was still, of course, the convenient international language, and would remain so well into the eighteenth century. Immensely popular works like *The Courtier* of Castiglione were translated into Latin.[22] But when it came to make its influence felt, immediately and directly, the vernacular became paramount. As of 1528, in some measure because of the *Ciceronianus*, the secular supremacy of Latin was already on the wane.

NOTES

1. See especially *Lectiones succisivae* (Basel, March 1540), vol. 3, chap. 4, pp. 253–54, by Franciscus Floridus Sabinus. Cf. Emile V. Telle, *L'Erasmianus sive Ciceronianus d'Etienne Dolet (1535)* (Geneva: Droz, 1974), p. 82, n. 11, and pp. 443–44.

2. See Augustin Renaudet, *Études Érasmiennes* (Paris, 1939), pp. 292-94, and Angiolo Gambaro, *Il Ciceroniano o dello stilo migliore*, [a critical edition with Italian translation] (Brescia, 1965), introduction. See also Pierre Mesnard, "Erasme," in *Philosophes de tous les temps* (Paris: Seghers, 1969), pp. 82-93; idem, "La bataille du *Ciceronianus*," *Etudes* (February 1968); idem, "La Religion d'Erasme dans le *Ciceronianus*," *Revue Thomiste* (1958), pp. 267-72. For an older but excellent study, see Gaston Feugère, *Erasme: Etude sur sa vie et ses ouvrages* (Paris, 1874), pp. 426-36.

3. As a satirist Erasmus is well known. His contemporaries as well as posterity granted him the dubious honor of being a new Lucian. In fact, the adjective *erasmicus* in Erasmus's time is usually the equivalent of lucianic. Comedy, however, though akin or tangent to satire, strains at veering fully into scoffing and sarcasm. See A. E. Douglas, "Erasmus as a Satirist," *Erasmus*, ed. T. A. Dorey (London, 1970), pp. 31-54, and C. A. Mayer, "Lucien et la Renaissance," *Bibliothèque de Littérature Comparée* (1973), 1: 5-22, and the bibliographical note 1, on p. 5.

4. *Bibliotheca Belgica*, 2d ser., Book 9. Fiche E 473 (2d ed.). The September 1529 edition, printed by Froben, Hervagius, and Episcopius (Fiche + 475), is a 917-page octavo, plus *Index colloquiorum* (Folger Library: 182027). This edition does not have the *Ciceronianus* or the other pieces that appeared in the first edition of March 1528 (in Bibliothèque Nationale, Paris: Rés. PX 431; formerly X. 7008). See also Gambaro, *Il Ciceroniano,* pp. xii-xiii; facing p. cxii is a facsimile of the title page of the second edition of the *Ciceronianus* (March 1529), appearing with the *Colloquia*.

5. The only English translation, as far as I know, is that by Izorra Scott in the Columbia University Contributions to Education series, Teachers College, no. 21 (New York, 1908). A new English translation of the *Ciceronianus* is planned for the Toronto CWE edition. It seems odd that no English translation appeared (in print) in the sixteenth century. See E. J. Devereux, *A Checklist of English Translations of Erasmus to 1700* (Oxford: Oxford Bibliographical Society, 1968). We now have a French version by Pierre Mesnard in *La Philosophie Chrétienne* (Paris, 1970), pp. 261-358; an Italian version by A. Gambaro; a German one, with Latin text, by Theresia Payr (Ausgewählte Schriften, vol. 7, Darmstadt, 1972); an extract in Spanish by Lorenzo Riber, "Obras escogidas," in *Erasmo* (Madrid, 1956), pp. 1163-85.

6. Gambaro, *Il Ciceroniano,* ll. 148-49. I suggested Padua as the city where Erasmus sets the stage on the strength (weak indeed) of the word *porticu* in the first line; "Quem video nobis procul in extrema porticu deambulantem?" See also: "Les portiques qui sont continuels a Paduve et servent d'une grande commodité pour se promener en tous temps a

couvert et sans crotes," *Journal de Voyage de Montaigne,* ed. Armaingaud, *Oeuvres,* vol. 7, p. 153.

7. Gambaro, ll. 389–405.

8. Ibid., ll. 409–27.

9. "Qui vere amat, praeter unam amare non potest." Ibid., l. 437.

10. "Neque enim me fugit, hoc ipso colloquio, quod vobiscum nunc habetur, quantum flagitiorum admittam, quantum detrimenti capiam ad id quod molior. Itaque ad sarciendum vix menstria suffecerit lectio." Ibid., ll. 559–72. Molière's Misanthrope could not be more outspoken!

11. Ibid., ll. 872-74. This is a notable joke on Erasmus by Erasmus himself. Cf. note 16. "Non est magnum grammatice dicere, sed divinum est Tulliane loqui." Cf. Ibid., ll. 255–66.

12. Ibid. ll. 1302–11.

13. Ibid., ll. 1327-30; ll. 1380–1410. See Marcel Bataillon, "Erasme: Conteur-Folklore et Invention Narrative," in *Mélanges P. Le Gentil* (Paris: S.E.D.E.S., 1973), pp. 85-104.

14. Ibid., l. 165; ll. 200–01; l. 299. Margolin (ed., *De Pueris statim instituendis* [Geneva, 1966], pp. 618-19), and D. F. S. Thomson ("The Latinity of Erasmus," in *Erasmus,* ed. T. A. Dorey, p. 126) have underlined Erasmus's use of diminutives, mainly to express irony or disparagement.

15. Gambaro, *Il Ciceroniano,* ll. 359–63; l. 376; l. 441; ll. 416–29. Cf. Claude Baduel, *De ratione vitae studiosae ac literatae in matrimonio collocandae et degendae* (Lyons: Sebastian Gryphius, 1544). Translated into French by Guy de la Garde in 1548.

16. "Quid agat furor poeticus, nihil ad nos. Ciceronianum esse sobria res est." Ibid., ll. 449-50.

17. Ibid., ll. 3490–3515. Up to the end of his life, Erasmus's friends and adversaries begged him to "amend" his significant works. He never obliged.

18. Ibid., l. 1227.

19. See Telle, *L'Erasmianus sive Ciceronianus e'Etienne Dolet,* pp. 349-50. Let us recall one of the printer's mottoes and the device used by Dolet, a champion of Ciceronianism, which "nobody defended better than he (P. de Nolhac, *Ronsard et l'Humanisme* [Paris, 1921], p. 266, note): "Scabra et impolita ad amussim Dolo atque Perpolio." La Doloire: the cooper's adze. See Roger Trinquet, *La Jeunesse de Montaigne* (Paris, 1972), pp. 277-81.

20. See especially *Encomium Moriae,* chaps. 49 and 50: satire on professors and professional writers.

21. Molière's *Précieuses Ridicules* had a like effect on Préciosité itself. *Le Tartuffe,* while mocking the "faux dévots," brought into question devotion itself as well as the sincerely religious person. Joseph de Maistre used to say that so called "superstitious practices" may be the outer bulwark of religion itself ("les ouvrages avancés de la religion").

22. One by a German, Jerome Turler (1550-1602): *Aulicus Balthasaris Castiglionii* (Wittenberg, 1569). Another translation by an Englishman, Bartholomew Clerke (1537?-90), *De Curiali sive Aulico* (London, 1571), dedicated to Queen Elizabeth. Such translations raised the issue of using terms not to be found in classical Latin or Nizolius's dictionary of Cicero's vocabulary (1535). Erasmian freedom had already given the answer: "Dabis mihi veniam (erudite lector) si verbis utar nunc obsoletis, nunc plane fictitijs: idem tute faceres, si de istis scriberes: idem Marcus Cicero faciendum putaret, *si nunc viveret. Novis siquidem rebus nova nomina sunt imponenda* (my italics). See "Bartholomeus Clerke Lectori," f. A 8ᵛ (*S. T. C.* 4782).

12 The Method of "Words and Things" in Erasmus's *De Pueris Instituendis* (1529) and Comenius's *Orbis Sensualium Pictus* (1658)

JEAN-CLAUDE MARGOLIN

I have already had the opportunity[1] to show the exceptional importance of the *Treatise on the Liberal Education of Children* in the development of Erasmus's pedagogical thought,[2] as well as in the history of education during the Renaissance.[3] I have even outlined, in the introduction of my 1966 edition[4] and in a few notes,[5] some general points on the influence of the *De Pueris Instituendis* beyond the age of humanism and the Renaissance, evoking the names of Comenius, Locke, Basedow,[6] Rousseau, Pestalozzi,[7] Christophe (alias George Colomb)—better known for his *Savant Cosinus* or his *Sapeur Camembert* than for his *Leçons de choses en 650 gravures*[8]—and proceeding down to the most current methods of audiovisual instruction. But the influence of this book—rarely published since 1561[9] despite the renown of its author and his rather remarkable attempt at ideological and religious neutrality—is certainly more profound for the reactions it aroused, the pedagogical institutions it helped to create, the transformations in social customs it may have caused, and a whole series of works it engendered which spread its ideas throughout Europe and as far as America,[10] than for its literary commentaries.

On the other hand, we must realize that economic, social, and cultural facts do not change with an identical rhythm, and that the weight of history as well as geographical data, to say nothing of the destiny of individuals, often hinder the direct transmission of ideas, even in the bosom of a republic of letters already strongly established, and more so in the bosom of a Christian republic swaying on its foundations and, as during the seventeenth-century in Europe, irremediably divided. It is therefore a noteworthy fact that—the same causes sometimes producing the same effects—we find, three or four generations apart and through very diverse historical influences, identical concepts, similar methods, the same attitude toward the child, toward man, and toward man's relationship with the world and with God, in the pedagogical work of the Dutchman Erasmus and in that of the Czech Jan Amos Comenius,[11] who, in

Translated from the French by Louise M. Kamenjar and Simone Ferguson.

fact, in 1670 came to live his last days in Amsterdam, the city he described, in the dedication to his *Great Didactic,* as "admirable, the pride of Holland, the joy of Europe," or "the flower of cities."

Similarities are not lacking between the sixteenth-century humanist and Christian pedagogue and the seventeenth-century pedagogue and theologian of the Czech Union of Brothers.[12] They were both orphaned at an early age,[13] abandoned by their tutors, irresistibly attracted to the inexhaustible sources of knowledge, especially to the classical authors, and profoundly religious. They were equally rebellious against both the scholasticism of the theologians and the lack of culture or the immorality of certain monks, for one had become an Augustinian canon and remained a priest throughout his wandering life[14] and the other had been ordained a priest in the Community of Brothers, of which he later became a bishop. Both men fought with all their strength to assure or restore peace within the church—the Roman church or the Evangelical church being above all, for one as for the other, the church of Christ. They were equally irreconcilable enemies of war[15]—of which their epochs gave them so many examples, one as horrible as the other, the Peasant's War or Battle of White Mountain—and faithful all their lives to the same ideal of tolerance and of human brotherhood under the guardian eye of God. Cosmopolitan by nature or necessity—for the Czech patriotism of Komensky was certainly of finer mettle than that of the "homo Batavus"[16] who thought and experimented with the concept *Ubi bene, ibi patria*[17]—they both died in a foreign land where the misfortunes of the times and of religious dissension had led them.

One could say, finally, that the pedagogical plan of Erasmus—like that of Comenius, inseparable in fact as in substance from moral, political, religious, and social concerns—nourished itself from all his other plans, as he assigned a particularly vigorous foundation to each. To teach children how to read and write from the most tender age was important to the author of the *De pueris instituendis*. At the same time, he wanted children to grasp the elementary precepts of religion and the maxims of the great ancient thinkers. Such knowledge would promote their entrance into civil life, provide them with polished intellectual and spiritual tools that would enable a small number of them to become either a Christian prince—that is, an enemy of fraud—or a bishop who would accomplish his pastoral mission to the best of his ability, or a sovereign pontiff who was in agreement with the doctrine of Christ. Such training would also help all of them to become "more human," in the literal sense of the "humaniores litterae."

For the author of the *Janua linguarum reserata,* the *Litterarum tirocinium,* or the *Orbis sensualium pictus,*[18] the learning of languages, the spectacle of the world illustrated in a manual filled with drawings described in Latin and German (before the competitive appearance of Czech, French, English, Russian, Hungarian editions),[19] and the theatrical presentations[20] based on a few pages of school manuals had no other objective, on the individual or collective plane, than the happiness of man. Did he not call himself "the man with aspirations"? Did he not think, in the manner of Erasmus and the greatest minds of the Renaissance, that freedom had been granted to man so that he could arrange a more fraternal world, organize a juster society, expressing his ideal through formulas varied and resonant like the following, which could have been written by the author of the *Institutio principis Christiani:* "All people must strive toward a common good, seek peace and truth, and practice love of neighbor"?[21]

What we must now underline, as much for the particular problem concerning us as for the pedagogical thought of the author of the *Opera didactica,* is that, to Erasmus's pedagogical empiricism[22] and moral pragmatism, there corresponds in Comenius a true experimentalism. More than a century after the death of the Dutch humanist, educational institutions had been able to test the effectiveness or ineffectiveness of the principles he had set forth in his pedagogical treatises. Comenius himself, more than Erasmus, had been in contact with children to whom he could apply those principles. It has often been noted that Erasmus acted as a pedagogical counselor or theoretician of practical pedagogy rather than as a pedagogical practitioner.

Comenius, on the other hand, when he was twenty-two years old practiced the profession of teaching in Prerov[23] and four years later in the small Moravian town of Fulnek. It was as rector of the German school of Fulnek[24] that he would lead the children along roads and through meadows and sit with them under a thick-leaved beech in order to acquaint them with the curiosities of nature. Later, after seven years of clandestine life and incredible misfortunes,[25] he once again became a teacher in the Polish city of Leszno, and he had every opportunity to observe children "experimentally," and at the same time to draw up pedagogical plans for their benefit. Animated by the patriotic desire to write a *Didactic* in Czech which would provide a scientific basis for the general and joyful education of the children of his people once they had recovered their independence, he applied himself immediately to reforming the teaching of Latin. It is here, in the *Janua*—rapidly assigned the honorary epithet of *liber aureus*[26]—that he was to outline, in a practical and natural way and without using more than 8,000 words, the rules of correlation between the study of language and the knowledge of things.

For, unlike the intuitive—perhaps inspired—empiricism of Erasmus, who always took nuances and individual cases into account—the *De pueris* stresses on nearly every page the idiosyncratic cases of which the teacher should be made aware—a systematic mind and a sense of the universal led the Czech educator to establish a real pedagogical science whose laws would be drawn up by analogy to those of life. The international scientific Latin he intended to promote was destined, according to his own terms, to create "the general art of teaching everything to everyone,[27] in an active, efficient, and carefully chosen way, in every village, town, and community, where Christian schools can be established." A restriction, some will say, but let us not forget that for a European intellectual, born a Christian—*a fortiori* for a preacher and theologian—the republic of letters was inseparable from the Christian republic, and that even in Descartes, who wrote in the enthusiasm of universal reason ("I speak also for the Turks"),[28] the rules of the method were inspired by a logico-philosophical tradition marked by precise stages in cultural history.

In basing his theoretical teaching on constant practical experience, recommending everywhere the good use of nature and spontaneity (his motto was *Omnia sponte fluant, absit violentia rebus*), and according a prominent position to the teacher, Comenius followed or rediscovered through personal means Erasmus's pedagogical ideas; but at the same time he brought them to an absolute. By advocating the establishment of the infant school[29] and defining the principles of what he called the *autopsia,* which was no other than an intuitive method combined with a direct and sensitive observation of things, he laid the foundation for what we mean today by "didactic activism."

As in Erasmus, but with the self-assurance he had acquired all during his agitated life from the direct experience of teaching, we find in Comenius the idea that education is a living dialectic between teacher and pupil (between "a teaching rationalism" and a "taught rationalism," to use the words of the philosopher Bachelard,[30] another pedagogue of exceptional quality). Whether instruction is given in the home, as Erasmus wished, maintaining an individualistic and aristocratic view that he never wanted to deny, or whether the teacher makes the elementary school a real "laboratory of humanity," as Comenius wanted and practiced, the two men shared a common method: the "method of words and things," remembering a precise passage of the *De pueris instituendis,*[31] another from the *De ratione studii,*[32] the whole Erasmian treatise *De duplici copia verborum ac rerum,*[33] the colloquy *De rebus ac vocabulis,*[34] and, for Comenius, all his ideas set forth in the prologue[35] and in the very body of the *Orbis pictus.*

Let us not be deterred by the fact that the Czech pedagogue does not mention his predecessor in the prologue to his work, nor in the preface to the readers (*Lectoribus . . .*) of his *Great Didactic,* in which he tells us that he studied the most important theoreticians of pedagogy.[36] We know that he had a personal and direct knowledge of some of Erasmus's pedagogical works, as one can easily see by opening the *De civilitate morum puerilium* of 1530 and glancing through the *Praecepta morum in usum juventutis collecta anno 1653*[37]: same inspiration, same content, same expressions (in the short chapters *De vultu totiusque corporis statu et gestu, De Cultu et Vestitu, De Incessu, Mores matutini, Ad Mensam,* or *Mores vespertini*).[38] According to August Israel and Hermann Tögel[39] (to whom he had given this information), Comenius had even written a preface for a 1652 edition of the *De ratione studii,* but we were not able to locate this edition; neither was Marcelle Denis in her "Bibliographie des Oeuvres de Comenius," nor E. van Gulik, curator of the Rotterdam library, in his descriptive card catalogue of Erasmus's works. But what does it matter? The real Erasmianism of Comenius—not to speak of the "Comenianism" of Erasmus!—is simultaneously the aggressive criticism of artificial and emaciated imitation of Cicero's style[40] (imitation known by the name of "Ciceronianism") and the attentive and assiduous application of the "natural relation"—a term that must be elucidated—between words and things.

Words and things: two terms which in effect represent three, especially in an age where the "lessons on things"—of which we spoke earlier with respect to Christophe—have been replaced by the natural or experimental sciences, and where the new pedagogues no longer give courses or exercises on vocabulary. One can speak more readily—since Saussure and especially since the recent vogue of linguistics—of the "signifier" (the word, as bearer of the meaning) and the "signified" (the thing, or rather the *idea* of the thing, that is, its intellectual content). Between the enunciation or the "word" (the expressed word) or the vocable—in Latin *verbum* or *vox*—and the perception (let us say, to simplify, the visual, auditory, and tactile experience, the "meeting" of the subject with the sensible world—*orbis sensualium*), there has to be in some way a third term, that is to say, the idea, the concept or image—in other words, the meaning or sense of the thing; it should be understood that such a general and vague term as "things"—*res* in Latin—can designate natural phenomena, man-made objects, or living beings, as well as entities, rational beings, actions or "facts" directly connected to the understanding or even to the imagination, but certainly not to man's brain or sensory zones (think, for example, of the "things" we know as liberty, virtue, wisdom, mind, nothingness, contradiction, or identity).

But for a pedagogue like Erasmus, preoccupied above all with practical effectiveness and rather removed from abstract speculations—by natural reluctance as well as by will—the major problems in the education of the young, and primarily the very young, are: the simultaneous experience of words and things,[41] in other words, of language—or the language par excellence, Latin; and acquiring the knowledge contained in the books of the ancients (since they

had dealt with every subject) as it is dispersed over the surface of the globe, in
surrounding nature immediately perceived, which is itself nothing but a large
open book—the book of the world[42]—which the tutor must teach children to
read or decipher. Preestablished harmony? Happy encounter between word
and thing? Erasmus, like every user of language, quickly realized the utopian
nature of this congruity: the experience of discourse teaches us equivocation,
ambiguity, or, as we say today, polysemy of words; and the experience of life,
of men, and of things, their necessary proliferation. This is what Erasmus expressed, in a slightly different form, more rhetorical than philosophical, when
he spoke of the "double abundance of words and things,"[43] the multiplicity of
expressions, of phrases or of "figures" serving to designate a single thing—or a
single idea—compared to the multiplicity of things—or of ideas—contained
within a single vocable.

But at three or four—the age of the children to whom the precepts of the
De pueris apply and of those in the infant schools Comenius was thinking of—
reality is simpler, or rather the teacher works at simplifying it. So he would not
dream of giving lectures only, but directs elementary scenes in which his students are the actors who portray animals. In this way, he teaches his pupils
while amusing them. The word and the thing that it describes is in perfectly
adequate, transparent, and reciprocal correspondence. But the whole passage
must be quoted:

> As for fables and apologues, the child will more willingly learn them and
> remember them better if the subjects are presented to him before his very
> eyes, cleverly illustrated, and if all that the story relates is shown to him in
> the picture. The same method will be equally valuable in learning the names
> of trees, herbs, and animals, and at the same time what is natural to them,
> especially those animals that are not found everywhere, such as the rhi-
> noceros, the tragelaphus, the pelican, the donkey of the Indies, and the
> elephant. For example, a picture will show an elephant which a dragon has
> grasped in his coils while winding his tail around his front feet. This new
> presentation (*nova picturae species*) delights the little one: What will the
> teacher do then? He will teach him that the huge animal is called ἐλέρας
> in Greek and that in Latin, according to the forms of the Latin declension,
> we sometimes say *elephantus* or *elephanti*. He will then show him what the
> Greeks call προζοσχιδα (a trunk) and the Latins call *manum* (hand), be-
> cause it is with his trunk that the elephant grabs his food. He will have him
> observe that this animal does not breathe through his mouth, as we do, but
> through his trunk; he will show him his tusks, projecting on either side, from
> which ivory is obtained (a commodity greatly appreciated by the rich), and

at the same time he will show him an ivory comb. He will teach him next that there are dragons in the Indies, just as enormous, that *dracon* (dragon) [snake] is a word common to Greek and Latin, that we decline it as we are accustomed to, when the Greeks say δράκοντος, based on the model of λέοντος, whence we get the feminine *dracaena,* based on the model of *leaena.* He will also teach him that an inexpiable war is forever declared between these dragons and the elephants. And if the child is eager for more knowledge, the teacher can relate many other characteristics about the nature of elephants and dragons.[44]

Several ideas can be drawn from this model lesson on things, which clearly shows the effectiveness, for the youngest school-age child, of the method of "words and things." Let us organize these ideas.

1. If we apply to this text the statement of the *De ratione studii* to which I have already referred ("In general, knowledge appears as double, knowledge of things, and knowledge of words"),[45] we see that, while being double, this knowledge of the "signified" and the "signifiers" is simultaneous; for the child, as he discovers in a figurative scene a pelican or a tragelaphus[46]—animals of which he has no direct or familiar knowledge, not encountering them in his daily life—learns their respective names while perceiving their morphology. But, in the treatise concerning older children—since it is for pupils thirteen and fourteen that Erasmus composed the *De ratione studii*—it is specified that the knowledge of words—or rather the use of discourse, or again the practice of language—has a priority,[47] both logical and chronological, with respect to the knowledge of things. The two works having been written at about the same time,[48] it must be admitted that the difference in perspective we note between these two respective passages is due to the different stages foreseen on the road to knowledge.

2. If the term *verba*—more rarely *voces*—is the one Erasmus uses in the *De ratione studii,* the *De duplici copia,* and the colloquy on words and things, he uses, at the beginning of the paragraph just before the passage quoted above, the term *lingua* ("Ad linguae cognitionem . . ."); it is this term which gave him the title and the material for his famous treatise on speech or language (*Lingua,* 1525)[49] and which is nearly always used by Comenius (*Vestibulum rerum et linguae fundamenta ponens, Eruditionis scholasticae pars, rerum et latinae linguae exhibens,* for example). Both knew that the connotations of these two terms were not identical: not only does *verbum* have a precise character while *lingua* sometimes designates discourse in its most general form or the very act of speaking, sometimes the verbal or linguistic system, and finally an institution-alized national language (French or Latin, for example), but also *verbum* and *res*

maintain theoretically biunivocal and transparent relations (*dragon* designates a particular animal, *vase* represents this manufactured object and no other, *sun* designates the star of the day, and *moon,* the star of the night), while the area of discourse does not exactly cover—far from it—the spectacle of the world, a spectacle which, moreover, does not cover all that on which discourse can bear. But, here again, it is a question of presenting things simply; and, at the risk of using false symmetries, *verbum* and *lingua* will be intermingled *practically,* for the use of very young children.

3. This very elementary method of teaching through pictures, used by Comenius, restored in the eighteenth century by the German Basedow,[50] and again by modern pedagogues who have specialized in the teaching of sciences in the primary schools, is based on *dramatization*[51] of the scene presented and not only on *animation* of the characters (in this case, pictured animals). Great progress has been made today in animated drawing, but the fact of presenting to the child simultaneously and in action (that is to say, engaged in their instinctive and natural struggle)[52] two animals such as the dragon (or serpent) and the elephant is a happy educational initiative. Also, by having children play the role of real or imaginary characters destined to illustrate the "living Encyclopedia" of the "world of images," Comenius had discovered or rediscovered this elementary theatrical "praxeology" (*praxis scenica*). In both cases, it is a question of creating associations of ideas and of guiding the memory to real or natural associations, at least those which have been fixed in the mind by the present state of knowledge or the tradition which inspired this knowledge.

4. In a more general way, this method of teaching by word and image derives from a more general concept, to which Erasmus, like all the great humanists of the Quattrocento and the pedagogues of his time, was particularly attached: that of teaching through play, of teaching through joy. In several passages of the *De pueris*[53] Erasmus stresses that point. He evokes, for example, the method practiced by the ancients: "Some gave the shape of letters to little cakes children are fond of, so that they would, in this way, devour the letters."[54] Or again, take the method of this father of a British family: "The English have a particularly strong liking for archery, and it is the first thing they teach their children. That is why a father with an inventive mind, observing in his son an extraordinary attraction to this sport, bought him a very fine bow and beautiful arrows, with letters painted everywhere, on the bow as well as on the arrows. Then, as targets, he first gave him the characters of the Greek alphabet, then the Latin characters. When the boy struck the target and pronounced the name of the letter, he would be applauded and would also receive as a reward a cherry or some other delicacy which delights all little ones."[55] This little game is, if you wish, a variation on the method of words and things; but here the "things" are the very letters of the

Greek and Latin alphabet, the letters as drawings to be recognized. The point is to establish a biunivocal correspondence (or approximately biunivocal, for every letter, or rather every Latin phoneme, and a fortiori English, has no exact correspondent in Greek) between the two series of letters, or rather between a series of familiar sounds and a series of less familiar drawings.

5. One must have noticed the constant use of analogous relationships (the hand and the trunk, the Latin declension and the Greek, the serpent's size and the elephant's, etc.), and the continual transition from the experience familiar to children to new understanding, and from this new understanding to a reliable knowledge whose strength is tested at the proper time. In this way, the arbitrary bond between the "signifier" and the "signified" is balanced by a whole network of analogies, contrasts, morphological affinities or dissimilarities, in both the natural and the logical-verbal order.

Comenius's encyclopedic ideal and pedagogical methods merge with Erasmus's concerns. The study of languages, particularly of the three fundamental languages (Latin, Greek, and Hebrew), is, for him also, a necessary and preliminary condition of the knowledge of reality. The universe is translated precisely in the universe of things, an intuition Comenius shared not only with Erasmus but with most sixteenth-century authors[56] who have reflected upon the relationship between words and things. Did he not write: "Januam linguarum et Encyclopaediam debere esse idem" [The door to languages and the Encyclopedia ought to be the same]?[57] And, in his vivid language, which itself experiments with what it wants to demonstrate, he continues: "To open the door of languages is to go to the source of all languages and all sciences, that is, to formulate a method of learning at the same time the Latin language and the foundation of all sciences and of all arts."[58]

I could multiply the didactic formulas of the *Janua* (and other pedagogical works by Comenius) that express the correspondence of word and thing. Its author could even be suspected of having considerably simplified the problem of the relationship between language and reality for purely pedagogical ends. Here, for example, is a simple and brief definition of the learned man or the scholar, taken from the *Introitus* ("in Januam linguae latinae"): "Is qui perdidicit nomenclaturam rerum,"[59] he who knows thoroughly the nomenclature of things! And he continues: (4) "Vocabula sunt notae rerum: verbis recte perceptis, res percipiuntur; et utrumque discitur melius junctim quam separatim" [Names are signs of things: through words correctly perceived, things are perceived; both are better learned jointly than separately].[60] Let us retain this last formula, of which the *Orbis pictus* will make a literal application (if one may say so) and which merges exactly with what Erasmus declared in some of the canonical texts we quoted above: the study of language must not be separated from the study of things. And this is so, even if in practice and in the psychical evolution of the child a certain (sensorimotor) experience of the world precedes the linguistic mastery that will allow him to account for it. Also, invariably a conceptual knowledge or a linguistic pattern does not immediately or adequately apply to the data of experience (or of one particular experience).

But, as we have already noted, what is in question here is a practical presentation for the use of children, an organizing of knowledge. The teacher has learned during his wandering life that artisans and soldiers acquire the practical knowledge of a foreign language more rapidly than schoolchildren who are administered strong doses of grammar. He would like to apply to the school the methods drawn from life, improving them if possible. It is thus that he will abandon "verbal chicanery" and synonyms more subtle than necessary; he will rely on "things and on strong and truly useful words," while searching through this "inextricable labyrinth"[61] of knowledge for the thread that will allow the ordering of factual knowledge. This method considerably resembles that of Bacon, who influenced him profoundly. It is known that, for Comenius, all things "which are and can be thought, must, by a true anatomy of reality (vera instituta anatome),[62] be brought back to their order and species." This rational will to organize the diversity of experience is often translated in his work by the elaboration of a picture where dichotomous divisions and subdivisions are multiplied. It is not, then, long and obscure lectures which are suitable to the minds of young children (or all children), but rather this autopsy we have already mentioned. He prefers to the uninterrupted exercise of memory the constant practice of the direct observation of things.

Of course, everything cannot be presented directly to the senses. So the study of objects or of phenomena which cannot be seen, heard, smelled, touched, tasted—nor drawn, like abstract ideas, will be temporarily neglected. "The picture of the elephant," Comenius writes further, using again in this passage from his Pansophia the example of the De pueris, "the picture of the elephant if I have seen the animal, were it only a single time—even as an effigy—will remain fixed in me more easily and more strongly than if it had been described to me ten times."[63] We find again the Erasmian idea of animated pictures and of natural associations in Comenius's attempt to organize the encyclopedia of knowledge according to nature. It is once more from the Pansophia that I shall quote: "Everyone exclaims that we must progress according to natural order, going from what is first to what is last, from the more general to the more particular, from what is known to what is unknown. But who respects that order?"[64]

Comenius respected it when he composed this tableau of sensations in the form of a small book that is truly "the book of the world," the Orbis sensualium *pictus* of 1657–58, the ultimate expression and the summary of his method. As he believed and as he advocated after his *Janua* or the encyclopedic program of his *Pansophia*,[65] it is a matter of teaching words and things simultaneously. The *Orbis pictus* is, then, at the same time a picture of the world and a vocabulary book; but since words and things are reversible or interchangeable, the world and the book are one. "A very small book," as Comenius himself wrote in his *Janua*, "can include the universe of things and that of the Latin language."[66]

Let us recall that the teaching of Latin was done in the pupils' mother tongue, which formed in a way a "metalanguage" in respect to the language whose vocabulary was favored. In the *Orbis pictus*, Latin is treated as a living language, since we are dealing with a manual of ordinary conversation, no longer a dryly didactic formulary. Consequently, if the teacher speaks exclusively in Latin or if, like most of our current teachers of living languages, he has recourse from time to time to the pupil's mother tongue, these "crutches" are quickly forgotten by the student who is attentive and caught up in the game because of the pictures and illustrations, the perception of which is the practical equivalent of the intuition of the thing. The subtitle of the *Orbis pictus*, moreover, expresses strongly the proposed method: "Omnium fundamentalium in Mundo rerum et in Vita actionum Nomenclatura ad ocularem demonstrationem deducta,"[67] that is to say, the nomenclature presented as visual demonstrations (*demonstrationem* might better be translated as "presentations") of all the foundations of the universe and of action: beings, things, objects or phenomena, as well as the different modalities of human action, such as technical gestures, games, moral behavior. For the use of his pupils, but thinking also of the universal school, Comenius adopted again the fundamental theme of Tommaso Campanella's *La Città del Sole*, that of a library-city, whose walls displayed on illustrated pages a section of the encyclopedia of knowledge. The universe reduced to a school, or better yet to a picture book; utopia here joins, in Comenius's eyes, the most day-to-day reality.

This "breviary of the entire world and of language as a whole,"[68] as he called the *Orbis pictus*, is made up, then, of pictures, of nomenclatures, and of descriptions. In his famous preface he defined each of these terms: "the pictures (*picturae*) set on small boards, are illustrations (*icones*) of visible things (to which even the invisible things are related in a way); the nomenclatures are made up of inscriptions corresponding to each picture, in other words, of terms which express, through a general vocable, the totality of the thing; as for the descriptions, they are explanations of parts of a picture (in fact, images corresponding to objects which form part of the whole represented by the picture, that is to say, the animated scene: the farmer in his field, the king on his throne, the painter in his studio, the house, the mine, Adam and Eve in Paradise, etc.).[69] It will be noted, moreover, that these *explanations*—if we so render the Latin *explicationes*—are in fact *designations*.

Comenius himself explained, by example, how his living tableaux should be used. He chose as "painted picture" that of the world (*Mundus*),[70] the picture number 2 which comes immediately after the number 1 of God (*Deus*), at once simple and general. The circle of the world, inscribed within a square, is described as follows:

Heaven has fire, stars (a number 1 is represented in the picture and affixed to the word *coelum*). Clouds (number 2) hang in the air (no number appears, perhaps because air is invisible, therefore not depictable in itself in the drawing). Birds (number 3) are flying under the clouds (a second use of a term already identified, and a good opportunity for the student to have a fore-taste of the declensions). Fish (number 4) are swimming in water. *Terra*, earth (followed by f.1, that is to say, a feminine noun of the first declension, whereas *coelum* was followed by n.2, that is, a neuter noun of the second declension), has mountains (5), woods (6), fields (7), animals (8), men (9).

And the brief lesson on things ends with a summary, which at the same time extends the knowledge already acquired: "Ita sunt plena *habitatoribus* suis, quatuor *elementa*, quae sunt *mundi* maxima corpora" [Thus their complete surroundings consisted of four elements, which are the largest bodies in the world] (the four elements are, of course, fire, air, water, and earth, which will make up the next four illustrated chapters, or rather, chapters 4, 5, 6, and 8, the third being reserved for the Heavens, and the chapter *Nubes*[71] having been placed between the chapter *Aqua*[72] and the chapter *Terra*.)[73]

One could have discovered Comenius's method, so close to that of Erasmus in the passage from the *De pueris* translated and commented on above: short, simple sentences, which animate the subjects of the action through the verb ("pendent" [hanging], "volant" [flying], "natant" [swimming], or even the neutral "habet [has]) since the *vision*, or the *visualization*, of the world is at the same time a very schematic abridgment of its *creation*; the quick, but not superfluous, indication of grammatical points, such as the gender of nouns (or at least of two of them, in order not to overload the child's memory) and the use of three cases (out of six) of the declension (the nominative, accusative, and ablative), and of the singular and plural of nouns and of verbal forms.

I could extend this analysis, but it seems more appropriate to examine rapidly two or three pictures whose motives are related to those used by Erasmus in his

method "of words and things": for example, picture 27 *Jumenta* [mule],
picture 29 *Ferae bestiae* [savage beasts], and picture 30 *Serpentes et reptilia*
[serpents and reptiles]. What captures our attention is not the use of the same
examples, for besides being expected, they are inspired, here as there, by the
nomenclatures and descriptions—with or without pictures—by Pliny's *Natural
History*. Even the epithets of *immanissima* [most monstrous] applied to the
tiger, of *rapax* [insatiable] applied to the wolf, of *villosus* [most hairy] applied
to the bear, or of *astutissima* [most astute] applied to the fox, offer little
interest. But, here again, what strikes us in Comenius is his vivid or dynamic
way of depicting these animals by characterizing them either by a physical or
moral trait (the ant is industrious, the hare trembles, the crocodile is monstrous
and a plunderer, etc.), or by their habitat (the snake in the woods, the water
snake in water, the viper on a rock, the asp in the field, etc.), or by their specific
activity as gnawing for worms or invertebrates that can be described by the noun
vermes, regardless of what they gnaw—fruits in the case of the grasshopper, earth
for the earthworm, clothes for the moth, flesh and cheese for termites, or books
for the cockroach).

However, unlike Erasmus, whose animation is a universal dramatization, as
we have shown in the scene where an elephant was struggling with a serpent who
had coiled his tail around his front legs, and where technical objects made from
ivory were shown perhaps in the foreground or background, Comenius used a
more linear—not to say precise—representation: he voluntarily limited himself
to a schematization, to repetitions or parallels that gained, perhaps, in mnemonic
fixation what they lost in affective atony. Thus, the column of various gnawing
or horned animals, represented most often by a noun—the name of the animal—
followed by a verb or noun enriched by an epithet (seldom with both at the
same time), makes us think more of a diorama than of a stage. He has just named
the rabbit (*cuniculus*) who "digs in the ground"; he adds immediately, "like the
mole (*talpa*) who builds mounds." He names mortally dangerous snakes; the
same verb, *necat* [kill], applies to the dragon, the basilisk, and the scorpion; but
while the first kills with his breath (*halitu*), the second kills with his glance
(*oculis*), and the third with his poisoned tail (*venenata cauda*). We spoke of a
column; we could almost have said that they are arranged for a parade. But we
should also recognize that as the teacher and pupils progress in the discovery
of the world—we mean in the reading of the book and the observation of the
pictures—their vocabulary is enriched (see, for example, picture 63 depicting the
trade of the carpenter,[74] scene 90 of the shipwreck,[75] of the rich display (number 100) of musical instruments),[76] while the sentences become more varied and
the drawings themselves seem less static.

In any case—and this is the fundamental lesson of the *Orbis pictus* as well as the mark of its originality compared to other pedagogical writings by Comenius—the spectacle of the world and of all the creatures inhabiting it requires the total participation of the child spectator, and to his active and scrutinizing gaze corresponds a dynamic experience of vocabulary, through the fixation in the memory of short sentences which are themselves elements of action.

In his deservedly famous work entitled *Les mots et les choses*,[77] Michel Foucault brilliantly supported the thesis of an appropriate correspondence of words and things in the sixteenth century. In his preface he speaks of language "as a spontaneous tableau and as the foremost structuring of things,"[78] or again "as the indispensable relay between the representation and the 'beings.'" He also evokes, in his chapter on "The prose of the world," the infinite interlacing of nature and word, "forming one great single text for whoever can read."[79] We have already had the opportunity[80] to show the importance of Foucault's analysis of resemblance as the key category of the cultural history of the sixteenth century, but also the limits imposed by its avoidance of the anthropological dimension. The total or partial equivalency of words to things, even their inequivalency, does not constitute objective data. Did he not, moreover, add these four little words, "For whoever can read," which reintroduce the active presence of the reader—therefore of man—and thus imply the necessity for a hermeneutic?

Even at the elementary pedagogical level where Erasmus and Comenius placed themselves in the texts upon which we have commented, even at the age when the child learns how to read, write, and observe nature, synonymic patterns can appear and, with them, a principle of choice and therefore a distortion of the correspondence between words and things. The *Orbis sensualium pictus* is able to assimilate the world into a tableau of images only through metaphor. As for the fables, they are not integrally transposable into pictures. It is only after a long apprenticeship, of which the *De pueris* gives us some idea but whose value Erasmus spent his whole life discovering, that a difficult and problematic correspondence can be "established between words and things." What this passage in the *De pueris* proposed to teachers and pupils of yesterday and today is an empirical method of basic and vital instruction. But this method should not be unduly prolonged, for, though wanting to give simple ideas to the pupil, it would then inculcate false ones; by postponing too long the necessary training in abstraction, it would risk depriving its user of both the knowledge of nature and the science of language.

NOTES

1. Especially in my thesis: *Erasmus, Declamatio de pueris statim ac liberaliter instituendis: Etude critique, traduction et commentaire.* Travaux d'Humanisme et Renaissance, no. 77 (Geneva: Droz, 1966). See also my article, "Philosophie et pédagogie dans le *De pueris instituendis* d'Erasme," *Paedagogica Historica* 4, no. 2 (Ghent, 1964): 370-91, and essay, *L'idée de nature dans la pensée d'Erasme* (Basel: Helbling and Lichtenhan, 1967).

2. Erasmus, *De pueris instituendis,* ed. Margolin, chap. 5, pp. 48-62. See also A. Gambaro, "La Pedagogia di Erasmo da Rotterdam," *Il Saggiatore,* March, June, July to December (Turin, 1951); and the bibliography in my edition of Erasmus's *De pueris instituendis* (1966), pp. 661-64.

3. See, among others, Eugenio Garin, *L'educazione umanistica in Italia* (Laterza, 1949). This work has also been translated into French under the title *L'éducation de l'homme moderne: La pédagogie de la Renaissance (1400-1600)* (Paris: Fayard, 1968).

4. Erasmus, *De pueris instituendis,* ed. Margolin, chap. 9, pp. 104 et seq.

5. Ibid., pp. 108-17 and notes 725-35 on pp. 572-74.

6. The German pedagogue Johann-Bernhard Basedow dedicated in particular his *Book of Method for Fathers and Mothers of Families and of Nations* (Frankfort and Leipzig, 1771) to Catherine II of Russia. It was the result of his teaching and pedagogical experiences.

7. The bibliography of the great Swiss educator, Johann-Heinrich Pestalozzi, is immense. See the references in my edition of Erasmus's *De pueris instituendis,* pp. 320-23, with regard to the works of A. Israel in *Monumenta Germaniae Paedagogica* (Berlin: Hofmann, 1903-04), in 3 vols. (25, 29, 31).

8. Paris, 1897.

9. Edited by Johann Oridryus and Alb. Buysius (Düsseldorf). This edition has been described in detail in my article, "Deux éditions inconnues du *De pueris instituendis* d'Erasme," in *Gutenberg-Jahrbuch* (1969), pp. 117-28.

10. See especially Marcel Bataillon's "Erasmo y el Nuevo Mondo", appendix to the Spanish translation of his work, *Erasmo y Espana,* 2d ed. (Buenos Aires and Mexico, 1966), pp. 807-31.

11. The literature on Comenius is very rich but very uneven, depending on the periods and the culture: the bibliography in the French language is notably deficient. Let me point out, however, a recent, dissertation of Marcelle Denis, "Komensky: sa pensée, son système," followed by a "Bibliographie de l'oeuvre de Komensky" (University of Tours, 1974).

12. There are several studies on the life and thought of Comenius in the *Acta Comeniana* pt. 1 (25) and pt. 2 (26) (Prague: Academia Praha, 1969 and 1970).

13. See Comenius, *Opera Didactica Omnia* (hereafter cited as *ODO*) (Prague: Academia Scientiarum Bohemoslovenica, 1957), 1:442: "Admodum enim puer parente utroque orbatus, tutorumque supinitate ita fui neglectus, ut demum aetatis anno decimo sexto Latina elementa gustare contigerit."

14. Among the most recent biographies, see Roland H. Bainton, *Erasmus of Christendom* (New York: Charles Scribner's, 1969), James D. Tracy, *Erasmus: The Growth of a Mind* (Geneva: Droz, 1972), as well as the second edition of Albert Hyma's *The Youth of Erasmus* (New York: Russell and Russell, 1968).

15. For Erasmus, see my *Guerre et Paix dans le pensée d'Erasme de Rotterdam* (Paris: Aubier, 1973). For Comenius, see his *ODO,* as well as P. Bovet, *Jean Amos Comenius, un patriote cosmopolite* (Geneva, 1943) and J. Polisensky, "Comenius: The Angel of Peace and the Netherlands in 1687," *Acta Comenia* (1969), vol. 1. See also Karl Mämpel, *Die Interkonfessionellen Friedensideale des Johan Amos Comenius* (Monatshefte der Comenius-Gesellschaft, 1892), pp. 93-108.

16. See also Aloïs Gerlo, "Erasme, homo Batavus," in *Commémoration nationale d'Erasme* (Brussels: Bibliothèque Royale, 1970), pp. 61–80.

17. One of his favorite adages (*LB*, 2:481B-D, no. 1193). See my study, "Erasme et la psychologie des peuples," in *Ethno-Psychologie* 4 (December 1970): 373–424.

18. See the different editions of these works in the bibliography of Denis, "Komensky" (n. 11 above), as well as in the study by Joseph Müller, "Zur Bücherkunde des Comenius," *Monatshefte der Comenius-Gesellschaft* (March 1892), pp. 19–53.

19. The *Janua linguarum reserata* (or "the training center of all languages") was even translated into twelve oriental languages. As for the *Orbis sensualium pictus*, which was composed between 1653 and 1654 and published at Nuremberg in 1658, it enjoyed, along with the *Janua*, the largest number of editions and translations (especially in the seventeenth century). A German translation appeared in 1658, an English one in the same year, and one in Bohemian in 1685.

20. See especially Comenius's *ODO*, pt. 3, p. 836 et seq., as well as pts. 1 to 8 (Prague: Academia Scientiarum Bohemoslovenica, 1957). These inducements of a pedagogical order are most often blended with elements of a religious nature; for many of these plays are drawn from passages in the *Psalms* or from the *Proverbs of Solomon*, and are accompanied by music with a chorus of students—particularly in Protestant countries of Germany and central Europe, according to a widespread custom.

21. This calls to mind Erasmus's phrase (in his dedicatory letter to Jean de Carondelet, archbishop of Palermo, Allen, *EE*, vol. 5, Ep. 1334, p. 177): "The foundation of our religion is peace and harmony." And for him the search for truth and love of neighbor became one.

22. See in this connection, Hermann Tögel, *Die pädagogischen Anschauungen des Erasmus in ihrer psychologischen Bergründung* (Dresden, 1896) and chapter 4 of the introduction to my edition of the *De pueris instituendis*, pp. 41 et seq.

23. "Ut . . . ego in Moraviam (Anno 1614) reversus Scholaeque Praeroviensi praefectus." See *ODO*, 1:3.

24. "Anno autem 1618 ad Ecclesiae Fulnecensis Pastoratum Scholaeque ibidem recens erectae Curaturam vocatus." Ibid.

25. See the account of his misfortunes in a letter to Montanus in *ODO*, 1:75–80.

26. *Janus linguarum reserata aurea: sive Seminarium linguarum et scientiarum omnium, hoc est compendiosa Latinam (et quamlibet aliam) linguam, una cum scientiarum artiumque omnium fundamentis, perdiscendi Methodus.* The preface is dated: "Scribebam in exilio 4 Martii 1631."

27. That is what he calls the *pansophia* (sometimes *pansophiola*), a practical equivalent of the *Encyclopaedia* (sometimes called *encyclopaediola*). It is the meaning that he gives to his *Didactica Magna* "sive *Omnes omnia docendi artificium.*" (In this connection, see the preface to this *Didactic*, addressed to "Christian readers" or to the "pious and discerning readers," in *ODO*, 1:3).

28. Luther himself adds in his *Table Talk*, after attacking Erasmus and reproaching him for his pieces of mockery, his impiety, his ambiguous and amphibolus words: "ut etiam ejus libri a Turcis legi possint." Did Descartes know this text?

29. "Schola materni gremii," as he said.

30. In his *Rationalisme appliqué* (Paris, 1949).

31. Precisely the passage we shall study: Erasmus, *De pueris instituendis*, ed. Margolin, in *ASD*, vol. 1, pt. 2, p. 67, l. 19 and p. 68, l. 18.

32. Ibid., *ASD*, vol. 1, pt. 2, p. 113, ll. 4 et seq.

33. *LB*, vol. 1, l. 110.

34. Erasmus, *Colloquia*, ed. L.-E. Halkin, in *ASD*, vol. 1, pt. 3, pp. 566–71.

35. *ODO*, vol. 1, bk. 2, pt. 3, p. 803 ("Nomenclatura, ad ocularem demonstrationem deducta"). In opposition to *res* and *verba* is added that of *sensualia* and *sensus*.

36. *ODO*, 1 : 3-4 (with the account of his exiled life). He refers especially to the educator Wolfgang Ratichius, who exerted a great influence on his thought and methodology. On this subject, see August Israel, "Das Verhältnis der *Didactica magna* des Comenius zu der Didaktik Ratkes," in *Monatshefte der Comenius-Gesellschaft* (November 1892), pt. 3, pp. 173-204 and 242-74.

37. *ODO*, vol. 2, cols. 776-83.

38. For example: "Quoties in conspectu cujuspiam honesti es, ita tegeres" (*C*) and "Si quis occurrerit in via, vel senio venerandus . . . de via decedere" (*E*); "oculi non vagi, non limi, non distorti, non procaciter huc illuc jactati, aut rursum nescio quo defixi" (*C*) and "non vagi ac volubiles, quod est insaniae . . . nec immodice diducti, quod est stolidorum" (*E*); "Comam nutrire prolixam, quae frontem tegat, aut involitet humectu, Apostolus vetat" (*C*) and "Coma nec frontem tegat, nec humeris involitet" (*E*); "Verbum Dei, cum praelegitur, nunquam aliter quam stando, capiteque nudato, audiet" (*C*) and "dum peraguntur mysteria, toto corpore ad religionem composito ad altaria versa sit facies (*E*); or further, "Manus ablue, os prolue, dentes defrica, ut sis purus" (*C*) and "Dentium mundities curanda est. . . . Os mane pura aqua proluere, et urbanum est et salubre" (*E*); The parallels could be multiplied, but this demonstration seems sufficiently convincing. *C* stands for Comenius *E*, for Erasmus.

39. A. Israel, "Eine Ausgabe von *De ratione studii* von 1652 hat ein Vorwort von Comenius," in *Monatshefte der Comenius-Gesellschaft*, pt. 3, p. 127, as well as note 7. H. Tögel alludes to the "last" edition of the *De pueris instituendis*, which he dates as 1556, confusing the *De pueris instituendis* and the *De ratione studii* (following F. Van der Haeghen's *Bibliotheca Erasmiana* [Ghent, 1893]) and ignoring the 1561 edition.

40. See the Italian translation of the *Ciceronianus* by Angiolo Gambaro (Brescia, 1965) and the critical edition by Pierre Mesnard in *ASD*, I-2, pp. 583 et seq. Ciceronianism has been ably discussed by Mesnard during the last few years in: "La Bataille du Cicéronianisme," *Etudes* (February 1968); in the essay *Erasme ou le christianisme critiqué* (Paris: Seghers, 1969), pp. 80-93; and in his French translation, "Le véritable Cicéronien," *La Philosophie chrétienne* (Paris: Vrin, 1969).

41. See especially the beginning of the major expansion of the *De ratione studii*.

42. A metaphor extraordinarily popular during the Renaissance.

43. *De duplici copia verborum ac rerum.*

44. The edition of *De pueris instituendis* (*LB*, 1:510D-E; Geneva: Droz, p. 447; *ASD*, vol. 1, pt. 2, p. 67, l. 20 and p. 68, l. 15), translated into French by J.-C. Margolin.

45. *ASD*, vol. 1, pt. 2, p. 113, ll. 4-5.

46. A kind of ibex or antelope (more precisely; a "stag-goat") from tropical Africa, described by Solinus.

47. "Verborum *prior*, rerum potior."

48. For the dates of composition, see, in addition to my respective editions (Geneva, 1966; Amsterdam, 1971) the article by James D. Tracy, "On the Composition Dates of Seven of Erasmus' Writings," *Bibliothèque d'Humanisme et Renaissance* 31, no. 2 (1969): 355-71.

49. See the edition by Fritz Schalk in *ASD*, vol. 4, pt. 1, pp. 221-370.

50. See note 6, above. In addition to Erasmus's *Colloquies*, Basedow recommended Comenius's *The Visible World in Pictures* (1658) for the use of twelve-year-olds. See Basedow's 1775 edition, which was published at Leipzig and Frankfurt: *Encyclopaedia philanthropica Colloquiorum Erasmi, demtis illis partibus quae erant adolescentum moribus nocivae ordini sacro et militari . . .* and the advice of Basedow: "Oro atque oro ut Erasmiana quotidiana lectione versetis." The pedagogical method of Basedow is found again in Wolke's book, *The Natural Method of Instruction*. (Wolke was the inspector of the school at Dessau, founded by Basedow.)

51. Here again, the Basedow-Wolke method was directly inspired by it, as is seen, for example, in the description of plate 8 (sketches by M. D. Chodowiecki, designed for the elementary work by Basedow): "I see a four-footed animal who is carrying a goose. Do you see it too? It certainly is some carnivorous beast that threw himself on the goose, killed her, and ate her. Would this be a wolf or a lion? Neither: it is a fox, an adroit and cunning animal. . . . The goose, who is stupid, and does not know how to fly."

52. To be compared with Erasmus's colloquy, *Amicitia* (*ASD*, vol. 1, pt. 3, pp. 700-69). This colloquy, which dates from 1530 and borrows certain phrases from the *De pueris instituendis* on the friendship or instinctive hostility of animals, is in fact inspired (as is the other text) by the *Natural History* of Pliny, of which Ephorinus—one of the characters of the dialogue with Johannes, alias John Boner, his pupil—had given him an edition in 1530. Erasmus himself edited Pliny in 1525. See his statement in the preface of *Ciceronianus, ASD*, vol. 1, pt. 2, p. 708: "Mundum docet Plinius."

53. See my edition of the *De pueris instituendis* (1966) for the terms *ludus* and *lusus* in the index on p. 629.

54. Ibid., p. 451: *ASD*, vol. 1, pt. 2, p. 70, ll. 18-20.

55. Ibid., p. 451; *ASD*, vol. 1, pt. 2, p. 70, ll. 22-28.

56. Not forgetting Bacon.

57. Quoted by Eugenio Garin, *L'Education de l'homme moderne*, trans. Fayard (Paris, 1968), p. 201. This expression is used in several passages of different editions of his *Janua*. Cf. *ODO*, vol. 2 passim.

58. Cf. *ODO*, 1:p. 250. The subtitle of *Janua* is *Seminarium linguarum et scientiarum omnium*.

59. *ODO*, vol. 2, col. 476.

60. Ibid.

61. As he writes in the *Pansophia ODO*, vol. 1, col. 413.

62. Ibid., col. 413.

63. Ibid., col. 414.

64. Ibid., cols. 414-15.

65. Defined as "viva universi imago."

66. *ODO*, vol. 1, col. 253.

67. Ibid., vol. 2, cols. 802-03.

68. "Libellus est, ut videtis, haud magnae molis, Mundi tamen totius et totius Linguae breviarium" (*ODO*, vol. 2, col. 803).

69. Ibid., cols. 803 and 829 (*sic*).

70. The edition of the *Orbis pictus* I used—because the edition of 1657, reproduced in the Prague edition of 1957, curiously does not include the text of the book whose preface it reproduced—is a Latin-Hungarian edition of 1675, republished in 1970 in Budapest ("In Aedibus Academiae Scientiarum Hungaricae Budapestini"). See *Mundus* pp. 8-9.

71. Comenius, *Orbis pictus* (1675), pp. 18-19.

72. Ibid., pp. 16-17.

73. Ibid., p. 20.

74. *Faber lignarius.*

75. *Naufragium.*

76. *Instrumenta musica.*

77. Paris: Gallimard, 1966.

78. Preface, p. 14.

79. Chap. 2, p. 49.

80. Margolin, "Tribut d'un antihumaniste aux études d'Humanisme et Renaissance: Note sur l'oeuvre de Michel Foucault," *Bibliothèque d'Humanisme et Renaissance* 29, no. 3 (1967): 701-11.

13 Erasmus at School:
The *De Civilitate Morum Puerilium Libellus*

FRANZ BIERLAIRE

Thus far Erasmian specialists have been little interested in *De civilitate morum puerilium libellus,*[1] as though they were afraid that this minor work might decrease the reputation of the prince of humanists. Guillaume Budé reproached Erasmus during his own lifetime for wasting his eloquence and his talent on such insignificant subjects:[2] "And, great gods, you will tell me again that you corrected the little Cato (*Catonis disticha,* 1514) and that you do not regret the short day's work devoted to that trivial task; as if so many little books do not risk tarnishing the brilliancy of your name."[3]

The editor of the *Disticha moralia* (attributed to Cato the Censor), a work not without similarity to the *De civilitate,* did not at all share the fears of his French friend. On the contrary, he estimated that "in the domain of belles-lettres, there is nothing on earth, even the most vulgar, which is to be scorned, and especially not these verses of the pseudo-Cato that so adorn the Latin language and serve as the means to good manners."[4] Adrien Barland had well understood this when he wrote to his brother: "This book, as I explain every day to my students, is for the purpose of forming their minds to virtue and their language to the art of expressing themselves correctly; for to teach one without the other is truly rather to corrupt than to teach."[5]

The theologian[6] Erasmus feels repugnant neither at "becoming a child again" nor at being occupied with subjects that may appear marginal:[7] "For whoever may seek to render service only and not to attract attention," Erasmus writes to Budé, "the brilliancy of the material is less important than its utility. I will not reject any work, not even that scornfully wretched *Catunculus,* if I determine that it is useful in bringing about progress in studies. I do not write for Persius nor Laelius, I write for children and for the unlettered [*pueris et crassulis scribuntur*]."[8]

The *De civilitate morum puerilium libellus* was destined for children, and although it was dedicated to the *crassissima philosophiae pars,*[9] it is far from being the least important of Erasmus's pedagogical works: the *civilitas morum* being for Professor Telle a way of "utilizing the medium of the printing

Translated from the French by Louise M. Kamenjar.

press,"[10] the indispensable complement to intellectual and religious formation: "The task of instructing the young consists of several things," Erasmus
writes, "the first and, therefore, the principal one is to inculcate in tender
minds the seeds of piety; the second, to have them love and study the liberal
arts; the third, to acquaint them with life's duties; the fourth, to accustom them
from their first steps to courtesy in their manners."[11]

One page of the *De pueris,* a work published only a few months before the
De civilitate, illustrates this fine definition of education: "If the young child
does something unsuitable at table, he is admonished and, after this warning,
he sets up for himself a code of deportment, conforming himself to the example
that was proposed to him. He is led to church; he learns how to kneel, to join his
little hands, to discover and to give to his whole body an attitude proper to
devotion; he is ordered to be silent when the mysteries are being performed, and
he is made to turn his head towards the altar. The child learns these rudiments
of modesty and piety before knowing how to speak, and, as they remain fixed in
him as he grows up, such rudiments profit true religion. The child learns that
he must rise before an old person and remove his hat before the representation of the cross. Those who imagine that these rudiments of virtue, such as they
are, have no moral value, commit, in my opinion at least, a grave error."[12]

Beginning as soon as possible the apprenticeship in propriety continues parallel
with the initiation into Latin conversation, as in witness whereof the first
edition, formally recognized, of the *Familiarium colloquiorum formulae* (March
1522). Indeed, Erasmus reserves a very important place there for the rules of
public well-being and city life *(urbanitas)*[13] before teaching his young readers
how to behave in the street, at play, in school, at table, in bed, in church: the
two short colloquies, entitled *Confabulatio pia* (The Whole Duty of Youth) and
Monita paedagogica (A Lesson in Manners), the latter being a true lesson in good
manners, constitute the outline of the *De civilitate.*[14]

This work, which Erasmus carried with him for several years, appeared in
Basel, in March 1530, in the form of a letter addressed "to the very noble son of
Prince Adolph of Veere."[15] The humanist who had utilized the epistolary genre
to exhort the father to virtue began again thirty years later in order to indicate
to the son the kind of manners suitable to boys his age. That child "who offered
the greatest expectations" was not Maximilian of Burgundy, to whom Erasmus
dedicated the *De pronuntiatione,* but his brother Henry of Burgundy, who was
then eleven years old.

According to Erasmus, Henry did not have a great need for his counsels on
good manners: the son of a prince, born to rule, he was raised from the cradle
in the midst of courtiers and had been recently instructed by a remarkably gifted

teacher.[16] In writing those lines, the humanist was only obeying the rules of a literary genre in which he excelled. Is not one of the characteristics of the *epistola monitoria* "to point out to the inexperienced the behavior that should be followed while pretending to have nothing to teach him?"[17] The remarks on comportment which suits a well-born boy,[18] and especially the admonitions against the manners recommended occasionally by certain courtiers,[19] prove that the *De civilitate* was not destined only for children of the lower classes.[20] Erasmus was concerned with children of noble ancestry as well, for the milieu in which they lived was generally not a nursery for well-bred individuals: "Some still send the young into the prince's courtyard, so that they may learn civility and especially princely manners. By what, pray then, are princely manners? Let nothing be added: everyone decides for himself."[21]

In seven chapters, Erasmus applies himself to a survey of all the social situations, and even some intimate details, in the life of the child. In succeeding chapters he becomes interested in the exterior aspect and behavior (*De corpore*), in dress (*De cultu*), in the manner of behaving in church (*De moribus in templo*), in how one serves and behaves at the table (*De conviviis*), in meetings and conversation (*De congressibus*), in comportment at play (*De lusu*), and in the bedroom (*De cubiculo*), speaking in the same way of how to expectorate or snuff out a candle, not hestitating to study and to "name some functions of the body that our sensibility no longer permits us to discuss in public, much less in treatises on good manners."[22] He considers the most familiar gestures as well as the most unusual, trying to foresee all the particular circumstances in which the child can be found. In passing, he points out proper or absurd attitudes he has observed around him: those he has noted in the course of his reading or his travels; even those he has noticed in some paintings. Certain countenances or facial expressions inspired in him some comparisons with the behavior of certain animals and some remarks on character: Erasmus obviously believed in physiognomy, but he did not seem to be inspired by ancient practitioners of this art.

The well-bred child whose portrait appears in filigree in the *De civilitate* resembles Gaspar, the hero of the *Whole Duty of Youth*. Modest, deferential, and smiling under all circumstances, he behaved according to nature and reason,[23] respecting the customs of different areas he was called to frequent and avoiding the temptation to singularize himself by exaggerating the signs of politeness. He constantly worried about the image that he reflected. He knew how to close his eyes to the defects of others,[24] and he attached more importance to his health than to courtesy itself: "But it is not proper to make yourself ill in an effort to be seen as a man refined in manners."[25]

Today's reader cannot fail to be struck by the universality and the reality of the counsels and admonitions of Erasmus. Formulated for children—*nos puerum formamus*—[26] these rules of conduct have a universal significance: they apply even to a preacher and, with some exceptions, remain valuable in our own age.

The work of a moralist with his eyes wide open, the *De civilitate* is an important document, not only for the history of manners and mentalities, but equally for the history of pedagogy, since this work was the most esteemed school manual in the sixteenth century and even in the following century. Several generations of children learned how to read and to write with this little book, which was usually printed with characters—in imitation of actual handwriting—and owed its name to it, "characters of civility."[28] Moreover, long before the invention of these characters, the *De civilitate* was used in schools as a manual of good breeding and as an introduction to the Latin language. If, in the Middle Ages, and even at the beginning of the Renaissance, the knowledge necessary for living in society was not learned at school but with an outside family—preferably noble—or even at some princely court where the child, representing a miniature valet, served his apprenticeship in contact with adults,[29] all of this had begun to change in Erasmus's time,[30] and this humanist is without doubt the one who contributed the most to the development of instruction in courtesy for the various classes.[31]

Most of the school programs of the sixteenth century required that one class be dedicated to mores or that a special meeting be set aside which defined the behavior to be adopted and the rules to be respected inside as well as outside the institution.[32] Almost all of these elementary disciplinary rules seem to have been inspired by the *De civilitate*, the reading of which was recommended frequently by the schools. Indeed, the use of this Erasmian manual is attested in the statutes of the schools in the following cities or regions: Wittenberg[33] (1533), Brunswick[34] (1535), Speyer[35] (1538), Bury Saint Edmunds[36] (1550), the Duchy of Mecklenburg[37] (1552), Neubrandenburg[38] (1553), Magdeburg[39] (1553), Augsburg[40] (1557), the Duchy of Deux-Ponts[41] (1557), Neuburg-on-Danube[42] (before 1559), Braunau[43] (1560), Ingolstadt[44] (about 1560), Nördlingen[45] (1561), Landshut[46] (about 1562), Winchester[47] (between 1561 and 1569), Wassenberg[48] (1562), Pomerania[49] (1563), Brandenburg[50] (1564), Deventer (1564) and Utrecht[51] (1565), Wismar[52] (1566), Regensburg[53] (1567), Lindau[54] (1568), Bangor[55] (1569), Breslau[56] (1570), Oettingen[57] (1575), Utrecht[58] (1578), Höningen[59] (about 1580), Brieg[60] (1581), Kampen[61] (1587), Annaberg[62] (1594), Brunswick[63] (1596, 1598, 1599).

The *De civilitate* serves obviously to teach good manners:[64] "Sometimes . . . some rules will be taken out of Erasmus' manual on civility of manner or the *De disciplina puerorum*, so that manners may more properly be formed."[65] Children must refer to this code of behavior in every circumstance: "Every child's

behavior in all circumstances represents the kind of manners that Erasmus'
book, written for erudite civility, illustrates," according to the rules of the
Gymnasium poeticum of Regensburg.[66] The statutes of the *schola Martiniana*
of Brunswick foresaw that this manual would be read every Thursday to pupils
gathered together from three classes.[67] As for the rules of the school of Neubrandenburg, they did not insist on the means to remove from the school
barbarities in manners and in conversation, since they insisted that Erasmus's
"*De civilitate morum puerilium libellus* is always in the hands of our school
children."[68] The manual appears, then, as one of the instruments in the struggle against the coarseness of manners as well as language: "Henceforth, pure
conversation and acceptable manners are to be learned and harmful ones are to
be avoided," stipulated the statutes of Brandenburg.[69] Those of Ingolstadt bore
witness to the same concern: "For this reason in this class, albeit gradually, let
the same, formed jointly in the courtesy of manners, be instructed in the perfection of the Latin language."[70]

The use of the *De civilitate* for grammatical and stylistic ends took several
forms. Sometimes the teacher helped the children to find "Latin phrases and
names of numerous things"[71] in the book; sometimes he used the text to illustrate a lesson in morphology or syntax:[72] "The other two classes should be combined, and the schoolmaster should explain to them the *De civilitate morum . . .*
and on the other days one should make constructions and declensions out of it,"
so ordered the statutes of the school at Wittenberg.[73] The grade in which the
manual was studied was generally neither the first nor the last, but an interme-
diary one, most often the third—that is to say, the one in which children who
read perfectly were admitted[74] and who knew fairly well the declensions and
conjugations.[75] In certain schools, they still spent the major part of their time
declining and conjugating,[76] and they completed their grammatical formation
by practicing the application of rules, which the teacher showed them how to
use. The study of Latin grammar was accompanied by the use of the *De civilitate:*
at Bury Saint Edmunds and at Bangor, for example, the *King's Grammar* was
one of the other manuals used in the third form. Certain school statutes did not
mention any specific grammar, but they did not forget to remind the teacher
how to use "the little book," so that the precepts of Latin grammar might be
added."[77]

Without any doubt the *De civilitate* answered a social need: its immediate
success—twelve editions at least in a single year, 1530—its early translation into
the major vernacular languages, its utilization in schools, are all incontestable
proofs of this need. The extraordinary diffusion of this little book can be explained by the fact that it came at the right moment and that it presented some
models of comportment that were suitable to its time.[78] However, its adoption

not only as a guide to decorum for use by children but also as a book for reading—"whence the knowledge and use of Latin conversation becomes self-evident"[79] —is certainly not unrelated to the multiplication of reissues of the original and of school or annotated editions as well.

The most celebrated and widespread of these editions, accompanied by annotations, is, unquestionably, that of Gisbertus Longolius which Johann Gymnicus published at Cologne in October of 1531. It was not the first effort of the editor, who became rector of the school at Deventer, then professor at the University of Cologne, since scarcely a few months after the appearance of the *De civilitate,* he published an edition of the work enriched by some marginal notes.[80] The other annotators are less well known and less interesting than he: one of them, however, was William Hachusanus, another citizen of Deventer.[81]

Most of the editions of the *De civilitate* were the work of pedagogues, who carefully placed at the disposal of their students a manual designed especially for them. Dedicated to a son of a prince who had been instructed by a tutor and had not attended school, the *De civilitate* did not discuss school behavior and set before the student some rules that could only be memorized with great difficulty. Beginning in 1534, a teacher at the school of Marburg, Reinhard Hadamarius, transformed the work into a kind of catechism in the form of questions and answers, "so that the young might learn by heart more easily and be able to remember it."[82] He also introduced a supplementary chapter, entitled "De moribus in paedogogio et inter praelegendum servandis," thus filling a gap in the original version.

In 1536, another pedagogue, Ewaldus Gallus, drew a series of brief *Leges morales* from the principal chapters of the *De civilitate*. Less complete than the work by his German colleague, this rector of the Latin school at Weert was interested neither in children's clothes nor in school conduct. Thus he reserved only a few lines for comportment at play and at bedtime.[83] Like the question-and-answer manual designed for schoolchildren at Marburg, this edition was nevertheless a faithful adaptation of the text of Erasmus:

Erasmus

A naribus absit purulentia, quod est sordidorum. Id vicium Socrati philosopho datum est probro.

Inflectere cervicem et adducere scapulas pigritiam arguit, resupinare corpus fastus indicium est; molliter erectum decet. Cervix nec in levum nec in dextrum vergat: hypocriticum enim, nisi colloquium aut aliud simile postulet.

Hadamarius

Quales debent esse nares? Mundae, et ab omni mucoris purulentia alienae.

Qualis debet esse cervix? Nec inflexa, non in laevum nec in dextrum vergens, sed (ut etiam corpus) molliter sit erecta.

Gallus

A naribus abesto mucor, ab ore saliva.

Cervicem nec in laevum humerum, nec in dextrum, nisi ad colloquium non reflectito: nec scapulas adducito, nec resupinato corpus.

In order that children might more easily memorize the rules they were to know by heart and to recite before their fellow classmates,[84] certain teachers had the idea of putting the *De civilitate* in verse form. Requiring that his pupils respect scrupulously the Erasmian precepts, the rector of the *Gymnasium poeticum* at Regensburg added: "Wherefore and indeed this composition being translated by us into poetry on a favorable occasion, we offer it to the students of the highest class."[85] This rhymed version is no longer extant, but we possess several others, among which is one by Francois Heeme, teacher in the chapter school of Notre Dame at Courtrai.[86]

The diffusion of these adaptations proves that the *De civilitate* was utilized in many more schools than our list indicates. Students in regions that remained faithful to Rome had nothing to envy in students in German-Lutheran schools or in British grammar schools: Did not the *De civilitate* appear in 1550 among the school books recommended by the University of Louvain?[87] The acts of censorship took effect only very slowly. Speaking of instruction in propriety in a letter to Vérépée dated January 3, 1574, the regent of the college of the Jesuits at Cologne wrote to this effect: "This matter must be drawn from books which treat specifically of the civility of manners. Why have you not written a work of this type! Teachers and students would read it in the place of Erasmus's *Civilitas morum*."[88]

It is known that the Jesuits disclaimed with difficulty certain Erasmian manuals and that they continued to use them somtimes, but without citing the name of the author. Responding to Johann von Rheitt, Vérépée pointed out to him the existence of the *Leges morales* of Ewald Gallus, which *ex Erasmo fere collectas,* and he announced his intention of inserting them in his *Progymnasmata,* after giving them a form better adapted to young children and suppressing the name of a certain person (*suppresso cuiusquam nomine*).[89] Thirty years later, in 1593, a certain Jean Houtveus of Vlierden published in Brussels a small book entitled *De civilitate morum puerilium libellus, de integro in breviores redactus quaestiones memoriae iuvandae gratia.* The *Librorum censor* gave his approval to the publication of this version, scarcely altered in its question-and-answer approach by Reinhard Hadamarius and destined for Jesuit pupils. The name of the teacher at Marburg appears nowhere, nor does that of Erasmus, from whom the plagiarist borrowed not only the title and the contents but the appendixes of the small book as well.[90]

Thus, a long time after his death Erasmus continued to teach fine manners to little schoolchildren, and his career as textbook writer was far from terminated. In 1625, the famous *Schoolordre* promulgated by the States of Holland prescribed the utilization of the *De civilitate* in all the schools of Holland and Friesland, and it ordered the printing of an edition "corrected in some places" that would be reproduced in a thousand copies. Reedited several times, this manual was still used in Amsterdam[91] in 1677. In the school at Stralsund, at the edge of the Baltic, the *De civilitate* appeared in the 1643 curriculum of the second and third classes: the teacher read the work to his pupils and used the occasion to teach them things that were not found in the manual but concerned the issues treated.[92] In an ordonnance of 1651, enforced in all the schools of his jurisdiction, Duke Augustus of Brunswick concluded the chapter devoted to the "censure of manners" with the words: "Let whoever may be either holding onto or fleeing tradition in daily living with others be instructed especially by Erasmus of Rotterdam's work on the civility of manners."[93] At the end of the eighteenth century, the German pedagogue Joachim-Henry Campe, the successor of Basedow as head of the *Philanthropinum* at Dessau, drew from the *De civilitate* and from the *Introductio ad sapientiam* by Vives a *Compendium artis vivendi*, which well served his pupils, first at Hamburg, then at Brunswick.[94]

We could multiply these examples[95] and could likewise evoke here the *Bonne habitude nouvelle*, a book of Erasmian counsels in verse, published in 1829 by a Rumanian teacher,[96] as well as the innumerable adaptations, imitations, translations of the manual—these *Civilités puériles et honnêtes,* more or less inspired by Erasmus, who was in effect "the model for these inept little books which for two centuries have multiplied rapidly in the schools"[97] and made fortunes for the book trade.[98] The history of this literature remains to be written. He who charges himself with the task will have to return often to Erasmus, concerning whom Melanchthon underlined in 1522 his permanent concern for the *civilitas* and the *boni mores:* "Erasmus nearly always teaches this."[99]

NOTES

1. The most recent and the most complete study is by Herman de la Fontaine Verwey, "The First 'Book of Etiquette' for Children," *Quaerendo* 1 (1971): 19-30.

2. P. S. Allen et al., *Opus Epistolarum Desiderii Erasmi . . .* (Oxford, 1906–58), vol. 2, Ep. 403, p. 232, ll. 122-23; hereafter referred to as *EE.*

3. *EE,* vol. 2, Ep. 435, p. 275, ll. 88–91.

4. Ibid., Ep. 298, p. 2, ll. 17-20.

5. Ibid., Ep. 492, p. 389, ll. 115-18.

6. Ibid., Ep. 298, p. 2, ll. 16-17: "Sed interim clamabit vitilitigator aliquis, Hui theologum in tam frivolis versari nugis?" An explication by Gisbertus Longolius illustrates this remark of Erasmus: "Fuere tamen quorum ineptam et loquacem temeritatem hic praeterire non possum, quibus incomparabilis hic puerorum thesaurus quum primum aeditus esset, ansam calumniandi autorem dedit. Deum immortalem quo supercilio Erasmum grammaticum (nam Erasmum theologum dicere, apud eos verecundum est, et capitulari censura dignum) pro consuetudine sua damnarunt, iam apud omnes, inquiunt, evulgatum est, quod hactenus in homine latuit, ô intempestivam stultitiam, iam senex se ad pueros erudiendos demisit...." (see the edition of the *De civilitate* printed at Cologne: Johann Gymnicus, October 1531, p. 5).

7. Erasmus, *De civilitate,* in *Opera Omnia* . . . , ed. J. Clericus (Leiden, 1703) henceforth cited as *LB,* 1:1033A: "Si ter maximum illum Paulum non piguit omnia fieri omnibus, quo prodesse posset omnibus, quanto minus ego gravari debeo iuvandae inventutis amore subinde repuerascere." See also *De utilitate colloquiorum,* ed. L.-E. Halkin et al., in *Opera Omnia Desiderii Erasmi* . . . (Amsterdam, 1969-), vol. 1, pt. 3, p. 741, ll. 16-17: "Quod si quis clamet indecorum homini sic pueriliter ludere, nihil moror quam pueriliter, modo utiliter." Henceforth *ASD.*

8. *EE,* vol. 2, Ep. 480, p. 364, ll. 69-74.

9. *De civilitate, LB,* 1:1033C.

10. Emile V. Telle, *Erasme de Rotterdam et le septième sacrement* (Geneva, 1954), p. 299.

11. *De civilitate, LB,* 1:1033B–C. See also *Institutio christiani matrimonii, LB,* 5:713C: "Est autem duplex institutionis cura, altera quae pertinet ad disciplinarum cognitionem, altera quae pertinet ad pietatem ac bonos mores."

12. *Declamatio de pueris statim ac liberaliter instituendis,* ed. J.-C. Margolin (Geneva, 1966), pp. 412-14.

13. *Colloquia, ASD,* vol. 1, pt. 3, pp. 125-30. See also *De conscribendis epistolis,* ed. J.-C. Margolin, *ASD,* vol. 1, pt. 2, pp. 276-85 ("De salutatione").

14. Ibid., pp. 171-81 and 161-63.

15. We take the liberty of sending the reader to our critical edition of the *De civilitate,* which will appear in *ASD.*

16. *De civilitate, LB,* 1:1033B.

17. *De conscribendis epistolis, ASD,* vol. 1, pt. 2, p. 488, ll. 5-6.

18. *De civilitate, LB,* 1:1033C and 1043B.

19. Ibid., 1035A, 1038C, and 1038E.

20. Ibid., 1033D.

21. *Ecclesiastes, LB,* 5:909F.

22. N. Elias, *La civilisation des moeurs* (Paris, 1973), p. 193. An excellent analysis of the Erasmian manual and of other treatises of the same genre will be found in this work, whose first edition (German) appeared in 1939.

23. *De civilitate, LB,* 1:1036B: "At non statim honestum est quod stultis placuit, sed quod naturae et rationi consentaneum est."

24. Ibid., 1044A: "Maxima civilitatis pars est, quum ipse nusquam delinquas, aliorum delictis facile ignoscere, nec ideo sodalem minus habere charum, si quos habet mores inconditiores. Sunt enim qui morum ruditatem aliis compensent dotibus."

25. Ibid., 1036C.

26. Ibid., 1035A.

27. The advice given to teachers in *Ecclesiastes* (*LB,* 5:963A-967A) blends with that lavished on Henry of Burgogne.

28. See especially Harry Carter and H. D. L. Vervliet, *Civilité Types* (Oxford, 1966).

29. Valuable information and numerous texts will be found in the works of F. J. Furnivall, *The Babees Book* . . . (London, 1868) and *Queene Elisabethes Achademy* . . . (London, 1869).

30. Contrary to what Philippe Ariès thinks in *L'enfant et la vie familiale sous l'Ancien Régime,* 2d ed. (Paris, 1973), p. 429.

31. Foster Watson, *The English Grammar Schools to 1660: Their Curriculum and Practice* (London, 1908), p. 104.

32. See especially R. Vormbaum, *Die evangelischen Schulordnungen des sechszehnten Jahrhunderts* (Gütersloh, 1860), pp. 57-58, 426-27, 569-71; E. E. Fabian, "M. Petrus Plateanus, Rector der Zwickauer Schule von 1535 bis 1546," in *Gymnasium zu Zwickau* (Zwickau, 1878), p. 31. The statutes of the school at East Redford (1552) specify that the purpose of the institution is to teach "not only grammar and virtuous doctrine but also good manners." See T. W. Baldwin, *William Shakspere's Small Latine and Lesse Greeke* (Urbana, Ill., 1944), 1:315. Let us note finally that among the exercises of the pupils of the college of the Jeromites in Liège appear two letters which concern good manners. See M. Delcourt and J. Hoyoux, "Documents inédits sur le Collège liégeois des Jéromites (1524–1526)," in *Annuaire d'histoire liégeoise* (Liège, 1957), 5:933-79.

33. Vormbaum, *Die evangelischen Schulordnungen,* p. 29; Karl Hartfelder, *Philipp Melanchthon als Praeceptor Germaniae* (Berlin, 1889), p. 427.

34. Friedrich Koldewey, *Braunschweigische Schulordnungen von den ältesten Zeiten bis zum Jahre 1828* (Berlin, 1886), 1:50 and 54.

35. K. Reissinger, *Dokumente zur Geschichte der humanistischen Schulen im Gebiet der Bayerische Pfalz* (Berlin, 1911), 2:371.

36. T. W. Baldwin, *William Shakspere's Small Latine,* 1:298.

37. Vormbaum, *Die evangelischen Schulordnungen,* p. 63; Heinrich Schnell, *Urkunden und Akten zur Geschichte des Mecklenburgischen Unterrichtswesen* (Berlin, 1907), 1:206.

38. Vormbaum, p. 434; Schnell 1:240 and 242.

39. Vormbaum, p. 415.

40. H. Ockel, *Geschichte des höheren Schulwesens in Bayerisch-Schwaben während der vorbayerischen Zeit* (Berlin, 1931), pp. 35 and 323.

41. Reissinger, *Dokumente zur Geschichte,* 2:6.

42. Ockel, *Geschichte des höheren Schulwesens,* p. 249.

43. G. Lurz, *Mittelschulgeschichtliche Dokumente Altbayerns, einschliesslich Regensburgs* (Berlin, 1907), 1:290.

44. Ibid., 1:308-09.

45. Ockel, p. 128.

46. Lurz, *Mittelschulgeschichtliche,* 1:324.

47. Baldwin, *William Shakspere's Small Latine,* 1:330.

48. Lurz, 1:318.

49. Vormbaum, p. 172.

50. Ibid., p. 529.

51. P. N. M. Bot, *Humanisme en onderwijs in Nederland* (Antwerp and Utrecht, 1955), p. 143.

52. Schnell, *Urkunden und Akten,* 1:287.

53. Lurz, 2:407-08 and 416.

54. Ockel, pp. 177-78. The work was still in use in 1624.

55. Baldwin, *William Shakspere's Small Latine,* 1:305.

56. Vormbaum, pp. 196 and 219.

57. Ockel, pp. 262-63.

58. Bot, *Humanisme en onderwijs in Nederland,* p. 143.

59. Reissinger, 2:341.

60. Vormbaum, pp. 306 and 309.

61. Bot, p. 143.

62. P. Bartusch, *Die Annaberger Lateinschule zur Zeit der ersten Blüte der Stadt und ihrer Schule im XVI. Jahrhundert* (Annaberg, 1897), p. 137.

63. Koldewey, *Braunschweigische Schulordnungen*, 1:127, 158-59, and 162.

64. "Ad morum institutionem": see Lurz, 1:309 (Ingolstadt, ca. 1560).

65. Vormbaum, p. 529. The other text to which this rule makes allusion is without doubt the *De disciplina et institutione puerorum* by the German humanist and reformer Othon Brunfels. This work, which was inserted in 1529 in the *Catechesis puerorum in fide, in literis et in moribus* by the same author, was published in 1525. It consisted of a judicious collection of texts, borrowed mostly from Erasmus: *Confabulatio pia, Monitoria, Epistola de ratione studii, Modus repetendae lectionis. . . .* See F. Cohrs, *Die evangelischen Katechismusversuche vor Luthers Enchiridion* (Berlin, 1901), 3:194-220. It is to be noted that the first French edition of the *De civilitate* printed with symbols of courtesy was accompanied by a translation of the *De disciplina: La civilité puerile distribuée par petits chapitres et sommaires. A laquelle nous avons ajouté la discipline et institution des enfants, traduits par Jean Louveau* (Lyons: Robert Granjon, 1558). See H. de la Fontaine Verwey, "Typografische schrijfboeken. Een hoofdstuk uit de geschiedenis van de civilité-letter" in *De gulden passer* 39 (1961):300-01.

66. Lurz, 2:416.

67. Koldewey, 1:50.

68. Schnell, 1:242.

69. Vormbaum, p. 530.

70. Lurz, 1:308.

71. Ibid., 2:407 (Regensburg, 1567). See also Vormbaum, p. 172 (Pomerania, 1563). In the seventeenth century, certain printers thought of giving a list of these forms at the end of the volume. See especially the bilingual edition (Amsterdam, 1678), of which a reproduction in facsimile was published in 1969 by H. de la Fontaine Verwey: it ends with a long enumeration of the *Phrases sive Formulae loquendi, e Libello de morum puerilium Civilitate collectae, cum ad elegantiam, tum ad meliorem constructionem.* To illustrate the "multarum rerum appellationes" that the school statutes of Regensburg refer to, I shall point out the great richness of the Erasmian vocabulary. A single example will be sufficient. Erasmus devotes only a few lines to the care that a boy should give to his hair, but he succeeds in using three different words: "coma," "capillitium," and "caesaries." See *De civilitate, LB*, 1:1035F.

72. "Etymologiam cum Syntaxi e libello Erasmi de civilitate morum," precisely the *Leges et disciplina scholae Daventriensis* of 1564. See J. I. Van Doorninck, "Bouwstoffen voor eene Geschiedenis van het Onderwijs in Overijssel," in *Bijdragen tot de Geschiedenis van Overijssel* (Zwolle, 1880), 6:207.

73. Vormbaum, p. 29.

74. Lurz, 1:324: "Confluant in hanc classem omnes qui perfecte legunt" (Landshut, ca. 1562). See also ibid., p. 308 (Ingolstadt, ca. 1560).

75. Reissinger, *Dokumente zur Geschichte*, 2:371: "iam Grammaticae precepta mediocriter tenent" (Speyer, 1538); Vormbaum, p. 172: "Hierin sollen sein die knaben, die Etymologiam . . . ziemlich wissen und nun ferner lernen sollen Syntaxin und linguam latinam" (Pomerania, 1563); and p. 527: "Cum enim Elementa Grammatices et Syntaxis, formulas coniugandi et declinandi mediocriter tenent" (Brandenburg, 1564).

76. Lurz, 1:324 (Landshut, ca. 1562).

77. Reissinger, 1:371 (Speyer, 1538).

78. See Elias, *La civilisation des moeurs*, p. 102 et seq.

79. Vormbaum, p. 530 (Brandenburg, 1564).

80. See F. Bierlaire and R. Hoven, "L'école latine de Deventer vers 1536: un règlement oublié," in *Archives et Bibliothèques de Belgique* 45 (1974): 602-17.

81. I consulted an edition published at Cologne: Martin Gymnicus, 1549.

82. The first edition that uses this question-and-answer format (Marburg: E. Cervicorn, May 1537) is entitled: *Elegantissimus D. Erasmi Roterodami libellus, de morum puerilium Civilitate. Eadem in succinctas et ad puerilem aetatem cum primis adpositas Quaestiones Latinas et Germanicas olim digesta, iam recognita, et locupletata, per Reinhardum Hadamarium. In Marpurgensis usum paedagogii* (University Library of Ghent: Th. 2662/1). Erasmus's text precedes the adaptation and German translation. The prefaces of the two versions are dated Sept. 8, 1534 and Sept. 13, 1536, respectively. Before becoming a teacher, then rector, at Marburg, R. Loerich Hadamarius had attended the University of Cologne. See H. Keussen, *Die Matrikel der Universität Koln* (Bonn, 1931), vol. 3, no. 1745, p. 103.

83. See Wouter Nijhoff and M. E. Kronenberg, *Nederlandsche bibliographie van 1500 tot 1540* (The Hague, 1923), vol. 1, no. 951, pp. 334-35. We have consulted another edition dated: "Antverpiae, apud Antonium Tilenium Brechtanum, Anno 1569."

84. Vormbaum, p. 219: "Recitabitur memoriter Civilitas morum a pueris . . ." (Breslau, 1570).

85. Lurz, 2: 416.

86. This "elegiacum carmen" appeared for the first time in an edition of *Poemata* by the author that was published in Antwerp, at Plantin's, in 1578 (pp. 246-75).

87. *Les Catalogues des liures reprouuez, Et de ceulx que lon pourra enseigner par laduis de Luniuersite de Louuain* (Louvain: Servais Sassenus, 1550), folio C^4r^o. The work is classified among "Les autheurs en lart de Retoricque et Oratoirre."

88. M. A. Nauwelaerts, "La correspondance de Simon Verepaeus (1522-1598)," in *Humanistica Lovaniensia* 24 (1974): 282.

89. Ibid., p. 294. See also idem, *Latijnse school en onderwijs te 's-Hertogenbosch tot 1629* (Tilburg, 1974), p. 257.

90. This work is to be found at the Library of the University of Liège (shelfmark: 6487-A). Among the appendixes is a brief text entitled *Repetendae lectionis modus,* which previously appeared in one of the first editions of the *Familiarum colloquiorum formulae.* See the *Colloquia, ASD,* vol. 1, pt. 3, pp. 119-20.

91. H. de la Fontaine Verwey, "The First 'book of etiquette' for Children," pp. 28-29; E. J. Kuiper, *De hollandsche Schoolordre van 1625* (Groningen, 1958); W. H. Van Seters, "De historische achtergrond van de uitgave van een Grieks-latijns schoolboekje, volgens decreet der Staten van Holland in 1626 verschenen, en tot 1727 in gebruik gebleven," in *Het Boek,* 3d ser., 33 (1958-59), pp. 84-105.

92. R. Vormbaum, *Die evangelischen Schulordnungen des siebenzehnten Jahrhunderts* (Gütersloh, 1873), pp. 380-81.

93. Koldewey, *Braunschweigische Schulordnungen,* 2: 157.

94. The Municipal Library of Rotterdam possesses two editions of this work: one is dated 1778 (7 H 29), the other is dated 1797 (7 H 1/1).

95. The work was used at Güstrow in 1602 (Schnell, *Urkunden und Akten,* 1:439), at Görlitz in 1609, at Beuthen in 1614, at Soest in 1618 (Vormbaum, *Die evangelischen Schulordnungen,* pp. 95, 118, 204), at Speyer in 1612 (Reissinger, *Dokumente zur Geschichte,* 2:407), at Augsburg in 1665 and in 1670 (Ockel, *Geschichte des höheren Schulwesens,* p. 66). In the middle of the seventeenth century, Nicolas Mercier, assistant principal of the Collège of Navarre in Paris, published the *De civilitate* and the rhymed version by François Heeme as an appendix to his *De officiis scholasticorum sive de recta ratione proficiendi in litteris, virtute et moribus* (Paris: Claude Thiboust, 1657 and 1664).

There is a copy at the University Library at Ghent (shelfmark: BL 1648) and at the Municipal Library of Rotterdam (shelfmark: 9 H 16). This same author published an expurgated edition of the *Colloquies* as well.

96. Constantin Crisan, "Erasme en Roumanie," in the *Colloquia Erasmiana Turonensia*, ed. J.-C. Margolin (Paris, 1972), 1:178-79.

97. Alcide Bonneau, *La Civilité puérile par Erasme de Rotterdam. Traduction nouvelle, texte latin en regard, précédée d'une notice sur les livres de civilité dupuis le XVIe siècle* (Paris, 1877), p. vii.

98. See, for example, Georges Wildenstein, "L'imprimeur-libraire Richard Breton et son inventaire après décès, 1571," in *Bibliothèque d'Humanisme et Renaissance* 21 (1959):371: "Item mil six cens livre *La civilité honneste.*"

99. The text is cited by Allen, *EE,* vol. 5, Ep. 1496, p. 545, nn. 26-27.

14 *Ecclesiastes sive de Ratione Concionandi*

ROBERT G. KLEINHANS

While the *Ecclesiastes sive de ratione concionandi* was one of the last works Erasmus saw through the press, he had agreed to undertake its composition when it was suggested to him by an admirer in 1519. Erasmus began work on this manual for preachers as early as 1523, and it seems to have preoccupied him until it was finally published the year before his death. Undoubtedly this was partially due to the importance his friends and admirers, especially John Fisher, seemed to have placed on the work.

The *Ecclesiastes* is perhaps more important to the Erasmian corpus than current scholarship recognizes.[1] As John Becar, dean of the College of Zandenburg at Veere, had indicated when he first suggested the work to Erasmus, such a handbook for Christian preachers would be an excellent complement to Erasmus's handbooks for the Christian layman (*Enchiridion Militis Christiani*) and the Christian prince (*Institutio Principis Christiani*).[2] Or to paraphrase Becar more accurately, Erasmus had educated Christian laymen, Christian princes, and Christian educators; now he should educate Christian preachers.[3] Erasmus seems to take up this theme in the opening pages of the *Ecclesiastes*, where he discusses the twofold order of society that falls under the twofold leadership of princes (for the external order) and of bishops (for the internal order). Erasmus believes that it is the mutual task of both orders to establish peace in society in order for Christian piety to flourish, and he adds the complaint that those working in the external realm are better trained for their work than those in the ecclesiastical realm. In order to rectify this situation, Erasmus plans to speak first of the dignity, difficulties, and usefulness of the ecclesiastical preacher.[4]

From this it may be inferred that Erasmus did see the *Ecclesiastes* as an educational tool to be used to train the clergy for their task of developing that Christian piety which alone would ensure a tranquil society. Certainly neither the pressure of papal authority nor the bickerings of the theologians, whether scholastics or reformers, could in Erasmus's estimation achieve this noble end. The *Ecclesiastes*, then, is a complement to Erasmus's other works on Christian piety, to his editions of the New Testament and the Fathers, the reflection on which was to form the basis of this Christian piety, and to his innumerable works associated with pedagogy. It is best, however, to view the *Ecclesiastes* as a

work combining all these elements, since its purpose is to establish the importance of the role of the preacher in the church and to aid him in understanding
and communicating the word of God found in the holy writings that will nourish
true Christian piety.

If Becar's suggestion concerning the relationship of the as yet unwritten
Ecclesiastes to the Erasmian corpus seems strained, the importance of this
work for a study of Erasmus's thought has been well illustrated by James Weiss's
contention that the model of the rhetorician presented by Erasmus represents
his characteristic way of dealing with Christian truths.

> *Ecclesiastes'* style and method reveal not only the richness of the rhetorical
> approach in itself but also the very texture of Erasmus' mind. We find this
> thread of method running through the fabric of all his thought. Or rather,
> this thread discloses the seamless quality of the fabric. . . .
>
>   . . . . Ideally, the Christian orator is one who strives for holiness and who
> champions eloquence for Christ. In so doing, he deploys a vast reserve of
> Scriptural, classical, and patristic learning. . . . He infuses abstract discussions
> with the fundamentals of piety.
>
>   . . . . Thus the mirror of the Christian orator reflects the full-length image
> of Erasmus himself.[5]

Weiss's theory is intriguing and calls for further reflection. Whatever may be the
ultimate evaluation of his position, which seems in contrast to other current
Erasmian scholarship,[6] it should be noted that the *Ecclesiastes* is one of the few
major outlines of a theological perspective undertaken by Erasmus. Most of his
theological and religious works consisted of editions of the Fathers and the New
Testament, paraphrases on the latter, polemical justifications of his own work,
or brief treatises which attempted to indicate a way to harmony amid the
disastrous divisions within Christianity in the sixteenth century. It is true that
many of these works, like the *Colloquies,* are studded with asides on the state of
theology and the church, but it is clear that Erasmus's discussions of these topics
are controlled by the text he is paraphrasing or the author he is editing. There
are few works in which he presents a more organized, and perhaps original, perspective on religion.

The *Ecclesiastes,* as a late work and one not bound by the structure of someone else's text or the confines of a particular polemic, offers the possibility of
seeing Erasmus's mature thought in an organizational framework that is perhaps more congenial to his own mental outlook and that synthesizes in an
unique way his classical, patristic, and scriptural erudition with his concern for
transforming Christendom by establishing true Christian piety in the hearts

of all Christians. As such, this work may provide an interpretive tool for eluci-
dating remarks on theology and the church which appear in previously written
works, for at the time of their composition Erasmus was already intermittently
engaged in the composition of the *Ecclesiastes* and his basic perspective was
presumably being formulated, though less clearly stated.[7]

While the possible value of the *Ecclesiastes* as a hermeneutic resource for the
rest of the Erasmian corpus must be explored before one can actually eval-
uate its worth, two factors seem to militate against even undertaking this task.
First, scholars are generally influenced by Huizinga's characterization of the
Ecclesiastes as "the work of a mind fatigued,"[8] though Huizinga's qualifying
clause "which no longer sharply reacts upon the needs of his times" is overlooked. Huizinga generally viewed Erasmus's later writings as divorced from the
flow of events, and one is left with the impression of a major character of the
sixteenth-century drama gradually retreating from center stage. Huizinga's
criteria for such a judgment is implied by his contrasting of the *Ecclesiastes* with
the first edition of Calvin's *Institutes* which appeared in the same year. Both
Huizinga's judgment on the relation of Erasmus to central events and trends
concurrent with his later years, and his criteria for such a judgment, are subject
to debate; but even if one accepts this evaluation, it does not lessen the probability of the *Ecclesiastes* serving as a hermeneutic tool to uncover the presuppositions and orientations of Erasmus's previous works, which presumably would
have been showing signs of the developing "fatigue." Whether, indeed, the
Ecclesiastes is the work of a "mind fatigued" or of a "mature spirit" needs
further discussion. In any event, this last major work may well give clues to the
gradual "degeneration" or "elaboration" of Erasmus's basic world-view from
which other writings proceeded.

The other factor militating against the employment of the *Ecclesiastes* as a
hermeneutic tool is the natural tendency of scholars to use an author's treatise
on methodology as a starting point for a reconstruction of his "system," "overview," or method. Thus, in a study of Erasmus the *Ratio verae theologiae* seems
at first a more logical starting point for constructing a hermeneutic for the Erasmian corpus. Certainly the *Ratio* should not be overlooked, but caveats must be
heeded in using it to explicate Erasmus's thought. Blessed indeed is the scholar
whose methodology perfectly correlates with his method. There is no guarantee
that the *Ratio* per se is a better key to the Erasmian corpus than the *Ecclesiastes*.
It would be incorrect to read all of Erasmus's works subsequent to the *Ratio* in
light of its major premises, just as it would be incorrect to attempt to project all
major themes of the *Ecclesiastes* into his earlier works. Only the attempt to use
both of these works will ultimately verify the worth of each for the purpose of

clarifying Erasmus's thought. Neither the judgment of Huizinga nor the scholarly temptations to proceed from stated methodology to actual works or from the earlier works to the later writings should militate against attempting to use the *Ecclesiastes* as a possible interpretative tool for the works of Erasmus.

While the importance of the *Ecclesiastes* to the Erasmian corpus is an intriguing question, another which deserves equal consideration is the place of this work in the sixteenth-century Reformation setting.

While contemporary historiography, particularly that colored by the theological presuppositions of twentieth-century neo-Orthodoxy, has perhaps given too much emphasis to the role of preaching in Protestant reform movements without proper qualifications drawn from institutional, social, and cultural history, it is clear that both Lutheran and Reformed traditions reestablished preaching as an integral aspect of Christian worship. But preaching was more than an important element in sixteenth-century liturgical reform; it was also a basic tool and method of reform. In 1522 Luther mounted the pulpit in Wittenberg to correct the liturgical changes introduced by the enthusiast Andreas Bodenstein von Karlstadt. In that same year Zwingli used the pulpit to justify Christoph Froschauer's disregard for the Lenten fast regulations. It was in the following year that Erasmus undertook a preliminary outline for his work on preaching.

The reading public was aware of Erasmus's earlier promise to Becar to produce the work, since the correspondence had been published and, as Allen notes, Erasmus's June first letter to Justus Jonas seems to indicate "that Erasmus may already have had in mind the *Opus Concionandi.*"[9] In January 1523 Erasmus indicated that he hoped to have the manuscript in the press by the end of the year, that is, if the Lord blessed him with life and serenity.[10] At least the latter must have been lacking, for Erasmus's response to Luther, the *De libero arbitrio,* rather than the *Ecclesiastes,* appeared in 1524.

Having entered the list with Luther, Erasmus then wished to withdraw from dogmatic controversies and to return to the work on preaching, which he admitted, however, would touch on dogmatic questions.[11] Perhaps Erasmus's own perception of the importance of preaching was heightened by the importance the reformers placed upon it. If so, there is no indication of this in his letters. His remarks continually refer to the requests for the work from friends, requests which are well attested to by his correspondence.[12] Erasmus was increasingly conscious of the failure to produce the work promised in 1519. The pressure of work and lack of good health are usually given as excuses for the delay, but Erasmus does allude to one other possible cause for the consistent postponement of its completion—the charge that one who never preaches is presumptuous in teaching others how to preach.[13] Something more than the weight of work and ill health does seem to have caused Erasmus continually to set aside work on this project for other publications.[14] The *Ecclesiastes* was finally published in August 1535.

As we have seen, Erasmus began the work with a discussion of the role of the preacher in Christian society. Book 1 of the *Ecclesiastes* is a theological reflection on the dignity and importance of the preacher, and Erasmus initiates this discussion with observations on the importance of the Word of God made known primarily in Christ, who is the *Sermo Dei*. The stress on the Word of God and on preaching characterized the sixteenth-century ecclesiastical reform movements and it is obviously echoed here. E. Gordon Rupp has already reminded us that by 1524 Erasmus could identify "five evangelical slogans going the rounds, the words 'Gospel, Word of God, Faith, Christ, Spirit.'"[15] Erasmus knew he was addressing an issue of the day.

The reformers, however, changed not only the place and relative importance of preaching in the church, but they also developed a new theology of preaching. In their writings, Zwingli and Calvin placed special emphasis on the role of preaching the Word of God; Luther's concept of the Gospel and the subsequent necessity of proclaiming the good news of salvation placed considerable emphasis on the role of preaching and gave it a unique position in the development of Christianity; the conventicle communities of the radical Reformation seem to have continued the medieval sectarian replacement of a sacramental liturgical piety with one formed by the Word made known in preaching, and in so doing conferred upon preaching a singular importance for the church. Even the Council of Trent undertook a clarification of the role of preaching in church life, while at the same time restating the traditional Roman adherence to a sacramental piety. Its canons dealing with pulpit reform cannot be overlooked in a general assessment of its reforming activity.

While the Tridentine reformers viewed the sacraments as instrumental causes of salvation, they were concerned that good preachers be numbered among the church's ministering clergy. For their part, the Protestant confessions of the Reformation stressed the twofold ministry of preaching the Word and administering the sacraments. They seemed, however, to have added a quasi-sacramental value to preaching itself. Preaching was not mere instruction; it was the declaration of the forgiveness of sins. As such, it served as a parallel to absolution in the Roman practice of confession, the sacrament which received such extensive discussion by the Council of Trent and which seemed to be a locus of piety for Catholic reformers as diverse as Theresa of Avila and Philip Neri.

While among Protestant traditions, then, divisions arose over the interpretation of the precise content of the Word to be preached, there was a consensus concerning the importance of preaching. It is clear that during the early decades of the sixteenth century continental Europe was brought to a new awareness of the importance of both the practice of preaching and the theology which justified its place in church life. While Erasmus concurred with sixteenth-century cries for the reform of preaching, and while he seems to have granted an even greater importance to a preaching ministry as opposed to a sacramental ministry than even Luther would have condoned, the *Ecclesiastes* clearly indicates that Erasmus had a concept of the role of preaching which varied greatly from that of his Protestant contemporaries.

Erasmus indicates the general outline of his doctrine of preaching in the brief synopsis of the *Ecclesiastes* found in its dedicatory epistle.

> We have divided the entire subject into four books. In the first we show the dignity of the office and indicate the virtues which ought to be possessed by a preacher. In the second and third we adapt for the use of preaching material which is found in the principles of the rhetoricians, dialecticians, and theologians. The fourth book is a catalogue which shows the preacher what topics he ought to seek and the places in Scripture from whence he can draw them. When we have completed this much, some other matters which do not constitute a small book by themselves are added merely to inform the eager reader.[16]

From this schema and an actual review of the contents of the work, it is clear that the *Ecclesiastes* is really a collection of three books: (1) a theological treatise on the importance of preaching in the church; (2) a textbook in homiletics and hermeneutics which is to give the preacher the basic tools necessary for the interpretation of Scripture and the construction of sermons based on its doctrine; and (3) an outline of sermon topics with an explanation of how some of them should be developed. From this organization of the work it seems clear that Erasmus believed that the theoretical theological foundation of the task of preaching and the practical art of homiletics should not be separated. Just as Renaissance humanism stressed the importance of the role of the rhetorician in society as well as the theory of rhetoric, so Erasmus combined the theological justification of the dignity and role of the preacher with an application of the theories of classical rhetoric to homiletics.[17]

It is in Book 1 of the *Ecclesiastes,* however, that Erasmus seems to give the clearest outline of his theology of preaching. For Erasmus the preacher is to establish peace in individual souls by announcing the doctrine of Christ, the celestial philosophy, and by encouraging individuals to live according to this doctrine. This will enable men to establish the divine law in their lives and thus fulfill their very nature. Thus men will live in peace with God.[18]

For Erasmus both the political and the ecclesiastical hierarchies have the same function, namely of establishing peace in the Christian commonwealth;

but they accomplish their tasks in different ways. The king and the political hierarchy protect a society from calamities of nature and human enemies. But this is insufficient to establish peace if the souls of the citizens are infected with vice. Thus the ecclesiastical hierarchy attempts to establish a peaceful relationship between individuals and God.[19] Peace is the aim of both hierarchies, and the establishment of order in the external realm can frequently aid that of religion. While there is a clear distinction between the work of the king, his legates and officials, and that of the bishops and their pastors,[20] peace is the common goal of the secular and ecclesiastical hierarchies.

The concept of peace is a common theme in Erasmus's writings; the centrality of this concept in his doctrine of individual sanctification is a parallel theme. In the *Enchiridion Militis Christiani* Erasmus begins with a discussion of the need for vigilance in the war against vice. This is followed by an explanation of the armor of the Christian soldier. When in chapter 3 he begins his discussion of the Christian life, the opening word is *Pax*. Peace is the highest good sought by all men, but only Christ can give true peace, for God alone can give man virtue.[21] In the *Ecclesiastes,* Erasmus returned to this theme. The peace of the external order will be established by the proclamations of the king's will, while the ecclesiastical preachers will explain God's law, His promises, and His will to the people. The preachers will also persuade the people to live according to God's will. The combined actions of the secular legates and the ecclesiastical preachers will establish peace in the commonwealth.[22] The centrality of the doctrine of peace, order, and harmony can also be seen in Erasmus's selection of this topic as the theme of the model sermon which closes the *Ecclesiastes.*[23]

All peace will be established by law, by the ordering of society from above, but especially by the ordering of man according to his highest faculty, the mind. Thus the secular legates announce the king's edicts while the preacher proclaims God's laws, His promises, and His will. Certainly Erasmus must have considered the promise of salvation as one of the most important ones, and he could agree with Luther that the promise of the free forgiveness of sins is integral to Christian doctrine. Nevertheless, Erasmus's concept of Christian doctrine seems to focus on law. Law is the second principle of division of the topics in Book 4 of the *Ecclesiastes.* The material in the book is divided between persons and law. The section on persons is divided according to the hierarchies of Pseudo-Dionysius. The latter section on law begins with the statement that in any well-run republic law is the first authority.[24] Erasmus then offers the reader a brief discourse on divine law. Since law provides the basis for sin and since sins are listed in the general category of vices as opposed to virtues, Erasmus turns from a discussion of law to an explanation of virtue.[25] This is followed by a discussion of the ideal Christian death, which is the ultimate perfection of virtue.[26]

The complementary topics of law and virtue thus form the basic framework for the second section of Erasmus's summary of Christian doctrine.

Complementary to this theme of peace established by law is Erasmus's Christology. As Christ is the archetype of divine truth necessary for establishing proper order in men's lives,[27] so the *Sermo Dei*—Christ—is the perfect image of the Father. Through him the Father creates and governs the universe; through him the Father redeems fallen man and binds together the church. Through Christ God is made known to the world, gives life to the dead, bestows the gifts of the Holy Spirit and the power of the sacraments. Through Christ God will judge the world; through him he will create a new heaven and earth; through him God will finally satisfy the hunger and thirst of the angels and the entire celestial Jerusalem.[28] In short, through the Son, all of God's relationships with the world are established; and all other revelations of God to men, those through creation and the Old Testament prophets, come through Christ.[29]

But in order to grasp the truth revealed in the *Sermo Dei* and proclaimed by Christ, man must have something in his nature which has an affinity with the divine. This is man's mind. The mind is in some way an image of God.[30] The mind of man is reflected in his words, and even in his corporeal demeanor.[31] Thus the preacher must have Christ, the true image of the Father, in his heart so that the will of God may be reflected in his sermons. One must have the spirit of Christ in one's soul or heart in order that Christ will be in one's preaching.[32] Christ is the greatest preacher since he is the proto-image of the Father and since he is God's Word addressed to men. All Christians partake in this role of Christ, but the preacher especially must imitate Christ by performing this ministry.[33]

This emphasis on the preaching ministry of each Christian, or rather the very definition of a Christian as a preacher, harmonizes Erasmus's *Sermo Dei* and his Christology, and correlates with both his Christian anthropology and his concept of peace as the ultimate fulfillment of human existence. In this lies the essential character of a Christian as well as the way to harmony in the world and the much divided church of Erasmus's day. The ordained preacher has a special responsibility to proclaim God's will, and it is his task in society to establish peace and concord by drawing souls to Christ.[34] All this echoes the observations and advice Erasmus offered to John Becar when he first suggested the *Ecclesiastes* in 1519: "We don't lack those who praise papal authority which I confess ought to be held as most holy. Nor do we lack those who proclaim the principles of the Scotists and the Thomists which I also do not reject straight away. But as for you, instill in the minds of those committed to you that pure and unspoiled Christ, since we see this done by so few."[35]

It is clear that this theological position presupposes not only the Neoplatonic concepts of hierarchy, order, and peace, but also the general concept of the transformation and salvation of man by revelatory knowledge. Christ is the Word expressed by the mind of the Father. When the preacher contemplates this Word and proclaims it to the people, their minds grasp it and reorder their lives according to its image. Thus they find the ultimate fulfillment of their nature and perfect peace.

This theological framework to which Erasmus alludes in justifying the role of the preacher gives evidence of a more clearly defined statement of his general conception of Christianity and its major doctrines than is found in most of his other works. It exhibits a unity which is frequently lacking in other contexts and, as has been noted above, it may be useful to employ it as an interpretive framework to elucidate remarks made in other works in order to comprehend their true implications. It also serves as a foil to the theology of both the Protestant reformers and those who like Erasmus maintained a loyalty to the Roman church.

It is clear from the above synopsis that Erasmus refused to accept the contention of his contemporaries that the doctrine of justification was the central issue of Christianity. While Luther isolated and developed the Pauline theme of justification by faith and then employed it as the major, if not sole, criterion and organizing principle of theology; and while Calvin unified the strains of a broader humanist interpretation and presentation of the Scriptures with a basically Lutheran concept of justification; and while Trent accepted justification as the center of the debate but proclaimed the sacraments and ecclesiastical structures as true channels of the grace of salvation, Erasmus developed a different overview which refused to order all theology around the concept of justification. His doctrine, which stressed the acquisition of peace through virtue attainable by union with Christ through meditation upon the documents of the early church's witness to him, found little popularity with the major representatives of sixteenth-century reform movements, either among Protestants or Roman Catholics.

Despite the light which the above analysis of the *Ecclesiastes* may shed on Erasmus's own theological perspective, it is evident that he undertook its composition to bring about a reform in preaching rather than to elucidate his own theology. It is also clear that Erasmus's primary suggestion for the improvement of preaching was the episcopal establishment of competent training for the preaching ministry.[36] At one time the role of the bishop in educating the clergy centered in his own household, which was a veritable school of piety,[37] but Erasmus believed that in his own day this responsibility could best be discharged by the establishment of good colleges for the training of preachers. He stressed the necessity of schools oriented to the training of preachers as opposed to those which produced theologians,[38] recalling the work of Warham in this regard and praising it warmly. This bishop had not only founded schools but he had also constantly attempted to weed out unsuitable candidates for the clergy while he encouraged the more promising students with financial aid.[39] Erasmus continually returned to the topic of the training of preachers. He stressed the need for this education and compared it to the training for athletes and musicians;[40] he encouraged parents and educators to begin as early as possible the training in character and knowledge required for the preacher;[41] and in words reminiscent of his arguments for the necessity of good preachers, he cited the related need for competent educators of these men.[42]

In order that the bishops might fulfill their duties in this regard, Erasmus provided them with a clearly outlined program of study, a suggested library for the course, and in Warham, a model of episcopal concern and action in this matter. But more importantly he provided them with a textbook, the *Ecclesiastes*.

It should be noted that Erasmus refers to the fact that this work is for preachers and not mere orators.[43] Thus Erasmus adapts the principles and techniques of the rhetoricians to the specific function of preaching, and he produces a book the proper scope of which is homiletics and not rhetoric. This is clearly a textbook to be used by the bishops in their attempt to improve the state of preaching. As such, it is dedicated to a bishop known for his interest in preaching and church reform, Christoph von Stadion, and it recalls the death of another renowned bishop, preacher, reformer, and patron of the education of preachers, John Fisher of Rochester, to whom the book seems to have been originally dedicated.

Erasmus had always had a high regard for the educator's role in society and it seems he held that the scholar-educator's function in society was as important as those of the king and the bishop.[44] In addition, Erasmus's work in both literary and biblical studies frequently took the form of textbooks, editions of books important for education, and scholarly commentaries on such treatises. All this seems to indicate that Erasmus's own concept of his identity was that of the scholar-educator. But as De Vogel indicates, this was not an elitist position.

> Whatever may have been said on Erasmus's "aristocratic attitude of mind," the truth is that his life-work consciously aimed at serving the masses: the Gospel must be brought to everyone, and in the purest possible form. That is why he produced his edition of the New Testament in Greek and added his paraphrases. That is also why he wrote his elaborate work on the *Method of Preaching*, a work five times as large as the *Method of Theology*, for he considered the parish priest's task of bringing the Gospel to the people as extremely important.[45]

It should also be remembered that Becar first suggested the work on preaching in light of Erasmus's other handbooks for the Christian layman, the Christian prince, and educators.[46] Upon publication of the *Ecclesiastes,* Gilbert Cousin, Erasmus's former secretary and canon of St. Anthony at Nozeroy, wrote that he employed the new work as a companion to Erasmus's *Enchiridion.* He believed that those who formerly preached only from the scholastics would now turn to the preaching of the Gospel; Erasmus's three works, the *Paraphrases in Novum Testamentum,* the *Enchiridion,* and the *Ecclesiastes* would, according to Cousin, revitalize Christian preaching.[47] Perhaps the most laudatory comment concerning the book came from the Strasbourg preacher and reformer Capito. He stated that he could not remember having read any book which was more fruitful for him or for the age. Indeed, he found it second only to Paul in its ability to inspire and move him. Since this was written to Amerbach rather than Erasmus, Capito's enthusiastic language is less likely to be condemned as flattery.[48]

Because Erasmus believed that preaching needed reform and that the bishops were to undertake this reform both by the removal of incompetent clergymen and also by the establishment of proper training for candidates for the pulpit, Erasmus's *Ecclesiastes* should be viewed as a contribution to church reform. While many might disagree with its projected solutions to the problem of poor preaching in the Christian commonwealth, as well as to the very concept of a textbook in homiletics being considered as a means of church reform, there are clear indications that Erasmus's own concept of his role in society along with his concern for the reform of preaching are ample foundations for viewing the *Ecclesiastes* as an instrument for church reform.

The actual effect of the *Ecclesiastes* on the reform of preaching is impossible to assess. It is clear that it was a popular book in the years immediately following its first publication,[49] but it would be difficult to calculate its influence, if any, on a subsequent, alleged improvement of preaching. Also, while Erasmus's views concerning the bishops' role in reforming the state of preaching as well as the practical suggestions concerning the actual steps to be taken in this regard seem to have been adopted by the reform program of the Council of Trent, these ideas were not unique during this period. Trent's reform, however, recalls Erasmus's *Ecclesiastes.*[50] The bishops are reminded of their duty to preach and of the necessity of appointing men capable of preaching well; they are ordered to examine candidates for the priesthood to see if they possess suitable character and knowledge for their proposed work. In addition, preaching was to be a regular part of Sunday worship service.[51] Moreover, the *catechismus pro parochis,* compiled at the direction of the council, was to serve the same function as Erasmus's schema of sermon topics;[52] while the seminaries that were to be founded for the training of the clergy were to attempt to meet the long-felt need for an educated clergy.[53] Erasmus, of course, was not the sole inspiration for these canons even if they may have some relationship to his work. But it is clear that Erasmus's general views concerning the way in which to reform and improve preaching are echoed in the Tridentine legislation.

This last major work of Erasmus, the *Ecclesiastes sive de ratione concionandi*, has considerable importance for historical research. If Weiss's thesis is correct, and it seems more plausible than others currently proposed, the *Ecclesiastes* serves as a mirror in which we may view the full image of Erasmus. The work may thus serve not only as a synthesis of his thought but also as an interpretive tool for the rest of his works. In it the contrast with the thought of other religious movements of his day is most evident, while the book still serves as an example of Erasmus's own commitment to reform—a commitment conceived within a framework quite different from that of his equally famous contemporaries and executed in quite a different style.

NOTES

1. The only major studies of the *Ecclesiastes* are James Weiss, "*Ecclesiastes* and Erasmus, the Mirror and the Image," *Archive für Reformationsgeschichte* 65 (1974): 83–108, and Robert G. Kleinhans, "Erasmus' Doctrine of Preaching, A Study of *Ecclesiastes, sive de ratione concionandi*" (Th.D. thesis, Princeton Theological Seminary, 1968). John Payne has noted that even on a topic central to the *Ecclesiastes*, namely hermeneutics, "*Ecclesiastae* (1535), Erasmus' latest and most mature work on the subject, has received scant attention." "Toward the Hermeneutics of Erasmus," in *Scrinium Erasmianum*, ed. J. Coppens (Leiden: E. J. Brill, 1969), 1:14. Payne claims to remedy this situation, at least with regard to his topic, since he states that his "essay rests chiefly on the *Enchiridion* (1503), the introductory writings to the New Testament (1516 et seq.), and the *Ecclesiastae* (1535)," ibid. p. 17. There are, however, only two additional references to the *Ecclesiastes* in this article. Albert Rabil's *Erasmus and the New Testament: The Mind of a Christian Humanist* (San Antonio, Texas: Trinity University Press, 1972) develops its interpretation of Erasmus's hermeneutic from his early works, with occasional references to later works such as the *Ecclesiastes*. James Kelsey McConica does use the *Ecclesiastes* in developing his presentation of Erasmus's concept of peace, in "Erasmus and the Grammar of Consent," *Scrinium Erasmianum*, 2:77–79.

2. *Opus Epistolarum Des. Erasmi Roterodami*, ed. P. S. Allen, H. M. Allen, and H. W. Garrod (Oxford: Clarendon Press, 1906–58), vol. 3, 515, Ep. 932, ll. 18–22. Hereafter cited as *EE*. Letters are cited by volume, page, number, and lines.

3. Becar's allusion to Erasmus's works that educated the Christian layman, the Christian prince, and the Christian educator was probably an apt attempt to quote Erasmus himself as the foundation for Becar's request. In his *Institutio Principis Christiani* (Basel: Froben, 1516), Erasmus had said that, just as God is the source of all good in heaven, so the prince is the source of all good in the commonwealth, and the bishop of all good in the church (*LB*, 4:509F). In a preceding paragraph Erasmus had already stated that a major function of the bishop was to preach to the people concerning the mysteries of Christ (*LB*, 4:567F). Because Erasmus also developed the doctrine of the importance of education in this same treatise (*LB*, 4:562C–566A and 529E–F), Becar could easily say that three major forces for

establishing the type of Christian society Erasmus desired were the prince, the bishop-teacher, and the educator. Since Erasmus had already instructed the Christian prince and Christian educators it now remained for him to perfect and complete his corpus by penning a manual for Christian preachers.

4. *LB*, 5:769A.

5. Weiss, "*Ecclesiastes* and Erasmus," p. 107.

6. Weiss's interpretation may be contrasted with John Payne's "Erasmus as Theologian," in *Erasmus: His Theology of the Sacraments* (Richmond, Va.: John Knox Press, 1970), pp. 7–34, and E.-W. Kohls, *Die Theologie des Erasmus* (Basel: Reinhardt, 1966).

7. In his article "The Ecclesiology of Erasmus," in *Scrinium Erasmianum* (Leiden, 1969), vol. 2, C. Augustijn discusses the problem of reconstructing Erasmus's basic theological perspective from his various theologically unsystematic works (p. 137).

8. Johan Huizinga, *Erasmus and the Age of Reformation* (New York: Harper & Row, 1957), p. 182.

9. *Farrago Nova Epistolarum Des. Erasmi Roterdami ad alios et aliorum ad hunc: admixtis quibusdam quas scripsit etiam adolescens.* (Basel: Froben, 1519), p. 118 (to Justus Jonas); p. 149 (from Becar); p. 150 (to Becar). As attested by Allen *EE*, 3:610, 514, and 555.

10. *EE*, 1:34, ll. 19–22.

11. Ibid., 5:538, Ep. 1489, ll. 42–45.

12. Ibid., 7:252, Ep. 1907, ll. 36–38; 425; Ep. 2016, ll. 23–29; 186, Ep. 1881, ll. 50–54; 295, Ep. 1932, ll. 137–43, 334, Ep. 1954, ll. 58–59; 522–23, Ep. 2065, ll. 74–86; 8:12, Ep. 2083, ll. 16–23, 9:59, Ep. 2392, ll. 72–73; and 10:236, Ep. 2817, ll. 48–53.

13. Allen, *EE*, 7:454, Ep. 2033, ll. 45–48. During the debates with Nicholas Egmondanus at Louvain, his opponent hurled this same accusation at Erasmus during their interview with the rector of the university. *EE*, 4:385, Ep. 1162, ll. 56–70.

14. Erasmus had set aside the work on preaching to complete the edition of Augustine (*EE*, 8:189, Ep. 2225), the *Apophthegmata Plutarchi* (*EE*, 8:341, Ep. 2261, ll. 43–49), and *De sarcienda Ecclesiae* concordia (*EE*, 9:257, Ep. 2483, ll. 50–54).

15. Gordon Rupp, *The Old Reformation and the New* (Philadelphia: Fortress Press, 1967), p. 12.

16. *LB*, 5:767–68.

17. While Erasmus obviously sees Books 2 and 3 as closely related to Book 1, the content and style of these two major divisions of the *Ecclesiastes* differ. The opus does give the impression of three distinct works, as outlined above.

18. *LB*, 5:941A–B.

19. Ibid., pp. 769A–770A.

20. Ibid., pp. 770A–771A. The apostles are elsewhere described as legates sent by Christ the King to proclaim his edicts. *Paraphrases in Novum Testamentum* (Mark 3:4), *LB*, 7:182D.

21. Ibid., pp. 9F–11A.

22. Ibid., pp. 770A and 820D–E.

23. Ibid., pp. 1097E–1100C.

24. Ibid., p. 1074D.

25. Ibid., p. 1078E.

26. Ibid., p. 1083D–E.

27. Ibid., pp. 772D and 1008B–C.

28. Ibid., p. 772C–D.

29. Ibid., p. 772D.

30. Ibid., p. 772E–F.

31. Ibid., pp. 847F–848F.

32. Ibid., p. 773D.

33. Ibid., pp. 772A and 1016E.

34. Ibid., pp. 788B, 834E–835E, 1067C.

35. *EE*, 3:555, Ep. 952, ll. 44–48.

36. Ibid., p. 807E-F.

37. Ibid., p. 909D.

38. Ibid., p. 810E.

39. Ibid., p. 811D-E.

40. Ibid., p. 830C.

41. Ibid., pp. 800C and 849F.

42. Ibid., p. 806B-C.

43. Ibid., p. 894B-C.

44. *Institutio Principis Christiani, LB*, 4:562C–566A; 592E-F.

45. C. J. De Vogel, "Erasmus and His Attitude Towards Church Dogma," in *Scrinium Erasmianum*, 2:104.

46. *EE*, 3:515, Ep. 932, ll. 18–22.

47. *EE*, 11:3080, ll. 15–43.

48. *Die Amerbachkorrespondenz*, ed. Alfred Hartmann. (Basel: Verlag der Universi- tätsbibliothek, 1942), 4:375, Ep. 1980, ll. 1-6.

49. The first edition consisted of 2,600 copies, and it was followed immediately by pirated editions and reprintings (Antwerp: Mart. Caesar, 1535; Antwerp: Mich Hillenius, 1535; Basel: Froben, March 1536, August 1536; Antwerp: G. Montanus, 1539; Basel: Froben, 1539, in *Opera Omnia*, 1540; Leiden: S. Gryphius, 1543; Basel: Froben, 1544–45, 1554).

50. Hubert Jedin, who displays a certain animosity toward Erasmus, does not mention any evidence of Erasmus's influence on the participants at the Council of Trent. He does note, however, that Nausea's memorandum for the Colloquium at Worms (1540) includes a list of books which should constitute the groundwork of clerical education. It consisted of the *Bible*, Lombard's *Sententiae*, Augustine's *De doctrina christiana*, Aquinas's *Compendium*, and Erasmus's *Ecclesiastes*. Hubert Jedin, *Geschichte des Konzils von Trent* (Freiburg: Herder, 1957), 2:462–63, n. 1.

51. *Concilium Tridentium*, session 5, "Decretum: Super lectione et praedicatione" and session 24, "Decretum de reformatione," Canon 4 in *Conciliorum Oecumenicorum Decreta*, ed. Centro di Documentazione Instituto per le Scienze Religiose, Bologna, 2d ed. (Basel: Herder, 1962), pp. 643–46 and 739.

52. *Concilium Tridentium*, session 24, "Decretum de reformatione," Canon 7, ibid., p. 740.

53. *Concilium Tridentium*, session 23, "Decretum de reformatione," Canon 18, ibid., pp. 726–29.

Publications of Craig R. Thompson on Sixteenth-Century Subjects

BOOKS

The Translations of Lucian by Erasmus and St. Thomas More, Ithaca, N.Y., 1940.

Inquisitio de fide: A Colloquy by Desiderius Erasmus Roterodams, 1524, with introduction and commentary. Yale Studies in Religion 15. New Haven, 1950.

Ten Colloquies of Erasmus. New York, 1957. 174 pp. 7th printing, Indianapolis and New York, 1972.

The Bible in English 1525–1611. Washington, D.C.: Folger Shakespeare Library, 1958. 37 pp. 4th printing, 1975.

The English Church in the Sixteenth Century. Washington, D.C.: Folger Shakespeare Library, 1958. 37 pp. 4th printing, 1975.

Schools in Tudor England. Washington, D.C.: Folger Shakespeare Library, 1958. 48 pp. 4th printing, 1973.

Life and Letters in Tudor and Stuart England, edited by Louis B. Wright and Virginia A. LaMar. First Folger Series. Ithaca, N.Y., 1962. Reprints, pp. 185–382: *The Bible in English 1525–1611*, *The English Church in the Sixteenth Century*, *Schools in Tudor England*, and *Universities in Tudor England*.

The Colloquies of Erasmus. Chicago and London, 1965.

[Thomas More]. *Translations of Lucian*. Yale edition of the Complete Works of St. Thomas More, vol. 3, pt. 1. New Haven and London, 1974.

Inquisitio de fide: A Colloquy by Desiderius Erasmus Roterodamus, 1524. 2d ed., with introduction by Roland H. Bainton and bibliography. Hamden, Conn., 1975.

Editor, vols. 23 and 24 of *The Collected Works of Erasmus*. Literary and Educational Works Series. Toronto: University of Toronto Press, 1978.

ARTICLES

"The Date of the First Aldine Lucian." *Classical Journal* 35 (1940) 233–35.

"Erasmus' Translation of Lucian's *Longaevi*." *Classical Philology* 35 (1940): 397–415.

"Rabelais and *Iulius Exclusus*." *Philological Quarterly* 22 (1943): 80–82.

"Some Greek and Grecized Words in Renaissance Latin." *American Journal of Philology* 64 (1943): 333–35.

"Erasmus as Internationalist and Cosmopolitan." *Archiv für Refomations-geschichte* 46 (1955): 167–95.

"Erasmian Humanism." In *Society and History in the Renaissance*. Washington, D.C.: Folger Shakespeare Library, 1960. Pp. 20–26.

Foreword to William Harrison Woodward, *Desiderius Erasmus: Concerning the Aim and Method of Education* (1904). Classics in Education 19. New York: Teachers College, Columbia University, 1964. Pp. vii–xxiii.

"Better Teachers Than Scotus or Aquinas." *Medieval and Renaissance Studies* (Southeastern Institute of Medieval and Renaissance Studies, Durham, N.C.) 2 (1968): 114–45.

"Erasmus and Tudor England." *Actes du Congres Erasme*. Rotterdam, Oct. 27–29, 1969; Amsterdam and London, 1971. Pp. 29–68.

"Erasmus, More, and the Conjuration of Spirits. . . ." *Moreana*, no. 24 (1969), pp. 45–50.

"Erasmus Research in the United States." *Erasmus in English* (Newsletter of University of Toronto Press) 5 (1972): 1–5.

"The Humanism of More Reappraised." *Thought* 52 (September 1977): 231–48.

"Scripture for the Ploughboy and Some Others." In *Studies in the Continental Background of Renaissance English Literature: Essays Presented to John L. Lievsay*, edited by Dale B. J. Randall and George W. Williams, pp. 3–28. Durham, N.C., 1977.

REVIEWS

More's Utopia: The Biography of an Idea, by J. H. Hexter (Princeton, 1952). In *Archiv für Reformationsgeschichte* 44 (1953): 261–62.

Advocates of Reform from Wyclif to Erasmus, edited by Matthew Spinka. Library of Christian Classics 14 (Philadelphia, 1953). In *Archiv für Reformationsgeschichte* 45 (1954): 265–68.

Classical Myth and Legend in Renaissance Dictionaries, by DeWitt T. Starnes and Ernest W. Talbert (Chapel Hill, N.C., 1955). In *Shakespeare Quarterly* 8 (1957): 233–35.

A Fifteenth-Century School Book, edited by William Nelson (Oxford and New York, 1956). In *Journal of Modern History* 29 (1957): 288–89.

The Poems of Desiderius Erasmus, edited by C. Reedijk (Leiden, 1956). In *Renaissance News* 11 (1958): 16–19.

The Praise of Wisdom, by Edward L. Surtz (Chicago, 1957). In *Renaissance News* 12 (1959): 203–08.

A Life of John Colet . . . , By J. H. Lupton (1887, 1909; Hamden, Conn., 1961). In *American Historical Review* 67 (1962): 471.

Douze années de bibliographie érasmienne (1950-1961), edited by Jean-Claude Margolin (Paris, 1963). In *Renaissance News* 18 (1965): 24–26.

[Erasmus]. *On Copia of Words and Ideas*, translated by Donald B. King and H. David Rix (Milwaukee, 1963). In *Shakespeare Quarterly* 16 (1965): 267-68.

Colloquium Erasmianum. Actes du Colloque International réuni à Mons du 26 au 29 octobre 1967 à l'occasion du cinquième centenaire de la naissance d'Érasme (Mons, 1968). In *Church History* 39 (1970): 115-16.

[Erasmus]. *The dyaloge called Funus (1534) & A Very pleasaunt & fruitful Diologe called The Epicure (1545)*, edited by Robert R. Allen (Chicago, 1969); *Érasme et l'humanisme chrétien*, by Léon-E. Halkin (Paris, 1969); *Quatorze années de bibliographie érasmienne (1936-1949)*, edited by Jean-Claude Margolin (Paris, 1969). In *Renaissance Quarterly* 24 (1971): 372-79.

[Erasmus]. *Opera omnia, recognita et adnotatione critica instructa notisque illustrata:* vol. 1, pt. 1, edited by K. Kumaniecki, R. A. B. Mynors, J. H. Waszink, and C. Robinson; vol. 1, pt. 2, edited by J.-C. Margolin and P. Mesnard (Amsterdam, 1969, 1971). In *Renaissance Quarterly* 25 (1972): 192-209.

[Erasmus]. *Opera omnia, recognita et adnotatione critica instructa notisque illustrata*, vol. 1, pt. 3, edited by L.-E. Halkin, F. Bierlaire, and R. Hoven (Amsterdam, 1972). In *Renaissance Quarterly* 27 (1974): 196-98.

Colloquia Erasmiana Turonensia, edited by Jean-Claude Margolin (Paris and Toronto, 1972). In *Classical World* 68 (1975): 408-10.

The Contributors

FRANZ BIERLAIRE is a member of the Institute of the History of the Renaissance and the Reformation at Liège. He earned his doctorate at the University of Liège in 1976. He is the author of *La familia d'Erasme* (Paris, 1968) and has contributed to *Scrinium Erasmianum* (1969) and volume 3 (*The Colloquies*) of the Amsterdam edition of Erasmus's *Opera omnia* (1972).

VIRGINIA W. CALLAHAN is professor emerita of classical languages at Howard University. She received her Ph.D. in Greek from the University of Chicago in 1941. She is the author of *Types of Rulers in the Plays of Aeschylus* (Chicago, 1944) and editor of "Vita S. Macrinae" in *Gregorii Nysseni Opera Ascetica,* ed. Werner Jaeger (Leiden, 1952 and 1963), and *Saint Gregory of Nyssa: Ascetical Works* (Washington, D.C., 1967).

GEORGES G. CHANTRAINE, S.J., is professor of the history of dogma at the Institute of Theological Studies in Brussels. He obtained his *Docteur en Philosophie et Lettres* from the Catholic University of Louvain in 1968. His principal publications include *'Mystère' et Philosophie du Christ' selon Erasmus* (Gembloux, 1971) and articles on Erasmus in *Nouvelle revue théologique, Revue d'histoire ecclésiastique,* and *Recherches de science religieuse.*

The editor of this volume, RICHARD L. DeMOLEN, was awarded his Ph.D. in history by the University of Michigan in 1970. Among other works, he has published *Erasmus of Rotterdam: A Quincentennial Symposium* (New York, 1971), *Erasmus* (London and New York, 1973), and *The Meaning of the Renaissance and Reformation* (Boston and London, 1974). He has been engaged in research at the Folger Shakespeare Library since 1970.

B. A. GERRISH is professor of the history of theology and Reformation history at the Divinity School of the University of Chicago. He was awarded a Ph.D. in religion from Columbia University in 1958. He has written *Grace and Reason: A Study in the Theology of Luther* (Oxford, 1962), *The Faith of Christendom: A Source Book of Creeds and Confessions* (New York, 1963), and *Reformers in Profile* (Philadelphia, 1967).

MYRON P. GILMORE is professor of history at Harvard University. He received his Ph.D. from the same institution in 1937. He is the author of *Roman Law in Political Thought* (Cambridge, Mass., 1941), *The World of Humanism* (New York, 1952), and *Humanists and Jurists* (Cambridge, Mass., 1963), and has contributed articles on Erasmus to the E. H. Harbison and Paul O. Kristeller Festschrifts.

CATHERINE A. L. JARROTT is associate professor of English at Loyola University of Chicago. She obtained her Ph.D. in English from Stanford University in 1954. She has published articles on Erasmus and Sir Thomas More in the *American Benedictine Review, Studies in Philology,* and *Studies in the Renaissance.*

ROBERT G. KLEINHANS is associate professor of theology at Saint Xavier College in Chicago. He received his Th.D. from Princeton Theological Seminary in 1968. He has published articles on Erasmus in *Church History* and the *Historical Magazine of the Protestant Episcopal Church.* He also devoted his doctoral thesis to a study of Erasmus's *Ecclesiastes.*

ERNST-W. KOHLS is professor of church history at the University of Marburg. He was awarded his Th.D. by the University of Erlagen in 1962. His major works include *Die Theologie des Erasmus,* 2 vols. (Basel, 1966), *Die Schule bei Martin Bucer* (Heidelberg, 1963), and *Luther oder Erasmus,* vol. 1 (Basel, 1972).

JEAN-CLAUDE MARGOLIN is professor of philosophy at the University of Tours. He received his Doctorat d'Etat from the University of Paris in 1969. His major publications are an edition of Erasmus's *Declamatio de pueris statim ac liberaliter instituendis* (Geneva, 1966); volume 2 of the Amsterdam edition of Erasmus's *Opera omnia* (1971); and two volumes of *Bibliographie érasmienne,* covering the period from 1936 to 1961 (Paris, 1963, 1969).

CLARENCE H. MILLER is professor of English at Saint Louis University. He earned his Ph.D. from Harvard University in 1956. He is the editor of Sir Thomas Chaloner's 1549 translation of Erasmus's *The Praise of Folie* (Oxford, 1965) and has also edited the *Praise of Folly* for the Amsterdam edition of the *Opera omnia,* which will appear shortly.

MARGARET MANN PHILLIPS earned her *Docteur de l'Université* (Paris) in 1934. At present she is an honorary lecturer in French at University College, London. Her major studies are *Érasme et les Débuts de la Réforme Française (1517-1536)* (Paris, 1934); *Erasmus and the Northern Renaissance* (London and New York, 1949, 1950, 1965); and *The 'Adages' of Erasmus* (Cambridge, 1964).

ALBERT RABIL, JR., is professor of humanities at the State University of New York College at Old Westbury. He was awarded a Ph.D. in philosophy from Columbia University in 1964. He has published *Merleau-Ponty: Existentialist of the Social World* (New York, 1967) and *Erasmus and the New Testament* (San Antonio, Texas, 1972); and he is coeditor of Erasmus's Paraphrases and Annotations on Romans and Galatians for Toronto's *Collected Works of Erasmus.*

EMILE V. TELLE, professor emeritus of French at Catholic University of America, earned his *Docteur ès Lettres* (Toulouse) and *Doctorat d'Etat* (Paris) in 1937 and 1952 respectively. He is the author of *L'oeuvre de Marguerite d'Angoulême* . . . (Toulouse, 1937; reprinted in Geneva, 1969) and *Erasme de Rotterdam et le septième sacrement* (Geneva, 1954), and the editor of Etienne Dolet's *L'Erasmianus sive Ciceronianus (1535)* (Geneva, 1974).

SISTER M. GERALDINE THOMPSON, C.S.J., is professor emerita of English at St. Michael's College of the University of Toronto. She obtained her Ph.D. in English from there in 1955. She has written *Under Pretext of Praise: Satiric Mode in Erasmus's Fiction* (Toronto, 1973) and articles on Erasmus in *Studies in Philology, Erasmus in English,* and the *University of Toronto Quarterly.*

Index